THE AHMANSON FOUNDATION

has endowed this imprint
to honor the memory of

FRANKLIN D. MURPHY

who for half a century
served arts and letters,
beauty and learning, in
equal measure by shaping
with a brilliant devotion
those institutions upon
which they rely.

NUNS AS ARTISTS

Leonhard Beck (?), St. Erentrude, ca. 1517 (Albertina, Vienna), part of a genealogy celebrating the saintly ancestry of the Hapsburg emperor Maximilian I. Erentrude (d. 718), the first abbess of the Benedictine abbey of Nonnberg in Salzburg, meditates on the Passion in her cell. Her vision represents her ardent compassion for Christ's self-immolation on the cross.

NUNS AS ARTISTS

The Visual Culture of a Medieval Convent

JEFFREY F. HAMBURGER

UNIVERSITY OF CALIFORNIA PRESS

Berkeley   Los Angeles   London

Publication of this book has been aided by a grant from the Millard Meiss Publication Fund of the College Art Association of America.

University of California Press
Berkeley and Los Angeles, California

University of California Press, Ltd.
London, England

Library of Congress Cataloging-in-Publication Data

Hamburger, Jeffrey F., 1957–
Nuns as artists : the visual culture of a medieval convent / Jeffrey F. Hamburger.
p. cm. — (California studies in the history of art ; 37)
Includes bibliographical references and index.
ISBN 0-520-20386-0 (alk. paper)
1. Devotional objects—Germany—Eichstätt. 2. Devotional objects—Catholic Church. 3. Christian art and symbolism—Medieval, 500–1500—Germany—Eichstätt. 4. Nuns as artists—Germany—Eichstätt. 5. Benediktinerinnen-Abtei St. Walburg (Eichstätt, Germany) I. Title. II. Series.
NK1655.E35H36 1997
704.9′482′082—dc20 96-6045

Printed in the United States of America
9 8 7 6 5 4 3 2 1

The paper used in this publication meets the minimum requirements of American National Standard for Information Sciences—Permanence of Paper for Printed Library Materials, ANSI Z39.48-1984.

FOR DIETLINDE

Du bist min, ich bin din:
des solt du gewis sin.
du bist beslozzen
in minem herzen:
verloren ist daz slüzzelin:
du muost immer drinne sin

Loves mysteries in soules doe grow,
But yet the body is his booke.

John Donne, "The Extasie"

CONTENTS

ILLUSTRATIONS

Plates (following page 134)

Map

Figures

PREFACE AND ACKNOWLEDGMENTS

THIS BOOK IS IN LARGE MEASURE devoted to a group of drawings that I came across while conducting research on the art and architecture of female monasticism of the later Middle Ages. En route to Germany in the spring of 1992, I stopped in London, among other things to look at the manuscripts awaiting sale at Sotheby's. With his usual generosity, Christopher de Hamel allowed me to examine the lots assembled for auction. As always, the material promised the possibility of a serendipitous discovery. That June my eye was attracted less by the lavishly illuminated liturgical codices, Bibles, and Books of Hours than by a single leaf of paper with an unassuming drawing of an unusual subject: the heart as a house inhabited by a nun embraced by the Trinity. I made a mental note of the sheet, above all its idiosyncratic iconography, and then moved on to the more eye-catching tomes shelved nearby.

As it turned out, the drawing was not so easily set aside. On arriving in Würzburg four days later, within minutes of putting down my luggage, I wandered into the study of my father-in-law, Friedrich Röll, irresistibly drawn to the books strewn about. I immediately came across a catalogue of *Klosterfrauenarbeiten,* "nuns' handiwork" of the seventeenth and eighteenth centuries, consisting for the most part of devotional objects made by cloistered women for their own use. Unable to hold back, even though I had only just arrived, I began to thumb through it when, to my astonishment, I found myself confronted by the reproduction of a devotional drawing that, without any doubt, was the companion piece to the leaf offered for sale at Sotheby's. I could hardly believe my eyes—and my luck. This fortuitous—or fateful—discovery led to others and, in turn, to this volume.

Only in recent years have the works of art made both by and for nuns and semireligious women become the objects of intense scholarly scrutiny. One would have thought that the surge of interest in women's history, not least female spirituality, across numerous disciplines and, still more generally, in gender as a category of historical investigation would have led to a heightened curiosity concerning the material remains of female monasticism. With few exceptions, however, this has not been the case.[1] Despite the extensive and ever-expanding literature on devotional imagery, the role played by women in the formation of novel attitudes toward images remains largely unexplored.[2] Moreover, for all the interest professed in women as a marginalized group, many of their most characteristic products and forms of expression remain outside the purview of art history. Instead, scholars have too often contented themselves with the tired generalization that we cannot look beyond inevitably misogynistic representations of women. If nothing else, in this book I hope to demonstrate that we need not accept as Gospel truth such statements as that made by Margaret Miles as recently as 1985: "As far as we can determine, not a single image of any woman—saint, Mary, scriptural or apocryphal figure—was designed or created by a woman. The images we must deal with are images provided for women by men."[3] The neglected class of images generally known as *Nonnenarbeiten,* or "nuns' work," to which this study is devoted belies so bald—and blind—an assertion.

In contrast to decorated textiles, the drawings, miniatures, and other small-scale devotional objects manufactured by nuns have never found an established place in the history of art. Considered to exist outside the category "Art," they have remained the province of historians of folklore. With a single study I can hardly hope to redress this pattern of long-standing neglect, especially as the few drawings that form my focus probably represent no more than the tip of the proverbial iceberg. In some respects typical of material from other convents, in other, more interesting ways they are not. They nonetheless raise issues of interpretation that can be considered exemplary, not simply for the study of late medieval devotional imagery, but also for the history of spirituality, which too often disregards the import of images. Much of the material to which I relate the drawings—vernacular prayers and devotional tracts—similarly remains uncharted territory. As a result, some of my conjectures remain tentative. I have not, however, refrained from drawing sweeping conclusions.

After an introduction in which I review the two categories that ostensibly frame my topic—*Nonnenarbeiten* and *Andachtsbilder*—I turn in Chapter 1 to a group of late medieval drawings from the convent of St. Walburg, setting the stage for the four chapters that follow by analyzing the style and iconography of the images as a group as well as the visual culture of the convent.[4] By this I mean not simply the images integral to the nuns' devotional routines, but also the patterns and protocols of viewing that governed their devotional life.[5] In addition to identifying distinctive images, I set out to identify distinctive habits of visualization. The drawings from St. Walburg implicitly mandate certain devotional practices in which seeing assumed a role no less important than reading and in which both modes of experience were related to a wider sphere of pious performance.

Chapters 2–4, which form the heart of the book, explore these problems in detail. Around each image or group of images crystallizes a previously uncharted set of devotional practices particular in their elaboration, if not always in their content, to cloistered women in the German-speaking world of the later Middle Ages. Chapter 2, "The Sweet Rose of Sorrow," reconstructs the use of images of the Agony in the Garden as exemplars of prayer on the Passion and, hence, of the *imitatio Christi.* Chapter 3, "Wounding Sight," explores a set of interrelationships developed in images of the cross and the Crucifixion: on the one hand, between exegesis and experience, on the other, between sight and subjectivity. Chapter 4, "The House of the Heart," further explores the use of metaphors of introspection as the basis for devotional images that both structure subjective experience and take it as their subject.

Although the drawings from St. Walburg could be construed as foreshadowing the images of interiority developed in early modern emblems and tracts—be they Protestant, Pietist, or Post-Tridentine Catholic—there can be no question of direct affiliations. All major confessions of the sixteenth century appropriated elements of the medieval mystical tradition to suit their proselytizing strategies. The drawings, however, challenge the boundaries imposed by periodization, complicating the categories we use to distinguish Catholic and Protestant piety.[6] They also confound conventional characterizations of the relationship between text and image by suggesting the need for a third term, the expectations of the onlooker. Much of this study is devoted to defining, as precisely as possible, the horizon of expectations of the enclosed women for whom the drawings were made. Both the drawings and the larger mass of material to which they are related illuminate the contribution of female spirituality to a larger process of cultural transformation: by the end of the Western Middle Ages, images had joined texts as recognized sources of religious authority and devotional authenticity and served as an integral, even indispensable, part of the experience of prayer.

Throughout this book I plead for a contextual approach to the study of images. Like virtually every other methodology, contextual art history has recently come under criticism.[7] I conceive of context, however, not as a convenient catchall, but as a complex subject, itself to be construed by the historian, just as nuns and their advisers contested the proper framework for the function of images. As Dominick LaCapra observes: "An appeal to *the* context is deceptive: one never has—at least in the case of complex texts—*the* context."[8] In situating the drawings from St. Walburg amid modern as well as medieval debates over images, I look beyond the limits of enclosure to consider the various institutions—of spiritual instruction, monastic reform, or ecclesiastical control—that impinged on the convent, which was never an isolated entity. Context thus provides neither a background against which to read the images nor a matrix that deprives them of vitality. There is no need to consign the drawings to a passive role when, for the nuns who made them, they were an indispensable part of everyday religious routines.

In Chapter 5 I stand back from the intense scrutiny of individual images and return to problems of context, in particular, the functions of *Nonnenarbeiten* in the various institutional settings mandated by monastic reform and the pastoral care of nuns. The Conclusion relates the interpretation of the drawings to current critical inquiry: the interaction of text and image, of spirituality and sexuality, and of gender and the gaze. The drawings from St. Walburg invite such investigation, but also compel us to look beyond the horizon of present critical concerns. To quote LaCapra again, "even if one accepts the metaphor that presents interpretation as the 'voice' of the historical reader in the 'dialogue' with the past, it must be actively recognized that the past has its own 'voices' that must be respected, especially when they resist or qualify the interpretations we would like to place on them."[9] The voices of medieval nuns may be irretrievably lost, but the images that led me to write this book allow us to recapture some of their resonance.

The completion of any endeavor brings with it the happy chore of acknowledging the help of others. But in this case I can fairly say that had my father-in-law, Friedrich Röll, not left the right book in the right place at the right time, this project never would have been launched. To Hildegard as well as Fritz, I am greatly indebted, not only for their library, but also for their incomparable hospitality.

From London to Würzburg, my discoveries soon led me to the Abbey of St. Walburg in Eichstätt. To the abbess, M. Franziska Kloos, O.S.B.; the librarian, Sister Veronika; and the other nuns of St. Walburg, I am obliged for permission to study and photograph the drawings and manuscripts in their collections. Although I remain convinced that additional drawings await discovery at the abbey, I have decided that the material to which I was granted access was itself of sufficient coherence and interest to warrant its publication. I am no less grateful to the collector who generously allowed me to study the one drawing in the group no longer at Eichstätt, since acquired by the Staatsbibliothek in Berlin. Brun Appel, director of the Diözesanarchiv in Eichstätt, also granted me repeated access to the manuscripts in his care.

Obtaining some of the photographs for this book proved immensely frustrating. I am grateful to those who helped overcome obstacles at every step of the way—above all, Prof. Dr. Karl-August Wirth and Dr. Sibylle Appuhn-Radtke of the Zentralinstitut für Kunstgeschichte in Munich; Prof. Dr. Ernst Reiter of the Katholische Universität, Eichstätt; and Prof. Dr. Ludwig Wamser, director of the Prähistorische Sammlung, Munich, formerly of the Bayerisches Landesamt für Denkmalpflege, Außenstelle Würzburg.

I have incurred many other debts in my research. My wife, Dietlinde, to whom this book is dedicated, helped at every turn in ways too numerous to tally, not least by sharing in the delight of my discoveries. At times I fear she may have felt I would withdraw forever to the enclosure of my study. With his usual acumen and insight, James Marrow commented extensively on several earlier drafts. This book bears the indelible imprint of his example, enthusiasm, and unstinting generosity as both a friend and a scholar. I am also much indebted to Caroline Bynum and Michael Curschmann, both of whom commented on portions of my manuscript. In Del Kolve and Bernard McGinn I found two readers who parsed my text with uncommon care and wisdom.

My thanks extend to others who assisted with transcriptions, photographs, photocopies, and a myriad of miscellaneous queries: Janet Backhouse, Elisabeth Beare, Peter Jörg Becker, Birgitt Borkopp, François Boespflug, Bodo Brinckmann, Walter Cahn, Robert Deshman, Christopher de Hamel, Carmela Franklin, Christoph Gerhardt, Nina Gockerell, Kate Greenspan, my parents, Joseph and Lotte Hamburger, Christian Heck, Elisabeth Klemm, Joseph Koerner, Thom Kren, Annie Lyles, Werner Neuhauser, Reiner Nolden, Peter Ochsenbein, Nigel Palmer, Anny Raman, Joseph Romano, Deborah Rose-Lefmann, R.-D. Schmid, Gerhard Schmidt, Karin Schneider, Rainer Schoch, Gregory Sebastian, O.S.B., Elizabeth Sears, Sieglinde Sepp, John Seyfried, Fronia Simpson, Hiltrud Westermann-Angerhausen, Henrik von Achen, Jeffrey Weidman, Volcker von Volckamer, Leonie von Wilckens, Ulla Williams, and Werner Williams-Krapp.

To this long list I would also like to add the entire reference staff of the Oberlin College Library, who were a mainstay throughout. In addition to subsidizing some travel and photographic expenses early on, the college generously supported a special leave of absence to write the book. I am also greatly indebted to two other institutions: the National Endowment for the Humanities, which funded a major portion of my leave, and the Institute for Advanced Study in Princeton, which provided the ideal combination of isolation and intellectual community in which to write, not unlike a monastery itself (although hardly as austere). Throughout the year, Profs. Irving Lavin and Giles Constable, together with a congenial group of colleagues, among them Tom Noble, Philip Soergel, and John van Engen, provided a lively forum in which to test ideas. I owe much to the remarkable staff of the institute's library, especially Patricia Bernard, Gretchen Bogue, Mark Darby, Faridah Kassim, Marcia Tucker, and Eliot Shore, for their skill and speed in tracking down bibliographical arcana as I completed this manuscript during a year devoted in part to other projects.

Finally, my thanks to the staff of the University of California Press, especially Deborah Kirshman, Kim Darwin Manning, and Stephanie Fay, for the energy and enthusiasm with which they pursued this project.

All English quotations from the Vulgate Bible are from the Douay-Rheims version. With the exception of inscriptions in images or poetry, I have relegated the Latin and Middle High German of the original sources to the notes. Unless otherwise indicated, translations and transcriptions are all my own. Capitalization in inscriptions follows that in the originals. Familiar foreign names are anglicized; the remainder are not.

Readers should also be advised that throughout the book I use the term "convent" in the modern vernacular sense of "nunnery," not according to its medieval meaning, which denoted either a male or a female congregation.

Fig. 1. Crucifixion, Cologne, Schnütgen Museum, Inv. Nr. M340.

INTRODUCTION

EVEN IN A PREDOMINANTLY secular age, the Crucifixion remains an inescapable image, so familiar that it rarely, if ever, commands our attention. The same, however, cannot be said of the single-leaf drawing of the crucified Christ now in the Schnütgen Museum, Cologne (Fig. 1 and Plate 1). Attributed to a draftswoman working in the Rhineland in the fourteenth century, it rivets the eye. Difficult as it is to believe, this startling image has never before been reproduced in color so that we, like the nuns for whom it was made, can experience it in the flesh, Christ's as well as our own.[1]

Although usually classified as a *Kleines Andachtsbild,* or "small devotional image," the drawing in Cologne hardly qualifies as diminutive. Its dimensions, 25.5 × 18 centimeters, increase its impact.[2] Not an object intended for viewing at a disinterested distance, it asks to be handled and touched, even as the body of Christ is caressed in the image. Like St. Bernard at Christ's right and the nun at his left, we are compelled to identify with the body and blood of Christ through the sheer livid profusion of ruddy ink that saturates the paper.[3] Christ's head droops from the otherwise overscale corpus, sinking below the level of the shoulders and the stiff, twiglike arms. His body, almost entirely obscured by blood, appears as one enormous wound, with the only contrast the green band of the crown of thorns, itself dotted in red. Even Christ's halo takes on the sanguine tincture. The pigment—thick, viscous, unevenly applied—suggests a compact sealed in blood, like Christ's own assurance of salvation.[4]

This Crucifixion fascinates even as it repels us. Yet where we might see only an image of unbridled violence, the woman by (and perhaps for) whom it was made—represented by the nun at the foot of the cross—would have experienced more complex meanings and sensations. To see through her eyes and those of her contemporaries, we must forget any preconceived notion of "Art." Instead we must try to inhabit her world, removed from our own by the passage of time and the seclusion of the cloister.

Sermons delivered to nuns offer insight into the confined spaces inhabited by cloistered women in late medieval Germany. We can juxtapose with the drawing of the Crucifixion a sermon on the wound in Christ's side and the sacrament of the Eucharist by Konrad von Eßlingen, twice Dominican prior provincial of Teutonia (1277–81, 1290–93).[5] Delivered in 1318 to the female community at Adelhausen in Freiburg, his words survive as a precis recorded by the nuns, who heard him only through a grille.[6] Konrad's homily offers an analogy to the drawing without, however, accounting for its visceral power. In good scholastic fashion, the Dominican enumerates the qualities of Christ's blood: its heat, fluidity, and color. Likening the Eucharist to a pigment, Konrad argues that the red color of Christ's blood

> restores and renews the divine image imprinted in the soul; a person may never erase that image, whether he goes to heaven or to hell. With our sins, however, we often act like the man who took the emperor's shield and dunked it in a puddle so that the image was besmirched and yet remained as it was. The red of the blood restores and revarnishes that [the divine image of the sinner].[7]

The shield not only denotes the *imago Dei* imprinted on the soul but also signifies a piece of military gear that safeguards the soul against the ravages of sin. In German, however, *Schild* refers specifically to a coat of arms of the kind often emblazoned on shields, in this instance, the *arma Christi,* the heraldic insignia of Christ's Passion. Painting itself provides an emblem of the process of creation and redemption, with Christ's blood as the medium that binds image and artist, man and his Maker.[8] Man—or, in this case, the women who make up Konrad's listeners—commit through their sins an act of collective lèse majesté. Christ, however, works through the sacraments to restore his image in the soul.

In the drawing the blood-drenched body of Christ assumes sacramental significance. The vivifying fluid rains down in great gouts and gathers in a pool between Christ's devotees. Bernard and the nun, however, maintain both decorum and distance; for all their fervor, they remain untouched, as if to signify their purity now that they have been cleansed by Christ's sacrifice. Where the Cistercian saint grasps the upright beam of the cross with his left hand, the torrent of blood flows under, not over, his fingers, suggesting that no matter how close he is to Christ, he remains distant in time. The nun is still further removed. Even as the image portrays such intimate and privileged proximity to the divine, it bars the participants from complete immersion in the Godhead.

In a time when professional artists increasingly mass-produced images—prints, paintings, even entire altarpieces—for the market, the drawing of the Crucifixion with St. Bernard and a nun and other works like it stand apart by virtue of their singular and unprofessional character.[9] The majority of such images were intended for those who made them, most often nuns lacking both systematic training in art and wide-ranging contact with images outside the convent. They are generally known as *Nonnenarbeiten,* "nuns' works." [10] We would never assign a *Sacra conversatione* by Fra Angelico and a portrait by Fra Filippo Lippi to the same genre simply because both happen to have been painted by friars. Nor would we assume that in identifying both artists as mendicants we had succeeded in identifying all that was typical of their oeuvres. Far from providing an apt, let alone productive, characterization of the images it seeks to define, *Nonnenarbeit* stands by definition for deficiency: a lack of both skill and sophistication.

On close examination, however, drawings such as the Crucifixion address their onlookers in surprisingly complex, and—more important—compelling ways. To write them off as *Nonnenarbeiten* implicitly asks them to meet criteria to which they did not and could not aspire. Such anachronistic considerations need not interfere with our appreciation of these objects any more than they do with our response to other genres, once disdained, that have found a fixed place in the art-historical firmament.[11] As Otto Pächt acknowledged, iconographic imagination does not necessarily go hand in hand with aesthetic accomplishment, nor, to paraphrase Francis Wormald, need we limit our investigations of "popular" images to what they can tell us about their "rich relations." [12] In medieval art what we might set aside as "ugly" constituted as much a moral, social, even religious category, associated not simply with the representation of evil or rustic characters but with the *summum bonum,* Christ himself, the paradoxical figure of the defiled and degraded Godhead who, on behalf of mankind, underwent the ultimate humiliation.[13]

The neologism *Andachtsbild* is no less misleading than *Nonnenarbeit* as a way of coming to terms with the images made by and for nuns. Originally it designated a small group of sculptural types distinguished by their iconography and, it was thought, their exclusive association with convents in southwestern Germany. It has since lost whatever precision it could ever lay claim to, having been applied to virtually any object that might have been used to stimulate devotional experience.[14] The addition of the qualifier, "small," as in *Kleines Andachtsbild,* to this umbrella term implies that size alone allows for a meaningful distinction between works of this type and others belonging to the same supposed family. Yet *Kleine Andachtsbilder* come in the most varied shapes and sizes. The term has been attached to almost any image drawn, painted, or printed on single leaves of either parchment or paper, as well as to a host of other objects (the majority of the sixteenth century or later), sculpted, embroidered, or constructed from such diverse materials as wax and lace.[15]

Instead of supplying coherent categories, *Kleines Andachtsbild* and *Nonnenarbeit* define dumping grounds for images, often made by and for women, with which art history would rather not be bothered.[16] Inaccessible to conventional aesthetics, these unassuming images remain more or less intractable to other forms of inquiry: neither the abstractions of iconography nor the particulars of context seem to explain their significance. Modern variants come dangerously close to *Kitsch,* in Germany linked with the feminine categories of *Heim und Herz* ("hearth and heart"), that is, domesticity and sentimentality.[17] Pigeonholed as examples of popular imagery, *Nonnenarbeiten* and *Kleine Andachtsbilder* sink below the horizon of art-historical regard to remain the concern of pious collectors or the chroniclers of *Volkskunde.*[18] To the extent they have been harnessed to art history, such small-scale devotional images have been used to secure reliable points of reference to date and localize single-leaf woodcuts.[19] Their idiosyncratic imagery also provides precedents for some early modern emblems.[20] *Nonnenarbeiten,* however, had their own rationale, independent of their relationship to other genres and media. Between the medieval and early modern materials there are decisive differences of audience and function.

Rather than discard *Nonnenarbeit* as an outmoded epithet, we can instead, faute de mieux, accept it as an affirmation of difference, just as nuns, in contrast to clerical culture, unapologetically affirmed the role of images in their own spirituality. Whereas theologians rarely mentioned works of art except to criticize them or, on occasion, to concede their utility for pastoral purposes, nuns made them an integral, even indispensable, part of their piety.[21] *Nonnenarbeiten* owe their power in part to their idiosyncratic imagery, in part to the beliefs of the women who made them, but they represent more than mere talismans or curiosities. They gain their vitality from their visual language, a mode of expression as distinctive as the spirituality that informed them.

Far from effusions of "popular piety," *Nonnenarbeiten* can only be understood in relation to the monastic culture that produced them, insofar as it can be reconstructed. "Reconstruction" has become a suspect term, and rightly so: even if St. Walburg, the abbey at the center of this study, had been preserved in a time capsule, we would still confront problems of interpretation. It is difficult, however, to deconstruct the art history of female monasticism, which has yet to be assembled, even in a rudimentary fashion. The principal construction, if one so wishes to state the issue, has been one of exclusion and disregard. If, however, we set aside established historiographical frameworks and grant these overlooked drawings our regard, we see how images that supposedly make up the prehistories of later genres turn out to have histories all their own. *Nonnenarbeiten* can be seen as their makers saw them, as ends in themselves, not as antecedents or analogues. No works of art speak directly in the manner once assumed for all so-called primitives. Yet the artless images from late medieval convents express with an uncommon immediacy the aspirations of the nuns who made them.

Eichstätt and its surroundings.

I

PATTERNS OF PIETY — PROTOCOLS OF VISION

THE VISUAL CULTURE OF ST. WALBURG

IN THEORY, THE BEST WAY to rewrite the history of the images known as *Nonnenarbeiten* would be to explore the contexts in which they were drawn and distributed as aids to devotion. In practice, however, these single-leaf images are notoriously difficult to date, let alone localize, accurately. Their simple, if bold, visual vocabulary generally hinders any but the broadest comparisons with other works of art; their status as independent images, for the most part without marks of ownership or origin, obstructs correlations with a specific context. Thus the survival of a group of at least a dozen drawings closely related in style and, for the most part, iconography, all traceable to the hand of an anonymous nun working in a Franconian convent at the turn of the sixteenth century, represents an unprecedented opportunity to reexamine the significance of this entire class of image.

Produced around 1500 at the venerable Benedictine abbey of St. Walburg, situated in the Altmühl gorge on a hillock overlooking the city of Eichstätt, the drawings, with a single exception, have survived as a group in the convent's possession.[1] Although virtually unknown, they have not altogether escaped attention: in the 1930s some were used to illustrate articles in the abbey's pastoral newsletter, the *Walburgis-Blätter.*[2] More recently, a few have been reproduced for distribution to modern-day visitors to the convent, mostly female pilgrims. Only three have ever been displayed to a wider public—in an exhibition of *Klosterfrauenarbeiten* of the seventeenth, eighteenth, and nineteenth centuries.[3] Modern mores cannot be projected back onto medieval objects, but the continued use of these images today as devotional aids and spiritual souvenirs implies a continuity of function across close to five hundred years. In some respects, the shift to photomechanical reproduction merely represents an increase in efficiency; the use of the images as aids to meditative prayer remains little changed.[4]

The abbey of St. Walburg takes its name from the saintly sister of the Anglo-Saxon missionaries Wynnebald and Willibald, the latter the first bishop of Eichstätt.[5] Apart from her family, however, Walburga had few ties to Eichstätt, either during her lifetime or following her death, probably in 779. Born in England around 710, she was raised at the aristocratic convent of Wimborne in South Dorset. Following her brothers, Walburga came, sometime during the 740s, to the Continent, where in 761, within a week of Wynnebald's death, she took over the direction of the Benedictine monastery at Heidenheim, in Bavaria, founding soon after a sister house of Benedictine nuns. Only in about 870–79, at the instigation of Bishop Otgar of Eichstätt (ca. 847–80), were her relics translated from Heidenheim to the site of the future abbey, where they were enshrined in a chapel. As part of the effort to promulgate her cult, the priest Wolfhard composed a vita devoted to her miracles in 888;[6] five years later Bishop Erchanbald (882–912) permitted the abbess Liubila to remove to the convent she had founded a few years earlier at Monheim a portion of Walburga's remains. From this moment, Walburga's cult grew rapidly, soon spreading, like her relics, all over southern Germany.[7]

In Eichstätt itself Walburga's remains were tended by a community of canonesses. Permitted to own private property and not bound by vows to a cloistered life, the canonesses exercised privileges in keeping with their wealth and status.[8] By the eleventh century, however, the foundation had fallen on hard times. With the encouragement of Bishop Heribert of Eichstätt (1022–42), Leodegar, count of Lechsgemünd-Graisbach, fulfilled a vow by providing for the conversion of the *Damenstift* into a Benedictine convent. In 1035 Walburga's bones were removed from the chapel and installed in the crypt of the newly constructed church. A miniature from the *Salbuch,* or account book of the abbey, dated 1360, depicts Leodegar, who eventually became a priest and was buried in the church, presenting his foundation to the saint (Fig. 2).[9] Walburga sits on a throne resembling an altar, raised on an arched pedestal, just as in the abbey itself her relics reside above the vaulted *confessio,* or burial chapel, in the crypt (see Figs. 39, 40).

By the mid fifteenth century, Leodegar's foundation was once again in urgent need of renewal. At the direction of the bishop, Johann III von Eych, the abbey was reformed, a process that got under way on March 24, 1456—but, as was often the case, only in the face of considerable resistance from its aristocratic inhabitants, led by Abbess Elisabeth von Seckendorff.[10] Reform generally entailed a reimposition (or initial imposition) of traditional monastic discipline. At St. Walburg, the bishop's efforts included an ambitious program of artistic patronage to make the abbey once again the center of a significant cult. Then as now pilgrims were at-

Fig. 2. Leodegar presenting the abbey to St. Walburga, *Salbuch,* 1360, Eichstätt, St. Walburg.

tracted by the water (the so-called Walburgis-Öl, or oil) that collects in the cavity below the relics between October and February; visitors can carry it home with them in small vials prepared by the nuns.[11]

Given the extensive rebuilding and renovation (and even outright destruction) of the abbey, the survival of a considerable number of ephemeral scraps of paper from its inventory is little short of miraculous. Rebuilt in the midst of the Thirty Years' War to accommodate growing throngs of visitors—but pillaged and burned by marauding Swedish troops on February 6, 1634, almost immediately after—the abbey retains few traces of its medieval origins.[12] Virtually nothing remains of the premodern fabric apart from portions of the crypt and a few funerary monuments. That the drawings have survived in the convent for approximately half a millennium provides the surest indication of their origins. No less important, their survival testifies to a tradition of uninterrupted use and veneration. Even if art historians have overlooked the drawings, the nuns of St. Walburg have held them in ceaseless regard.

DELINEATING DEVOTIONS

In 1936 as many as twenty-five drawings, all attributable to a single nun, were still in the possession of St. Walburg.[13] Unfortunately, it is uncertain how many of them still remain there.[14] At the abbey itself, at least eleven drawings survive. Of these, six have relatively conventional subjects, even if they are not always conventionally treated: the Entombment, a St. Kümmernis, the *Gnadenstuhl,* the *Arbor virginis,* or "Tree of the Virgin," the Presentation in the Temple, and a St. Barbara with the Virgin and Child (see Plates 2–4; Figs. 5, 11, 33). The remaining five are more unusual, even idiosyncratic: the Consecration of Virgins, the Agony in the Garden, a Symbolic Crucifixion, the Heart on the Cross, and the Eucharistic Banquet (see Plates 7–11). One additional drawing, of the Heart as a House, was sold at Sotheby's, London, and passed through a private collection before being acquired in 1993 by the Staatsbibliothek in Berlin (see Plate 12).[15] Whether the drawing that came to auction was among the number tabulated in 1936 can no longer be determined; probably it had been alienated from the convent's collection by that time—conceivably as recently as 1930, when, in response to fears of contamination, some of the convent's older furnishings and devotional objects were cleared out or destroyed.[16] More likely, however, it was removed during the secularization of the convent, which lasted from 1806 to 1835.[17] Whatever the fate of the other drawings, that only one seems ever to have left the convent strongly suggests that the remainder were intended for use within its walls.

Almost all the images in St. Walburg's possession were either produced by professional artists or copied from models supplied from outside the convent. In contrast, the drawings the nuns themselves produced show scant regard for the conventions of professional scriptoria and workshops. Their awkward technique and idiosyncratic imagery indicate the relative isolation in which the nuns worshiped and worked. Aesthetically, their quality may be marginal, and they can at best be said—with unavoidable condescension—to have a certain "childlike" charm. Once we adopt the nuns' point of view and look at the images from the inside out, rather than from the outside in, however, little about them is naive. Making a virtue of necessity, the nuns developed a visual culture of their own that was, if not entirely independent, then at least governed by its own requirements and protocols.

Some of the drawings are unique; their unconventional character demands from

Fig. 3. Entombment, Eichstätt, St. Walburg.

us an unconventional response. But among even the images with nominally commonplace subjects, none can be identified as an outright copy. Of the twelve drawings, only two, the Presentation in the Temple (see Fig. 11) and the Entombment (Fig. 3 and Plate 2) illustrate narrative themes. More typical are cult images: a Trinity adored by angels (see Fig. 5) and a Virgin and Child with St. Barbara, with two female devotees kneeling in prayer at their feet (see Plate 6). In addition, there is an effigy of St. Kümmernis, better known as St. Wilgefortis (Fig. 4 and Plate 3).[18] Although this drawing lacks narrative detail, it can be correlated with the legend of the female martyr included in a miscellany from the convent's library

Fig. 4. St. Kümmernis, Eichstätt, St. Walburg.

that recounts how the saint grew a beard and suffered crucifixion to avoid marriage and preserve her virginity.[19] Based on a misinterpretation of the *Volto Santo* and its copies, which depicted Christ crucified in a full-length *colombium* rather than a loincloth, the legend enjoyed a special veneration among nuns because it celebrated female virginity and martyrdom in the imitation of Christ.[20]

Most, if not all, of these images contain unconventional elements, telltale indicators of the spiritual climate in which they were made. For example, only the inscription ("Sancta Barbara virgo et martir") identifies the female saint in the drawing of the Virgin with St. Barbara. She appears without the tower in which she was enclosed, her customary attribute, which would have had resonance for an audience of nuns (see Plate 6). In its stead, she displays the palm of martyrdom and holds a golden chalice crowned with a Host, corresponding to the Child, held by the Virgin, who, in addition to a small coral bracelet, wears a cross pendant around his neck. As if to underscore the words of the canon of the Mass *hoc est enim corpus meum,* "for this is my body," the Child points demonstratively toward the chalice, reenforcing the parallel established by the symmetrical composition, which in turn likens the saint to the Virgin.[21]

Still more idiosyncratic is the drawing of the Trinity surrounded by a glory of angels (Fig. 5). At first glance, the configuration appears to represent the *Gnadenstuhl,* a form of the Trinity in which God the Father displays his crucified Son (Fig. 6).[22] On closer examination, however, the subject appears less straightforward. Even as the drawing takes the hieratic *Gnadenstuhl* as its point of departure, it imparts to it an unusual animation: the image transforms a static cult image into an epiphany. God the Father, off center, presents his Son to the heavenly host. Only the dove of the Holy Ghost, perched on God's wrist, remains frontal. Leaning forward from a window or niche, God, who bears a cross halo, displays an orb with a cross and the crucified Jesus, symbols that refer to the divine and human natures unified in Christ. The architectural framework serves as a monstrance for the *corpus Christi,* which "demonstrates" the Incarnation. The adoring angels, their hands clasped in prayer, acknowledge and affirm the exaltation of the cross, which, by extending to the lower border, stands in a space separate from the otherworldly realm occupied by the Father.

Two other images in the set combine the narrative and diagrammatic modes. One represents the family tree of the Virgin, with her parents, Joachim and Anna, seated in a garden, a double stem growing from their chests leading up to the Virgin and Christ (see Plate 4).[23] Christ, however, is shown, not "life-size," but rather in the form of the crucifix Mary clasps in her hands. In the second such image Mary assumes a similarly prominent position (see Plate 9). A symbolic Crucifixion bristling with inscriptions, the drawing incorporates three smaller scenes representing the life of the Savior: his infancy (the Christ Child lying in a tiny manger enclosed in a wattle fence), his adulthood or ministry (the clothed Christ, standing erect), and his death (the Crucifixion itself). Removed from her usual position beneath the cross, the Virgin Mary crowns the composition as an emblem of compassionate response, five symbolic swords of compassion converging on her heart.

Two additional drawings that appear to focus on moments of narrative in fact take ritual and devotion themselves as their themes. The first, an image of the

Fig. 5. *Gnadenstuhl,* Eichstätt, St. Walburg.

Agony in the Garden set in a red rose blossom presents a reflexive image of prayer (see Plate 8). Like a rosary itself, the representation of the rose serves as both an emblem of prayer and an object of devotion. The rose, a symbol of Christ's sacrifice, presents the viewer with Christ as her exemplar contemplating his own Passion in the garden of Gethsemane, even as it reminds her to meditate on the same subject. No less complex is the drawing that recalls illustrations of the Adoration of the Magi—except that in it, instead of three kings, two files of women, only one of them crowned, kneel before the Virgin and Child enthroned in front of a red and gold cloth of honor (see Plate 7). The drawing represents, not an epiphany,

Fig. 6. Christ in the Winepress and the *Gnadenstuhl,* embroidery, ca. 1490.

but the defining moment in the liturgical life of any nun: her consecration as a virgin.

The three remaining drawings are even more exceptional. Although analogous images may once have existed, each now represents a unicum. All three drawings take the heart as their central theme, even though they interpret it in different ways. The first, another symbolic Crucifixion, turns Christ's body inside out, concealing the torso, which normally displays the side wound, behind a huge heart (see Plate 10). Images of the wounded heart are commonplace. In this case, however, the yawning gash opens to reveal a nun and the Christ Child; he offers her a small golden container of uncertain identity, probably a pyx.[24] A ladder with rungs identified as virtues illustrates the arduous ascent of the soul that aspires to join Christ on the cross. The second drawing, which focuses on the heart alone, presents, as it were, a close-up of this place of spiritual refuge: now the nun joins the entire Trinity at a eucharistic banquet (see Plate 11). Having taken his bride, Christ introduces her to his Father.[25]

The third drawing in this group configures the heart as a house in which the soul finds rest in the embrace of the Trinity (see Plate 12). Ablaze in a threefold aureole, the Triune God is seen through a window, as in the drawing of the Trinity adored by angels. In the upper right corner, the choir of virgins recalls that in the drawing of the consecration; at the lower left, the steps leading up to the door bring to mind the ladder in the second symbolic Crucifixion. As in the drawing of the Eucharistic Banquet, the nun joins the Trinity at the altar table, identified by the Hosts and chalice to the right. The three images in this group, like many of the others, present Christ as both an offering and an exemplar. At the same time, they develop a visual rhetoric that makes the viewer's union with the Godhead their unifying theme.

The twelve images form a close-knit group. Joseph Lechner, who catalogued the manuscripts from St. Walburg in the 1930s, recognized their common authorship, although he did not describe them or their subject matter. He dubbed the otherwise unknown artist the "Kümmernis painter" after one of the most conventional images in the set, perhaps because it could be correlated with a legend of the saint included in one of the convent's *Sammelhandschriften* (see Fig. 4 and Plate 3), or devotional miscellanies.[26] To call the nun who made these images the Master or even the Mistress of St. Walburg is clearly inappropriate. Perhaps we should settle for the designation she and her community would have employed: *Malerin,* or "painter."

The twelve drawings, while uniform in manner, could hardly be more varied in other respects, most notably size and format. Some are square, others rectangular. The images also vary in technique and support. A few—the Heart as a House, the Symbolic Crucifixion, and the St. Kümmernis (Plates 12, 9, 3; Fig. 4)—are on paper, the remainder on parchment.[27] Those on vellum are more elaborately embellished, a distinction that might indicate recipients of varying rank or resources. Whereas the drawings on paper are outlined in ink, then tinted with pale, translucent colors, those on parchment are worked up with opaque pigments and gold leaf. All, however, are worn, suggesting extensive handling and use. Eight of the drawings have parti-colored frames—of two different types—that in some cases have been trimmed. Three others—the Presentation of Christ in the Temple, the Trinity adored by angels, and the *Arbor virginis*—have floral borders that emulate the decorative margins of illuminated manuscripts (see Figs. 11, 5; Plate 4). If it was trimmed, the remaining drawing, the Virgin and Child with St. Barbara, may also have been of this type (see Plate 6). The variety of format and technique indicates that no matter how closely related in function or how deeply informed by a shared set of concerns, the dozen drawings that have come down to us were not created as a set. Moreover, the categories and relationships we see in them may not have been typical of what was once, perhaps, a much larger number of drawings. The extant images probably represent no more than a fraction of a far more extensive production.

Beyond variations in format and content, the drawings share a distinctive decorative vocabulary, reminiscent, at least at first, of some single-leaf woodcuts: simple compositions drawn in outline, then filled in with unmodulated blocks of color. The figures are rigid, with small heads and hands, and wear garments whose folds are defined by stiff, parallel striations. The faces are especially distinctive, with small noses, long arched eyebrows, button eyes, undefined chins, and pursed lips. Almost all the drawings have as a setting a carpet of schematically rendered greenery that rises to approximately half the height of the figures. The plants, which recur with such regularity that they could be considered a hallmark of the artist, do not overlap but are set in neat parallel rows, one stacked above the other, as if in a tapestry. Except for the drawing of the Heart as a House (see Plate 12), which remains virtually untinted, the palette is similar from one drawing to the next: a bright orange, used principally for figures, a deep blue, a pinkish beige, yellow (in lieu of gold), green, and, in lesser quantities, brown and black, the latter used exclusively for the habits of the Benedictine nuns.

Because the drawings from St. Walburg all look as if they were stamped from the same mold, it seems reasonable to assume that they represent the handiwork of a single nun. German convent communities often assigned the task of painting or repairing images, miniature or monumental, to a *Malerin,* not simply out of economic necessity, but to forestall, whenever possible, the entry of workmen into the convent. At Wienhausen in Saxony, three nuns, all named Gertrude, were active as painters: in 1488 they repainted (in fact, restored) the murals in the choir.[28] The chronicle of the Dominican convent of Töß in Switzerland specifies that it owed many "pictures"—whether wall paintings or panels is not clear—to the hand (not simply the patronage) of Sister Mezzi von Klingenberg: "We had many of our good pictures from her; she illuminated many German books." [29] The implied distinction between German books ("tüscher bůcher") and Latin service books identifies illustrated vernacular devotional literature—little of which survives from the fourteenth century—as Mezzi's speciality and also intimates that she and, by implication, other nuns active as artists needed to understand the texts they were illustrating.

As far as content is concerned, the draftswoman from St. Walburg speaks her own language; by any measure, her images are "originals." Although most of her drawings cannot be pigeonholed as unambiguous copies or even as adaptations of sources, the same cannot be said of her stylistic vocabulary. Although unlikely, it is not inconceivable that the drawings stem from several hands. Were we to try to distinguish between the contributions of the three Gertrudes who reworked the murals at Wienhausen—a task admittedly made more difficult by subsequent restorations—we would soon be defeated; to judge from appearances alone, the three sisters might as well have been one.[30] The drawings' style, moreover, is not typical of one house, let alone a single hand. Many of the stylistic conventions that mark the work of the *Malerin* of St. Walburg recur in drawings and miniatures from other convents, for example, a drawing of the Christ Child in a basket, formerly in the Figdor collection in Vienna (see Fig. 47).[31]

Drawings and miniatures less closely related to the material from St. Walburg, but nonetheless akin in manner and expression, come from convents across the German-speaking world. A fifteenth-century cutting from a choir book, perhaps from Alsace, offers a representative example (Fig. 7).[32] A trio of female saints—Martha, Agatha, and Elizabeth of Hungary—in a flower-filled meadow present a picture of blissful beatitude. These figures, with their garlands, rosy red cheeks, pursed lips, and button eyes, combine with the overall pattern produced by the even distribution of the dominant colors blue, red, and green to give the initial the quality of a decorated textile. A drawing of the Crucifixion in an early-sixteenth-century prayer book from Strasbourg—according to the colophon, written for her own use by sister "Elysabeth bißnerin zü sanct Katharinen zü Strossburg"—exhibits a similar schematic vocabulary and bright, gaudy palette (Fig. 8).[33] The illustration, which prefaces "a very pretty prayer about the holy, worthy Sacrament" to be said before Communion ("ein vil hübster gebet von dem heiligen wirdigen sacrament"), shows the soul as a young woman with a garland in her hair bathing naked in a tub of blood at the foot of the cross, thus combining allusions to the soul as Christ's bride and the cleansing power of the Sacrament (cf. Fig. 14).[34] As in the drawings from St. Walburg, the stylized foliage does more than supply a foil for the figures; it identifies Golgotha as a garden in which the chaste soul is made immaculate by Christ. The affinities, however, extend beyond means to ends. In its bright colors and boldly silhouetted forms, the drawing recalls a sampler. In spite of the gruesome subject, its pretty conventions conjure up a paradisiacal mood.

All these images participate in a conventual mode of representation. Readily recognizable, it cannot be accounted simply a borrowing from the dominant visual culture, which, especially in Germany, was marked by a profusion of highly articulated local dialects. Nor can it be discounted as the primitive and spontaneous reflex of untrained artists. The draftswoman from St. Walburg adopted conventions from a range of media, primarily prints, tapestries, and illuminated manuscripts, all of which she would have known from her immediate environment. These media, however, also include textiles, sculpture, metalwork, and even the architecture of the abbey itself. The stylistic and iconographic affinities raise sig-

Fig. 7. SS. Martha, Agatha, and Elizabeth of Hungary, cutting from a choir book, German, fifteenth century, detail. Art Museum, Princeton University. y1031. Museum purchase.

Fig. 8. Crucifixion, prayer book, Strasbourg, early sixteenth century, Karlsruhe, Badische Landesbibliothek, Ms. St. Peter pap. 4, f. 30v.

nificant questions about the models available to the nuns and about their training, because enclosure strictly limited what the nuns could and could not see.[35] At issue is the extent to which the images express the nuns' own spirituality or result from the community's contact with the world outside the walls. The passage of images to and from the convent serves as a paradigm for the effectiveness and limitations of enclosure itself.[36]

Classified by medium, genre, style, or iconography, the abbey's disparate images cannot coalesce into a coherent picture. The tapestries and what remains of the illuminated manuscripts are, for the most part, unrelated in style; the vernacular manuscripts that make up the small but significant collection of *Sammelhandschriften* are unillustrated except for a few images, primarily prints, inserted with little regard for their relation to the texts; and of these writings, few can be precisely correlated with the imagery in the drawings.[37] The conventional categories of art history and the fine arts, however, were not those of the nuns themselves. Organized according to overarching patterns of piety and paraliturgical performance, their images interacted with one another in a larger theater of devotion. Objects most museums would divide among different departments (or relegate to storage) in the convent's shared ritual spaces performed complementary liturgical, commemorative, and devotional functions. As part of such a mixed mise-en-scène, the drawings from St. Walburg assumed their place in a complex constellation of art and devotion. Created to complement the large number of professionally produced objects purchased or otherwise acquired by the abbey, the drawings met needs that the community's rich and varied inventory of imported imagery left unfulfilled. If they do not qualify as "Art," at least as conventionally defined, it need not follow that the nun who drew them did so naively. With their sophisticated visual rhetoric and highly unusual subject matter, the drawings display a premeditated and self-conscious resourcefulness. The nun who made them sought nothing less than to reshape the religious imagination of fellow nuns in their collective image.

PRINTED EXEMPLARS

Nonnenarbeiten inevitably invite comparison with prints, largely because devotional drawings are usually characterized as derivative images. Presuppositions about their "secondhand" nature shape their definition as "second-class" objects. Adolf Spamer, in *Das Kleine Andachtsbild,* the standard work on small-scale devotional imagery, characterized the majority as naive copies of "better" models, either miniatures or prints.[38] The innovative and idiosyncratic imagery of many of the drawings from St. Walburg should put us on guard against such a tired generalization.[39] Although we place a premium on innovation, in context even rote repetition can be meaningful. The history of medieval art is full of indications that reproduction, mechanical or otherwise, did not necessarily deprive images of their aura.[40]

None of the drawings from St. Walburg survives as a multiple original, or even as a close variant of another design. Some internal evidence, however, suggests that at least one of the images (see Plate 12), on its face the most unusual, could be a copy or at least a variation on a previous pattern. In the upper left corner of the leaf sold at Sotheby's, the scribe, probably identical with the draftswoman, inadvertently repeated the word "mensch," "person," following the verb "vernewet," "it renews," breaking the borders of the scroll.[41] In theory, she might have realized—too late—that if she continued writing from left to right across the top of the drawing, she would run out of space. In practice, however, this possibility can be ruled out, and with it, the hypothesis that the rather unruly inscriptions were added ad hoc, as afterthoughts. The way the scrolls overlap all other parts of the image, not only their outlines but also the hatching, indicates that they were planned from the start. It seems that the draftswoman lost sight of the curvilinear track, perhaps when she looked up to read the next portion of the text she was transcribing. If the texts she was copying were integral to the design of the drawing, then it follows that the drawing itself was copied. And if this drawing is a duplicate, the others might be as well.

If we proceed on the premise that the drawings from St. Walburg were produced as multiples (if not in quantity, then at least as variants on loosely defined themes), the first analogy that comes to mind is prints in the form of single-leaf woodcuts. Printed on both parchment and paper, single-leaf impressions were commonplace objects by the end of the fifteenth century. Moreover, once they were finished, they rarely remained uniform. A painter usually added a patchwork of color to the inked lines, varying it from one image to the next. Rarely does one find two fifteenth-century prints that are exactly alike. In some convents nuns not only collected but may also have produced prints for themselves, occasionally even cutting their own blocks.[42] Although there is no evidence of in-house production at St. Walburg, the prints in the abbey's collection indicate that the nuns were familiar with mass-produced images.[43] One of the tapestries the nuns produced incorporates a motif borrowed directly from a print, a process that can be documented at other convents.[44]

The closer we look, however, the less satisfactory the comparison between the drawings and prints becomes. Unlike woodcuts, which often leave open large ex-

Fig. 9. The *Arbor virginis,* Eichstätt, St. Walburg.

Fig. 10. The *Arbor virginis,* Munich, Bayerische Staatsbibliothek, Cgm. 105, f. 1r.

panses of blank paper as a foil for the inked parts of the image, the drawings from St. Walburg fill and crowd the surface, indicating a visual *horror vacui.* Stylistic conventions aside, only one drawing, the *Arbor virginis* (Fig. 9 and Plate 4), seems possibly to echo a printed model:[45] a late-fifteenth-century woodcut of the same subject. One exemplar of this composition was printed directly from the block onto the opening parchment folio of a German prayer book (Fig. 10).[46] The iconography is closely related: Christ's grandparents serve as the "roots" of the tree, which loops upward around Mary before culminating in Christ. Similar renditions of the subject are too common to permit firm conclusions, but in this case the draftswoman appears to have taken her inspiration from a model—if not this one, then one very much like it.[47] The drawing appears to simplify the print, eliminating the angels, cutting back the trunk of the tree, and consolidating the remaining figures.

We should be wary, however, of characterizing these and other changes as misunderstandings. In removing Joachim and Anna from the bench to the foreground, the draftswoman converts their stool into the barrier wall of a *hortus conclusus,* or enclosed garden, an image of virginity with special resonance for a cloistered nun. Punning on the relation between *virgo* (virgin) and *virga* (rod), the image shifts the burden of meaning from Christ on the *arbor vitae* to the immaculate stock of the Virgin.[48] The amalgamation of the Virgin and Child and the crucified Christ into the single figure of the Virgin at the center makes Mary the focal point of the image. In addition, by eliminating the Christ Child and replacing him, not just with the crucified Christ, but with a diminutive image of the Crucifixion that the Virgin holds as she prays, the artist presents the viewer with an exemplar of prayer, as in the drawing of Christ at Gethsemane (see Plate 8), where Christ prays before a crucifix.[49] The image of the Holy Genealogy presents not only a model of prayer but an exemplar of prayer before images. The alteration lends the drawing a reflexive character that its ostensible prototype does not possess. Whatever models it depends on, the drawing also functions as a model, not for other images, but for the life of prayer itself.

MANUSCRIPT MODELS

If we look beyond the image of the Holy Genealogy to its setting, the analogy to prints becomes even less convincing. The drawing (see Fig. 9 and Plate 4) simulates a leaf from an illuminated manuscript. The arched frame around the composition is a common device in fifteenth-century manuscript painting; still more suggestive of an illuminated prayer book is the elaborate floral border, filled with large buds, blossoms, and pods that grow from a single curling vine. Similar frames and borders occur in two of the other drawings, neither of which bears any known relation to prints: the Presentation in the Temple and the Trinity (Fig. 11; see Fig. 5). Of the dozen drawings that survive, these three are also the only ones that include no inscriptions, an absence of text that reinforces their character as "illustrations." Among the most conventional in their iconography, these drawings are also the most easily imagined as single-leaf miniatures tipped into manuscripts.

The frames and floral borders of this subgroup of drawings immediately bring to mind the characteristic *mise-en-page* of innumerable French, Flemish, and Netherlandish Books of Hours. More specifically, the objects, primarily fruits and flowers, strewn around the periphery of each leaf recall the ornamentation typical of "Ghent-Bruges" illumination, widely distributed outside the Low Countries.[50] Single leaves facilitated the dissemination of this type of ornament and resemble the drawings in format as well as decorative vocabulary. The nuns of St. Walburg may have seen leaves similar to a set of four produced circa 1500 by the Master of the Suffrages, affiliated with the Augustinian convent of Hieronymusdael in the

Fig. 11. Presentation in the Temple, Eichstätt, St. Walburg.

Northern Netherlands (Fig. 12).[51] Each leaf of this set bears an inscription in Dutch and has been mounted in an elaborately embroidered frame, suggesting that even if they were originally intended for insertion in a prayer book, they were adapted early on to serve nuns as isolated devotional images.

The drawings from St. Walburg have a much more tenuous relation to German manuscript illumination, especially from the region surrounding Eichstätt. Contrary to what one might expect, they cannot be characterized as customary or even as straightforward derivations from a local style. The tradition that flourished in the diocese of Augsburg and its environs offers parallels in neither format nor

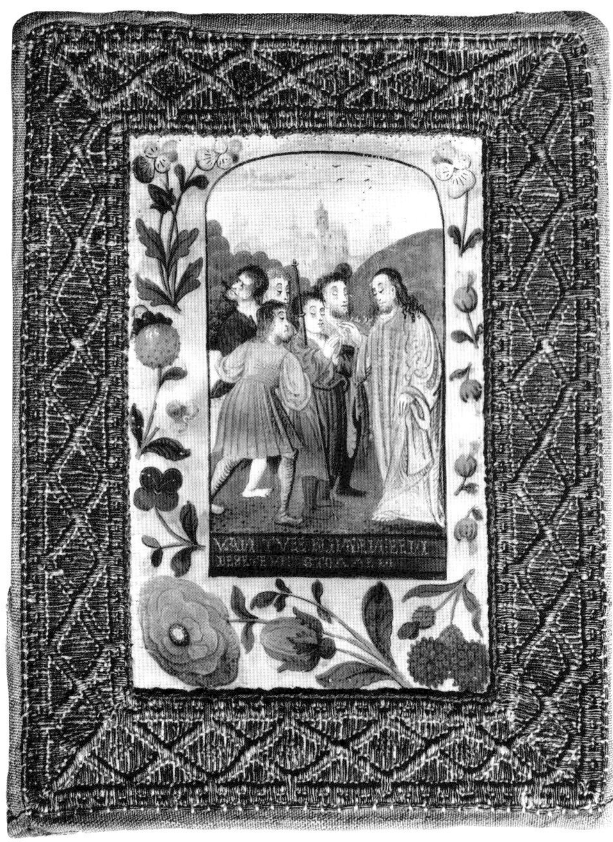

Fig. 12. Christ Healing the Blind, single leaf in embroidered mount, Master of the Suffrages, Leiden, ca. 1500. Sam Fogg Rare Books, London.

decorative vocabulary.[52] Manuscripts from Augsburg are celebrated for the exuberant embellishment of their margins, in some books so dense and luxuriant that it threatens to overwhelm the text.[53] The sumptuous Pontifical-Missal of William of Reichenau, commissioned in 1466 by the bishop of Eichstätt to commemorate his assumption of office in 1464, offers a representative example, striking not only for the flamboyance but also for the variety of its marginal ornament (Fig. 13; see Figs. 16, 23, 26, 27).[54] The borders include both small vignettes that complement the central narrative and a profusion of plants, ranging from highly stylized vines to blossoms of identifiable species, each one a nature study of the kind that reached full flower in the work of Schongauer and Dürer.[55] By comparison, in the drawings from St. Walburg the borders are reserved and restrained, the floral specimens stiff and scattered.

The decoration of the leaves from St. Walburg is not entirely anomalous, how-

Fig. 13. Feast of the Ascension, Pontifical-Missal of William of Reichenau, Eichstätt, Diözesanarchiv, Ordinariatsbibliothek, Ms. 131, f. 52v.

ever. A few German manuscripts offer astonishingly faithful emulations, if not outright replicas, of Flemish and Netherlandish models.[56] In Eichstätt itself, the *Gundekarianum,* a pontifical cumulatively commissioned by the bishops of Eichstätt from the eleventh century onward, contains several mid-fifteenth-century miniatures that emulate Netherlandish exemplars.[57] On occasion, German scribes collaborated with French artists, or at least completed manuscripts imported from France. For example, only the German text distinguishes a Book of Hours made for a well-to-do woman of Nuremberg around 1500 (Fig. 14) from a typical Parisian or Rouen Book of Hours of the same period.[58] This prayer book, illuminated by French artists, either at home or abroad, belongs to a genre rarely produced in Germanic-speaking regions, where more loosely organized prayer miscellanies remained the norm.[59] It stands out as a hothouse plant, the product of an unusual and perhaps fortuitous commission or collaboration.

Fig. 14. Augsburg, Universitätsbibliothek, Ms. Cod. I. 3 8° 2, f. 261r.

The nuns of St. Walburg may have had in their collection, by way of inheritance or donation, a similar Book of Hours that served them as a point of artistic departure. Their contact with works of art produced outside the convent, however, was hardly so haphazard. The manuscripts still in the abbey's possession suggest that the nuns either commissioned or received a small but steady stream of codices illuminated by professional craftsmen. Unlike the unadorned devotional miscellanies in the abbey's library, the liturgical manuscripts in the sacristy were extensively embellished. Unfortunately, they survive only as fragments, incorporated into a later set of books for the Mass and the Divine Office (Fig. 15).[60] The three imposing volumes (a Gradual and an Antiphonary in two parts) were written by the nun Maria Magdalena Hübschin (d. 1634) in the decade 1620–30.[61] Although a fine calligrapher, Maria Magdalena decorated the books with dozens of historiated and ornamental initials removed from medieval manuscripts. As in a Vic-

Fig. 15. Eichstätt, St. Walburg, Ms. Lat. 3, p. 262.

torian pastiche or scrapbook, the initials have been pasted in without regard for chronology.

The fragments from St. Walburg date from as early as the fourteenth and as late as the mid sixteenth century. Only the fifteenth- and sixteenth-century cuttings furnish a context in which to evaluate the relationship between the drawings and the manuscript models available to the nuns.[62] Illuminated from around 1470 to 1540, they fall on the basis of style into three distinct groups that come from at least as many manuscripts. Although hardly of the same quality as the Pontifical-Missal of William of Reichenau, the first group is of approximately the same generation as the episcopal manuscript, as can be seen from a comparison of the cutting of the Resurrection with its counterpart in the missal (Figs. 16, 17). These cuttings probably date from approximately 1475 to 1486, the years when William's sister, Ursula of Reichenau, served as abbess. Painted in a stiffer shorthand version

Figs. 16 and 17. Resurrection: (*above, left*) Pontifical-Missal of William of Reichenau, Eichstätt, Diözesanarchiv, Ordinariatsbibliothek, Ms. 131, f. 44v; and Eichstätt, St. Walburg, Ms. Lat. 3, p. 214.

of the fluid style exhibited in William's missal, they conceivably came from liturgical books presented to the abbey by the bishop as part of his efforts at reform. A second set of cuttings, interspersed with the others, is distinct in style, even though it shares with the first an ornamental vocabulary, including the simulated beveling of the frames and the curling acanthus in the initials. In comparison with the elegant figures from the first set—for example, the *imago pietatis* that illustrates the Office for the Dedication of a Church—the Judging Christ in the gradual who introduces the first Sunday in Advent is both angular and awkward (Figs. 18, 19).

Despite their differences, all the later cuttings can be associated with a large and heterogeneous group of manuscripts assigned, on the basis of their apparent origin in Austria and southeastern Germany, to the "Salzburg-Augsburg Workshop."[63] Engaged primarily in the mass production of missals, this loosely affiliated group of craftsmen has been traced from circa 1460 to the early sixteenth century.[64] The production associated with this enterprise varies greatly in quality, but a missal of the use of the diocese of Brixen, dated approximately 1490 (Fig. 20), suggests how the fragments from St. Walburg would have looked before they were cut from their original context.[65] Whereas the Christ in Judgment (Fig. 21), illustrating the first Sunday in Advent, is a virtual twin of the initial pasted into the seventeenth-century gradual at St. Walburg (see Fig. 19), the script and border decoration more closely resemble those found in the Pontifical-Missal of William of Reichenau of 1466. The continuities and connections among manuscripts spanning well over half a century suggest that the artists and scribes who constituted the "workshop"

Figs. 18 and 19. Man of Sorrows (*above, left*), Eichstätt, St. Walburg, Ms. Lat. 4, p. 519; and Christ in Judgment, Eichstätt, Ms. Lat. 3, p. 1.

collaborated on a wide variety of commissions in ever-changing constellations.[66]

The cuttings from St. Walburg indicate that this consortium of craftsmen continued to produce manuscripts, albeit of lower quality, well into the sixteenth century. Proof comes from cuttings in the gradual that combine a coat of arms and a portrait of St. Willibald, the patron saint of Eichstätt, both executed by the same illuminator as the Judgment initial (Fig. 22).[67] The arms belong to Christoph Marshall von Pappenheim, bishop of Eichstätt from 1535 to 1539.[68] The cuttings reiterate late-fifteenth-century conventions—for example, those exhibited in the effigy of Willibald, brother of St. Walburga and the first bishop of Eichstätt, ensconced in the margin of the Pontifical-Missal of William of Reichenau (Fig. 23). Although the evidence is literally fragmentary, it suggests that as late as about 1535–40, the workshop that supplied St. Walburg continued to employ fifteenth-century exemplars. In their isolation, however, the nuns may not have minded; similar retrospective tendencies in iconography and style characterize the products of many convent scriptoria.[69]

In contrast to the books belonging to the bishops of Eichstätt, which betray an increasing reliance on the conventions and standards of print culture, the devotional drawings produced by the nuns for their own purposes stand apart from both the printed and illuminated imagery of their day. Even those drawings that emulate manuscripts most closely reshape their forms. Unlike the fifteenth-century fragments, they do not ape contemporary cosmopolitan models; unlike the sixteenth-century set, they do not fall back on outdated models. Instead, they invite com-

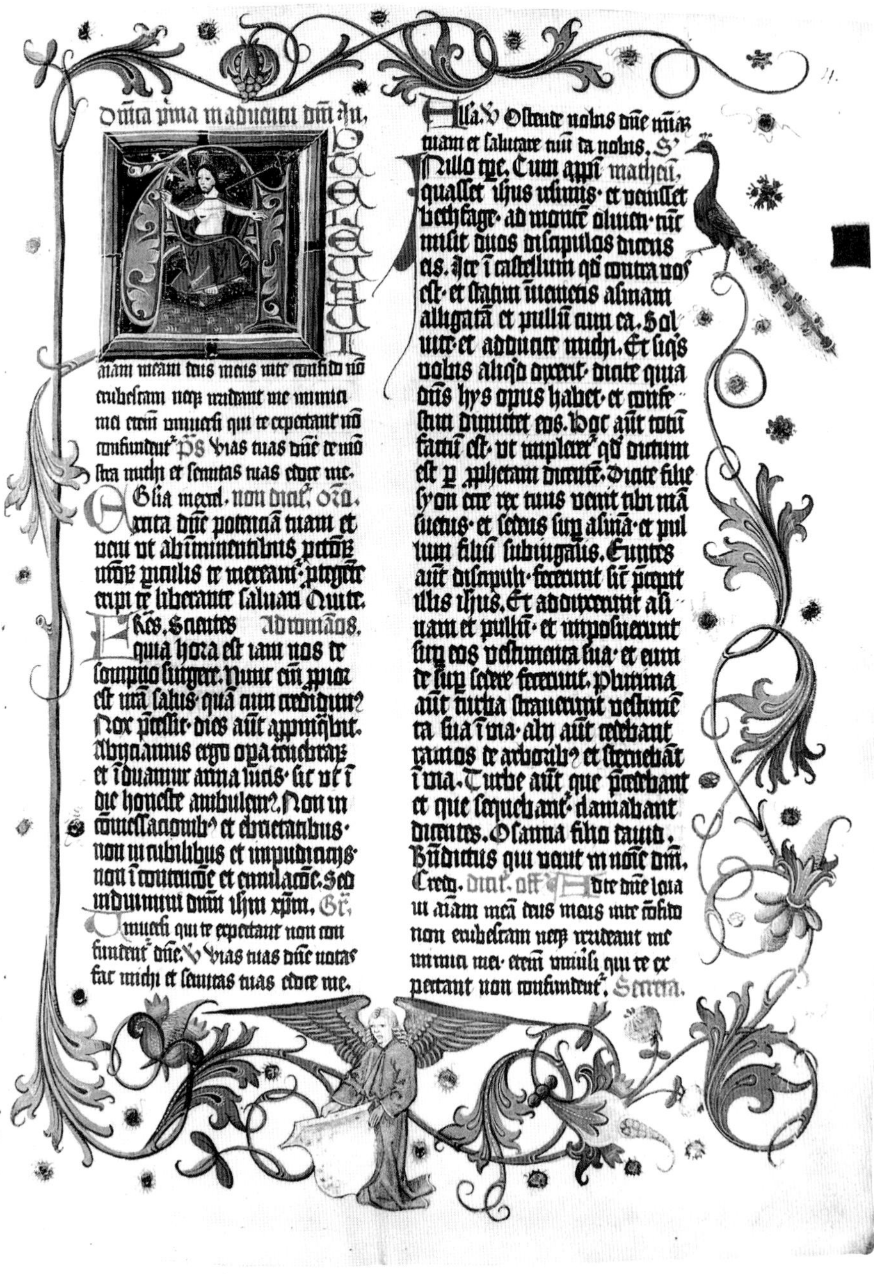

Fig. 20. Missal, use of Brixen, Innsbruck, Universitätsbibliothek, Cod. 15, f. 4r.

Fig. 21. Missal, use of Brixen, Innsbruck, Universitätsbibliothek, Cod. 15, f. 4r, detail.

parison to a third group of cuttings, easily overlooked because they include no figural decoration: scraps of borders assembled in a finicky hodgepodge around small gold initials from a late-fourteenth-century manuscript, occasionally with small strips of fourteenth-century filigree added along the edges (Fig. 24). Among these assemblages occur the only elements analogous to the floral ornament in the borders of the drawings that simulate miniatures (see Figs. 5, 9, 11; Plate 6). In both, for example, we find small red poppy flowers and stubby leaves that protrude directly from stems. If these cuttings represent remnants of a separate group of manuscripts, they provide the only indication that whichever nun made the drawings not only emulated manuscript decoration but practiced it as well.

As with prints, however, various considerations militate against pressing the analogy with manuscripts too far. Even if the drawings resemble miniatures and openly imitate some of their conventions, the vernacular prayer books in the convent's library contain only the most rudimentary decoration, usually the plainest scribal initials. The dramatically differing dimensions of the drawings also argue against their inclusion in manuscripts: they range from as large as 201 × 121 to as small as 74 × 63 millimeters.[70] If the drawings were intended as illustrations, then they were meant for many different books, some of extremely unconventional format. Lechner's catalogue of the convent's library, published in 1937, mentions a number of prints and drawings interleaved, attached to stubs, or otherwise affixed to the books, but to judge from the blank spaces in the manuscripts and the annotations in the convent's copy of the catalogue, all but a few were removed to

Fig. 22. St. Willibald and arms of Bishop Christoph Marshall von Pappenheim, Eichstätt, St. Walburg, Ms. Lat. 3, p. 439.

Fig. 23. St. Willibald of Eichstätt, Pontifical-Missal of William of Reichenau, Eichstätt, Diözesanarchiv, Ordinariatsbibliothek, Ms. 131, f. 165v, detail.

Fig. 24. Composite initial, Eichstätt, St. Walburg, Ms. Lat. 4, p. 94.

the convent's *Bildchensammlung* in 1974. Certainly most are no longer in place. The only drawing still integrated into a manuscript, the Symbolic Crucifixion, is attached to a stub. The manuscript itself, a collection of Marian devotions, was written around 1600.[71]

The relation of the drawings to manuscript models can at best be characterized as equivocal. Rather than ineptly or incompletely imitating miniatures, the drawings self-consciously distance themselves from a format inadequate or inappropriate to their function. Most of them employ unconventional iconography; the liturgical fragments, in contrast, employ exactly the narrative and cult imagery the drawings avoid. And contrary to what we might expect, whereas only one drawing can be identified as deriving from a print, an illuminator such as the Master of the Pontifical-Missal of William of Reichenau relied extensively on printed books for models. Many of the historiated initials and borders in the episcopal missal derive directly from an edition of the forty-page *Biblia pauperum,* printed no earlier than circa 1460.[72] For example, the initial that introduces the Mass for Ascension Day is copied with only minor changes from the printed page demonstrating the typology of Christ's return to heaven (Figs. 25, 26). The two scenes in the lower margin—on the left, the translation of Enoch, on the right, Elijah in his fiery chariot (Fig. 27)—derive directly from the Old Testament types that in the block book are set to either side of the Ascension.[73] The landscape vignette, which recedes to a high, hazy horizon, creates the illusion that the two episodes form part of a common, continuous narrative. Whereas in the typological handbook they are separated by the architectural framework, in the manuscript border they are joined by roads that converge at the center.

The changes introduced by the illuminator indicate that he did not copy slavishly. Nonetheless, if originality alone determines the value of a work of art, then the drawings from St. Walburg are far more innovative and independent than the manuscript the bishop of Eichstätt commissioned to celebrate his assumption of office. To champion the drawings in this way, however, would itself be an anachronism. No stigma attached to copying prints; moreover, the copying process linked the prestigious commission of 1466 to the most up-to-date development in contemporary visual culture, the emergence of printed books.[74] The forty-page *Biblia pauperum* had been in circulation for no more than about six years when the artist employed by William of Reichenau turned to it as a model for the missal. The inspiration and impetus almost certainly came from the bishop of Eichstätt himself. William was celebrated in his own day as a patron of printing. An episcopal chronicle notes that he "industriously saw to it with great care that everything pertaining to the liturgy was properly conducted, and to that end he had the priests' mass and prayer books reformed and prepared in print."[75] The production of printed books was a concomitant of the bishop's interest in humanism.[76] Improved, standardized texts went hand in hand with the bishop's commitment to monastic and liturgical reform. In contrast, the autonomy of the drawings from St. Walburg indicates the degree to which the abbey's draftswoman deliberately distanced herself from contemporary artistic developments.[77]

WOVEN WORK

Each drawing from St. Walburg was produced ad hoc—neither envisioned nor commissioned as part of a series. The drawings should be seen as independent works, not as the detritus of manuscripts that have been broken up or as illustrations to be added to texts. But even if contemporary manuscript illumination and prints offer few parallels to their stiff, schematic mannerisms, they were not produced in complete isolation. The drawings find a visual community where, upon reflection, we should most expect to encounter it: among the tapestries that, like the drawings, the nuns made for themselves.[78]

As opposed to embroidery, tapestry production was less common in convents than is often supposed.[79] It demanded both considerable training and a sizable investment in equipment. The Dominican convent of St. Katharina in Nuremberg was among the few convents engaged in the commercial production of tapestries.[80] Shortly after the reform of St. Walburg in 1456, perhaps as late as 1465, the nuns or their patrons commissioned from the Katharinenkloster a tapestry depicting the life of their patron (Fig. 28). Known as the *Ältere Walburga Teppich* (The older tapestry of St. Walburga), it served as a model for a second tapestry devoted to the same subject, known in turn as the *Jüngere* (younger) *Walburga Teppich* (Fig. 29).[81] The later tapestry, dated 1519, is usually written off as a less accomplished copy of the earlier work.[82] This, however, is to give it short shrift. In turning back to a model of the mid fifteenth century, the nuns acted on the same principles that led them to emulate earlier manuscripts. Characteristic of the "copy" is the freedom with which it treats its exemplar. Besides including two additional episodes, it uses modeling and color more schematically and emphasizes surface pattern rather than illusionistic space—traits that bring to mind the style of the drawings.

Like the drawings, the *Jüngere Walburga Teppich* is an "in-house" production, one of at least seven such textiles executed under the aegis of Walburga von Absberg, abbess of St. Walburg from 1508 to 1538.[83] The scant evidence for a tradition of textile manufacture at the abbey suggests the ambition of such an undertaking.[84] In addition to the expanded version of the *Ältere Walburga Teppich*, the set included

Fig. 25. Ascension, forty-page *Biblia pauperum,* Munich, Bayerische Staatsbibliothek, Xyl. 20, p. 34.

a pair of panels representing SS. Lucy and Apollonia (Fig. 30), the *Leodegarteppich*—a decorative "shroud" with commemorative inscriptions that was laid over the tomb of Leodegar, the abbey's founder—and a full-length portrait of St. Walburga that hung in the refectory or the choir directly above the throne of the abbess (Fig. 31 and Plate 5).[85] Other surviving works include a fragment depicting the Virgin Mary with the unicorn resting its horn in her lap, a larger panel of the

Figs. 26 and 27. Ascension (*left*) and Elijah and Enoch (*below*), Pontifical-Missal of William of Reichenau, Eichstätt, Diözesanarchiv, Ordinariatsbibliothek, Ms. 131, f. 52v, details.

Mission of the Apostles, and a Genealogy of St. Walburga (Fig. 32), now divided into two pieces, that celebrates the saint's royal ancestry.[86] Self-consciously marking the analogy with Christ's royal lineage (a reference reinforced by the echo of Matthew 1 : 1 in the inscription "Hec est generacio"), the designer crowned the composition with the figure of Walburga, who herself is crowned by angels, an action that likens her to Christ, the fruit and flower of the royal Tree of Jesse.

Fig. 28. Older Walburga Tapestry, Harburg über Donauwörth, Fürstliche Oettingen-Wallerstein'sche Sammlung, Schloss Harburg.

Fig. 29. Newer Walburga Tapestry, Harburg über Donauwörth, Fürstliche Oettingen-Wallerstein'sche Sammlung, Schloss Harburg.

Fig. 30. SS. Lucy and Apollonia, Munich, Bayerisches Nationalmuseum.

Fig. 31. St. Walburga, Munich, Bayerisches Nationalmuseum.

Fig. 32. Genealogy of St. Walburga, Munich, Bayerisches Nationalmuseum.

Some of the textiles produced by the nuns of St. Walburg bear direct comparison with their devotional drawings. For example, the relatively small panels of SS. Lucy and Apollonia (both about 34 × 90 cm.) resemble the image of St. Barbara and the Virgin in the disposition of the two female figures that confront each other across the central divide and in the use of a decorative ground dotted with schematic flowers (Fig. 33 and Plate 6; see Fig. 30).[87] The same drawing can be compared with the monumental portrait of St. Walburga (110 × 134 cm.), still imposing despite extensive restoration, which expresses the ideal kinship between the abbess and the patron of the community whose name she assumed (see Fig. 31 and Plate 5). Crowned by angels, the saint holds on a cushion a vial of her miraculous "oil." Two groups of veiled women kneel reverently at her feet: on her left, a group of seven lay sisters, on her right, nine nuns, with the abbess at their head, identified by her coat of arms. The second coat of arms at the foot of the saint is that of the abbey. In the drawing, a single representative of each group, distinguished by her garments, appears in the identical posture.

The similarities between the textiles and the drawings extend from content and

Fig. 33. St. Barbara with the Virgin and Child, Eichstätt, St. Walburg.

composition to minutiae of style. Were it possible to recover the *Bildner,* or cartoons, that underlay the images, the resemblances would be stronger still.[88] For example, in the tapestry of St. Walburga as protectress of the convent, we find the same angular conventions for describing garments, gestures, and faces as in the drawings (see Fig. 31 and Plate 5). Where they fall uninterrupted, the folds and creases run in parallel lines, reinforced by strong shadows. Not that the tapestries and the drawings necessarily were designed by the same nun, but they betray an unmistakable kinship. The analogies carry further if one considers the broad floral border beneath the nuns; restricted to one side of the drawing, it resembles nothing so much as the floral borders conventionally employed to frame tapestries. Even the green paneled backgrounds that recur from one drawing to the next seem to depend on the conventions of decorated textiles; they recall, for example, the stereotypical rows of schematic blossoms in the panels of SS. Lucy and Apollonia (see Fig. 30).[89]

The textiles from the abbey give the devotional drawings from St. Walburg an authoritative point of reference in the artistic and religious experience of the nuns. Although it has been arbitrarily asserted that *Nonnenarbeiten* were no longer produced after 1500, comparisons of the drawings and textiles provide strong evidence to date the surviving drawings no earlier than circa 1500 (a proposal that need not, however, preclude the production of other drawings, no longer extant, in the years immediately following the reform of the abbey).[90] The exact date of the drawings, however, is a secondary issue. Like the textiles, they represent a realm of imagery in which the nuns could develop a language that directly addressed their own concerns.

The most unusual of the abbey's textiles testifies to the nuns' artistic independence even when they relied on models from outside (Fig. 34). Produced earlier than the other surviving tapestries, perhaps as early as 1475, the tapestry sets a cluster of tiny figures and symbols against the "pomegranate" ground typical of many of the textiles from St. Walburg.[91] At the center a scroll unfurls from the beak of an eagle with a halo. Previously identified as either the dove of the Holy Ghost or the symbol of John the Evangelist, the eagle represents the resurrected Christ: three sets of striations form a cross within the halo.[92] As if in a cartoon, the eagle's scroll unfurls from a "bubble" beginning at his beak.[93] It reads, or rather proclaims: "misericordias domini in eternum cantabo," "I will sing the mercies of the Lord for ever," a direct quotation of the opening verse of Psalm 88. Angels playing a rebeck, a lute, and two psalteries accompany this chant of praise. Between and above the uppermost pair of angels is a second, smaller, symbolic ensemble (Fig. 35): the Christ Child with the *arma Christi* in a circular band and,

Fig. 34 Christ as an Eagle with the Infants Christ and John the Baptist, Munich, Bayerisches Nationalmuseum.

seated just below, his head overlapping the border, John the Baptist with the Agnus Dei.[94] Beneath the eagle, St. Ursula with her arrow and St. Agnes with her lamb complete the assembly.

Interwoven into this intricate composition is a borrowing from a print. The group of Christ and St. John near the top center of the tapestry depends directly on a woodcut that similarly presents the infant Christ with St. John the Baptist (Fig. 36).[95] This printed source brings the textile's imagery into focus. In the woodcut, as in the tapestry, Christ appears twice, in symbolic form as the Lamb and in human form as the incarnate Infant. In an implicit reference to the paradox of the Incarnation, the symbolic Lamb appears in an expansive landscape setting, whereas his "real" counterpart is set apart in the symbolic sphere.

In theory, the woodcut might depend on the tapestry or its model, rather than the tapestry on the print. The two media had always been closely related; indeed, in western Europe the technique of printing per se probably derived from the transfer of patterns to textiles using inked blocks.[96] But aside from the unlikelihood of a printmaker's gaining access to a model housed in a cloister, several details in the two works dictate the print's priority. First, the roundel in the tapestry and the associated figures of John and the Agnus Dei are exactly the same size as their

Fig. 35. The Infants Christ and John the Baptist, detail, Munich, Bayerisches Nationalmuseum.

counterparts in the print (albeit reversed). The single-leaf woodcut was used not only as a model but also as a cartoon.[97] Other particulars confirm the primacy of the print. Although often dismissed as "crude" images, woodcuts can display a high level of visual and technical sophistication. In this case, whereas the print shows the toes on Christ's left foot head-on in dramatic foreshortening, the woven adaptation omits this feature. No less indicative, the infant John is right-handed in the print, left-handed in the reversed textile copy.

Fig. 36. The Infants Christ and John the Baptist with the Instruments of the Passion and the Sacrificial Lamb, Swabian, ca. 1455–70, Munich, Staatliche Graphische Sammlung, Inv. Nr. 174032.

Far from suggesting a mechanical approach to the production of images, the process of copying indicates the self-consciousness with which the nuns approached their task. In transferring the design from paper to linen, the nuns reversed the figures and their attributes, omitting the lettering, which would have been illegible in reverse. Moreover, the letters, no more than half a centimeter high, would have been extremely difficult to weave. Instead, they were embroidered.[98] Although the words added over the tapestry's woven ground can no longer be read, the few remaining traces suggest that the inscription on St. John's scroll reproduced the one on the woodcut: "Ecce agnus dei q[ui tollit peccata mundi]," "Behold the lamb of God who [taketh away the sins of the world]" (John 1 : 29). Another scroll immediately behind the head of the Baptist identifies him. The circular inscription surrounding his companion also derives from Scripture: "vias eius tu propheta altissimi vocaberis praeibis enim ante faciem domini parare." It paraphrases Luke 1 : 76: "And thou, child, shalt be called the prophet of the Highest: for thou shalt go before the face of the Lord to prepare his ways." In the print, the Lord remains unseen; only the hand in the upper left corner alludes to his presence.[99]

In appropriating the woodcut, the nuns altered their model, at the same time transforming its meaning. The shift in significance comes in part with the change in context and function. Given its shape and size (161 × 89 cm.), the tapestry probably served as an altar frontal or hanging. In this large format, the figures taken from the print are reproduced one to one; there is no attempt to alter their size to fit the scale of their new setting. But the figures now form part of a more elaborate composition, in turn embedded in an extensive nonfigural ground. On the altar hanging, the field of stylized flowers symbolically connotes the paradise of Christ and his saints and the cloister itself as a *hortus conclusus* in which the nuns celebrate their sacrifice. In the print, the Christ Child at the center of the circle (itself a symbol of creation), the hand of God outside its compass, and the dove that mediates between them by overlapping its circumference combine to form a carefully differentiated depiction of the Trinity. Together, the various elements represent the fulfillment of the prophetic plan of salvation ordained by the Trinity, foretold by the Baptist, initiated by the Incarnation, and fulfilled through the sacraments, above all, the Eucharist, instituted through the Passion, reenacted at the Mass, and dispensed from the chalice prominently displayed at the lower center. The superimposed hand of God, the dove, and the infant John refer to Christ's baptism, the moment at which the Trinity first made itself manifest. In the textile, the oversize eagle plays a comparable role. The bird, which dominates the tapestry and represents Christ's divinity, mediates the promise of salvation to the female community represented by Ursula and Agnes.

By joining the nuns in reciting the Psalms, the eagle provided the community at St. Walburg with a powerful image of liturgical performance. Prominently displayed on the altar, the tapestry would have reminded the nuns, who gathered in the choir eight times a day, of their duty and its higher significance. Its imagery recalls one of the visions of the Cistercian Mechthild of Hackeborn (1241/42–1299),[100] related in the *Liber specialis gratiae:*

At Mass she saw the Lord on the altar in the form of a golden eagle, and she recognized that just as the eagle has the highest flight and thus the most profound sight, so, in like fashion, Christ sees into the humble heart. And it appeared to her that that eagle had a curved beak and an exceedingly sweet voice. The beak signified the eloquence of the Lord, which, through devotion, pricks the heart of the soul. In truth, the tongue signified sweetness, for, just as the eagle always seeks the sweetest prey, that is, the heart, so too God always desires our heart, so that we will offer it to him with delight.[101]

For a comparable vision the nuns of St. Walburg need have looked no further than the tapestry they had made to adorn their own altar.[102] Just like the eagle who spoke to Mechthild in a dulcet voice, the bird in the tapestry would have appeared to speak directly to them. The image initiates a devotional dialogue between Christ and the nuns. The tapestry joins their chant with the song of the saints and angels. Like the heavenly choir, the nuns sing the Sanctus, in the words of the inscription, "ante faciem domini," before the face of the Lord.

CONSECRATION AND ENCLOSURE

We are accustomed to thinking of devotional imagery as personal, private, even intimate. The small scale and meditative subjects of the drawings from St. Walburg reflect the essential inwardness and detachment of the cloistered life. But even as devotional images, the drawings have a communal as well as a private dimension. Several of them take shared ceremonies, above all the sacrament of the Eucharist, as their point of devotional departure. Even if they were held as private possessions, the drawings echoed customs that engaged the entire community acting in unison.

None of the images from the convent or the devotions in which they were used could have been fully "private" in the modern sense of that term. According to rules that may not always have been followed, all images in the abbey, including the drawings, would have remained common property; nuns were forbidden private possessions.[103] After the reforms of the mid fifteenth century, moreover, there would have been no private spaces in the convent, except, perhaps, the apartment of the abbess. Even where nuns no longer shared a common dormitory, statutes forbade the locking of cells and provided for officers, known as the *circatrices* or *Zirkarinnen,* who monitored the behavior of the nuns by carrying out inspections that amounted to a continual internal visitation.[104]

In place of the term "private," we might better employ the designation "paraliturgical" to describe the devotions in which the drawings played a part. By defi-

Fig. 37. Older Walburga Tapestry, detail, Fürstliche Oettingen-Wallerstein'sche Sammlung, Schloss Harburg.

nition, paraliturgical piety was enacted "next to" or alongside the liturgy proper, in tandem with the Mass or the Divine Office. The piety of nuns was intrinsically paraliturgical in that enclosure often denied them direct access to the high altar. At St. Walburg, as elsewhere, the nuns would have been separated by barriers not only from the laity but from the clergy as well. The nuns would have participated in the sacraments of Communion and confession through windows or grilles provided especially for those purposes. Only on rare occasions, for example, when novices took their final vows, would a priest or a bishop actually join the nuns in celebration.[105]

The seclusion of nuns represented an ideal that was rarely imposed with absolute stringency. Its strict enforcement was more often a radical innovation than the "return" to origins envisaged by reformers.[106] When the reform of St. Walburg itself was carried out in 1456, Johann III von Eych, bishop of the city from 1445 to 1464, invited the reforming "cell" from the Rhenish convent of Marienberg bei Boppard.[107] Architecture and images together ensured that the bishop's reform remained a living legacy. His burial chapel, dedicated to St. Agnes, which was

Fig. 38. Newer Walburga Tapestry, detail, Fürstliche Oettingen-Wallerstein'sche Sammlung, Schloss Harburg.

added to the convent circa 1465, celebrated him as a second founder. The *Ältere Walburga Teppich,* probably commissioned for this chapel, kept his memory alive by linking his remains with those of St. Walburga herself.[108] In the last scene of the tapestry, the bishop kneels at her shrine, the words "Ora pro nobis walpurga," "Walburga pray for us," rising from his lips (Fig. 37). In the later version of the tapestry, his place has been taken by two pilgrims, joined in their devotions by two nuns, a lay sister, and the abbess Walburga (Fig. 38). Both scenes idealize the convent's liturgical arrangements. Whereas in the earlier tapestry the rear corner of the high altar is just visible through the door at the top of the steps to the right, in the sixteenth-century copy, a third pilgrim, staff in hand, strides down the steps. On the other side, one can just make out the choir stalls of the nuns. The tapestries cannot represent the actual arrangement in either 1465 or 1520: in neither the crypt nor the church could the nuns and the laity have shared the same space, especially following the reform. Each, however, accurately represents the relics of the saint as the devotional focus of the nuns as well as outsiders. Both groups would have had access to the bones in the crypt, if not necessarily at the same time.

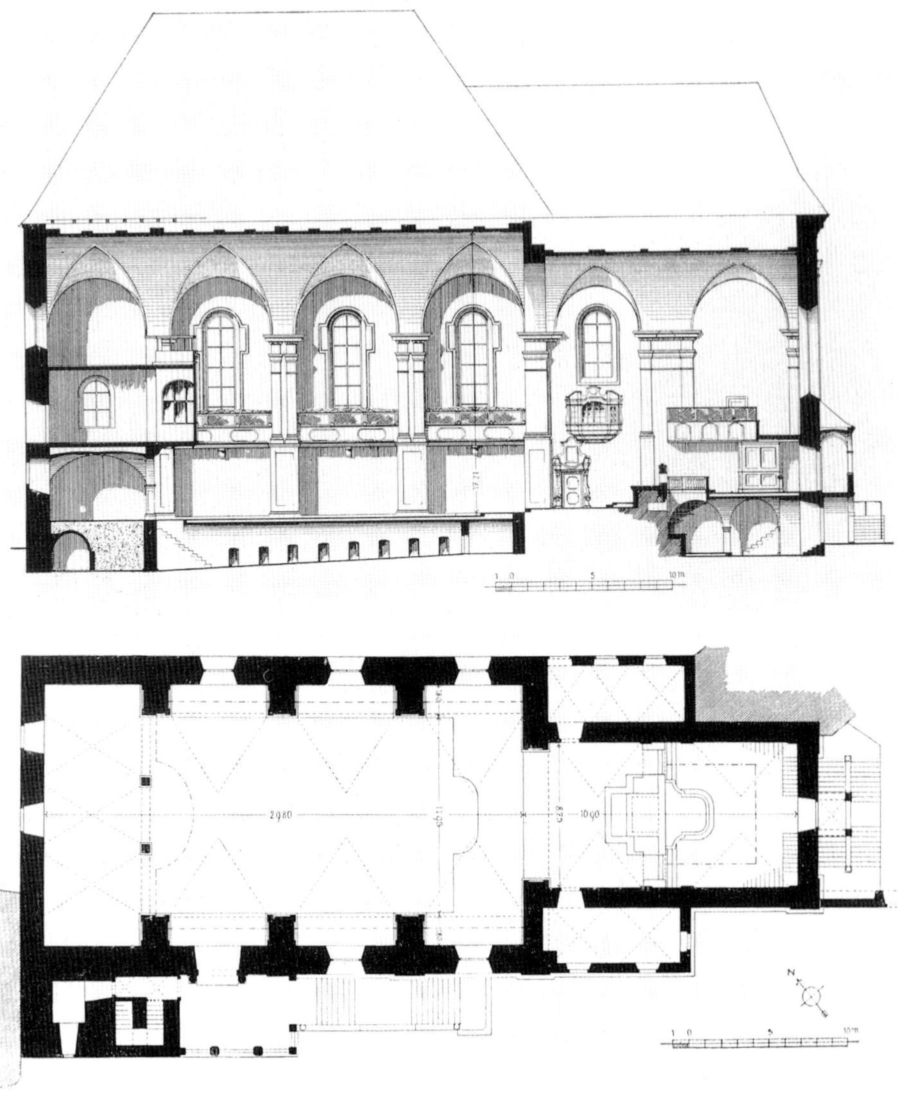

Fig. 39. Eichstätt, St. Walburg, section and plan.

Unlike the tapestries, the devotional drawings that survive make almost no reference to the cult of the saint. But in the drawing of the Eucharistic Banquet, Walburga's relics appear as the convent's identifying emblem (see Plate 11). Easily overlooked, the large gold object above the head of Christ and just to the left of the convent itself represents the shrine of the saint.[109] Housed behind and beneath the high altar and accessible from both the church to the west and the crypt to the east (Figs. 39, 40), the relics were preserved in a manner adapted to their curative

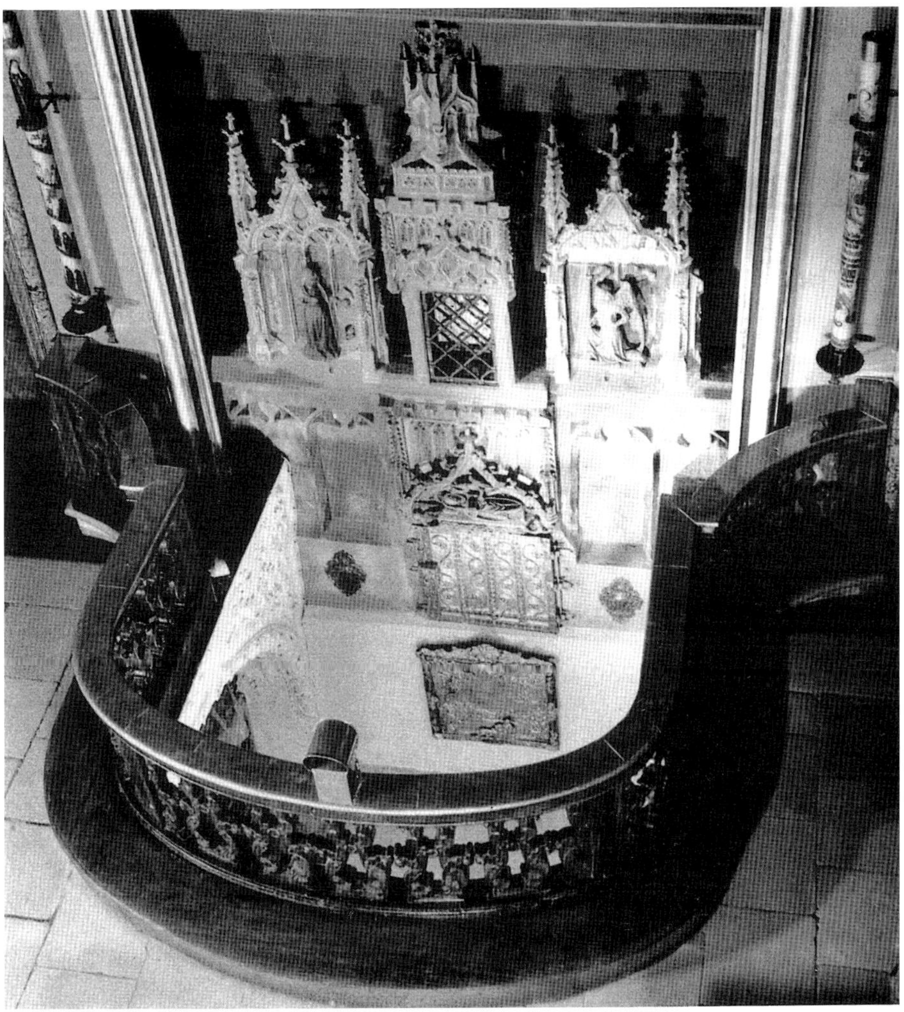

Fig. 40. Eichstätt, St. Walburg, view into crypt.

powers.[110] The saint is enshrined beneath the high altar, but above an enclosed space behind whose open doors the miraculous "Walburgis oil" can be collected at certain times of the year in the large basin that features prominently at the center of both scenes. In the crypt only the bottom of the sarcophagus and the doors—or, when they are open, the walls—of the collecting cavity immediately below it are apparent to the onlooker; the body itself remains invisible. The "oil" collects on these surfaces, which are covered in metal, before running down to the basin at the bottom.

The reference to the shrine in the drawing of the Eucharistic Banquet (see Plate 11)—an image ostensibly intended for private devotion—not only reminds the viewer of Walburga's miraculous powers but also serves as a symbol of collective identity. With this image in hand, a nun could pray for her own salvation and for that of her entire community. Taking up a traditional topos, the drawing suggests that the convent is already a paradise.[111] The heart, itself an image of enclosure and containment, embraces the whole of the convent, just as the shrine envelops the body of the saint. The related image of the Heart as a House carries the analogies further (see Plate 12). It imagines the heart of the nun as a house within which she dwells with the Divinity, protected from the travails of the world outside. In effect, both images turn the idea of enclosure inside out. In the Eucharistic Banquet, the interior of the heart opens onto a landscape containing an exterior view of the church. Rather than present the viewpoint of the outsider who cannot look in, the drawings adopt the viewpoint of the nuns, who are enclosed and, ideally, uninterested in looking beyond the confines of the convent.

Of all the drawings from St. Walburg, that of the Consecration of Virgins expresses the bond between public ritual and private devotion most explicitly (Fig. 41 and Plate 7). Its horizontal format, unique among the surviving images, itself suggests the procession at the heart of the ceremony. And it is the only drawing whose inscription refers to the liturgy. The scroll reads, "Accipe puerum Istum et nutri michi. ego dabo tibi mercedem tuam," "Take this boy and take care of [literally, suckle] me. I will give you your reward." The first part of the injunction, in which Mary issues the imperative "Take this boy," conveys the essence of the consecration rite, in which the nun accepts Christ as her spiritual husband in a vow of eternal marriage. The words paraphrase a thrice-repeated formula from the liturgy of consecration in which the bishop first offers the assembled virgins the veil ("Accipe velamen sacrum"), then a ring ("Accipe ergo annulum fidei"), and finally a crown, which in the actual ceremony usually took the form of a torque ("Accipe coronam").[112] The language of this last injunction—"Come, O bride of Christ, accept the crown that the Lord has prepared for you in eternity"—comes closest to matching the sense of the drawing.[113]

The Virgin's proclamation, however, is countered with an unexpected change of voice. After Mary commands the assembled virgins to accept her Child, the infant Christ issues an imperative of his own: "nutri michi," "Suckle me!" Having first allowed the nun to identify herself with Mary in her role as Christ's bride, the drawing now encourages her to identify with her ultimate exemplar, the Virgin, as Christ's mother. The imagery of suckling provided a common figure of spiritual inspiration and mystical union. Usually, however, it was the soul that played the role of nursling.[114] For example, in a play on words—offensive to Panofsky as a "pun scarcely pardonable in even a saint" but in fact conventional—Abbot Suger

Fig. 41. Consecration of Virgins, Eichstätt, St. Walburg.

of St.-Denis described himself as suckling (in Latin, "sugo") at the breasts of Divine Wisdom.[115] In the drawing of the Consecration of Virgins, however, the soul is urged to identify with Mary as the source, rather than the recipient, of divine nourishment.[116] Christ appears, not as a mature, marriageable male, but as a strapping, beefy boy, the object of exalted maternal instincts rather than sublimated sexual desire.[117] Although hardly unique to images made for nuns, the infantilization of Christ was a strategy especially appropriate for an audience of cloistered women. A similar transformation and transferal of desire marks many of the drawings from St. Walburg, in which the adult Christ rarely appears without the Christ Child.[118]

The drawing of the Consecration of Virgins, in suggesting the transformation as well as the consummation of devotional desire, does not illustrate the ritual literally but rather represents its deeper meaning. Its imagery corresponds, not to one element in the rite, but to many. In the ceremony the virgins, in parallel rows, approached the bishop, who sat on a folding stool (a traditional attribute of authority); then they knelt to receive the veil, ring, and crown.[119] In the drawing, all these actions occur simultaneously. The foremost virgin—perhaps St. Walburga herself—already wears a crown. The infant Christ extends her his left hand, as if in compliance with the pontifical rubric: "Then the bishop taking the ring with his right hand and with his left hand the right hand of the virgin, and putting this ring on the ring finger of the virgin's right hand, marries her to Jesus Christ."[120] In addition to conflating several moments of the ceremony into a unified image, the drawing also represents its ideal incarnation; Mary, not a bishop, officiates.[121] The ceremony ends with the Mass; the nuns symbolically consummate the spiritual marriage by receiving the Host. In the drawing, Mary offers the virgins Christ himself. In place of habits, moreover, the virgins wear richly brocaded garments. Reform statutes explicitly prohibited nuns from wearing anything other than their habits in the cloister, a clear indication that such prohibitions were honored in the breach. For example, the *ordo* dated April 5, 1458, sent by Johann III von Eych, bishop of Eichstätt, to the Benedictine nuns at Bergen, just south of Eichstätt, prescribed that the nuns "wear their clothing, habits, and all else according to spiritual custom and not according to cost or superfluity, as is taught in the Rule."[122] In the drawing, however, the nuns appear already adorned in their heavenly garb, much like St. Walburga herself, who in the early-thirteenth-century bust reliquary formerly kept in the crypt wears a sumptuous jewel-studded gown (Fig. 42).[123]

By idealizing the participants, the drawing of the Consecration of Virgins represents the fulfillment of the ceremony's eschatological promise. In this sense, it resembles an anonymous woodcut from Augsburg dated circa 1475, in which the infant Christ offers a crown to a kneeling Brigittine nun (Fig. 43).[124] In response to her request, "trahe me post te," "Draw me after you," a paraphrase of Song of Songs 1 : 3, Christ replies, "Veni sponsa Christi accipe coronam," "Come, O bride of Christ, take the crown." The inscriptions referring to numerous virtues identify the crown as a metaphor for the reward of the righteous. The consecration liturgy illuminates many of the drawings from St. Walburg. Replete with metaphors of mystical marriage, the rite is less a "source" in any immediate sense than an underlying point of reference for their imagery. The closing section of the ritual, during which the Mass is celebrated, is especially rich in references to enclosure and containment. As the bishop distributes the Eucharist, he enjoins the virgins to enter gladly into the bridal chamber of the cloister.[125] He then entreats Christ that the virgins be allowed to enter through the doors of the heavenly kingdom.[126] The ceremony even employs the imagery of the heart. Following Communion, the bishop invokes God as he who establishes his dwelling place in the hearts of the chaste.[127] The rite defines enclosure as a contemplative as well as a physical state.

As if acting out the imagery of the ritual, the rows of virgins in the drawing of the consecration ceremony reappear in the upper right corner of the drawing of the Heart as a House (see Plate 12). Once again the woman at the head of the file wears a crown. In the drawing of the heart, "die junckfrowen," the virgins, "fol-

Fig. 42. Reliquary bust of St. Walburga, Eichstätt, St. Walburg.

Fig. 43. The Infant Christ offering a crown to a nun, Augsburg, ca. 1475.

gen nach dem lemlein wo es hin geet," a paraphrase of Revelation 14:4: "These are they who were not defiled with women . . . who follow the lamb whithersoever he goeth." The passage was a commonplace in the monastic literature of profession and imitation, but especially in writings for and about nuns.[128] For example, Bishop Johann III von Eych employed its imagery in his pastoral letter of 1457 to the new abbess, Sophie von Cölln bei Erfurt, in which he exhorted her flock to emulate the female martyrs, Lucy and Agnes and, through them, Christ the Lamb.[129] In the liturgy the bishop prays that the virgins he consecrates be allowed to join the company of the 144,000 virgins in heaven who are not defiled with women.[130] The consecration rite concludes as the nuns act out the metaphor of enclosure: they enter the convent and withdraw behind its walls.[131]

In the third Exercise of Gertrude the Great (1256–1301/2), the Cistercian nun from Helfta also draws on the language of the consecration liturgy to describe the process of mystical union.[132] No less than the liturgy, her words could serve as a description of the action in the drawing from St. Walburg: "Holy Mary, Mother of the King, of the Lamb, of the Spouse of the virgins, ah! lead me with clean heart and body into dwelling together with your son, Jesus. All holy angels and archangels, ah! obtain entrance for me, in angelic purity, into the inner chamber of Jesus my Spouse."[133] The drawings from St. Walburg are the visual equivalent of this mode of devotional entreaty, freely elaborating interrelated references to the liturgy and Scripture. Like Gertrude's Exercise, they provide exemplars of devotion, vehicles for meditative experience. For the nuns, contemplation of the drawings—including contemplation in the simple sense of looking with rapt attention—itself constituted an act of devotion. The drawings did not simply supplement devotional texts; they served as equal avenues of access to the divine.

2

THE SWEET ROSE OF SORROW

THE ROSE IS THE MOST BANAL of modern romantic symbols, conveying saccharine sentiment without depth of feeling. Once a pledge of heartfelt affection, it has become a mere token of love, as hackneyed as a Valentine's card. During the late Middle Ages, the rose was no less omnipresent an icon and, at times, in no less danger of degenerating into a cliché. Yet it carried complex connotations. To appreciate them we need to look beyond Gertrude Stein's celebrated refusal of metaphorical meaning: "Rose is a rose is a rose is a rose." For medieval readers, a rose was anything but a rose; it had not one name, but many. Its meanings were manifold, shifting and, at times, deliberately contradictory.

Nearly all the governing metaphors of late medieval piety can be distilled from imagery of this single flower.[1] If Mary was the *rosa sine spina,* "the rose without thorns," its blooms could also serve as the emblem par excellence of Christ's exquisite sorrow, of ecstasy and agony conjoined.[2] With the transient beauty of its blood red blossoms and the sharp prick of its thorns, the rose stood for passion in both its senses, ardent desire and desperate adversity. Such sweet sorrow was exemplified by Christ's own Passion, in which, according to Catholic faith, the Son of God expressed the greatest love through the greatest suffering.[3] Spiritual authors made this paradox resonate by coupling the love poetry of the Song of Songs with the four narratives of the Evangelists, thereby creating from this combination a new gospel of devotional experience.[4] Paraphrasing the vivid metaphors of the Canticle, they spoke incessantly of the "sweetness" of the Passion and all its instruments: the nails of the cross, the crown of thorns, the side wound, indeed, of the "sweet death" of God.[5] In fusing this strand of religious symbolism with imagery from the literature of courtly love, sacred verse acquired an unprecedented erotic charge, and secular lyrics, a newfound religious dimension.[6] Shakespeare gently mocked this tradition when Romeo, the shallow lover who has yet to learn the meaning of true suffering, bids Juliet adieu, saying, "Parting is such sweet sorrow."[7] He, too, however, dies for love: Christ becomes Adonis.

Medieval theologians emphasized the other side of this coin, agape instead of eros. Mystics, however, especially female mystics, fused the imagery of *caritas* and *cupiditas,* charity and courtly love.[8] In seeking to define ineffable states of religious rapture, they developed a language epitomized in Donne's wry yet rhapsodic poem "The Extasie": "Loves mysteries in soules doe grow, / But yet the body is his booke."[9] Donne translates the body into terms of art even as he defines spiritual growth as an inherently organic process. In a manner no less paradoxical, mystics characterized the love expressed by Christ's self-sacrifice as a form of *concordia discors,* an oxymoron whose implications extended beyond Christ's own experience to that of his followers. Christ's death, as reported in the Gospels and expanded on in exegesis, raised a fundamental theological question: how could a God who came in the name of Charity endure so much suffering?[10] Invoking the trope of *formosa deformitas,* "beautiful ugliness," Christians could reply with the words of the bride in Song of Songs 1 : 5: "Nigra sum, sed formosa," "I am black, but beautiful."[11] Christ's triumph in and over death matched and made good the oxymoron of the *felix culpa* of the Fall; in the words of Augustine: "He hung deformed on the cross; but his deformity was our beauty."[12]

In late medieval Germany, all these contradictions came together in the image of the rose. Its manifold meanings are codified in the writings of the Rhenish mystic Henry Suso (ca. 1295 – 1366), who devoted much of his career and the majority of his writings to the nuns in the care of the Dominican order.[13] The red rose served as Suso's self-styled attribute. It recurs as a leitmotif in both the illustrations and the text of his "autobiography," the first book of the collection known as *The Exemplar.* In almost all the images, which were integral to Suso's design for the book, the Dominican friar appears in the guise of a bride, crowned with a garland of red and white roses, bearing his other "attribute," the monogram of Christ, on his chest (Fig. 44).[14] Both symbols are written in blood, for the roses represent the stigmata on the friar's hands and shoes (his feet remain covered). In one of the visions recorded in the narrative, the noblewoman Anna, who asks an angel the meaning of the flowers, is told that

> the white roses signify his purity and the red roses his patience in the various kinds of suffering he must endure. And just as the golden halo that one usually paints around the head of saints signifies the eternal happiness which they possess in God, so this bright crown of roses signifies the various sufferings the dear friends of God have to bear as long as they are serving God with knightly endeavor.[15]

Fig. 44. Anna's vision of Suso crowned with a rose garland, Henry Suso, *The Exemplar,* Strasbourg, Bibliothèque Nationale et Universitaire, Ms. 2929, f. 28v.

In describing Suso as a *miles Christianus* and the *imitatio Christi* as a "ritterliche ůbung," or "knightly exercise," the angel identifies ascetic athleticism as a pursuit worthier than the feats of arms championed in secular romance.[16] The parody of courtly conventions extends to the characterization of Suso himself, who in the illustration appears in feminine guise. Not only does he wear a chaplet of flowers and adopt the pudic pose and swaying S-curve stance customarily reserved for figures of female saints, above all the Virgin Mary, but he also, like her, sways in response to an angelic salutation, as if in an Annunciation. In body as in mind Suso represents himself as an exemplar for his female audience.

The complex interaction between image and vision in Suso's *Exemplar* itself exemplifies the changing relationship between images and their audience in late medieval devotions. Suso gives his female readers and viewers an example, not only of how to behave, but also of how to read and to see. In referring to the halo "that one usually paints," Suso likens himself, not simply to a saint, but also to an image of a saint, thereby identifying himself with a legitimate source of religious authority. Suso becomes saint-like in that he appears like a picture.

The drawings from St. Walburg rely on a similar interaction between image and audience, mediated by vision. They force us to bring to the traditional pairing of text and image our own experience as onlookers as well as that of the nuns for whom they were made. Like the illustrations of *The Exemplar,* they invite the viewer to assimilate pictorial models whose grounding in visions invests them with authenticity. In turn, the images and the devotions of which they form an indispensable part invest visual experience with religious power and authority.

ROSES AND REMEMBRANCE

Suffering and love, pain and pleasure, spirituality and sexuality: all these apparent opposites conjoin in the image of the rose, which provides the pattern for one of the drawings from St. Walburg (Fig. 45 and Plate 8). In light of the flower's rampant proliferation as a symbol, the bold simplicity of the drawing comes as something of a surprise. It presents the rose as a single blossom set, but not quite centered, between two closed buds and isolated against a green, grassy ground. At the heart of the flower appears a diminutive depiction of the Agony in the Garden. At first glance the drawing, like the leaf itself, seems a fragment: the large blossom atop its severed stem looks like a cutting. The apparent incompleteness of the rose, along with its scale, gives it the character of a small handheld object, much like the single leaf on which it is drawn. The rose sheds its appearance as an image to serve as a token of remembrance, as much a keepsake as if it were a real flower.[17]

In its singular detachment, the rose recalls the flowers featured in New Year's greetings, where they served as emblems of rebirth and renewal. For example, a single-leaf woodcut dated around 1490–1500 and inscribed "Ein guot selig ior" ("A good and blessed year") depicts the Christ Child, his groin ostentatiously disclosed by his parted garment, standing before the cross, which is not dry wood but the fruit of the flower, a symbol, in turn, of Mary's miraculous conception (Fig. 46).[18] A similar conceit underlies a nun's drawing formerly in the Figdor collection in Vienna that depicts the naked Christ Child lying in a basket ensconced in a bower of blossoms (Fig. 47).[19] The inscription in the garland proclaims, "Ver-

Non quod ego volo sed quod tu. Marci

Fig. 45. Agony in the Garden, Eichstätt, St. Walburg.

Fig. 46. The Infant Christ with New Year's greetings, Paris, Louvre, Département des Arts graphiques, Collection Edmond de Rothschild, 31 LR (© Photo R.M.N.).

bum Caro factum est," "The Word was made Flesh." In the image, word and flesh sit cheek by jowl.

The drawing from St. Walburg relies on a similar strategy of simplification and intensification. By isolating a moment in Christ's life and identifying it with an object, it also brings to mind the piecemeal representations of the *arma Christi,* which reduce Christ's sufferings to a collection of things, each no more than a part, that the onlooker regards as a series of nonlinear, interconnected cues to a larger context of devotion (Fig. 48).[20] The context, however, is not prescribed; the viewer is invited to imagine it for herself. The drawing from St. Walburg adopts a similar strategy, but in inverted form: the object envelops its context, framing and enclosing the narrative of the Agony, itself a foretelling of the whole of Christ's Passion.

The isolated rose inevitably recalls for us, as it would have for most viewers of the later Middle Ages, the rosary, itself an instrument of memory, in which each bead stood for a single blossom and enumerated a prayer evoking an event

Fig. 47. The Christ Child in a basket, formerly Figdor Collection, Vienna.

in the history of salvation.[21] Just as some strings of rosary beads culminated in a hollowed-out ball or "nut" containing an extraordinarily detailed depiction of the Passion (Fig. 49)—the viewer's wonder only working to secure her attention—so too the rose from St. Walburg contains the image it is intended to evoke. The drawing seems like a snippet cut from the historiated rosaries depicted in prints (Figs. 50, 51), themselves reproduced on a monumental scale in works such as the *Engelische Grüß,* or "Angelic salutation," of Veit Stoß, suspended in the crossing of the church of St. Lorenz in Nuremberg (Fig. 52).[22] In all these images, each salient event from the life of the Virgin is contained in a chaplet of blossoms or, as in the print and the drawing, the petals of a single rose (see Fig. 51).[23] Like a single bead detached from its string, the flower provides a mnemonic device designed to trigger an ever-expanding array of associations.

Fig. 48. *Arma Christi,* passional of the Abbess Kunigunde, ca. 1321, Prague, National Library, XIV A 17, f. 10r.

Fig. 49. Boxwood rosary bead, open, Flemish, early sixteenth century, New York, Metropolitan Museum of Art, Gift of J. Pierpont Morgan, 1917, 17.190.474 ab.

Fig. 50. Madonna with the rosary, woodcut, German, 1485, Rosenwald Collection, National Gallery of Art, Washington.

Fig. 51. Madonna and Child in the rosary, detail, Rosenwald Collection, National Gallery of Art, Washington.

Fig. 52. Veit Stoß, The Annunciation, St. Lorenzkirche, Nuremberg.

In female devotions, the interchangeability of objects and prayers came to stand for the process of prayer itself. No object of devotion was more familiar than the rose. The phrase "to say the rosary" captures this reciprocity: it refers to both the device and the invocations it recalls. Even those for whom prayer is no longer a daily habit can probably imagine using a string of beads to structure a cycle of prayers. The reverse process, however, of prayers crystallizing into objects, even if only imaginary ones, is more remote from our experience. Yet in the tradition of prayers known as *Handwerkliches Beten* that was common in, if not exclusive to, convents, supplicants offered up make-believe gifts fashioned, not from gold, silk, or beads, but from prayer formulas reiterated so often that the words took on the character of an incantation.[24] A panel from the Rosary altar of the Dominicans in Frankfurt depicts this process of prayer in action: as the kneeling monk says his prayers, Mary plucks each Ave Maria from his mouth in the form of a rose and weaves it into the chaplet that she holds in her hand (Fig. 53).[25] A story from the childhood of the Franciscan tertiary Joanna Maria of Maillé (1331–1414) reverses the process: after collecting roses with her playmates, she imagines them images of the saints and joins them into a chain, with which she crowns a statue of the Madonna.[26] In the Rosary panel from Frankfurt, the representation of prayer itself is enclosed in a chaplet of roses, decorated in turn with small roundels containing scenes of the Passion.[27] Just as in the painting the praying monk confronts a vision of the Virgin, so too the viewer of the panel, who can imagine that the Virgin plucks prayers from his mouth in the form of the flowers that make up the frame.

Pictorial prayer obviated material sacrifice of the kind offered up by the Beguines of Lille, who pledged to "deliver, in return for the right of relief, a garland of roses or violets or other flowers according to the season that will be given to and placed upon the primary Virgin in the chapel called 'à la Treille.'"[28] A devotee, regardless of the season (or of income), could make an immaterial offering. In an anonymous tract, "Von zwei bayerischen Klosterfrauen Leben," "The life of two Bavarian nuns," the author—a "Friend of God" associated with Rulman Merswin (1307–1382)—relates how the sisters prayed so intently that they fell into an ecstatic trance in which Christ rewarded them with rose garlands. When the nuns awoke, however, they discovered that their chaplets were not merely the stuff of visions. Unbeknownst to them, their fellow nuns had removed the garlands to the sacristy and placed them alongside the other relics.[29]

In these and other stories the rose emerges as the consummate emblem and instrument of prayer, both an image and the means by which images are honored. A vision that the Praemonstratensian nun Christina von Hane (1269–1292) experienced on Christmas day, 1280, condenses all these meanings into a single story.

Fig. 53. The monk and the rosary, antependium of the Rosary Altar from the Church of the Dominicans in Frankfurt, ca. 1484, Heidelberg, Kurpfälzisches Museum.

Despite the season, her biographer likens Christina, not to the Magi who come to the manger, but to Mary Magdalen, who visits the tomb in search of the dead Christ. Exhausted from her devotions, six hundred Paternosters, she falls into a trance in which she sees the Christ Child, first playing in the stalls, then covered with roses in the *lectulus noster floridus,* the flowery bed of Song of Songs 1 : 15:

> In the dream she had a spiritual vision in which the most beloved little child Jesus was playing in front of her on the stalls, and all about him the most beautiful roses that ever were on earth. They were not earthly roses, they were heavenly. . . . There she saw the tender, most beautiful Child standing in front of the altar in a cradle, and it was blanketed with a cover of roses, and on each and every rose petal was written: "Pater noster." And on his head was a garland of twelve beautiful roses. God gave her to understand that these were the twelve times fifty "Paternosters" that she had said to the Christ Child.[30]

The vision translates Christina's orations into visual terms. At the same time, the vivid imagery of the text provides the reader with a memorable exemplum of prayer.

An unpublished *Sendbrief,* or devotional epistle, from the first half of the fifteenth century introduces a similar combination of imagery. Entitled "Von Jhesus pettlein," "On the little bed of Jesus," the tract, preserved in a single manuscript from the Katharinenkloster in Nuremberg,[31] takes as its theme, not the crèche of the Nativity its name might imply, but the flower-strewn bed of the Canticle on which the nun should consummate her love for Christ, just as he consummated his love for mankind on the bed of the cross:

> Let Jesus, the son of the Virgin Mary, the wonderfully beautiful, fragrant rosebush, be your comfort who must always gladden your heart, and also your pleasure for the short time that you are here in this false world, your first sight as you rise and go walking below; and collect in the little basket of your heart the rose petals that the rosebush of Christ let fall in the fear of his suffering as he knelt on the Mount of Olives and as he carried up the cross.[32]

The rose serves simultaneously as a symbol of suffering and of love: Christ is the rosebush, and each drop of his precious blood is like one of its blossoms, tokens of affection the bride should gather into the basket of her heart.[33] Statuettes depicting Mary holding the Christ Child surrounded by roses similarly identify Christ as a rosebush rooted in his mother's virginal stock (Fig. 54).[34] Like the drawing from St. Walburg, however, the tract from the Katharinenkloster condenses the idea of "sweet suffering" around the figure of Christ at Gethsemane.

Authors of spiritual literature never tired of labeling Christ's life-giving blood *rosenfarbig,* "rose colored."[35] The metaphor takes visual form in the statues of the Pietà, or *Vesperbild* (a term that refers to the early evening hour at which Mary mourned the dead Christ), of which the abbey of St. Walburg owns an example dating to the mid fourteenth century (Fig. 55).[36] The sculpture's inconsistencies of scale and expression only reinforce its underlying message: the fortunate paradox of Christ's having been born to suffer a horrible death on behalf of mankind. Mary's unflinching stance and the childlike size of the lifeless Christ bring to mind images of the *sedes sapientiae,* in which the Virgin sits stock still with the Christ Child on her knees. Mary's pursed lips, drawn up at the corners in the slightest trace of a smile, also seem incongruous.[37] But the Virgin, who delights in the necessity of the Passion, herself embodies "sweet sorrow." Intensifying the imagery of Christ's sacrifice as a *Liebestod,* gouts of blood flow from the wounds in his hands, feet, and side, congealing into roseate blooms centered on the perfora-

Fig. 54. Madonna with rosebush, Munich, Bayerisches Nationalmuseum.

Figs. 55 and 56. Pietà (*left*) and detail (*below*), St. Walburg. (Photos: © 1995 Belser Wissenschaftliche Dienst, Germany).

tions in his flesh.[38] To cement the comparison, a garland of roses applied in relief runs around the base of Mary's throne (Fig. 56).[39]

Just as the wounds in Christ's body were imagined as openings from which the sacraments flowed and through which the mystic could penetrate to the mysteries of Christ's heart, so too the rose in the drawing from St. Walburg unfolds at its center, inviting deeper examination. Like images of Christ's disembodied wounds, it provides an isolated focal point for intense and ardent scrutiny. At the center of the drawing we penetrate, as if peering from the wrong end of a telescope, to the small-scale view of the Agony in the Garden. As the event that inaugurated the Passion, the Agony stood, *pars pro toto,* for the whole of Christ's suffering. In the drawing from St. Walburg, it also provides an archetypal image of prayer.

PASSIONATE PRAYER

Just as Christ foresaw the Passion as he prayed in the garden, so the medieval viewer saw in the Agony in the Garden the sum of Christ's sorrow. In medieval prayer books the scene appeared most often with the opening plea of Psalm 101, the fifth penitential psalm, an important formal and devotional marker, for it denoted the beginning of the final third of the Psalter (Fig. 57).[40] The familiar words—"Hear, O Lord, my prayer: and let my cry come unto thee"—would have served as an exemplar for the experience of prayer.

In addition to Psalters, images of the Agony occur in devotional miscellanies. The nun from the ancient Benedictine convent of Nonnberg, in Salzburg, who searched her prayer book for a meditation on the Agony found it at the woodcut, not inserted, as was customary, but printed directly on the page (Fig. 58).[41] The invocation on the verso, part of a cycle composed about 1426–32 by the Augustinian canon Johannes von Indersdorf (1382–1470) for Elisabeth Ebran, echoes, at least metaphorically, the process by which the image was imprinted on the page:

> Write in my heart the memory of your bitter fear and martyrdom and especially the unworthiness and shame that you suffered in your wretched imprisonment for my sake; free my poor soul from the bonds of sin, and protect her henceforth from eternal imprisonment. Allow my soul to contemplate your great suffering, your outpouring of blood that you spilled at the Flagellation, at the Crowning with Thorns, and on the holy cross, where your holy body was injured and your innocent heart was bound. Help my sick soul and give her medicine from your wounded heart so that she may enter into Being.[42]

The prayer is replete with reciprocal imagery: Christ suffers imprisonment to liberate the soul, which pleads in turn that Christ fill her heart with the fear he felt at the prospect of the Passion. As in the book, so too in the prayer: the nun petitions Christ to impress word and image on her heart.

The drawing from St. Walburg of the Agony in the Garden presents its viewer with a still more compact combination of image and text. Beneath the rose, a short but central passage from Mark 14:36 serves as a caption: "Non quod ego volo, sed quod tu," "Not what I will, but what thou wilt." The drawing, however, does not simply illustrate this declaration or even the episode from which it is taken. Any

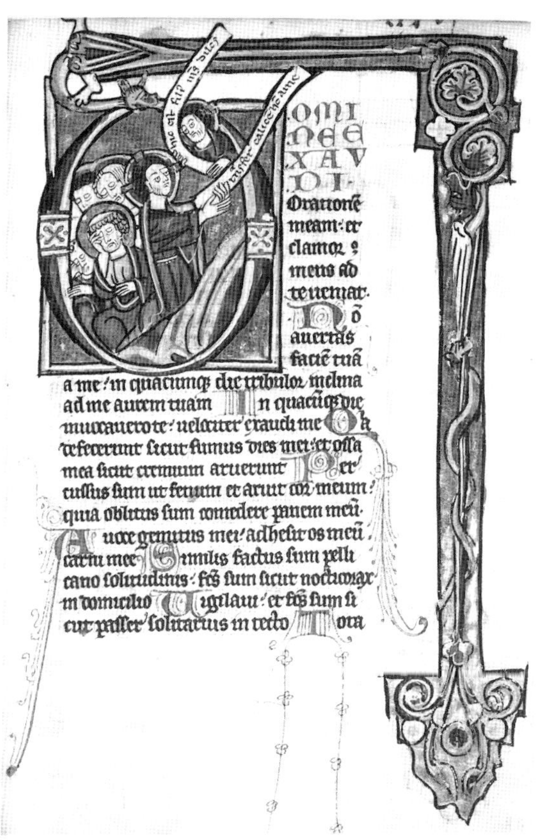

Fig. 57. Agony in the Garden, Psalter, Huy, early 1250s, Brussels, Bibliothèque Royale Albert Ier, Ms. IV-36, f. 84r.

Fig. 58. Agony in the Garden, prayer book, Nonnberg, Pasadena, Calif., Huntington Library, HM 195, f. 83r.

reference to the surrounding narrative is removed; all that remains is Christ's petition, which the viewer takes as her own. At best, the words serve as a cue with the image, whose rhetoric is far more compelling.

Turned to confront the onlooker, the rose opens to reveal Christ kneeling in the garden at Gethsemane. Christ reacts as if in response to the plea of Psalm 101 : 2–3: "Turn not away thy face from me: in the day when I am in trouble, incline thy ear to me in what day soever I shall call upon thee, hear me speedily."[43] Looking out to meet our gaze, however, is Christ, who breaks the containment of the narrative by imploring us, in the words of the psalm, to "turn not away."[44] In startling contrast, the three Apostles to Christ's left, Peter, James, and John, lie asleep. Above, amid blue clouds, appears the angel, holding a red crucifix as a foreshadowing of the Passion, whose onset the Agony announces. By duplicating the stylized stems that dot the lawn in the surrounding framework, the "plants" in the garden collapse time and space. Christ's gaze, encountered by our own, bridges both gaps, creating the effect of immediate presence.

The nun who held this drawing in her hands worshiped in tandem with Christ. Even as she said her own prayers, she was confronted by an image of the Savior engaged in the archetypal act of prayer: Christ praying before his own Passion. The image has a similarly reflexive character. It functions much like the mirror it resembles. Seeking her reflection, the nun would instead have found the model whose actions hers reflect. Some devotional writings of the late Middle Ages actually compare the scene of Christ praying at Gethsemane to a *speculum orationis*. For example, Angela of Foligno (1248/49–1309)—or, more likely, the redactor of her *Liber vitae*—urges her readers to "place this mirror [Christ's prayer at Gethsemane] before your eyes and apply yourself to it as often as you have to, because with it he prayed for you, not for himself."[45] The drawing from St. Walburg enforces a similar process of imitation; by putting Christ's words into the viewer's mouth, the inscription at the bottom of the leaf dictates that the female onlooker identify with the kneeling Jesus. The identification, however, is not entirely reciprocal: Christ renounces his will in front of the Father; the nun, however, renounces hers in the name of Christ. Christ, himself a supplicant, also acts as an intercessor between the nun and the unseen God.

The reciprocity between Christ, who looks at the viewer, and the viewer, who returns his gaze, defines prayer itself as the subject of the image. The rhetoric of imitation developed by the drawing does not, however, rely on words alone. If anything, we notice the inscription at the bottom only as an afterthought. No less important, the image defines the act of looking as integral to prayer. Christ asked the Apostles (Luke 22 : 46), "Why sleep you? Arise, pray, lest you enter into temptation"; we answer this question, in effect, by saying, "But we did not sleep, we worshiped," and, by implication, "We gazed with our eyes wide open."[46] The visual dialogue at the center of the image entails a verbal dialogue which, when enacted by the viewer, lends the image the authority of revelation.

In this context, the crucifix displayed by the angel who appears to Christ, however tiny, plays a decisive role in identifying vision and, by extension, visionary experience inspired by images, as part of the subject matter to which the drawing refers. Crucifixes occasionally occur in other representations of the Agony, most often placed in or above the chalice mentioned by both Matthew (26:39) and Mark (14:36) in their accounts (Fig. 59).[47] The crucifix, however, does not simply substitute for the cup of sorrow, which during the fifteenth century became the predominant fixture in representations of the scene.[48] Instead, it affiliates Christ's invocation with the prayer of his most ardent imitator, Francis of Assisi, identified in his own lifetime as an *alter Christus* on account of the stigmata he received in 1224 as indelible marks of his identification with Christ.[49] As depicted in art and recounted in legend, the saint's charismatic authority stemmed, in part, from images of the cross, so it is hardly surprising to find that authority invested in representations of the saint and his stigmata.[50] If Francis himself supplied an *alter Christus,* then his effigy supplied, for many, a corresponding *alter crucifixus*.

For Franciscan exegetes and hagiographers, their patron's forty-day fast at Alverna conjured up a range of Old Testament prototypes.[51] But Francis's encounter with the angel on a mountaintop also paralleled Christ's Agony in the Garden on the Mount of Olives, part of a typology linking Francis to Christ that extended from his person to the places he had inhabited.[52] Representations of the stigmatization underscore the correspondence by echoing the pose and placement of both Christ and the sleeping Apostles in contemporary representations of the Agony (Fig. 60; see Fig. 59). By attaching to a cross the seraph that appeared to Francis, the image underscores the saint's identification with Christ at Gethsemane and suggests to the viewer that Francis's vision was inspired by a Crucifixion.[53] An illustration to a set of prayers on the Passion in a Flemish manuscript of Jean Miélot's French translation of the *Speculum humanae salvationis* encourages a comparable conflation with a pictorial exemplar: the viewer of the image sees himself close-up, his hands joined in prayer as he gazes at a vision of Christ, who adopts the same attitude before the angelic apparition (Fig. 61). The illustration provides both a model for, and a mirror of, the viewer's own devotional activity.[54]

The rhetoric of self-reference in the drawing from St. Walburg, which implicitly sanctions devotions that depend on images, could be read, at some level, as a response to the concerns of theologians and reformers about the proper use of art

Fig. 59. Christ on the Mount of Olives, woodcut, German, fifteenth century, Rosenwald Collection, National Gallery of Art, Washington.

in worship.[55] The nuns, however, are unlikely to have shared such anxieties. The woman who held the drawing of the rose as she prayed would simply have seen herself imitating Christ, who in the drawing sets an example by praying before an image of his own Passion. The drawing presents him as a model of meditation, indeed, of vision itself. Christ not only prays but also foresees in a vision his own suffering. An image takes the place of Scripture as a model for the life of prayer, and visionary experience takes the place of written revelation.

During the second half of the fifteenth century, sculptural groups of the Agony

Fig. 60. St. Francis receiving the stigmata, Munich, Bayerische Staatsbibliothek, Rar. 327, inside back cover.

in the Garden became common fixtures in churches across southern Germany, especially in their cemeteries and cloisters, where worshipers could pray outdoors throughout the year.[56] Devotions revolving around Christ's prayer in the garden of Gethsemane were especially popular, however, during Holy Week. The extensive rubrics in a fifteenth-century prayer book from the Benedictine convent of Engelberg in Switzerland testify to the importance of such devotions in or alongside the liturgy leading up to Easter.[57] For Holy Thursday, the day the Agony was commemorated, the rubric specifies that the community recite in unison a "dri-

Fig. 61. *Speculum humanae salvationis,* Paris, Bibliothèque Nationale, Ms. fr. 6275, f. 45r.

valtig pett," a "threefold prayer."[58] Meditations on individual events from the history of salvation, including from three to as many as seven parts, were a staple of devotions to the Passion in German vernacular prayer books of the later Middle Ages.[59] But in this case the threefold prayer refers specifically to Christ's tripartite prayer on the Mount of Olives as described in Matthew 26:39–44. No such set of petitions occurs as a standard part of the Mass for Holy Thursday.[60] The rubric, however, spells out exactly what is intended:

> [The threefold prayer] indicates that then our Lord God prayed on the mountain, and then he sweated bloody sweat, that he then sorrowfully went about his prayer and he sought comfort from his beloved disciples and he found no comfort in them. And [you] should first beseech and recall all the pain and mockery that he ever suffered on his holy head, so that he might have mercy on all the heads of Christendom. The second time we should recall all the pain and fatigue that he ever suffered in his

holy limbs, so that he might have mercy on all the limbs of Christendom. And third we should recall all the fear and distress that ever came into his holy soul, so that he might have mercy on all faithful souls.[61]

A woodcut of the Agony in the Garden (printed from the same block as the impression reproduced in Fig. 59 and pasted into the front cover of the manuscript) allowed the nuns to visualize Christ's sufferings as they prayed three times, thereby recapitulating as well as commemorating Christ's own threefold petition.[62] In addition to compelling imitation of Christ at Gethsemane, the threefold prayer practiced at Engelberg allowed for narrative, meditative, and even theological expansion in its glosses on each of Christ's actions.

An account of a threefold petition from the Dominican convent at Töß describes an analogous pattern. According to the chronicle—traditionally, if problematically, ascribed to Suso's "spiritual daughter," Elsbeth Stagel—Sister Margret Finkin would hold a vigil before matins and read three Paternosters, "as our Lord Jesus Christ did on the mountain."[63] Each part of her prayer carried a different connotation:

the first, the suffering that his tender heart endured as he withdrew from all human society and desired in all his hardships to be unaided by all creatures; the second, the great plight that his suffering heart endured as he went out from under the protection of his heavenly Father into all the merciless, evil power of his enemies; the third, that he departed from the comfort of the Holy Spirit so that his martyrdom and sufferings would rise up to the very highest.[64]

As laid out in the chronicle, Margret's prayer invokes the Trinity, with each of its component parts commemorating one of the three persons and his place in the plan of salvation. The models for Margret's prayer, however, are both Christ's prayer at Gethsemane and St. Francis's recapitulation of Christ's experience as described in Bonaventure's biography, the *Legenda maior.* Having retired to Mount Alverna, Francis prayed to God with the help of his companion, who took the Gospels from the altar and opened the book three times in the name of the Trinity. Each time, it fell open to the account of Christ's Passion, by which Francis understood that "just as he had imitated Christ in the actions of his life, so too he ought to conform himself to him in the afflictions and sufferings of the Passion before he passed from this world."[65]

The *Vita Jesu Christi* by Ludolf of Saxony (1295/1300–1378), a work heavily influenced by Bonaventure's biography of St. Francis, also provides an extended meditation on the Agony in the Garden, combining material from the three Gospels that include an account of it.[66] Ludolf spells out just what petitioners were to bring to their prayers on the subject. To enforce imitation and inscribe it on the body of the devotee, Ludolf specifies a trio of postures described in the Gospels.[67] Matthew 26:39 and Mark 14:35 refer to Christ prostrate, "on his face" or "flat on the ground"; Luke 22:41, to him "kneeling down."[68] Taking the fullest account in Matthew as the framework for his exemplary narration, Ludolf compares Christ's vigilance with the lassitude of the Apostles by enjoining the readers: "Be watchful and take heed, with the eye of the mind and the body, and pray piously with the words of the heart and the mouth."[69] According to Ludolf, to pray is to see as well as to speak. Combining references to the kneeling described in Luke and the prostration in Matthew and Mark, Ludolf prescribes an accord between outward comportment and interior disposition: "and kneeling, he fell flat on his face on the ground, in order to show his humility of mind in the appearance of his body, and prayed in his heart."[70] Not only must the devotee see as she prays, but her devotion must also be visible to others so that she too becomes an exemplar.

In this rhetoric of visible example, images of the Agony in the Garden such as the drawing from St. Walburg served as set-piece demonstrations of prayer gestures and attitudes.[71] The extensive cycle of narrative illustrations prefacing the early-thirteenth-century Bohemian prayer book known as the *Cursus Sanctae Mariae*—in all likelihood commissioned by Margravine Kunegund of Moravia for her niece, the princess of the Přemyslid dynasty Agnes of Bohemia (1211–1282)—contains an exceptional serial image of Christ's prayer at Gethsemane that corresponds closely to the pattern laid out in the prayer book from Engelberg and other allied material (Fig. 62).[72] In three separate scenes Christ appears, kneeling, prostrate, and standing. These representations of Christ at prayer mark a dramatic change of pace in the pictorial narrative, which includes ninety-five scenes running from Creation to Pentecost. The Middle High German inscription states simply: "Hie sprichet er sin gebet zu sine[m] vater. un[d] hie and[er] weide. unde hie criste stunt," "Here he speaks his prayer to his Father. And here, in another way. And here he stood." The tiny trilogy bears little, if any, relation to the iconography of the Agony in the Garden familiar from the Byzantine tradition, in which Christ, after admonishing the Apostles, prays in the two postures described in Scripture: kneeling and prostrate.[73] Nor do the three attitudes match the characterization of Christ's movements in the three Gospels that mention the episode. Instead, they both inculcate and echo a repertory of prayer gestures generated in the devotions for Holy Week of nuns in Germanic-speaking regions.[74] In relation to this tradition of prayer and pictorial representation, Dürer's depictions of the Agony in the Garden in the *Small Passion* of 1509–11 and a drawing of 1521, in

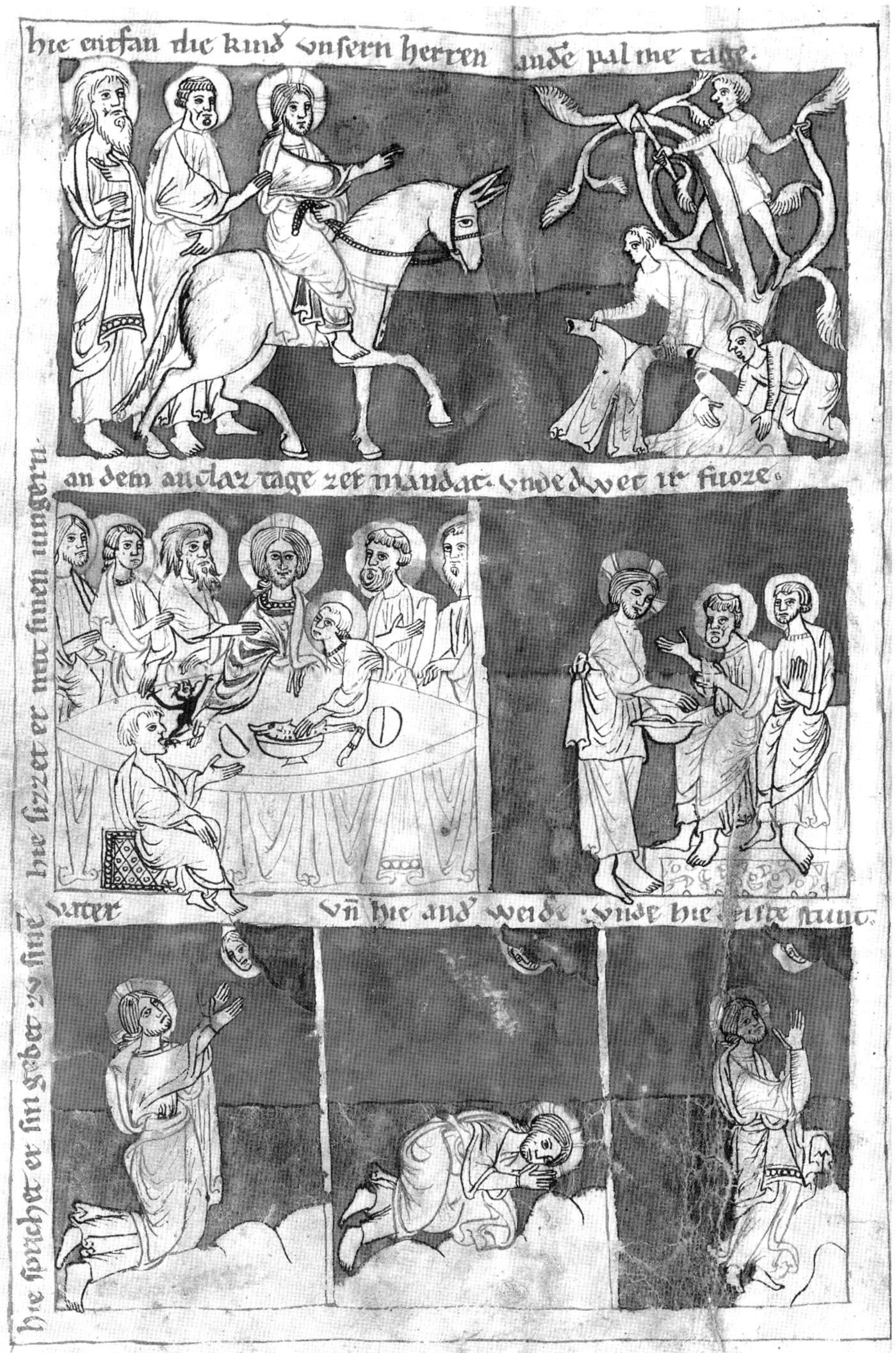

Fig. 62. *Cursus Sanctae Mariae,* New York, Pierpont Morgan Library, M. 739, f. 22v.

which Christ lies prostrate, represent less an iconographic innovation than a radical return to one of the postures described in Scripture (Fig. 63).[75]

Although the evidence is scattered, images of the Agony in the Garden appear to have enjoyed a special veneration among nuns.[76] In the elevated choir of the nuns at the Dominican Katharinenkloster in Nuremberg, there once were two paintings of the Agony in the Garden, one above each of the arches dividing the nave from the aisles. According to a reliable description made in 1925, both paintings, destroyed without trace in World War II, were executed around 1480.[77] The double depiction of an identical moment in the Passion narrative seems superfluous—until one considers the disposition, mental as well as physical, of the viewers. The opposing murals would not have been redundant but would have offered mirror images, not only of each other, but also of the nuns in the choir stalls below. Regardless of which side they were seated on, each time they looked up from their prayer books they would have seen an image of Christ praying on the eve of the Passion.

Rubrics and prayers in devotional books that belonged to nuns conform to similar patterns of use, as does the unusual iconography of the Agony in the *Cursus Sanctae Mariae*. For example, a rubric in a fifteenth-century devotional compendium from the Dominican convent of St. Nicolaus in undis, in Strasbourg, advises the reader: "When you feel sorrow and fear, prostrate yourself before the image of the fear of our Lord on the Mount of Olives and say the Psalm 'Miserere' with longing for the forgiveness of the sins with which you so burdened yourself."[78] The prayer is conjoined with the injunction, "stond krucz wiß," "stand crosswise."[79] Subsequent petitions, some also spoken before images, require other postures, either standing or kneeling, with hands either joined or upraised.[80] Exercises such as these in effect turned each nun's place in the stalls into a private space for a theatrical, even histrionic, reenactment of Christ's Passion, especially his prayer at Gethsemane.

The lives of holy women bear witness to the pervasiveness of such devotions.[81] For example, the Cistercian Lukardis of Oberweimar (ca. 1276–1309) wore herself out by reenacting Christ's death on the cross, finally emitting a sound perceived by her fellow nuns as an echo of Christ's "Heli, heli lema sabacthani," "My God, my God, why hast thou forsaken me?" (Matthew 27:46).[82] Still more dramatic were the devotions of the Prussian recluse Dorothy of Montau (1347–1394), documented in exhaustive detail by her spiritual supervisor, John Marienwerder (1342–1417).[83] Dorothy not only meditated in succession on episodes of the Passion but also accompanied each stage of her meditation with gestures or actions embodying her identification with Christ, in what Richard Kieckhefer has termed

Fig. 63. Albrecht Dürer, Agony in the Garden, 1521, Frankfurt, Städelsches Kunstinstitut.

"a kind of Christian yoga."[84] For example, in imitation of Christ's Crucifixion she stood for hours with her arms extended or suspended herself from nails in the wall.[85] This pantomime of the Passion was designed to drill Dorothy's body as well as discipline her mind.

Only once, however, in emulating the threefold prayer at Gethsemane, is Dorothy explicitly described as taking a painting as her model:

> Whence in memory of the threefold prayer of our Lord Jesus on the Mount of Olives, she was accustomed to practicing three prostrations. First she kneeled with her hands extended as if crucified, and this she called praying on the Mount of Olives. Second, she kneeled with her hands joined and raised toward heaven, as the Savior is depicted praying on the Mount of Olives. Third, she prostrated herself on her face with her hands extended in the manner of the cross, and this she called the prostration of the cross.[86]

Marienwerder singles out for comparison with a picture of Christ at Gethsemane the only part of the threefold prayer that remained current in fifteenth-century representations of the Agony in the Garden: Christ "kneeling with his hands joined and raised toward heaven." Confirming his own familiarity with representations of the Passion—and anticipating that of his readers—he takes a painting as his point of reference, even using it to reinforce the authority and authenticity of his narration.[87] To pray like Christ—in effect, to become Christlike—one must pray as he appears to pray in representations of his Passion.[88]

Others besides a mystical elite used images of Christ in the garden at Gethsemane as reflexive models of prayer. A set of instructions in a fifteenth-century manuscript in Dresden bids its reader, defined simply as a devout man ("devotus homo"), to imagine, with the "eyes of his heart" ("oculos cordis"), praying as Christ prayed on the Mount of Olives ("et ponat ante oculos cordis quomodo Christus oravit ad patrem in monte oliveti"). Like Christ, he should surrender his will to God, repeating Christ's words: "Non sic ego volo, sed sic tu vis pater."[89] The manuscript, however, supplies material for the exterior as well as the interior eye. A parallel set of directives in the same text begins: "first place Christ in his image before the eyes, as if one could see Christ corporeally."[90] In addition to invoking the established practice of meditative visualization, the injunction to look at Christ's body with corporeal eyes takes for granted the reader's acceptance of *acheiropoietoi,* images not made by human hand that revealed the true likeness of Christ.[91] In this construction, images do not so much confirm reality as establish the standard by which it is defined. And in case the reader cannot conjure up an iconic image, the manuscript supplies a sequence of twenty-four narrative scenes, the sole surviving set of engravings of the Passion by the Master of the Playing Cards.[92] They serve as the starting point for prayers that lead the devotee from grace and compassion to the imitation of the "exemplum" of Christ's Passion.[93]

Illustrations of the Agony in the Garden from the prayer books of nuns not only permitted a similar identification of viewer and subject but also anticipated and enforced it by including in the images "portraits" of nuns in postures of prayer indicative of their identification with Christ. For example, in an extensively illustrated Rhenish prayer book of the second half of the fifteenth century an illustration of the Agony includes among the sleeping Apostles an open-eyed female figure, most likely the *anima,* or soul, who, in conformity with Christ, joins her hands in prayer (Fig. 64).[94] In another Rhenish prayer book, compiled by a nun at St. Nicolaus in undis, in Strasbourg, about 1450 (Fig. 65), the artist uses different means to achieve the same end: instead of inserting a diminutive proxy into the narrative, she removes from the scene all accessory figures, leaving only Christ and a maiden, again representing the soul, whose posture of prayer provides a mirror image of Christ's, albeit on a smaller scale.[95] She appears to distract Christ from the primary object of his own vision, the chalice on the flower-decked outcrop of

Fig. 64. Agony in the Garden, prayer book, Upper Rhine, Karlsruhe, Badische Landesbibliothek, Ms. Donaueschingen 437, f. 74r.

Fig. 65. Prayer book, Upper Rhine, ca. 1450, Staatsbibliothek zu Berlin—Preußischer Kulturbesitz, Ms. germ. oct. 53, f. 2v.

Gethsemane, so that despite the rain of blood from his face, he looks at the virgin with a beatific smile. We can imagine the nun responding in the words of a prayer book of 1436 from the Dominican convent at Oetenbach in Zurich:

> O gentle Lord Jesus Christ, as you in the very greatest distress sweated bloody sweat on the Mount of Olives in your pious prayer for me and all mankind, I recall your fear and distress and beseech you grant that I become so inflamed and ardent in the memory of your holy suffering that in return for your bloody sweat I shed pious tears that will wash from me all my sins and protect me now and eternally from all evil.[96]

Not Christ's blood, but the nun's tears, shed in response to his sacrifice, will save her. The approximate symmetry of the two secretions reproduces a similar reciprocity of devotion in the image and, by implication, in the viewer.[97]

The drawing of the Agony from St. Walburg, no different in its aims, is more direct in engaging the viewer. Like the drawing in Berlin or the devotional practice of Dorothy of Montau, it depends on mimesis in reverse or, rather, an art of mimicry. Echoing its own rhetoric of inversion, the drawing directs that the viewer, rather than see the image itself as an imitation, imitate it, praying, not in the way the Gospels describe Christ, but in the way the image portrays him. The image confers on itself unambiguous powers of formation.

AGONY, ECSTASY, OBEDIENCE

The habit of using images as devotional exemplars was deeply ingrained in the practice of nuns. The drawing from St. Walburg brings to mind accounts in convent chronicles in which an image of Christ—most often a Crucifixion—appears and speaks to a nun in a vision. In many of these exempla, the evocation of the Agony in the Garden is at best indirect. Christ nonetheless teaches the same submission of will he exhibited in the garden of Gethsemane, often in the words inscribed on the drawing from St. Walburg: "Non quod ego volo, sed quod tu."

The chronicle of Adelhausen in Freiburg, compiled in 1318 by Anna von Munzingen, offers a representative example. Anna describes how, as the nun Metze Túschelin stood before a cross contemplating the Passion, "a voice spoke to her: 'That I stood on the cross naked and bare for your sake, of that you shall never make me think as well as you would were you to rob yourself of your own will.' "[98] From the same chronicle comes a comparable account of the nun Geri Küchlin:

> She especially liked to meditate on the martyrdom of our Lord. And one time, as she stood before a crucifix and prayed earnestly, our Lord inclined himself from the cross toward her. And she said: "O woe, Lord, this I have never deserved from you, and I

> am not deserving of it." . . . And afterward she underwent great affliction, and suffered so much that she thought it impossible to suffer any longer. And she feared that God had forgotten her, and she asked our Lord from the bottom of her heart and with many tears that he take the suffering from her. And she did that very often, and especially one time after Matins. . . .
>
> And so it was that her heart became completely open, and a great light came into her, and our Lord came with the light and stood before her with all the wounds that he ever suffered and said to her: "Oh! Will you not suffer a little bit for my sake?" And he took her by the hand and said to her: "Look at my fresh wounds and deny what I suffered for your sake." But then he said: "That which you must suffer, you should patiently endure. For I am with you and will be with you in all your works and will never leave you." And she said: "O Lord, I will endure all the more gladly what I must suffer for your sake." [99]

Neither of these stories from the Adelhausen chronicle can be read as an account of actual experience. Like the images to which they allude, however, they were designed to structure devotional response. In this case, they not only describe the dialogue that a nun might have initiated with an image—if not in a vision, then at least in her imagination—but also link her meditations to a discourse on the interrelated virtues of patience and obedience. The drawing of the rose makes much the same argument: the nun who seeks to imitate Christ's agony should not seek out suffering. Rather, she should follow the cardinal rule spelled out in the inscription: "Not what I will, but what thou wilt," that is, obedience, submission, and patience. Christ acquiesced to the Passion, but the abdication of his own will constituted the defining act.

In keeping with the fundamental precepts of monasticism, the literature of reform repeatedly underscores the importance of obedience over works, in a manner that demonstrates the degree to which Reformation theologians such as Calvin were indebted to Catholic tradition.[100] The prologue to the cornerstone of Western monasticism, the Rule of St. Benedict, begins with an exhortation: "Receive willingly and carry out effectively your loving father's advice, that by the labor of obedience you may return to him from whom you had departed by the sloth of disobedience." [101] To reinforce the point, the prologue concludes with a reminder that by "persevering in the monastery according to his teaching until death, we may by patience share in the sufferings of Christ and deserve to have a share also in His kingdom." [102] The section governing female novices in the Dominican Constitutions spells out the same principle: "Abandon your own will for the will of the majority, observe voluntary obedience in all things." [103]

Franciscan reform statutes speak with the same voice, as, for example, in the legislation imposed circa 1455 on the Poor Clares at Brixen:

All things shall occur with order among you. . . . In you should be observed and required more than in other and worldly people, who, as opposed to the spiritual person, sets himself apart from the community through his own will, special devotions, or works, and often brings much disorder and thus alienates himself from God. . . . Obedience [is] better than any sacrifice, and a relatively minor good work accomplished in obedience is much better than other good works done for one's own advancement.[104]

The Dominican Nicholas of Dinkelsbuhl (1360–1433), preaching to the nuns of Vienna on the evils of private possessions, was offended less by property per se than by the nuns' use of it "nach alem irem willen," "each according to her will."[105] Obedience—renunciation of the will—is the essential monastic virtue; all other virtues follow from it.

In this spirit, the drawing from St. Walburg is an exhortation, not so much to imitate Christ's acts through penance as to emulate the patience and obedience that inspired them. Read in this way, the words added at the bottom of the drawing contradict the image as much as they complement it. They rein in the imaginative possibilities unleashed by the image, in effect, tempering its invitation to understand imitation literally.

To interpret suffering as patience and obedience is entirely in tune with the tenets of monastic reform as it was preached in convents. Spiritual advisers condemned and sought to control what they regarded as the nuns' extravagant, even excessive, acts of self-mortification in imitation of the Passion.[106] In his "autobiography," Suso details his gruesome self-inflicted suffering only to castigate himself for taking the ideal of imitation too literally.[107] He aims this corrective primarily at the women in the care of his order. He takes up the same theme in his *Horologium sapientiae,* in chapters entitled "How useful it is for the servant of God to suffer many tribulations in this world" and "In what way the true disciple of Christ ought to conform himself with his sufferings."[108] In passing from the reader's tribulations to those of Christ, Suso speaks of proceeding "from roses to roses" ("De rosis ad rosas procedimus"); then, in a flowery invocation, he asks the reader to turn to the "most precious thesaurus of your Passion" ("pretiosissimo tuae passionis thesauro"), applying to Christ as Holy Wisdom epithets usually reserved for the Virgin Mary: "O flower of the field and rose without thorns, Eternal Wisdom, let us then turn the eyes of the heart back with the greatest desire to the rose blossoms of your sufferings."[109] The drawing from St. Walburg presents an analogous image, condensing the whole of the Passion into a single flower. But like Suso, the image stresses submission over suffering per se. Speaking with the same voice as the seraph who appeared to Suso and declared, "Receive suffering willingly," Wisdom states: "If tribulations do not afflict, they are not worthy of being called afflictions."[110] The point is hammered home with the inevitable tag from Scripture (Luke 22 : 42): "Accede and faithfully say unto him: 'My father, not my will, but thy will be done.' "[111]

Master Eckhart (ca. 1260–1328), Suso's teacher, provides the most extensive and most radical statement on the need for resignation and the abdication of the will. For example, in the *Buch der göttlichen Tröstung* (Book of divine comfort), written in about 1318 for Agnes of Hungary, co-founder of the Franciscan double monastery at Königsfelden in Switzerland, Eckhart preaches a theology of absolute submission to the will of God.[112] Citing Seneca as well as Scripture, he argues:

> A man cannot be good who does not wish for exactly what God wills, for it is im possible that God should will anything but good, and precisely in and because God wills it, it must be good and best. That is why our Lord taught the Apostles, and us through them, to pray every day that God's will be done. And yet, when God's will appears and is done we complain. . . . Therefore the masters declare that the blessed in heaven know creatures independently of an image of those creatures, knowing them in the one image that is God, in which God knows Himself and all things, and loves and wills them. And God Himself teaches us to pray for and desire this, when we say "Our Father," "hallowed be thy name"—that is, to know you alone—"thy kingdom come," that I may possess nothing I prize and regard as wealth but You, who are all riches. Therefore the Gospel says: "Blessed art the poor in spirit," that is in will, and so we pray to God that His will may be done "in earth," that is, in ourselves, and "in heaven," that is, in God himself. . . . Such suffering alone is perfect suffering, for it arises and springs from pure love of God's sheer goodness and joy.[113]

Taking the prayer most commonly recited by nuns apart from the Ave Maria, Eckhart turns it into the occasion for a profound meditation on coming to terms with God. In this theology of suffering, the teaching of the drawing from St. Walburg finds no place: all imitation, all images, are submerged in the striving for absolute conformity and union with God.

To Eckhart's treatise on the true imitation of suffering addressed to the nuns of Königsfelden, however, we can oppose the *Legatus divinae pietatis,* ascribed to Gertrude of Helfta but actually written in large measure by her immediate followers, who sought both to glorify her reputation and to hold her up as an exemplar of devotion.[114] This compilation, unlike Eckhart's text, grants a central, indeed indispensable, role to images of all kinds, including works of art. Among the many elaborate pious exercises attributed to Gertrude are several sets of devotions structured around the repeated recitation of Christ's prayer: "Non quod ego volo, sed quod tu." Two closely related passages in book IV, the first (chap. xxii) detailing devotions for the fifth Sunday in Lent, the second (chap. xxiii), those for the ensuing Palm Sunday, go beyond a straightforward enumeration of prayers, situating them in a wider context of paraliturgical use. Although neither passage can be attributed to Gertrude herself, and neither necessarily reflects her own devotional practice, they nevertheless represent the devotional conduct of the nuns at Helfta during the early fourteenth century, when the text was compiled as part of the effort to secure Gertrude's canonization.[115]

According to the *Legatus,* in the course of offering up a prayer to Christ's tortured body, Gertrude unexpectedly receives from one of his wounds (which one is not specified) an illumination in the form of a ray of light. In rhetoric reminiscent of the rubrics from Engelberg, Gertrude asks how she might best commemorate Christ's Passion in a manner he would find praiseworthy. In response, Christ describes a devotion centered on the words he uttered at Gethsemane, in this case as given, not by Mark, but by Luke:

> Namely, you should turn over more often in your mind with gratitude and compassion that anguish in which I, the Lord, your Creator and Savior, fixed in willing agony, prayed at great length, while, on account of an extreme anxiety of love and desire, I irrigated the earth's surface with bloody sweat. You should commend to me all your works and all that takes place around you in accord with the submission with which I spoke to the Father in that prayer, "But yet not my will, but thy will be done" [Luke 22 : 42]. And in this manner you will receive all prosperity and adversity in that love which made me send them to you for your salvation. You will therefore receive good fortune with gratitude, in accordance with the love that made me, your lover, grant it to you, out of condescension for your weakness, so that through it you might learn to think of hoping to obtain eternal happiness.[116]

The construction of the dialogue invests the devotion with the authority of revelation, so it comes as no surprise that Gertrude complies:

> On account of this she decided to read throughout that week a certain prayer by which she greeted each member, namely: "Hail, O exquisite limbs," etc. And she was aware that this greatly pleased the Lord. And let us not hesitate to do the same in order to be worthy of attaining a similar joy.[117]

The *Legatus* does not have Gertrude literally repeat Christ's own words, nor does she ask her readers to reiterate them. Rather, she has them recite an otherwise unknown petition in honor of Christ's limbs. Christ's invocation nevertheless defines the essence of the devotion, which, as she explains it, requires the passive acceptance of good and bad fortune, "prospera et adversa," just as Christ accepted them out of love for mankind. The internal echoes of the concluding injunction—

"ut consimilem beatudinem consequi mereamur"—captures the pattern of imitation that the prayer seeks to instill. The nuns at Helfta imitate Gertrude, and in imitating her, they imitate Christ.

In the ensuing chapter, the nun who claims to speak for Gertrude places Christ's words in her mouth, not just once, but 225 times in memory of what was believed to be the sum of the members—or parts—of Christ's body.[118] The impetus to pray in this manner comes from a vision, itself provoked by an image. On the eve of Palm Sunday—according to the text—Gertrude, inflamed by a desire to give refuge to the Lord, prays to an image of the crucifix and kisses the wound in its side with ardent devotion. Filling the wound with her desire for the Sacred Heart, Gertrude beseeches that Christ, in turn, might enter into the most unworthy and humble abode of her heart ("ad hospitiolum indignissimi cordis sui dignaretur declinare"). Christ asks what she can offer him in return, demanding nothing less than the key to her hospice (i.e., her heart), namely her will: "Voluntas tua propria."[119] Gertrude complies: "Then, divinely inspired, she read on account of all of his members that passage from the Gospel [Luke 22:42] 225 times: 'But yet not my will, but thy will be done.'"[120]

The pious procedures described in the *Legatus* offer fascinating analogies to the patterns of prayer suggested by the drawing from St. Walburg. The texts associated with Gertrude, however, cannot be regarded as the source either for the image or for associated devotional practices; there is no evidence to suggest that the nuns at St. Walburg knew the *Legatus*. Each prayer exercise represents an independent invention based on a shared substratum of paraliturgical and devotional custom. The available evidence indicates that this body of customs was especially common in convents; to the best of my knowledge, prior to the fifteenth century all the sources that either describe or prescribe devotions emulating Christ's prayer at Gethsemane come from texts written by, for, or about nuns. The devotions take as their point of departure the Gospels' account of the Agony and, although they can only be inferred from sources such as the rubrics from Engelberg, paraliturgical prayers incorporated into the services for Holy Week. The *Legatus* also identifies the Mass as the context in which these devotions were enacted.

The Gospel account of Christ's invocations at Gethsemane was preordained to serve as a model for prayer. To the words provided by this archetype, however, both the *Legatus* and the drawing from St. Walburg add a no less indispensable image. Although in each case the role of the image differs, the two devotions suggest parallel modes of devotional practice. The image and the texts represent opposite sides of the same devotional coin. Whereas the method of prayer laid out in the *Legatus* is inspired by an image, the drawing from Eichstätt uses imagery to inspire a similar pattern of devotion. In the exercises ascribed to Gertrude, her devotion to the side wound inspires the vision that instructs her in prayer. In the drawing from St. Walburg, the opposite obtains. An image based on the Agony inspires, if not a vision per se, then a visual experience that emulates visionary modes. The drawing of the rose from St. Walburg does not simply represent prayer in the words of its inscription; it also exemplifies and structures the viewer's devotional response. In analogous fashion, Gertrude's devotions, as described in the *Legatus,* present as a model for her female audience the whole of her practice—the objects she used as aids to devotion as well as the reactions they inspired. Gertrude's vision is like the scene of Christ in the garden in the drawing from Eichstätt, framed and then presented as an object for imitation.

Examined in context, the drawing of the Agony from St. Walburg reveals that in late medieval devotions a rose was never simply a rose. The blossoms evoked a dense array of metaphorical and mnemonic associations linking images and prayers in pious devotions. Although the rose from St. Walburg represents but a single cutting, it is one of the more exotic offshoots of this florid tradition. An iconographic unicum, it nevertheless distills the essence of prayer on the Passion.

3

WOUNDING SIGHT

SCHOLASTICS DEFINED PRAYER as the "ascensus mentis ad Deum," "the ascent of the mind to God."[1] Yet, in a paradox consistent with the oxymoron of the Incarnation, the path that led the devotee toward the summit of mystical experience required that she first descend with Christ to the depths of degradation. The formula "Per Christum hominem ad Christum Deum," "Through Christ the man to Christ the God," summarized this practice, which offered exaltation through humility and self-abnegation.[2] Mankind could ascend only because God himself had first condescended to take on human flesh. The Evangelist John laid out the principle in his Gospel (John 3 : 13): "And no man hath ascended into heaven, but he that descended from heaven, the Son of Man who is in heaven." Benedict of Nursia reiterated the principle, declaring in his chapter on humility: "Everyone who exalts himself shall be humbled, and he who humbles himself shall be exalted."[3] To imitate Christ was to recapitulate this cycle of ascent and descent: not simply to rise up to him, but to begin by subordinating the self. The mystic's path thus closed to form a circle, its point of origin one with its point of return.

Of all the images in the Bible, none more clearly expresses this rhythm of reciprocal decline and elevation, death and resurrection, than Jacob's ladder (Genesis 28 : 12–17):

> And he saw in his sleep a ladder standing upon the earth, and the top thereof touching heaven; the angels also of God ascending and descending by it, and the Lord leaning upon the ladder, saying to him: "I am the Lord God of Abraham thy father, and the God of Isaac; the land, wherein thou sleepest, I will give to thee and to thy seed. And thy seed shall be as the dust of the earth: thou shall spread abroad to the west, and to the east, and to the north and to the south: and in thee and thy seed all the tribes of the earth shall be blessed. And I will be thy keeper whithersoever thou goest, and will bring thee back into this land; neither will I leave thee, till I shall have accomplished all that I have said." And when Jacob awakened out of sleep he said:

"Indeed the Lord is in this place, and I knew it not . . . this is no other but the house of God, and the gate of heaven." [4]

Seizing on Jacob's vision, Benedict argued that "by descent and ascent we must surely understand nothing else than this: that we descend by self-exaltation and ascend by humility. And the ladder thus set up is our life in the world, which the Lord raises up to heaven if our heart is humbled." [5] For other exegetes, the ladder leading from heaven to earth and from earth to heaven was the cross itself, the nub of sacred time and space, elaborated in terms of Paul's exhortation in Ephesians 3 : 17–19:

That Christ may dwell by faith in your hearts; that by being rooted and founded in charity, you may be able to comprehend with all the saints, what is the breadth and length, and height, and depth: to know also the charity of Christ, which surpasseth all knowledge, that you may be filled unto all the fullness of God.

Aligned with the four dimensions specified in Ephesians ("latitudo et longitudo et sublimitas et profundum"), vertical and horizontal beams were in turn associated with the points of the compass cited in Genesis ("ad occidentem et orientem septentrionem et meridiem").[6] The dimensions indicated were temporal as well as spatial: just as Christ's death marked the midpoint in human history, so too the cross provided the allegorical as well as literal "crux" of the cosmos. The cross also had its moral dimensions: each arm stood for a different virtue or set of virtues, each personified by its ultimate exemplar, Christ himself.[7]

In keeping with these fundamental patterns of pious expression, the drawings from St. Walburg themselves serve as ladders, helping the viewer mount, step by step, toward union with Christ. They thus function as exemplars, models to be imitated, if not literally, then in spirit. At the same time, they supply a self-conscious commentary on the process of exemplification. With a view to the mystic's ultimate goal, the beatific vision, sight itself becomes not only the end, but also the means, of achieving union with God.

EXEMPLARY IMAGES

The tradition of allegorical exegesis devoted to the cross is among the most elaborate and extensive of the entire Middle Ages. Two closely related drawings from St. Walburg distill this tradition, without, however, merely repeating its well-worn formulas (Figs. 66, 67 and Plates 9, 10). Each image is a unicum. Although not conceived as pendants, they invite reading as a pair: both focus on the cross conceived as a vehicle for the *imitatio Christi*. They are still more closely integrated by their inscriptions, which overlap in many of their terms and which, with the exception of those in the drawing in Berlin (see Plate 12), are the most extensive in the group. From our point of view, the elaborate didactic apparatus detracts from the affective impact of the drawings. Without it, however, their abstruse imagery would have remained impenetrable. Rather than deter devotional response, the words incorporated into the images enhance their resonance and meaning.

The two Crucifixions provide variations on a central theme, the cross itself, which in each drawing takes the same T-square form. Painted to simulate gold, the two crucifixes assume the aura of the gilded processional crosses deployed in the liturgy. In each image, the cross has been removed from its natural narrative context. The green lawn that in all the drawings serves as the draftswoman's signature motif does not supply a stage space for the usual cast of characters present in Crucifixion scenes—Mary, John, and other mourners, in some cases joined by a motley assortment of Christ's tormentors. Instead, it identifies the cross as the *arbor vitae,* the tree of life, and, in addition, provides a foil for an array of related symbolic imagery. In the second Crucifixion (see Fig. 67 and Plate 10) the blood from Christ's wounds gives life to the poppies that dot the green and form an especially dense pattern at the foot of the ladder.

The inscriptions provide an indispensable gloss on the two allegorical Crucifixions. In the first, the legends identify the arms of the cross with Christ's exemplary virtues: to his right (our left), "Barmherczinkait," "Mercy"; to his left (our right), "Gerechtigkait," "Justice"; at the foot of the cross, immediately above the skull of Golgotha, "Laingmüetigkait, Gedult, Gehorsam," "Forbearance, Patience, and Obedience"; and, at the top, to the left of the tablet identifying Christ as "INRI" ("Jesus of Nazareth, King of the Jews"), the foremost virtue, "Lieb," "Charity." By juxtaposition, the tablet lends the inscriptions a scriptural authority.

At the apex of the composition, replacing the uppermost arm of the cross, Mary perches incongruously in the traditional pose of the Madonna of Humility. The swords arrayed around her heart identify her as the archetypal embodiment of compassion (literally "suffering with") and hence of the *imitatio Christi.*[8] A bright stroke of red highlights Christ's reciprocal wound, the gash in his side. Mary stands in for the nun, who in her capacity as *sponsa Christi,* provokes the cry of the bridegroom in Song of Songs 4:9: "Thou hast wounded my heart, my sister, my spouse, thou has wounded my heart with one of thy eyes."[9] As a figure of humility exalted, she provides a female exemplar of devotion whose paradoxical prominence would not have been lost on the nuns. Her exaltation represents the fulfillment of the prophetic promise encoded in the image of the *Arbor virginis;* the virginal flower bears fruit in the Passion.

Fig. 66. Symbolic Crucifixion, Eichstätt, St. Walburg.

Fig. 67. The Heart on the Cross, Eichstätt, St. Walburg.

To the Symbolic Crucifixion's vivid display of visual exegesis, derived from commentaries on Ephesians 3 : 18 and paralleled, if not duplicated, in other images, the artist adds an unusual pair of complementary figures: to the left, Christ in the manger, identified with the virtues "Armut, Ellendt, and Diemüetigkeit," "Poverty, Suffering, and Humility"; to the right, the adult Christ, associated with the trio "Senfftmüetigkait, Yainigkait, and Messigkait," "Tenderness, Unity, and Temperance."[10] The three labels "Anfang," "Das mitel," and "Endt," "beginning," "the middle," and "end," identify the infancy, maturity, and death of Christ as three successive stages or stations in a progress toward the fulfillment of the divine plan of salvation. The flanking figures identify the crucifix as the third stage in a narrative embracing Christ's earthly existence, just as the arms of the cross embrace the physical and moral universe.

In the Symbolic Crucifixion the prominence of the wound in Christ's side implies the presence of the figure who thrust in his lance. In historical representations, Christ's tormentor is the centurion Longinus, whose blindness was miraculously healed by the touch of Christ's blood.[11] The drawing from St. Walburg relies more directly on a long tradition of images that associated parts of the cross with Christ's exemplary virtues. Especially popular in late medieval Germany, these allegorical interpretations of the Crucifixion replace Longinus and the other tormentors of Christ with personified virtues that spell out the spiritual meaning of his sacrifice.[12] Most often it is Charity who thrusts the lance into Christ's side in a paradoxical expression of love consonant with the Passion. Elsewhere, for example in the lectionary from the Dominican convent of the Holy Cross at Regensburg, 1267–76, a female figure, Sponsa, assumes the same role (Fig. 68).[13] As *sponsae Christi,* the nuns could have identified all the more readily with an image of the bride who acts out the conception of wounding love.

The Symbolic Crucifixion from St. Walburg relies on this imagery but transforms it as well (see Fig. 66 and Plate 9). Especially unusual is the artist's inclusion of the whole of Christ's life in the allegory to suggest that each stage of it—not only the Passion—offers itself as an exemplum, and that each exemplifies a different set of virtues. The artist argues that the consummation of imitation does not take place in an instant; it is not a moment of self-immolation. Instead, in keeping with monastic discipline, it involves an arduous struggle that lasts a lifetime.

Despite its unconventional elements, the Symbolic Crucifixion from St. Walburg builds on traditional christological exegesis. In a sermon on John 3 : 13 ("And no man hath ascended into heaven, but he that descended from heaven, the Son of Man who is in heaven") Bernard of Clairvaux, the twelfth-century Cistercian, argued that the imitation of Christ involved a step-by-step process rather than

Fig. 68. Christ crucified by the Virtues, Lectionary of the Convent of the Holy Cross, Regensburg, 1267–76, Oxford, Keble College Library, Ms. 49, f. 7r.

union or identification achieved in an instant.[14] John, Bernard notes, deliberately chose the word "descend" rather than "died" because someone who dies simply falls, whereas one who descends necessarily proceeds gradually ("gradatim").[15] Bernard does not invoke Jacob's dream, but the motif of descent implies the possibility of movement in the opposite direction:

> There are, therefore, steps in descending as there are in ascending. In fact, in descending, the first step is from the height of heaven all the way to the flesh; the sec-

ond, all the way to the cross; the third, all the way to death. . . . As we have seen the descent, so we shall see the ascent. But that too is threefold, and its first step is the glory of the Resurrection; the second, the power of judgment; the third, admission to the right hand of the Father. And from death he [Christ] certainly deserved the resurrection from the cross, and from judgment, the power; so that, since in that injustice he was judged, from that he obtained the just censure of judgment, as he himself said after the Resurrection: "All power is given to me in heaven and in earth" (Matthew 28 : 18).[16]

Bernard divides ascent and descent into three equal stages embracing the whole of human history. Those of the downward path correspond precisely to the ones identified in the drawing: the first, "from the height of heaven all the way to the flesh"—what the drawing labels "Anfang"—corresponding to the Incarnation, embodied by the Christ Child in the manger; the second, "all the way to the cross"—what the drawing labels "Das mitel"—Christ's infancy and public ministry, corresponding to the standing figure of the adult Christ; and the third, "all the way to death"—what the drawing terms "Endt"—the Passion, summarized in the dominant figure of the crucified Christ. Exhorting his audience to imitate Christ, Bernard concludes this section of his sermon with a gloss on the words of Paul in Galatians 6 : 14: "But God forbid that I should glory, save in the cross of our Lord Jesus Christ."

Anything more sublime than this ascent, anything more glorious than this honor can neither be said nor imagined. For through the mystery of his Incarnation the Lord descended and ascended, leaving us an example so that we might follow in his footsteps.[17]

According to Bernard, just as Christ first descended, then ascended, so man, through grace, can recapitulate his actions.[18]

If the first Symbolic Crucifixion from St. Walburg can be compared to Bernard's allegory of descent, then the second corresponds to the reciprocal return to the Godhead (see Fig. 67 and Plate 10). Just as for Bernard "the essential work of Christ [was] to descend so that he may ascend," so the goal of the monk who followed in his footsteps was to emphasize the Resurrection over the Passion, the *amor spiritualis Christi* over the *amor carnalis Christi*.[19] The drawings from St. Walburg are no less elitist in their implications. The ladder, its ten rungs labeled virtues, makes ascent explicit. It is as if the image asks the viewer to recapitulate the movement choreographed in the imagery of Psalm 83 : 8, often cited as a parable of mystical ascent: "ibunt de virtute in virtutem videbitur Deus deorum in Sion," "They shall go from virtue to virtue: the God of gods shall be seen in Syon."[20] The virtues, however, do not correspond to any of the classical catalogues; the choice, if not arbitrary, is unconventional.[21] Nor is it clear which inscriptions correspond to which rungs; the two do not dovetail neatly. Those on the right, from bottom to top, are "Diemuetigkait, Senfftmuetigkait, Armut, Gehorsam, Rainigkait, Gelassenhait," "Humility, Tenderness, Poverty, Obedience, Purity," and, for lack of better terms, "Detachment or Resignation," the last, the virtue Christ embodied in the garden at Gethsemane.[22] The virtues on the left are "Golaub, Hoffnung, Gedult, Lieb," the cardinal virtues "Faith, Hope, and Charity," along with "Patience," again a virtue Christ exemplified in his Passion.[23]

During the late Middle Ages, edifying treatises with the word *scala,* or "ladder," in their titles, or at least referring to the idea of ascent, were second in popularity only to those with *speculum,* or "mirror."[24] Spiritual authors used steps or rungs to structure an ordered set of principles corresponding to the stages of the "itinerarium mentis in Deum." Most of these schemes originated in the Bible: some had seven steps (corresponding to the seven gifts of the Holy Spirit or the three cardinal and four theological virtues); others had twelve, corresponding to the twelve degrees of humility laid out in the Rule of St. Benedict. Among the most common were fifteenfold formulas corresponding to the Gradual Psalms (Psalms 119–133), such as the one associated with the *scala virtutum* in the *Hortus deliciarum* (Fig. 69).[25]

The drawing from St. Walburg evokes this tradition without, however, repeating its conventions by rote. Its tenfold scheme is rare, with one of the few parallels occurring in the unpublished pseudo-Bonaventurian tract *Decem gradus perfectae humilitatis.*[26] The number of rungs, however, is less important than the idea of gradual ascent. The image is also without roots in the iconographic sources, effectively summarized in a fifteenth-century Carthusian miscellany from Yorkshire (Figs. 70–72).[27] This profusely illustrated picture book contains, in addition to numerous tree diagrams that imply the idea of ascent, three images of ladders: the first with five rungs ("mekness," "pouerte," "obediens," "chastite," and "charite"), all leading to "the mounte of perfeccioun"; the second, a "scala celi" with nine rungs ("humiliacione," "conuersacione," "meditacione," "contricioune," "confession," "satisfaccion," "orison," "deuocion," and "contemplacion"); and the third, "the leddyr of heuen," with three rungs ("fayth," "hope," and "charite," the trio of virtues listed to the left of the ladder from St. Walburg).

Closer at hand, the nuns of St. Walburg may have known images such as *Der Weg zur Seligkeit,* an allegory of spiritual ascent printed in nearby Augsburg circa 1490 (Fig. 73).[28] Twelve scrolls, each bearing the name of a virtue, identify the twelve steps of the spiritual ascent, from "globen," or "faith," at the bottom, marked by a cross, to "gotliche lieb," or "divine love," at the top, marked by a small heart pierced by an arrow. Above, God and the angels await the soul with a

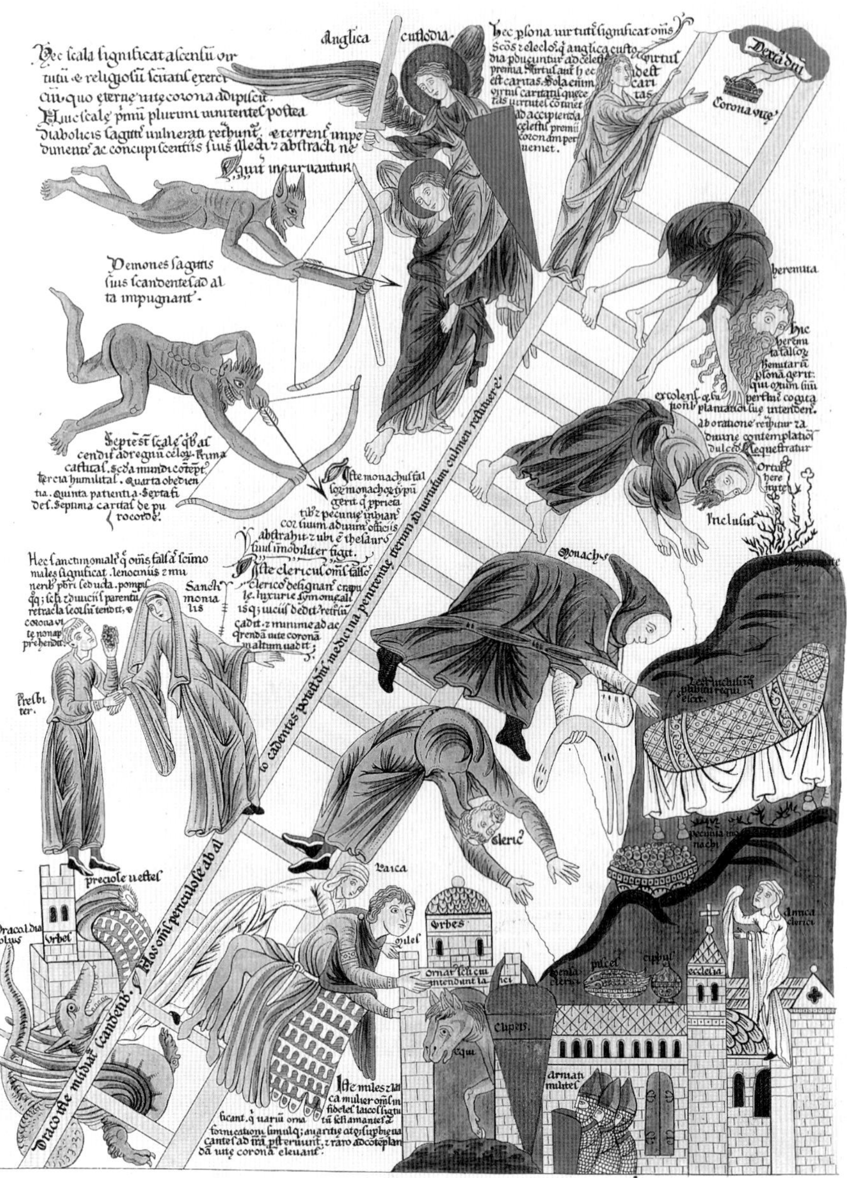

Fig. 69. Ladder of Virtues, *Hortus deliciarum*, f. 215v
(Photo: Metropolitan Museum of Art).

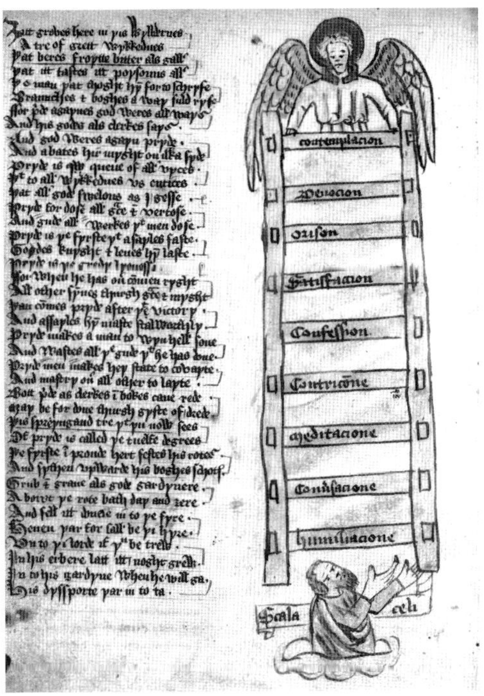

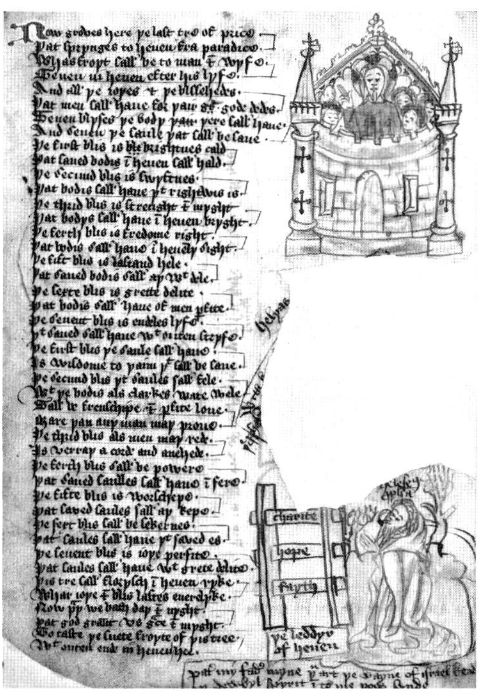

Figs. 70–72. Carthusian miscellany, Yorkshire, London, British Library, Ms. Add. 37049, f. 37v (*above, left*), f. 49v (*above*), and f. 65v (*left*).

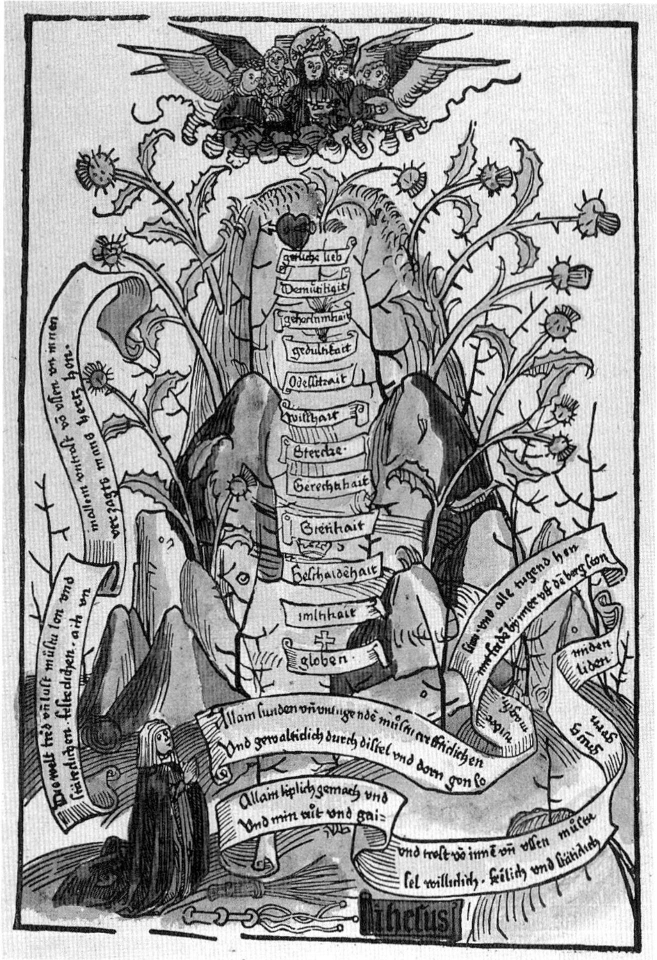

Fig. 73. *Der Weg zur Seligkeit,* Augsburg, ca. 1490, Mainz, Gutenberg-Museum, Inv. Nr. 18:4°/500.

crown; below, a nun kneels, a flail and scourge at her feet. Her presence indicates, not that nuns were the intended audience for the broadsheet, but that for late medieval viewers, as for us, the cloistered woman personified piety.

The drawing from St. Walburg implicitly compares the cross with the ladder that leads the soul to union with Christ. This common conceit appeared in another Augsburg incunabulum, the *Zwölf Früchte des Holzes des Lebens,* printed by Günther Zainter around 1477 (Fig. 74).[29] Based on Bonaventure's *Lignum vitae,* the tract illustrates the soul's ascent of a ladder with twelve rungs; the image identifies the soul with the Sponsa of Song of Songs 7:8: "dixi ascendam in palmam adprehendam fructus eius," "I said: I will go up into the palm tree, and will take

Fig. 74. *Zwölf Früchte des Holzes des Lebens,* Günther Zainter, Augsburg, ca. 1477, Munich, Bayerische Staatsbibliothek, Einblatt VII, 38.

hold of the fruit thereof."[30] Often glossed as a reference to Christ's own ascent of the cross, the motif also acquired a tropological, or moral, meaning. In climbing the ladder of the cross, the soul became Christlike.[31] The print gives the identification visual form by linking the twelve rungs of the ladder with the twelve branches of the living cross, each bearing fruit in a virtue.

Between the drawing from St. Walburg and all the images to which it can be compared, however, there is a decisive difference. Whereas in both the prints and the drawings of the Carthusian miscellany the worshiper consistently appears at the bottom, looking up, in the drawing from Eichstätt, she already occupies the apogee, nestled in God's heart like the souls in the Bosom of Abraham (see Fig. 67

and Plate 10). As Barbara Newman has noted, "The dedicated virgin did not have to climb a ladder so much as she had to beware of falling from the high rung she already occupied."[32] Her arrival is prefigured by the Virgin seated atop the cross in the Symbolic Crucifixion (see Fig. 66 and Plate 9). Like Mary, whom theologians compared to the ladder by which Christ had descended and by which man, in turn, could ascend, the nun in the drawing has already attained her goal.[33] The ladder itself is vestigial; its rungs merely serve as a reminder of the route she has traveled to reach her spiritual summit. Although the image refers to ascent (and hence hints at the prospect of falling), its primary purpose is to affirm the possibility of perfection.

The symbolic Crucifixions from St. Walburg epitomize an entire system of devotion, one predicated on the worshiper's ability to close the distance between herself and God through a step-by-step *imitatio Christi.* It was hardly by accident that Luther singled out the image of the ladder as an emblem of all that he scorned in the piety of works: "A great deal has been written about how man shall be divinized; there they have made ladders with which one climbs up to heaven and many such things. It is, however, vain begging work."[34] No doubt Luther would have been scandalized by the drawings from St. Walburg, which, like the remainder of the group to which they belong, were made within his lifetime (1483–1546). He would not, however, have taken exception to their existence as images per se; paintings and prints, bristling with inscriptions, that focused on the crucified Christ quickly became a staple of Protestant propaganda.[35] And, despite its rhetoric of absolute opposition, Lutheran and, later, Pietist polemic eventually adopted visual strategies first developed in fifteenth-century prints and devotional images, in some cases employing the very same plates and altering only their identifying inscriptions, as, for example, in the famous, if only recently identified, instance of Cranach's *Heavenly Ladder of Bonaventure,* initially printed around 1510–15 and reworked after 1531 (Fig. 75).[36] Rather, Luther would have been offended by the devotional premise underlying the drawings, that by pursuing the virtues, the soul can of its own accord ascend to union with God. For Luther, "Faith"—in the drawing from St. Walburg one of ten different rungs and not even the uppermost—was not merely the preeminent virtue but the only one that could justify man. In contrast, the drawing takes for granted that gradual imitation can lead to identification, the very nexus that Luther sought to deny.

In the drawings from St. Walburg, the cross, itself identified with the ladder and the suffering it stands for, is only a means to an end. The ultimate goal of the mystic is union with Christ.[37] Whereas the first Symbolic Crucifixion offers an intimation of this union, its "pendant" makes union the central theme (see Fig. 67

Fig. 75. Lucas Cranach, *Die Himmelsleiter des hl. Bonaventura,* after 1531, Coburg, Kunstsammlungen der Veste Coburg, Inv. Nr. I.44.82.

and Plate 10). In effect, the second drawing offers an extraordinary "close-up" of the first. The crossbar now defines the top of the drawing; even Christ's halo is truncated. We zoom in on the stunning, even shocking, image of the heart at the center, penetrating the gash to find ourselves—in the person of the nun, identified by her habit—nestled within it, exchanging vows with Christ. In a manner reminiscent of representations of the Coronation of the Virgin, the Infant Christ, at the right, places one hand behind the nun, as if to embrace her; with his other hand, he offers her a gift, not a ring, but a small golden pyx or container. As in the drawing of the Consecration of Virgins, Christ appears, not as a mature young man, but as a child. The image exemplifies the reciprocity of imitation as defined by Catherine of Siena, who advised her own adviser, Raymund of Capua: "Let your heart and soul be grafted onto the tree of the most holy cross—with Christ crucified. Make his wounds your home."[38] The oversize heart, no longer Christ's alone, also represents the interior of the nun's own being, into which she welcomes Christ, just as he admits her to heaven through the portal of his wounds.

If the image of the distended and crucified heart appears fantastic, even grotesque, the crucifixion of the disembodied heart is not without parallel; it appears, for example, in the elegant illustrations of René d'Anjou's *Mortifiement de vaine plaisance,* in which the penitent soul presents her bleeding heart, impaled on a cross, to personifications of contrition and the fear of God (Fig. 76).[39] The drawing from St. Walburg, however, is an independent invention that condenses and combines several biblical metaphors. The heart atop the ladder visualizes the foundational image from Ephesians 3:17–18 ("That Christ may dwell by faith in your hearts"). It also evokes the imagery that in Psalm 83 introduces the description of the soul "going from virtue to virtue," which, in turn, anticipates the images of the mystical heart (see Plates 11, 12). In each case, the central image evoked by the wound is less one of penetration than one of envelopment and enclosure.

> How lovely are thy tabernacles, O Lord of hosts! My soul longeth and fainteth for the courts of the Lord. My heart and my flesh have rejoiced in the living God, for the sparrow hath found herself a house, and the turtle dove a nest for herself where she may lay her young ones: Thy altars, O Lord of hosts, my king and my God. Blessed are they that dwell in thy house, O Lord: they shall praise thee for ever and ever.

The imagery of the soul nesting, like a bird, in Christ's wounds would in turn have evoked the dove "in the clefts of the rock, in the hollow places of the wall" of Canticles 2:14, each passage providing the impetus to an ongoing process of devotion.

In exploiting this method of reading and viewing, the drawings from St. Wal-

Fig. 76. Jean Colombe, the penitent soul presents her bleeding heart to Contrition and the Fear of God, René d'Anjou, *Le Mortifiement de vaine plaisance,* excised miniature, ca. 1470, Metz, Bibliothèque Municipale, Ms. 1486.

burg are more than merely ingenious; they imply a degree of self-consciousness on the part of the nun who made them that one would not instinctively associate with the naïveté of her draftsmanship. If the first drawing extends an invitation to follow Christ by imitating the Sponsa, the exemplar of compassion, the second offers a vision of fulfillment and identification: Christ and his bride conjoined in his mystical body. The very act of viewing is defined in scriptural terms. In irresistibly drawing our eye through the wound, the image compels us and, more specifically, the female viewer to whom it was originally addressed, to perform the act of penetration that in Canticles 4:9 prompts Christ to respond: "thou has wounded my heart with one of thy eyes." Simply in looking at the image, we fulfill the injunction and take on the role of the Virgin and bride.[40]

Few images of the wounded heart represent the reciprocal penetration of lover and beloved as effectively. The initial on a single leaf from a Westphalian manuscript of around 1475 incorporates the five wounds of Christ, the pierced hands and feet at the four corners and the Sacred Heart at the center (Fig. 77).[41] The

Fig. 77. The wounds of Christ, single leaf, Westphalian, ca. 1475.

heart bleeds from its wound, placed to Christ's right in deference to liturgical tradition.[42] On the viewer's right, however, a scroll inscribed "vulnerasti cor meum" pierces and penetrates a second slash, as if to demonstrate the words' cutting effect.[43] A similar interaction marks the opening folio of a life of Augustine copied and decorated in 1480 by a nun at the Magdalenakloster in Strasbourg (Fig. 78). At the lower left, the female donor or scribe, labeled with the cryptic initials k.i., utters a prayer beginning with the words "Vulneraverat caritas christi cor eius cor meum," which takes flight in the form of the arrow that pierces the heart in the initial, a monogram of the name of Jesus. The pierced heart represents not only that of Christ, but also that of his spiritual lover, Augustine.[44] The projectile's long shaft pointedly corresponds to that of the unicorn in the lower margin, aimed in the opposite direction.[45] As in the drawings from St. Walburg, the ensemble appeals to the viewer in terms provided by Scripture, specifically, the inherently visual imagery of Song of Songs 4:9. In the drawing from St. Walburg, however, the visual rhetoric translates the metaphor of piercing sight into a devotional performance enacted by the eye. The devout onlooker experiences her heartfelt compassion for Christ as an act, not simply of speech, but of penetrating vision.

In the drawing of the Heart on the Cross, the inscriptions that fan out from the heart do not simply function as labels; they also put words in the mouth of Christ

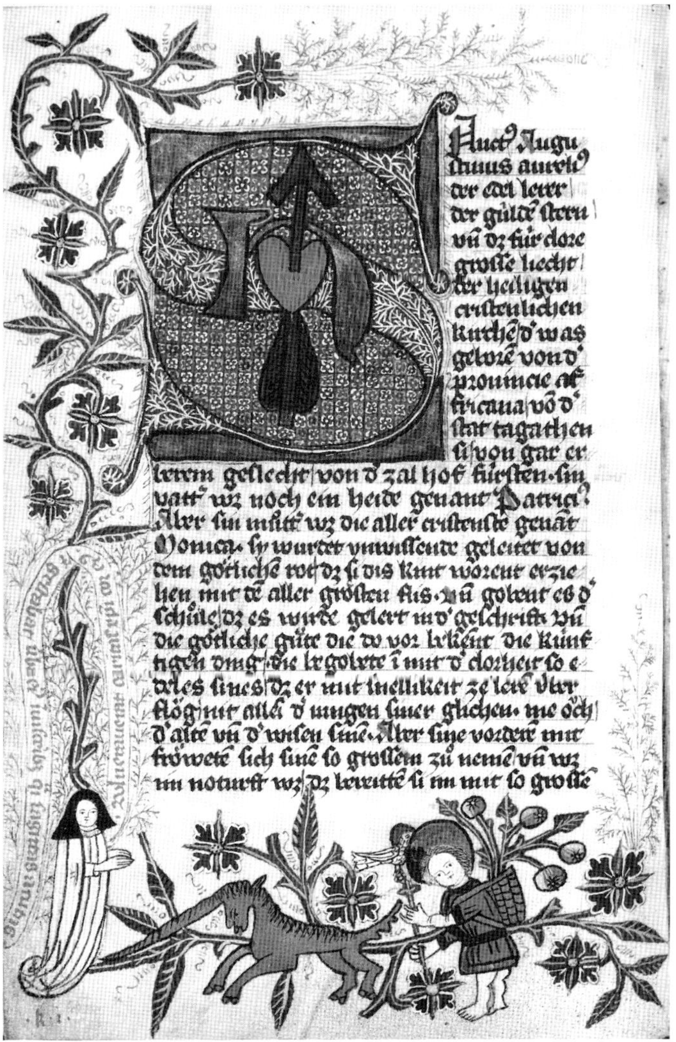

Fig. 78. Life of St. Augustine, Strasbourg, 1480, Staatsbibliothek zu Berlin—Preußischer Kulturbesitz, Ms. germ. qu. 1877, f. 2v.

and the viewer, thereby implying actions that the drawing completes and consummates. In effect, the image initiates a devotional dialogue that simulates the exchange the nun should re-create with Christ. The two inscriptions parallel to Christ's arms identify an offered embrace: the scroll to the left reads, "O herz zeuch mich zu dir In dich und nach dir," "O heart, draw me to you, into you, and after you," an echo of Song of Songs 1 : 3: "Draw me: we will run after thee," a passage usually glossed as an expression of the soul's desire to imitate Christ.[46] In light of the image at the center, the uncited remainder of the verse—"The king hath brought me into his storerooms; we will be glad and rejoice in thee, remembering thy breasts more than wine: the righteous love thee"—acquires immediate resonance. The heart, as the breast of the bridegroom, becomes the storeroom of Christ in which he gathers all his mystical secrets. In the drawing, the righteous nun rejoices literally within it.

In response to the bride's empassioned entreaty, the bridegroom replies in the words of the scroll that extends to the right: "Du bist gancz schon mein freundin," "You are completely beautiful, my beloved," a reminiscence of a refrain that recurs throughout the Song of Songs, for example, in 4 : 7, "Thou art all fair, O my love" (cf. 1 : 15, 4 : 1, and 7 : 6). The scroll that unfurls in a descending diagonal to the right corresponds to the ladder on the left, which represents the steps by which the soul ascends to Christ. It reads, "Das ist mein ruestat; darinn ich will ruen ewigklich on end," "That is my resting place, within which I will rest eternally without end." The words reinforce the identity of the heart as the bedchamber of the soul; they also add an eschatological note, defining mystical union as a foretaste of heavenly rest and repose.

A comparable concatenation of imagery forms the basis for a Middle High German song to the cross, which begins, "O du eddele sedderenbom," "O you noble cedar tree."[47] Known in manuscripts from several convents in Lower Saxony, among them Ebstorf and Wienhausen, the poem draws on a combination of secular and sacred sources in identifying the heart of Jesus as the mystical retreat of the soul:

Also du, here, hangedest
al an dem cruce breyt,
dyn gotlike mylde herte
eyn scharper sper dorsneyt.

As you hung, Lord,
on the wide cross,
your mild, divine heart
was pierced by a sharp spear.

Och were myn herte eyn garden
van den eddelen blomen fyn,
darin so wolde ik planten
mynem leve eyn krenselyn.

Oh! if only my heart were a garden
full of fine, noble flowers,
I would plant within it
a little chaplet for my love.

De blomen, de ik meyne,
de heten humilitas,
de anderen schullen heten
spes fides caritas.

The flowers that I have in mind
are called humility,
the others shall be called
hope, faith, and charity.

Ut mynes leves herten
dar springet eyn reverkyn,
dat reveriken wyl ik leyden
al an den garden myn.

From my beloved's heart
there springs a runnel.
I will channel that little river
directly into my garden.

Fig. 79. Christ crucified by the Virtues, Wienhausen, Cistercian convent, Lower Saxony, ca. 1330.

Mynes leves arme
stan wyt utgebreyt,
mochte ik dar anne rouwen,
vorgeyte ik al myn leyt.

My beloved's arms
stood wide outspread,
I would like to rest in them
so I could forget all my sorrow.[48]

In its evocation of the crucified Christ, arms outspread, as the exemplar of the cardinal virtues, the song recalls the small stained-glass window in the second-story walk of the cloister at Wienhausen that depicts Christ surrounded by virtues, in this case, the "four daughters of God" enumerated in Psalm 84 : 11 – 12: Mercy, Truth, Justice, and Peace (Fig. 79).[49] Caritas, however, juxtaposed with Mary as the embodiment of compassion, plays the leading role. Embraced by Christ, she reciprocates his love by thrusting a dagger deep into his heart.[50]

Like the drawings from St. Walburg, the poem from Wienhausen identifies the wound in Christ's side as both the source of redemption and the dwelling place of the soul. The song comes full circle, returning to the mystical experience of the devotee:

In mynes leven syden steyt eyn gulden schryn. ach were ik darin bescloten al na dem wyllen myn.	In my beloved's side stands a golden shrine. Oh! if only I were enclosed in it as I desire.
Ik bydde, sote Jhesu, dor dyner leve crafft, te du myn wilde herte al an des bomes ast.	I ask, sweet Jesus, that through the power of your love you place my wild heart upon the branch of the tree.
Dat myn herte rouwe al an den wunden dyn, al twischen dynen brusten alse eyn mirrenbundellyn.	So that my heart may rest entirely in your wounds, entirely between your breasts just like a bundle of myrrh.
Regere my, leve here, nu unde to aller stunt, dat ik dyne leve vinde in mynes herten grunt.	Lift me up, beloved Lord, now and for eternity, so that I may find your love in the ground of my heart.[51]

Identifying herself with the Sponsa of Song of Songs 1 : 12 ("a bundle of myrrh is my beloved to me, he shall abide between my breasts"), the nun pleads with Christ to seal her heart in his.[52] Similarly, the first of the two Crucifixions from Eichstätt presents Christ in a paradisiacal garden amid an allegory of salvation, and the second, like the second half of the poem, the fusion of Christ's heart and the viewer's into one.

One easily overlooked motif in the drawing of the heart on the cross underscores the organ's identity as the bridal chamber of the Canticle. Dangling from a cord attached to the lip of the wound and protruding over the uppermost rung of the ladder is a small round object that acquires meaning only in light of yet another uncited passage from the Song of Songs (8 : 6): "Put me as a seal upon thy heart, as a seal upon thy arm, for love is strong as death." The imagery of the heart sealed in and unto death carries many connotations: it takes up the eschatological tenor of the other inscriptions and adds to them the notion of Christ's sacrifice as a loving compact or covenant secured in blood. The twelfth-century Cistercian Baldwin of Ford dedicated a short sermon to the passage, interpreting it as a reference to the image of God implanted in the soul.[53] By the later Middle Ages, the seal set upon the heart more frequently served as a symbol of sacramental union.[54] The image is taken up in this spirit, albeit with a different emphasis, in one of the

Fig. 80. "The Charter of Human Redemption," Carthusian miscellany, Yorkshire, London, British Library, Ms. Add. 37049, f. 23r.

many drawings in the Carthusian collection from Yorkshire, in which the body of the crucified Christ is covered by "The Charter of Human Redemption," sealed at the bottom with a bleeding heart (Fig. 80).[55] To this soteriological message, mystics added a personal emphasis, speaking of Christ's pressing them so close to his breast that, like wax impressed by a seal, they took on his image.[56] The drawing from St. Walburg implies a similar embrace between God and the soul, but it reverses the relationship: rather than the soul bearing Christ's image, Christ bears the nun's body in his heart.

Many of the nuns at St. Walburg would no doubt have known these commonplace interpretations of the seal set upon the heart. Yet their reading of the drawing would have been shaped, if not set, by the devotional texts available to them in their own library. Although the collection is no longer intact—some manuscripts have been dispersed and others, presumably, have been lost—enough of it survives to define the range of the community's reading.[57] In addition to the obligatory Latin liturgical books and the statutes necessary for governance by the Rule, the collection consists mostly of vernacular compendia, or *Sammelhandschriften,* of prayers, meditations, saints' lives, edifying treatises, and sermons, including quite a number by Eckhart, Suso, and Tauler.[58]

Of these miscellanies, one, a late-fifteenth-century collection of mystical and devotional writings, contains an unidentified and unpublished tract that takes as its point of departure the verse "Pone me ut signaculum super cor tuum," which is inscribed in large letters across the top of the opening recto.[59] The tract opens with a simple explanation of Song of Songs 8 : 6: "These words are written in the book of love. Christ says them to his bride and in German they state: 'Lay me as a sign on your heart.'"[60] Then, at considerable length—138 folios!—it elaborates the image in eucharistic terms. For the author of the tract, union is accomplished through reception of the Host: "In these words, Christ teaches the soul, when he is present with you in the Sacrament, that you are the innermost thought of his love, which he has demonstrated to you, especially in his sorrows."[61] Most of the tract is devoted to an extended allegorical commentary on the narrative of the Last Supper; in addition to elaborating the self-evident meaning of Christ's actions, the author identifies each of the twelve Apostles with one of the virtues that the nun must embody to be worthy of receiving the consecrated Host. The virtues in this allegory serve much the same function as those inscribed in the drawing on the rungs of the ladder (which do not correspond, although there is some overlap); they constitute the steps necessary to the consummation of union effected in the heart.

Like the drawing, the tract on Song of Songs 8 : 6 defines vision itself as a vehicle of devotional experience.[62] Paraphrasing Song of Songs 4 : 9, it argues: "Your eyes should diligently pay attention, for there is nothing [in the soul] that escapes the Lord's attention. Look at him so lovingly that the Lord says: 'My sister, you have wounded my heart with one of your eyes.'"[63] In a paraphrase of Song of Songs 2 : 10–11 and 2 : 14, the treatise moves on from the eyes to engage the other senses, above all, hearing:

> Your ears listen attentively to the commandments of the Lord, and his speech and his loving words; listen especially to the loving voice as is written in the book of love (of the Canticles): There saith the Lord, "Arise, my beloved, my beautiful one, and come, my dove, in the clefts of the rock." And he says: "make haste to me, my beloved, for winter is now past."[64]

In the drawing a similar medley of paradisiacal metaphors is condensed into a single image of intimacy and enclosure: the heart serves simultaneously as bedchamber, wine cellar, storeroom, and the cleft in the rock where the soul takes shelter.

For all the parallels between the tract and the drawing of the Heart on the Cross, the text cannot be considered its source, even though it comes from the same library. In elaborating the image of the seal, the tract focuses on a single element of the complex image. Moreover, in the drawing, the eucharistic emphasis is more equivocal; unlike the other drawings of the heart, Christ and the nun do not sit at an altar. The object offered by Christ to the nun resembles a pyx, the small container used to reserve the consecrated Host, but its identification remains uncertain. The text, however, has some heuristic value; although it does not define the meaning of the drawing, it provides a context for interpreting it. At the very least, it establishes that the nuns of St. Walburg knew the imagery of Song of Songs 8 : 6 and could have identified the seal atop the ladder without the aid of an inscription. Moreover, it helps us look at the drawing in a manner that would have been familiar to the nuns themselves.

Eucharistic piety was the hallmark of female spirituality during the later Middle Ages, and the Sacred Heart, its exemplary emblem.[65] The disembodied heart not only stood, by synecdoche, for the whole of Christ's body; it also served, as in the drawing from St. Catherine's in Strasbourg (see Fig. 8), as the wellspring of the sacraments, the very source of salvation. Images developed in conjunction with the cult of the Sacred Heart, many of them prints, speak a devotional dialect similar to that of the drawings from St. Walburg. One woodcut, dated approximately 1472, suggests the type of image the draftswoman might have used as her model (Fig. 81). Inscribed "In mines vatters hertzen, fand ich disen schmerzen," "In my Father's heart I found these wounds," the print combines text and image into a symbolic representation of Christ's suffering yet glorified body. Grasping a scourge and flail as if to take an active role in his own Passion, the Infant Christ stands in an oversize heart suspended from a cross. To either side, Mary and John bear witness, not in person, but through their names, inscribed where normally they would stand in images of the Crucifixion. At the corners, Christ's wounded appendages stand apart from the nails to signify his Resurrection.

A second print resembles the drawing from St. Walburg still more closely. Depicting the crucified Christ in the guise of the Man of Sorrows, it shows Christ half-length, a wounded heart emblazoned across his groin, beneath which two angels collect in a chalice the blood that flows from his wounds (Fig. 82). Like the drawing of the crucified heart from St. Walburg, the image relies on the viewer's ability to recall other closely related images to make its full meaning felt: the five

Fig. 81. Sacred Heart, woodcut, Schreiber 797, Staatliche Museen zu Berlin—Preußischer Kulturbesitz, Kupferstichkabinett.

hearts, each embodying a different devotional response (in turn expounded in the inscriptions), mimic the familiar quincunx of Christ's five disembodied wounds. As in the drawings from St. Walburg, the bodies of Christ and the spectator merge into one.[66]

Accustomed to thinking of mind and body as poles apart, modern viewers find it difficult to accept the grotesque, even gruesome, imagery of late medieval piety as an expression of deeply felt devotion. The heart, however, functioned as a spiritual as well as a bodily organ. The conjoining of Christ and the soul, less a union than a reunion, demanded that the devotee "recollect herself" in concentrated self-reflection, both activities defined by the same Latin word, *recordor,* derived, in turn, from *cor,* or "heart." As the seat of memory, the heart represented the locus of devotional experience. The apostle Paul had himself defined the heart in these

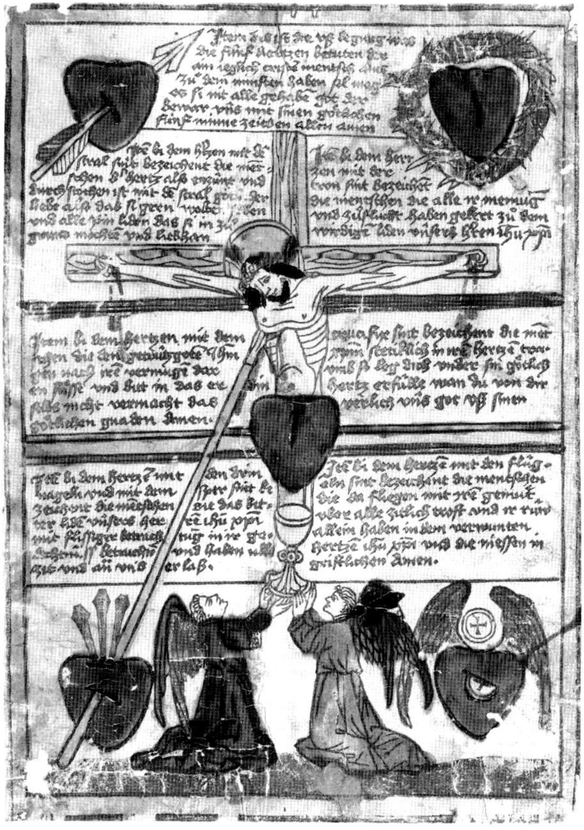

Fig. 82. "The explanation of what the five hearts signify," woodcut, Schreiber 1805, Staatliche Museen zu Berlin—Preußischer Kulturbesitz, Kupferstichkabinett.

terms when, in 2 Corinthians 3 : 3 he enjoined his audience to "show that you are a letter from Christ delivered by us, written not with ink but with the Spirit of the living God, not on tablets of stone, but on the tablets of the human heart."[67] In effect, the drawings from St. Walburg identify themselves as agents of a comparable transformation.

Taking up the imagery of return and recollection, the tract from the library of St. Walburg on the verse "Pone me ut signaculum" closes by defining devotion, not as a going out or ecstasy, but as a return to the "fatherland" of the soul:

> And my cross should also be your pilgrimage badge here in this vale of tears [literally, "sorrow"], from which you shall wander to the fatherland, and then I will be your crucified lover, your betrothed and little bed, in which you shall rest eternally with great joys, and love me, your lover, without intermediary.[68]

Even as the tract characterizes images as visible expressions of undying devotion to the crucified Christ, it has Christ himself describe paradise as a place where the nun, her pilgrimage complete, will no longer need their mediation. In the meantime, however, the drawings from St. Walburg identify the nun as a searcher after spiritual truth. Like an emblem affixed to the heart, the drawing seals her marriage with Christ, securing the compact until its consummation in heaven. Just as in the drawing of the Heart on the Cross Christ displays his heart as the visible sign of the bond of salvation, so too the nun who held the drawing in her hands might have considered it her "wallstecken," or "pilgrimage badge," as she progressed on her own itinerary from birth to a death conceived as rebirth. The drawing is a devotional keepsake, simultaneously a souvenir, a trophy, a token, and a memorial. By keeping the nun company in this life, it assured her that she would have Christ as her consort in the next.

PENETRATING VISION

Of all the images from St. Walburg, the two symbolic Crucifixions are the most explicitly exegetical, condensing in visual form a commentary on Christ's role in the salvation of mankind. They offer the viewer an outline of experience, a blueprint for the performance of prayer conceived as a step-by-step ascent to the Godhead. All allegories of religious experience imply a transition from idea to imitation, from exegesis to enactment. The drawings from St. Walburg, however, demand another, complementary, mode of apprehension. Unlike most mystical tracts or diagrams, the images set out, not to prescribe the worshiper's conduct or to describe a theory or method of mystical experience, but to initiate and transport the viewer; they do not diagram devotions but compel the onlooker to enact them with her eyes.

The most persuasive link between images of the Passion and passionate looking lay in Song of Songs 4:9—"Thou hast wounded my heart, my sister, my spouse, thou hast wounded my heart with one of thy eyes." In inviting the viewer to peer through the stigma, or wound, at its center, the drawing of the rose had made the connection implicitly.[69] But in compelling the viewer to act out the rhetoric of this key passage, the drawings of the heart explicitly define worship in terms of the wounding look of love.[70] By wounding vision, however, exegetes referred, not to corporeal or even spiritual sight, but rather to the vision of the contemplative for whom blindness constituted a form of insight. More specifically, Christian commentators identified the eye singled out in Song of Songs 4:9 as an emblem of contemplative love, arguing that the verse mentioned only one eye so as to distinguish between two modes of vision: the virgin's contemplative focus on eternal verities, and the married person's active admiration of God's creation.[71]

The rhetoric of affective piety employed sight as a metaphor but sanctioned corporeal vision only as the starting point of a process that led ultimately beyond it. Developing Neoplatonic conventions, Augustine spoke of the "oculus cordis," the eye of the heart, which served as the organ of an affective, interior vision.[72] Elaborating the Augustinian scheme, Hugh of St. Victor defined three gradations of vision, progressing from sight to insight, vision to blindness: "The eye of the flesh is open, the eye of reason runs, the eye of contemplation is closed and blind."[73] The closing exhortation of Bonaventure's *Itinerarium mentis in Deum* provides the most succinct statement of this doctrine of interior vision:

> Ask grace, not learning; desire, not understanding; the groaning of prayer, not diligence in reading; the Bridegroom, not the teacher; God, not man; darkness, not clarity; not light, but the fire that wholly inflames and carries one into God through transporting unctions and consuming affections.[74]

Affect is identified, not with the eye, but with the blinding light of interior illumination.

Late medieval devotional treatises frequently call on the reader to see with the eyes of the heart. Paul Saenger has linked this commonplace with the increasingly routine "references to the eyes and vision . . . in the rubrics of fifteenth-century prayers."[75] Yet the imagery of the interior eye—in affective piety associated less with the mind than with the heart as the seat of love and compassion—conflicted with the injunction to look that would have been reinforced and encouraged by the pictures that structured the content of late medieval prayer books.[76] The devotional images from St. Walburg resolve the inherent contradictions between interior and exterior vision by conjoining their imagery: the central metaphor of interior vision is presented visually, not simply as an allegory, but as an instrument that engages the eye. Looking becomes both the means and the end of the devotional act. The images present the nun with an opportunity to look into the heart of her spiritual bridegroom, an act of mystical intimacy not even envisaged by St. John, who saw more deeply than the other Apostles only by resting, eyes closed, on the heart of the Savior, as in the famous group of Christ and St. John from the Dominican convent of St. Katharinental (see Fig. 95).[77] In contrast, for the nuns of St. Walburg, vision provided both the means and the end of the devotional act. As defined by the drawings, to look is to love, and to love is to look.[78]

The notion that corporeal (as opposed to spiritual) sight could allow immediate access to the holy has few precedents in the art of the medieval West.[79] The closest analogies to vision as the drawings define it come from the devotional and visionary literature associated with nuns. The drawings, in creating a visual dialogue between viewer and subject, simulate the visionary experiences described in the literature of female monasticism in which a nun, often inspired by a work of art (most often a crucifix), engages in an intimate exchange with Christ.[80]

The chronicle of the Dominican convent at Weiler offers a typical example. It recounts how the nun Adelheid von Weiblingen, commanded by a voice to go into the choir, sees Christ floating above the altar; she is then drawn to the cross, where he embraces her body and soul, reassuring her: "I will always be with you and you with me, and will never separate myself from you."[81] The drawings from St. Walburg do not transcribe such visions, nor should the experience of viewing them be confused with visionary experience itself. The analogies are structural. They extend beyond straightforward parallels in imagery, the search for which reduces visionary accounts to no more than another set of textual sources or, conversely, the comparable works of art to little more than stimuli for hallucinations masquerading as authentic vatic phenomena.[82] Instead, the wide-ranging correspondences authorized the images as instruments of meditation, just as, on occasion, works of art could authenticate visions.[83] The analogies between works of art and visions enabled the images to inspire certain devotional experiences to which visualization and, on occasion, visionary experience were intrinsic.

Visionary texts go beyond lending authority to the seer and her vision to validating sight as a mode of spiritual perception. The person to whom insight is ascribed does not read but sees. Sometimes the sight is inward or imaginary; at other times, the texts insist, the visionary sees with "bodily eyes." In sanctioning sight and the senses as legitimate sources of revelation, visionary accounts subscribe to the authority of Scripture itself: in the Old Testament, all the major prophets, and, in the New Testament, none other than John the Evangelist experience their personal revelations through the medium of sight.[84] The texts describing these experiences cast themselves as secondary phenomena; seeing comes before writing. The drawings from St. Walburg seek to re-create the immediacy of this relation between seer and subject, even as they reverse the relation between image and text. The devotional drawings serve as the nun's point of departure, but she would have seen through the veil of scriptural imagery on which they rely. Sight itself becomes the subject of the image.

In invoking scriptural exemplars, visionary texts accrue authority without undermining their own authenticity. The allegorical drawings from St. Walburg rely on similar patterns and protocols of exemplification; like visionary texts, they draw on models and provide them in turn. For example, the presence of the ladder in one of the drawings immediately allies it with the account of Jacob's dream in Genesis 28. The twelfth-century Benedictine nun Elisabeth of Schönau (1129–1164) saw revealed to her a ladder leading from earth to heaven.[85] As reported by the *Golden Legend,* the Dominican Brother Guali had a similar vision of St. Dominic, founder of his order, ascending to heaven after his death, an event depicted in a miniature that soars along the margin of the Gradual of St. Katharinenthal near Zurich (Fig. 83).[86] The drawing of the ladder from St. Walburg provided its onlookers with a comparable example of ascent.

The ecstatic Cistercian Lukardis of Oberweimar saw a ladder leading from her heart to Christ, who returned her gaze and, like Christ in the drawing, stretched out his arms to receive her. The anonymous author of Lukardis's vita emphasizes vision by recounting his own recapitulation of her act of beholding:

> And, behold, she saw a golden ladder rising from her heart, whose summit reached the highest point of heaven; in whose summit she saw Christ her lover resting on the ladder and leaning down toward her, looking at her, moreover, gently with a loving glance. How many times afterward did she recall his tender glance, all the while seeking to renew for herself that miraculous consolation? Now I too saw that the rungs of that said ladder, by which she saw the angels of God descending, then ascending, were decorated with diverse beautiful gems.[87]

In the language of medieval allegory, the gems associated with the rungs stood for the virtues explicitly identified in the drawing from St. Walburg.[88] If in the drawing the imagery is reversed, with the ladder leading up to the open heart, its effect—one of ardent ascent met by the descent or declination of the Godhead—remains the same.

Christ's commentary on Lukardis's vision serves equally well as a gloss on the drawing of the Heart on the Cross:

> I know, my most beloved, I know because from the vale of tears you have disposed in your heart to ascend to me, at one time with your vows, at another time with your holy meditations and desires, at one time with your prayers, at another time with your patience and disagreeable sufferings, which rise lovingly up to me and draw me to you, and which in the embrace of your devotions gently touch [or wound] me. This ladder that you see has two golden sides: the one, right, side is the golden, ardent charity that you bear toward me, your God; the other, left, side is the golden, ardent love that you bear toward your neighbor. The rungs of the ladder, which you see so elaborately decorated, are your vows and holy desires, prayers and good works and various unpleasant sorrows, which you patiently endure. The angels you see climbing down do so to collect all of this diligently. Those you see ascending faithfully bring all they have gathered to me, and they offer it wholly for the salvation of

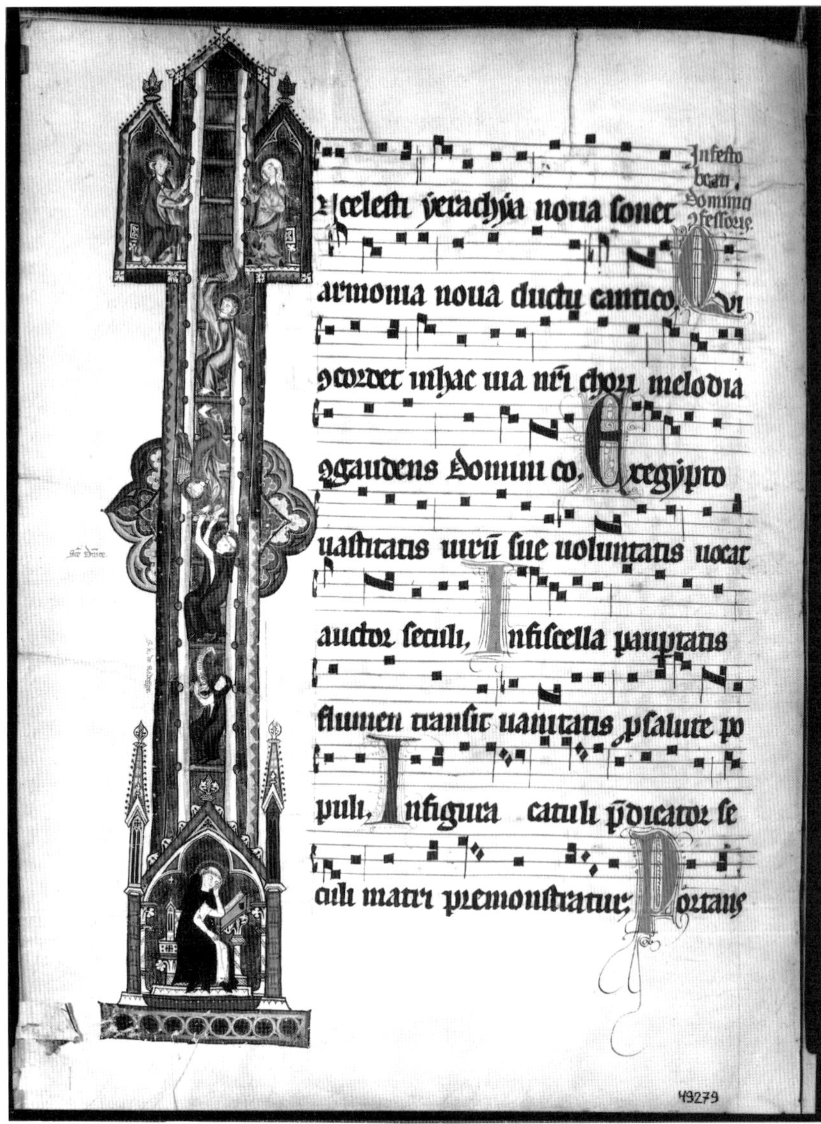

Fig. 83. The vision of St. Dominic, Gradual of St. Katharinenthal, 1312, Zurich, Swiss National Museum, Inv. Nr. LM 26117, f. 261v.

> all human kind. And just as I am always borne down to you by this ladder, so through this same ladder you will be carried swiftly to me from the vale of misery to eternal rest and reign with me in glory forever.[89]

In addition to modeling itself on the dream of Jacob in Genesis 28 : 12 – 17, Lukardis's vision takes up the imagery of Psalm 83, but not only the portion it paraphrases at the outset (verses 6 – 7: "Blessed is the man whose help is from thee; in his heart he hath disposed to ascend by steps, in the vale of tears"). The opening verse is no more than a cue that prompts the reader to remember the motif of the ladder implied by the subsequent verse ("ibunt de virtute in virtutem"). Bonaventure employed the very same verses to open his *Itinerarium mentis in Deum,* a paradigmatic treatise on the mystical ascent.[90] For Lukardis, the ladder represents a personalized vision of salvation, its rungs a means of transporting to God the offerings, prayers, meditations, good works, and suffering that lead her toward an embrace with her bridegroom in eternity. Lukardis, however, does not work only toward her own salvation; her sorrows, exemplified through her stigmatization, contribute, like Christ's, to the salvation "of all human kind." Her vita employs the language of return so that she, like Jacob, can hear God proclaim: "And I will be thy keeper whithersoever thou goest, and will bring thee back into this land" (Genesis 28 : 15).

The drawing from St. Walburg not only represents but itself serves as a ladder that leads the viewer to Christ. Despite its allegorical apparatus, it is not a static image but the vehicle for a devotional exercise that involves exertion and exchange. It also provides the nun with an image of the activity in which she is engaged. In the image, as in the text, the ladder signifies the complementary processes of descent and ascent: the nun not only climbs the ladder to Christ, just as Christ climbed the ladder of the cross, but also, like him, begins her ascent with the declination of humility.

The analogies between Lukardis's vision and the drawing from St. Walburg carry further, however. They share a set of symbolic sources, rooted in Scripture, and rely on common modes of address, visual as well as rhetorical. Christ speaks of Lukardis's prayers, "quibus in me affectuose ascendis et mi tibi adtrahis et in amplexus tuae devotionis me dulciter stringis," "which rise lovingly up to me and draw me to you, and which in the embrace of your devotions gently touch me."[91] No translation can convey the resonance of this passage, which also evokes the imagery of wounding love. The verb *stringo,* "to touch lightly," also means "to wound"; it thereby brings to mind the Sponsa who pierces the Sponsus with a look of her eye. Seen in this light, the vision casts Lukardis in the role of the blind centurion Longinus, who, having pierced Christ's heart with his lance, has his sight restored by the touch of Christ's blood (and who, in turn, according to John 19 : 34, fulfilled the prophecy of Zachariah 12 : 10: "And they shall look upon me whom they have pierced").[92] Sight and insight, palpable sensation and sacramental love, all are condensed into a single image. Just as the vision defines union as the meeting of Lukardis's and Christ's eyes, so too does the drawing, which allows the nun to embrace Christ with her eyes. Looking at the chamber nestled in the side wound, our eyes penetrate Christ's heart to experience the embrace enacted within it and spelled out by the flanking inscriptions that extend, along with the beams of the cross, like two open arms.

Of the visionary texts associated with female monasticism, none evokes the drawings from St. Walburg more directly than the visions attributed to the Cistercian nun Mechthild of Hackeborn, gathered in the *Liber specialis gratiae.*[93] Mechthild's visions were compiled, probably in German, during the last decade of the thirteenth century by several of her fellow nuns at the convent of Helfta in Saxony, celebrated as a center of mystical life and literary activity.[94] None of Mechthild's visions corresponds precisely to a drawing from St. Walburg, and a direct relationship is unlikely, even though by the fifteenth century Mechthild's book circulated widely in Franconia.[95] Both drawings and visions, however, rely on a similar range of imagery, combined in kindred ways, implying that they served comparable functions.

The heart is the leitmotif of Mechthild's religious imagination; she herself speaks of her "nimia devotio circa divinum Cor Jesu Christi," "excessive devotion to the divine heart of Jesus Christ."[96] Most modern critics have been inclined to agree, dismissing Mechthild's florid imagery as so bizarre and grotesque that it travesties whatever pretensions it has to transcendence.[97] Like the drawings from St. Walburg, however, the imagery in Mechthild's *Liber* functions less as a record than as an instrument of devotion. If it is aberrant, then so too is much of the pastoral imagery produced in vast quantities under ecclesiastical supervision during the Counter-Reformation.[98] "Excess" is an essential quality of Mechthild's devotional practice; it connotes, not a gratuitous surfeit, but a superabundant love and rapture whose absolute embodiment is Christ's heart.

Few, if any, of Mechthild's images of the heart are original; what lends them their allusive force is the shifting, kaleidoscopic complexity with which they are combined and elaborated. In the *Liber specialis gratiae,* as in the drawings, the heart connotes many things, among them the wellspring of the Eucharist. But in its foremost role it provides a place of interiority where Mechthild can withdraw in intimate dialogue with Christ. For example, in one vision Mechthild, missing her beloved, suddenly sees him standing beside her, his heart open like a door disclosing an interior paved with gold. At the center of this chamber, whose circular form represents eternity, Christ and the soul converse. Prompted by the Introit for the Mass of the Dead, "et tibi reddetur votum in Jerusalem," "and to you shall be given an offering in Jerusalem," Mechthild suddenly sees the Virgin sitting to her right, giving Christ a gold ring. Filled with desire, she wishes that she too could receive such a ring as a sign of her marriage to Christ.[99] Christ obliges by giving her a ring set with seven stones, each corresponding to a manifestation of his love

Plate 1. Crucifixion, Cologne, Schnütgen Museum, Inv. Nr. M340.

Plate 2. Entombment, Eichstätt, St. Walburg.

Plate 3. St. Kümmernis, Eichstätt, St. Walburg.

Plate 4. The *Arbor virginis,* Eichstätt, St. Walburg.

Plate 5. St. Walburga, Munich, Bayerisches Nationalmuseum.

Plate 6. St. Barbara with the Virgin and Child, Eichstätt, St. Walburg.

Plate 7. Consecration of Virgins, Eichstätt, St. Walburg.

Plate 8. Agony in the Garden, Eichstätt, St. Walburg.

Plate 9. Symbolic Crucifixion, Eichstätt, St. Walburg.

Plate 10. The Heart on the Cross, Eichstätt, St. Walburg.

Plate 11. The Eucharistic Banquet, Eichstätt, St. Walburg.

Plate 12. The Heart as a House, Staatsbibliothek zu Berlin—Preußischer Kulturbesitz, Handschriftenabteilung 417.

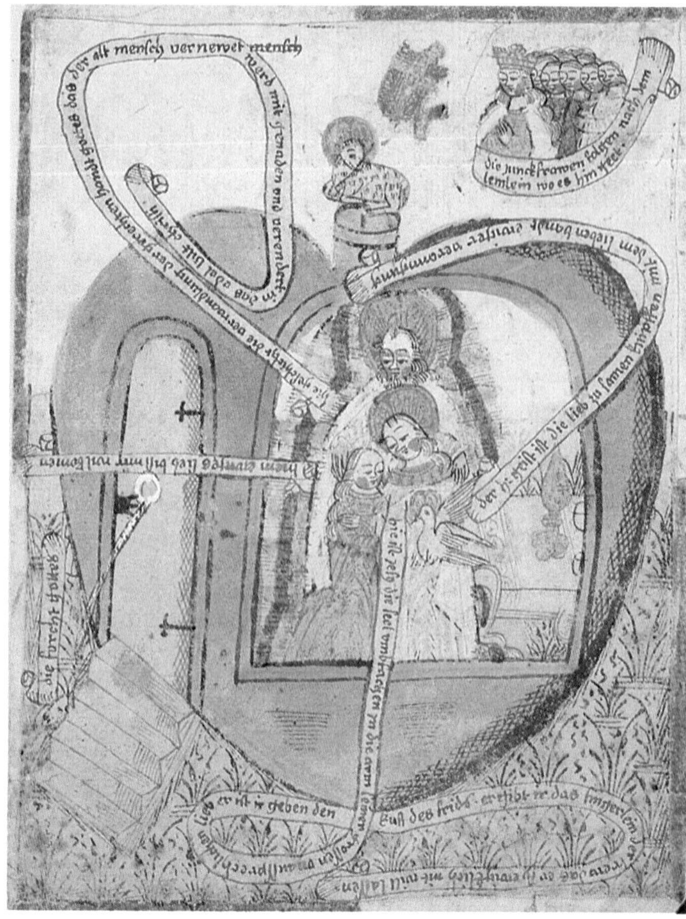

for mankind, beginning with what Christ calls his thirty-three years of "servitude" on behalf of mankind and ending with the opening of his heart when he died on the cross.[100]

The imagery of marriage, specifically the ring, brings to mind the Consecration of Virgins from St. Walburg (see Fig. 41 and Plate 7). Combined, however, with the image of the heart as the chamber where this union is consummated, it still more forcefully conjures up the heart atop the ladder where the Christ Child and the nun embrace as they exchange a love token. Speaking to Mechthild, Christ describes the cross itself as the bridal bedchamber ("thalamus") in which he consummated his love for mankind:

> You should remember how I entered the chamber of the cross; and just as the grooms give their garments to the players, so I gave my clothing to the soldiers, and my body to the crucifiers. Then I extended my arms with the hardest nails in your sweet embraces, singing to you in the chamber of love seven songs full of the most wonderful sweetness [a reference to Christ's seven last words on the cross]. After this I opened my heart so that you could enter as I, dying with you on the cross, suffered the sleep of love.[101]

In an oblique reference to the wound opened by Longinus's lance, the vision ends with Christ opening his heart so the soul can enter and join him in the "sleep of love."[102]

In elaborating imagery supplied by exegesis and the liturgy, the drawings from St. Walburg both reinforce and rely on habits of visualization comparable to those that underlie Mechthild's visions. Like the visionary texts from Helfta, the drawings are fundamentally paraliturgical. For example, prompted by the phrase in the Mass "Eamus in desertum interiorem," "Let us proceed into the interior solitude," Mechthild sees herself walking along a path in Christ's company and hears a voice saying: "I praise you in your eternity, immensity, beauty, truth, and justice." She then finds herself in an enclosed paradisiacal garden, filled with trees, the verdant ground covered with flowers. Grazing there is a lamb, standing for the soul, tethered to God by a gold and silver chain signifying the love of God and friends. Inspired by this sight, the soul asks, "O most beloved one, teach me to praise you," to which God replies, "Look into my heart." The heart then appears—but in the form of a most beautiful rose with five petals entirely covering Christ's chest. The meaning of the image, according to the Lord, is that Mechthild should praise God in all of his five senses, by which she understands that she should praise him for the loving regard with which he always looks at man.[103]

The imagery of Mechthild's vision summons up several of the drawings from

St. Walburg. The enumeration of Christ's qualities and virtues suggests the inscriptions identifying the four arms of the cross; the heart in the form of a sanguine flower that covers Christ's torso brings to mind not only the drawing of the crucified heart but also the image of the isolated rose (see Fig. 45 and Plate 8). More significant, however, than any specific component of Mechthild's vision, is Christ's injunction to look, issued in response to Mechthild's query how she might best love him: "Then the soul, desiring to praise God, said: 'O most beloved one, teach me to praise you.' To which the Lord replied, 'Look into my heart.'" In the drawings, as in Mechthild's visions, charity is defined as an act of piercing vision.

The correspondences between the visions of female mystics, such as Mechthild of Hackeborn and Lukardis of Oberweimar, and the drawings from St. Walburg indicate more than common literary or liturgical sources. Both the visionary accounts and the drawings provided the nuns who read or viewed them with vehicles for their religious imagination. Both also demand a response in which seeing or notions of sight are central: the visionary accounts, by inherently granting priority to the experience of vision, and the drawings, by compelling the devotee to see with an eye informed by their imagery. No matter how closely related, however, image and text function in different ways. As recorded and transformed for posterity, Mechthild's visions translate her experiences into exemplars for her readers, in all probability by a process of collaboration that we can no longer unravel. While no less mediated, the drawings reverse this process. Set into motion during the performance of prayer, the images transmute exemplars derived from exegesis and the liturgy back into the realm of visual experience. Inscriptions in the images may define the rungs of the ladder leading from earth to heaven as virtues, but the images themselves suggest that the senses, sanctified in Christ, are what lead the soul upward from this world to the next. In validating the realm of empirical experience, the drawings bring the imagery of the ladder full circle: if man can ascend only because Christ himself took on human flesh, then the body, through vision, itself provides the vehicle for mystical union. Employing the rhetoric of wounding sight, the drawings enact the *imitatio Christi* according to the script spelled out in the Song of Songs. The Canticle provides the cues for a passion consummated in the nun's body as well as Christ's, with the heart of each the place where this ecstatic introspection is enacted.

4

THE HOUSE OF THE HEART

OF ALL THE DRAWINGS from St. Walburg, those that depict the soul dwelling in the heart are the most deeply rooted in the spirituality of nuns. In evoking enclosure and the Eucharist, they bring into play distinctive modes of meaning, exemplifying the concerns of their female audience in both their content and the manner in which it is conveyed.

Although the drawings that focus, directly or indirectly, on the heart were not conceived as a set or a cycle, they can be read as a sequence. The four images depict stages in the union of the soul with Christ. If in the Symbolic Crucifixion we see Christ in the flesh, the wound in his side the center of the composition, in the drawing of the Heart on the Cross, we apprehend the meaning of his body laid bare (see Figs. 66, 67 and Plates 9, 10). As if at an even higher level of magnification, a third drawing shows only the heart, in which Christ and the nun commune at a eucharistic banquet (see Plate 11). Finally, a fourth drawing, in many respects the most complex and unusual in the entire ensemble, depicts the heart as a house, closed to the world, within which the soul rests secure in the embrace of the Trinity (see Plate 12).

Like the rungs of the mystical ladder, these four drawings offer the viewer a gradated approach to the innermost mysteries of the Godhead. As the sequence progresses symbolically, however, the response demanded from the viewer also changes. If the Symbolic Crucifixion invites an essentially intellectual analysis, focused on deciphering its inscriptions, the subsequent images increasingly emphasize the viewer's active participation, to the point of making affective response their explicit subject. The drawings serve as both mirrors and models of the viewer's own activity. With the removal of the intermediary figure of Mary in the drawing of the Heart on the Cross, nothing stands between Christ and the nun, now figured in the image. The next two drawings offer another perspective, in which the mental and physical space between the image and the onlooker appears to collapse. Viewer and image, subject and object, converge.

At this decisive point of transition, the identity of the heart also changes. Although the two drawings of the mystical heart are easily mistaken for representations of the Sacred Heart of Christ—an image omnipresent in late medieval devotional art and literature, especially in Germany—they do not belong to this tradition, with its less explicit mystical emphasis and its focus on the Passion, its exemplary emblem the *Cor Salvatoris.*[1] Whereas the devotion to the Sacred Heart emphasizes identification with the body of the suffering Christ, the drawings from St. Walburg focus on the union of the soul with the Son transcendent in the Trinity. All the images of the heart from St. Walburg carry eucharistic connotations. Their crux, however, is neither the Passion nor the sacraments but the mystical experience of Christ and the female devotee. The images, in addition to representing an exterior corporeal object whose meaning she must penetrate, metaphorically and physically, now also represent the nun's own heart, in effect her own consciousness, and make it the explicit subject of the image.[2] In place of the interior of Christ's body, the images now take as their subject the womblike enclosure at the heart of the nun's body and make it an image of her own subjec tivity. Having passed through the wound in Christ's side, the nun enters a metaphorical as well as physical interior; she passes from imitation to identification and from petition to contemplative union. The heart in which the nun embraces Christ and the Trinity is the seat of her own soul, a place where she can take her spiritual bridegroom into the core of her being.

UNION AND COMMUNION

Like the pair of symbolic Crucifixions, the two drawings of the mystical heart can be read as virtual, if not actual, pendants. In each, the heart dominates the drawing, providing the framework for a visionary interior. In the image of the Eucharistic Banquet, the small church immediately above the head of the kneeling nun that represents the abbey of St. Walburg associates her with the entire community (Fig. 84 and Plate 11). Exterior and interior views interpenetrate, in the end identifying the space enclosed by the nunnery as the *hortus conclusus* of the Song of Songs, a *locus amoenus* in which the nuns, by receiving the Sacrament, can sup with the Trinity at the altar table.[3]

In the affiliated image, the heart itself assumes the form of a small house with a large windowlike opening in front (Fig. 85 and Plate 12). Again the architecture identifies the convent as a paradisiacal place and its inhabitants, the nuns, as half-way to heaven. The structure combines references to entry and enclosure, central images in the life of any cloistered woman. Four steps lead to a closed door with hinges, a latch, and a circular knocker. A small animal tied to the knocker by a rope, presumably a dog, his head barely visible behind the steps, is identified by an inscription as "die furcht gottes," "the fear of God."[4] This is not a door at which visitors are welcome; it is designed, like the convent itself, to keep people out. In the house the soul is safe, like the nun in the convent; *timor Dei,* the root of other sundry virtues, keeps sin and the world at bay.

Both images place the nun at the center, at the table of the altar. In presenting her in the company of all three Persons of the Trinity, the drawings indicate her passage into a transcendent realm. In the Eucharistic Banquet, her assumption is expressed by her placement between Father and Son, echoing images of the Virgin Mary taken up into heaven and crowned by the Trinity or of the soul crowned by Christ and the Virgin (Fig. 86).[5] Here, however, Christ takes the most active role, presenting his bride to his Father, who is enthroned to the left. With Christ, the dove of the Holy Spirit proffers the chalice.

Comparable images of spiritual intimacy are extremely rare and appear to occur exclusively in manuscripts made both by and for women, for example an Alemannic (i.e., southwest German) translation of the life of St. Francis transcribed and illuminated circa 1470 by Sibilla von Bondorf, a Poor Clare in Freiburg (Fig. 87).[6] Previously identified as the translator as well as the transcriber of the text, Sibilla has since been denied any role in its authorship.[7] Through her many illustrations, however, she fashioned an original interpretation of the legend. For example, a small miniature of the soul embraced by the Trinity—unrelated to the text's account of how a falcon awakened the saint each morning for prayer—interrupts the narrative with a representation of the ideal the story itself merely exemplifies: St. Francis as a model of the interior life.[8] Whereas in Sibilla's miniature an angel presents the kneeling soul to the enthroned Trinity, in the drawing of the Eucharistic Banquet from St. Walburg the nun sits in its midst. United with Christ, she is taken up into the Godhead.

Still closer in spirit to the drawings from St. Walburg is an image in a late-fifteenth-century Alemannic codex containing the meditations on the Paternoster by the Poor Clare Magdalena of Freiburg (1407–1458), otherwise known as Magdalena Beutler (Fig. 88).[9] The crude but imaginative drawing—perhaps no more than a copy of an original from Magdalena's hand—immediately follows a prayer addressed to the Trinity and precedes the nun's account of her inspiration by the Holy Ghost: "The spirit of divine God spoke to my spirit and said: 'Write out the Paternoster for me in the little Psalter and fulfill those same words in the Pater-

Fig. 84. The Eucharistic Banquet, Eichstätt, St. Walburg.

Fig. 85. The Heart as a House, Staatsbibliothek zu Berlin—Preußischer Kulturbesitz, Handschriftenabteilung 417.

Fig. 86. Coronation of the soul by Christ and the Virgin, Gradual of St. Katharinenthal, 1312, Zurich, Swiss National Museum, Inv. Nr. LM 26117, f. 188r.

Fig. 87. Sibilla von Bondorf, The virgin soul praying to the Trinity, ca. 1470, London, British Library, Ms. Add. 15710, f. 111r.

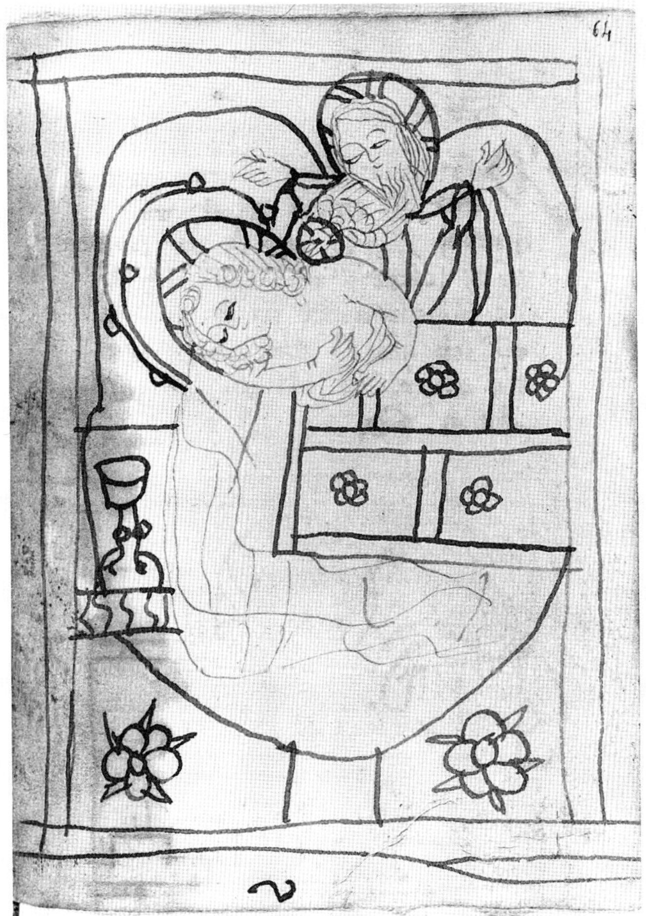

Fig. 88. Magdalena of Freiburg, Meditations on the Paternoster, Karlsruhe, Badische Landesbibliothek, Ms. Donaueschingen 298, 64r.

noster. And I heard them as gladly as the angelic hours and songs of praise."[10] Rather than illustrate either passage directly, the drawing shows the Trinity nestled in a heart, beside which stands an altar, identified by the chalice to the left. Christ, who appears as a child, detaches himself from the central group and leans to his right, much like the Evangelist in a group of Christ and St. John (see Fig. 95). The inchoate lines that flow from his head represent either the "vergiessen," "shedding," of Christ's blood invoked in the Trinitarian prayer or the outpouring of the Holy Spirit from which Magdalena takes her inspiration. Unlike the drawing from St. Walburg, the image does not show Magdalena or her soul as a figural presence in the embrace of the Trinity. Instead, it shows the Godhead's indwelling at the heart of her being.

The drawing of the Heart as a House from St. Walburg represents a comparable yet more complex crystallization of similar images and ideas. The central concept, however, is the same: mystical union achieved through interior prayer. As if to indicate that she is no longer of this world, the nun in the embrace of the Trinity sheds her monastic garb. She appears as a young woman with flowing, flaxen hair, dressed in a golden robe. The consummation is complete: watched over by God the Father, whose form encloses them both, the soul joins Christ in a mutual embrace. Just as God shelters Christ, so Christ shelters the soul, balanced to the right by the dove of the Holy Spirit. The tight-knit Trinity, bound together by a threefold green and yellow aureole, is set on an altar, identified by the chalice and the Hosts partially visible to the right.

By defining the altar as the locus of mystical union, both drawings link private prayer with communal celebration.[11] In the vernacular prayer books of nuns, preparatory prayers for the reception of the Sacrament, many of which speak of Communion as a banquet, often make up as much as half of the miscellaneous texts.[12] Moreover, the literature of female spirituality closely connects the Eucharist with the experience of mystical ecstasy.[13] It is not simply that the reception of the Host often triggers a vision; the drawings define the Eucharist as the sine qua non for any experience of union. The implications of this nexus are manifold: it makes the Mass the focus of mystical desire and inextricably binds "private" experience to the norms and prestige of the cult.[14] It also defines mystical experience in theological terms: Christ's assumption of the flesh, reenacted in the Mass, both figures and prefigures the possibility of mankind's elevation to eternity, of which mystical union itself provides a foretaste.

In relation to this complex of ideas and practices, the drawings perform multiple functions. By identifying the experience of union with the eschatological marriage banquet described in Revelation 19:9, the drawings define the mystical marriage in eschatological as well as eucharistic terms.[15] The drawings, however, do not simply translate everyday liturgical practice to a transcendental tier. Although the provisions of enclosure varied greatly from one house to another, the nuns of St. Walburg would have had limited access to the high altar; the frequency of Communion would also have been strictly curtailed.[16] In showing the nun seated with God at the altar, the drawings close gaps of both space and time.

The drawings of nuns participating with Christ at the altar represent the fulfillment of the desires to which visions gave vent. For example, after receiving the Host, the Dominican nun Adelheid Langmann saw the Christ Child playing in her heart, which, like a radiant monstrance, became as bright as the sun.[17] The life of the Cistercian nun Ida of Nivelles (1197/99–1231) describes how she passed from the "refectory" of the Eucharist to a "spiritual dormitory" in which, alienated from her bodily senses, she would sleep blissfully in the arms of her spouse.[18] The drawings from St. Walburg placed simulacra of comparable visions before the eyes of the nuns so that they could experience a vision like that enjoyed by Elsbeth von Stoffeln, prioress of the Dominican convent of St. Katharinental in Switzerland. According to the convent's chronicle,

> she had a habit of standing on a stall [or chair] when the convent received our Lord, so that she might see him well, and one time she was in great devotion as the convent received our Lord. And as she joined her heart entirely with God and looked at our Lord, he spoke to her out of the priest's hands in the form of the wafer: "Gaze at me and look at me with desire, if you shall gaze eternally at my divine visage according to all your heart's desire."[19]

Elsbeth's encounter suggests that despite the barrier separating nuns from the high altar, enclosed women sought and, on occasion, achieved direct visual access to the enactment of the Mass.[20] More important, the story defines the Host and the heart as twin focal points of visual and visionary longing. For nuns who were physically removed from the altar, vision itself served as a means of participating in the Mass and, hence, in clerical authority.[21] In similar fashion, the drawings depict eucharistic desire and its fulfillment in visual terms. In effect, the drawings provide the nun with a substitute for sacramental presence.

We can no longer know whether the drawings of the mystical heart succeeded in satisfying spiritual desire. In theory, however, the nuns looking at them beheld their own longings brought to fruition. In the absence of Communion or even access to the altar, the drawings could make present what the nuns would have missed most: communion with Christ understood simultaneously as mystical and corporeal.[22] The chronicle of the Dominican convent of Kirchberg bei Sulz describes how in the absence of a priest the nun Mechthilt von Waldeck received Christ spiritually:

> She desired also that God might let her understand whether it was possible for a person to receive our Lord spiritually as truly as the priest at the altar in the Mass. To which our Lord replied and said: "Many people go to mass out of habit. They receive in part according to their desire. But just as I give those persons my body and blood as food and drink spiritually in the soul, so I give myself as truly, God and man, to the priest at the altar. That is an extraordinary grace." . . . And indeed she had such a desire to receive our Lord's body at the altar that our Lord comforted her and said to her: "When you go to the altar, you do not receive what you see there, but what you believe. . . ." And He said: "Go up and open up the mouth of your desire.

'*Hoc est corpus meum.*'" With these same words she received God in all sweetness and grace as truly in her soul as if she had received him at the altar.[23]

Conjured up by her own desire, Christ rewards Mechthilt by celebrating a spiritual Mass. If in the standard eucharistic rite God is made flesh, in this visionary version the disembodied nun communes with an incorporeal Christ. The drawings from St. Walburg offer a similar opportunity for the independent celebration of spiritual Communion. By translating the Mass into mystical terms, they would have allowed the nuns, like Mechthilt, to take spiritual Communion, not only at Mass, but also in their solitary devotions.[24]

In each drawing, inscriptions spell out the interplay of the eschatological and eucharistic meanings. The scrolls voice the viewer's spiritual desire, commenting on the imagery without explaining it. References to the Sacrament are explicit in the image of the Eucharistic Banquet, which, like the visionary descriptions of eucharistic union, defines Communion as a foretaste of union with the Trinity in Heaven. According to the scroll across the top of the drawing, "hie wirdt gespeist das innig und ——— hercz mit haimsuchung gottlicher gnaden," "Here the ardent and ——— heart is nourished with the visitation of divine grace." In the second scroll, within the heart, God addresses the nun directly: "mein aller liebste fraindtin iß und trincket und wirdt truncken in meiner lieb," "My most beloved companion, eat and drink and become drunk in my love." Although one immediately associates these words with Christ, the image suggests that they are spoken by the Trinity as a whole, for God the Father holds out the paten, and the dove of the Holy Spirit proffers the chalice. The invitation to dine with the Divinity echoes and conflates various passages in the Song of Songs; like the king in Canticles 2:4, God invites the Sponsa into his wine cellar and, as in Canticles 5:1, he encourages her to eat and drink: "Eat, O friends, and drink: and be inebriated, my dearly beloved." The heart becomes all of these enclosed spaces combined: wine cellar, apocalyptic banqueting hall, paradisiacal garden, and bedchamber.

In the drawing of the House as a Heart, the scrolls express the consummation of these mystical longings. The inscriptions need not be read in any particular order, but as a group they speak the language of mystical renewal and transformation, mediated by the grace of the sacramental offering. Radiating from the center before winding in long, meandering loops, the scrolls compel the nun to turn the image over in her hands as she turns it figuratively in her mind. The inscription that originates at the center of the drawing identifies the couple on God's lap as Christ and the soul, wrapped in an eternal embrace ("hie ist Iesus die seel umbfachen in die arm seiner grossen unaussprechlichen lieb," "Here is Jesus embracing the soul in the arm of his great, ineffable love"), and adds the following gloss: "er ist ir geben den kuß des frids, ergibt ir das fingerlein der trew, das er sy ewigklich nit will lassen," "He gives her the kiss of peace, grants her the little finger of fidelity that he wishes never to leave her for all eternity." The words define mystical union in terms of the sacrament of marriage.

A second scroll carries similar sacramental overtones. Running up to the upper left corner before turning back on itself, it defines transubstantiation ("die verwandlung") as the process that transforms the "old man" ("der alt mensch"), that is, the sinner, through grace, renewing him "in the noble image of Christ" ("in das edel bilt Christi"): "hie geschieht die verwandlung der gerechten handt gottes das der alt mensch vernewet werd mit genaden und verendert in das edel bilt christi," "Here the transubstantiation takes place through the right hand of God so that the old man is renewed through grace and transformed into the noble image of Christ." Through its allusions first to God, then to grace, and finally to Christ, the inscription implicitly invokes the Trinity. In the short scroll beginning at the right hand of God (it can be read only if the drawing is turned on its head), the Trinity speaks as one in the voice of the Bridegroom: "O mein ewiges lieb biss mir wilkomen," "O my eternal love, be welcome unto me."

A third inscription, beginning just behind the outstretched wings of the dove, defines this passion: "der h[eilige] geist ist die lieb zu samen knipffen mit dem lieben bandt ewiger verainnigung," "The Holy Ghost binds love together with the loving bond of eternal union." According to this enigmatic phrase, the soul's union with God consists of one loving bond being formed with another, or, in more theological terms, of the soul entering into the inner relations of the Trinity. The reflexive image of the soul taken up into the Trinity and of the Trinity in turn contained in the heart of the nun expresses these complex reciprocal relationships. The mutual love of Christ and the soul reproduces the love that binds the Trinity together.

The inscriptions elucidate the drawings, but the images do not rely on the words alone for their meaning. The arrangement of the figures recalls that in other images. The mutual embrace of Christ and the soul on the lap of a larger encompassing figure brings to mind the drawing in Suso's *Exemplar* in which the Dominican opens his cloak to reveal his soul—depicted as a diminutive naked woman—embraced by Eternal Wisdom (Fig. 89). Although the nuns of St. Walburg may have known this image from the illustrations of the first printed edition, published in Augsburg by Anton Sorg in 1482, they could also have derived the formulation from other sources.[25] For example, in the drawing of the Heart as a House, the vertical alignment of Father, Son, and Holy Ghost recalls representa-

Fig. 89. Eternal Wisdom embracing the soul of Suso, Henry Suso, *The Exemplar,* Strasbourg, Bibliothèque Nationale et Universitaire, Ms. 2929, f. 8v.

tions of the *Gnadenstuhl* (see Fig. 6). In an equally appropriate reference, the soul at rest in the lap of the Trinity also echoes the commonplace image of souls ensconced in the Bosom of Abraham.

In disposition, however, the figures at the center of the drawing most closely resemble those in a cult image that, given its emphasis on Christ's female lineage, enjoyed particular popularity in female communities: the sculpted group of the type known as the *Anna Selbdritt,* in which Christ and the Virgin nestle on the lap of Mary's mother, St. Anne.[26] Three examples survive at St. Walburg.[27] In the

Fig. 90. *Anna Selbdritt,* Eichstätt, St. Walburg.

latest of them, from the early sixteenth century, roughly contemporary with the drawings, Mary and Christ perch on the knees of the monumental Anne, just as in the drawing Christ and the soul sit on the knees of God the Father (Fig. 90). The description of the drawing in the Sotheby's catalogue, indicating how easily the image can be misread, overlooked the information of the inscriptions and characterized the central group as "God the Father with the Virgin and Child with the Holy Ghost."[28] The mistake is nonetheless instructive; it underscores the change that is, in fact, essential to the image's message, namely that Christ has taken the

Fig. 91. Shrine Madonna, Nuremberg, Germanisches Nationalmuseum, Inv. Nr. Pl. 2397.

place of Mary, and the soul, the place of Christ. In carefully constructed inversions characteristic of mystical rhetoric, Christ—who, if not shown as a child, appears as a very young man—provides maternal shelter for the soul, which, of course, is gendered feminine.[29] At the same time, the nun can imitate Mary by regarding herself as succoring Christ, whom she has taken into her bosom.[30]

The drawings elaborate their speculations on the Trinity and the Eucharist with references to the Virgin and the Incarnation. The two ends of the devotional spectrum are united by both the Host, the nexus between heaven and earth, and the Virgin, in whom Christ took on flesh, a threefold relationship developed extensively in other devotional imagery, visual as well as verbal, from late medieval Germany.[31] For example, the image of the Trinity contained in the heart of the nun recalls those sculptures known as Shrine Madonnas in which the Trinity (usually of the *Gnadenstuhl* type) is ensconced in the core of the Virgin's body (Fig. 91).[32] Late medieval German devotional verse speaks of the Trinity in the shrine of the Virgin's heart, at the same time characterizing the Virgin as a mirror or model for the onlooker: "Du spiegelglaß, on allen rums, / den ein und den druvalten / versluß du in dins herzen schrein," "You, mirror, without any blot, you enclosed the one and threefold God in your heart."[33] In taking the Trinity into her heart, the nun could think of herself as imitating the Virgin, her ultimate exemplar.[34]

In mingling the imagery of union and communion, the drawings of the mystical heart liken Christ's union with the soul to the sacraments of marriage and the Eucharist, a double emphasis especially accessible to an audience of nuns. In turn, that imagery ensured that whatever paths the nuns pursued in their mystical meditations, their thoughts remained tethered to the norms of the cult. Through reception of the Host, a nun not only became Christ's guest at a mystical banquet but also partook literally of his body and blood. And in renewing her marriage with the heavenly Sponsus, she also took on the role of Mary, Christ's heavenly consort and bride. The drawings that place the nun in the circle of the Trinity display considerable daring: they project enclosed women into the heart of Christianity's deepest mysteries.

THE HEART AS A HOUSE

The drawing of the Heart as a House is the most intricate and enigmatic of the surviving drawings from St. Walburg (see Fig. 85 and Plate 12). Its complexity, however, is more than a function of its idiosyncratic iconography. Compared with the other drawings, it elicits a higher degree of reciprocity between viewer and image, and not simply because it makes devotional response its unambiguous subject. The drawing conjures up an interior space, mental as well as physical, where the nun could enter into an intimate devotional dialogue with Christ. Looking at the image, she would have been moved to recapitulate the colloquy that culminated in contemplative union. One can imagine her repeating the words of the Middle High German poem:

Du bist min, ich bin din:	You are mine, I am yours:
des solt du gewis sin.	Of that you should be certain.
du bist beslozzen	You are locked
in minem herzen:	in my heart;

verloren ist daz slüzzelin:	The little key is lost.
du muost immer drinne sin.	You must forever remain within.[35]

Strains of sacred and secular love poetry converge in the drawing as in the verses, commingling imagery from the Song of Songs and *Minnesang.*[36] Having entered Christ's heart, the nun can take Christ into her own.

None of the figures of interiority propagated in the early modern period proved more popular than the house as a heart.[37] Apologists, both Protestant and Catholic, elaborated the image in emblems and the didactic treatises that accompanied them.[38] Luther himself singled out the heart emblazoned with a cross as his personal pictorial device, or impresa: a potent symbol of faith in the saving power of Christ's sacrifice.[39] By far the most successful representations of the theme, however, were those by Antoine II Wierix (ca. 1555–1604), who in about 1585–86 engraved an influential series of prints depicting the human heart conquered by the infant Jesus.[40] The first state of the series incorporated as many as eighteen separate episodes of a sentimental, even melodramatic, psychomachia. The fourth engraving (Fig. 92) depicts the Christ Child knocking at the door of the human heart. Incorporated into the immensely popular, much imitated, and widely translated tract by the Jesuit Estienne Luzvic, *Le cœur dévot, trône royal de Jésus Pacifique Salomon,* published in Paris in 1626, Wierix's engravings translated the medieval metaphor of the house of the heart into a modern medium and assured its dissemination to the widest possible audience.[41]

In contrast, medieval readers, however familiar they were with the topos of the heart as a house, hardly ever encountered it translated into images.[42] In addition to the drawing from St. Walburg, only two other works present themselves for comparison—both marginally medieval in date and neither as complex. They come from German convents, a clear indication that the image had special, if not exclusive, resonance for nuns. The first occurs in a manuscript in Munich, where it is one of seven drawings of varied origin pasted in the book (Fig. 93). According to its colophon, the codex was copied in 1529 and belonged to "swester eufrosina gartnerin . . . in der pytrych regelhaus," that is, the Püttrich Regelhaus in Munich, a convent of Franciscan tertiaries.[43] Like the other drawings in the manuscript, the image bears no more than an indirect relation to the treatise it "illustrates," *Der gaistliche Mai* (The spiritual May), an allegorical treatise on the Passion by Stephan Fridolin, preacher and confessor to the Franciscan nuns of St. Klara in Nuremberg who is better known as the author of the richly illustrated *Schatzbehalter,* published in Nuremberg in 1491.[44] In the illustrations, the Christ Child stands before a diminutive convent church, strikes the door, and, speaking in verse, addresses the nun inside: "Ich ste vor der tur, / tue mir uff und laß mich ein, / du aller liebste mein," "I stand before the door. Open up and let me in, you, my most beloved." A paraphrase of the Song of Songs, this amorous dialogue serves as a model for the relationship between viewer and Christ.

Closely related to the drawing accompanying Fridolin's treatise is an engraving of around 1550, no longer traceable but published by Adolf Spamer when it was still in the von Kremer collection in Munich (Fig. 94). Known only from this impression, the print depicts three steps (labeled "gedechtnus," "erkantnus," and "frey willkur," "Memory, Intellect, and Free Will") rising to the door of a heart-shaped house. Like the ladder in the Symbolic Crucifixion from St. Walburg, the staircase embodies the virtuous ascent toward the Godhead, suggesting that the steps in the drawing of the Heart as a House carry a similar meaning (see Figs. 66, 85 and Plates 9, 12). At the entrance a nun extends her hands to greet the Christ Child, behind whom flutters the dove of the Holy Spirit. In bidding her bridegroom enter, the nun also welcomes the New Year; Christ declares, "Ich hab das neu Jar angesungen, / nun ist mir gar woll gelungen, / das ich bin gelaßen ein, / das freiet sich das hertze mein," "I have announced the New Year, now indeed I have succeeded in being let in, which makes my heart rejoice." The nun replies: "pis mir wilkum mein lieber herr, / Ich thue dir auff das hercze mein, / kum mit dein gnaden dreyn," "Be welcome, my dear Lord; I open up my heart to you. Come in with your blessings." [45]

Both the print and the drawing from Munich share the central conceit of the image from Eichstätt: a nun welcoming the Christ Child into her soul, depicted as a house. On closer inspection, however, the comparanda are actually quite different. They are not only less complex but also more sentimental and less mystical. In each, the emphasis lies less on the interior of the heart than on the encounter with Christ. The print in particular assimilates the image of the heart as a house to a popular genre, the New Year's greeting. Developed in the fifteenth century, New Year's prints served as the late medieval equivalent of the modern-day Christmas card.[46] According to a custom known as "Klopfan," "Knock (at the door)," on Thursdays during Advent parading revelers would knock at the doors and windows of strangers, then mock their replies.[47] In the print, the verses exchanged by Christ and the nun recall in miniature the poems that codified this custom. "Klopfan" verses, which were especially popular in Nuremberg, addressed men and women of all ages and stations; the lost engraving represents an adaptation intended especially for nuns. Once widely disseminated, it exemplifies one means by which the devotional imagery cultivated in convents entered the repertory of "folk art."

Fig. 92. Antoine II Wierix, *Cor Iesv Amanti Sacrvm*, Mauquoy-Hendrickx 432 I, Brussels, Bibliothèque Royale Albert Ier, Cabinet des Estampes.

Relatively few images resemble the drawings from St. Walburg closely enough to shed light on their content, let alone their function. Far more helpful, at least vis-à-vis the image of the Heart as a House, are the devotional texts written for nuns that develop the same metaphor. But if we seek to "unlock" the significance of the drawings by recourse to a single "source" text, the "key" to which iconographers traditionally have turned, our efforts will be frustrated. A more complex combination is required, one in which configurations of images, shaped by religious performance and mediated by institutional mechanisms, play the decisive role.[48] Assimilated through rote repetition, devotional tracts, and their metaphors, became part of the way in which nuns experienced the world. In turn, images such as the drawings from St. Walburg did not function as illustrations of texts; instead they served as the starting point for devotions in which any number of images, mediated by a variety of sources, might be brought into play.

Fig. 93. Christ knocking on the door of the heart, Munich, Bayerische Staatsbibliothek, Cgm. 4473, first flyleaf, verso.

Fig. 94. Christ knocking on the door of the heart, formerly von Kremer Collection.

The topos of the heart as the house or dwelling of the soul has roots in antiquity but was first fully exploited by Christian authors.[49] In Latin literature, the metaphor was grounded in part on the dual meanings of *educo,* "to raise up" and "to educate."[50] To edify the soul was to make it a spiritual edifice.[51] Etymology thus made the image of the heart as a house didactic, but its significance and function varied over the centuries. Elaborated in monastic meditational literature, the conceit of the soul as an architectural structure had become, by the end of the Middle Ages, one of the most useful and hence most familiar of devotional devices, as much an image of initiation as of instruction.

Of the texts that formed the devotional demeanor of nuns, few were more important than sermons. We assume that homilies were delivered from a pulpit; just as often, however, they were read in the refectory or collected in *Sammelhandschriften* for closer consultation.[52] The set of sermons associated with the so-called St. Georgener Prediger (in fact written by a number of preachers and assembled in southern Germany as early as the second half of the thirteenth century) reveals how easily a monastic audience could have absorbed the imagery of the heart as house and, at the same time, pinpoints some of its sources in Scripture.[53] For example, Sermon 57, "Vom dem wort Gottes," "On the word of God," identifies the heart as God's dwelling in the soul of the believer, translating Paul's words in Colossians 3 : 16 ("Let the word of Christ dwell in you abundantly") as "The word of our Lord should dwell in your hearts." Just as the drawing of the Heart as a House harks back to others in the set, so too the preacher's paraphrase of Paul recalls the related passage in Ephesians (3 : 17) that undergirds the imagery of the Symbolic Crucifixion: "That Christ may dwell by faith in your hearts, that being rooted and founded in charity you may be able to comprehend with all the saints, what is the breadth, and length, and height and depth"[54] (see Fig. 66 and Plate 9). The drawing of the Heart on the Cross embodies the Pauline metaphor still more effectively by displaying Christ dwelling in the heart of the onlooker. The "St. Georgener Prediger" cements the edifying architectural analogy with yet another paraphrase of Paul: "You are God's temple and a house."[55] In the drawing, the sole piece of furniture, the altar, clearly identifies the dwelling as a house of worship, so that the nun, together with the apostle, could know that the word of God dwelt in her heart.

Elaborating the imagery of the heart as a house, preachers encouraged their listeners to translate its allegory into action. For example, in addressing the topic "Von der beratung der sel" ("On the preparation of the soul"), the author of Sermon 31 in the St. Georgener collection (not identical with the author of Sermon 57) urged his audience:

> You should prepare the house, so that when the Lord comes he finds it beautiful and well prepared. This house is our heart; we should prepare it so that when our Lord comes, he finds it beautiful. That our heart is our Lord's house, he says himself: "My Father has given me this house as my proper inheritance" [Cf. Psalms 2 : 8 and 15 : 5]. This house we should prepare. In faith, we should drive out sin and the vice of sins. And then we should decorate it with virtuous works, and our hearts will really bloom with virtuous thoughts.[56]

Having imagined her heart as a bridal chamber, the nun could first cleanse it of vices, then embellish it with virtues, converting it into the *hortus conclusus* of the Song of Songs.[57]

The enclosed space of the heart as a house stood for the interior of the soul. By extension, however, it also signified the interior of the monastery, itself a symbol of interiority. As noted by Hans Blumenberg, who cites Anselm of Canterbury's *Prosologion,* "The small room and the monastic cell become, in the Middle Ages, places where truth is openly present, an indication that now everything can be expected *from within.* 'Intra in cubiculum mentis tuae, exclude omnia praeter Deum,' 'Enter the bedchamber of your mind; shut out all things except God.' "[58] The altars in the drawings of the heart from St. Walburg insist on a similar notion of contemplative withdrawal by identifying the spaces they enclose as ecclesiastical interiors. In the drawing of the Eucharistic Banquet, the identification of the heart and mind of the nun with monastic enclosure is made still more explicit by the placement of the church, probably the abbey of St. Walburg itself, directly above the head of the praying woman.

The image of the heart as a monastic house received its most expansive elaboration in a series of texts known generally as *Herzklosterallegorien.*[59] In these edifying treatises—addressed, virtually without exception, to monastic readers—the heart was allegorized as architecture. There are some early medieval examples, but the tradition first flourished in the twelfth century in the context of monastic reform.[60] Among the most influential of these twelfth-century tracts was *De claustro animae* (On the cloister of the soul), commonly attributed to Bernard of Clairvaux or Hugh of St. Victor but written, in fact, in the second half of the century by an Augustinian canon, John, prior of Saint-Jean-des-Vignes near Soissons. John's influential treatise translates each architectural element, not only of the cloister, but also of the lavabo, chapter house, oratory, refectory, and infirmary, into spiritual terms.[61] Taking as his point of departure Canticles 2 : 4 ("The king introduced me into his wine cellar"), John describes the monastery as a paradisiacal place, whose walls enclose and protect virtue from the blandishments of vice.

Vernacular adaptations of these allegories of monastic virtue were particularly popular in Germany. At least one version is known from the house of Augustinian canons at Rebdorf, which regularly supplied the nearby abbey of St. Walburg with manuscripts for transcription.[62] Another example, from the Katharinenkloster in Nuremberg, gives a sense of the genre in summary form. The tract begins: "Now learn about a spiritual monastery and how and where you should build it in yourself according to the teaching of Saint Bernard." It continues, "A peaceful heart is a spiritual monastery in which God himself is the abbot."[63] There follows a list of virtues, each associated with either a different part of the monastic complex or, in this version, one of the various posts occupied by the enclosed woman. As God is the abbot, the abbess must resign herself to playing the role of "Bescheidenheit," or "discernment." Humility is the prioress, Patience the custodian, Mildness the director of the infirmary, and so on. As in the drawing of the Heart as a House, Divine Fear plays the porter. Grace, of course, is reserved for the priest. As telling as the pairing of virtues and duties is the characterization of various places in the convent: "Resignation is the church, devotion the choir, meditation the cloister, remembrance of death the graveyard, . . . chastity the dormitory."[64]

The simple structure of *Herzklosterallegorien* made them easy to remember, and nuns would have had no trouble taking their colorful imagery to heart. The drawings from St. Walburg epitomize such an allegory: the convent is depicted as a house and a garden, and the chalice on the altar table, elaborated in the drawing of the Eucharistic Banquet in the imagery of Canticles 2 : 4 and 5 : 1, implies that the interior of the house doubles as the mystical wine cellar. The drawings not only reinforced the nun's identification with the institution of the monastery but also encouraged her to imagine her heart—that is, her inner self—as a microcosm of the convent and all its institutionalized virtues. Like the texts, the drawings presented the onlooker with a memorable image of the meaning of her monastic vocation.

KNOCKING AT HEAVEN'S GATE

The drawings of the heart as a house (see Figs. 84, 85 and Plates 11, 12) identify the heart as the site of a mystical encounter defined in sacramental terms. In both drawings, however, all movement has come to a halt; instead of a diagram of the path leading the worshiper to God, we are treated to an image of the soul at rest in the embrace of the Trinity. The heart-shaped spaces represent, in addition to banqueting houses, nuptial chambers in which Christ consummates his marriage to the soul. Although the steps in the drawing of the Heart as a House identify the heart as a liminal place, the point of passage between Christ and the soul, the entrance is no more than a vestige of the *itinerarium mentis in Deum.* Whereas in the sixteenth-century engraving formerly in the von Kremer collection (see Fig. 94) and in the drawing from the manuscript in Munich (see Fig. 93) the door of the heart, and by implication the convent, stands wide open, in the drawing from Eichstätt, the entrance is firmly shut. In the drawing's companion piece, the image of the Eucharistic Banquet, the framework of the heart has been reduced to a shell; nothing remains to suggest that the soul had ever left its innermost dwelling.

To understand the inward-looking imagery of the drawings we have to adopt the point of view of an idealized nun and imagine looking, not from the outside in, but from the inside out. The combination of a sealed door and open window would immediately have reminded a nun in enclosure of her own situation. Most convents had, not one door, but as many as three, separating them from outsiders, with whom, at least in theory, they could only communicate through a series of windows dedicated to such specific duties as confession, consultation, and Communion.[65] The literature of formation addressed to nuns seized on this complex apparatus of confinement, characterizing enclosure as a state of mind as well as body, with each nun in her person a microcosm of the convent. For example, in the *Buch der Reformatio Predigerordens,* a chronicle of the Dominican Observance compiled by Johannes Meyer (d. 1485), Clara von Ostren, a founding member of the reformed house of Schönensteinbach in Alsace, compares herself to a series of locked chambers:

> I enclose myself every day in three locks: the first lock is the pure, clear, and maidenly heart of the noble Virgin Mary against all temptation of the evil spirit. The second lock is the good heart of our beloved Lord, Jesus Christ, against all temptation of the body. . . . The third lock is the Holy Sepulcher, in which I hide myself with our Lord from the world and all harmful creatures.[66]

The three locks ("druy sloss") stand by synecdoche for three chambers and correspond to the three doors—inner, middle, and outer—prescribed for Dominican convents, the innermost of which had three locks with three keys kept by three separate persons.[67] By offering an allegory of the very circumstances in which the nuns found themselves, Meyer's text seeks to ensure that their minds as well as their bodies would not wander. If the convent is the tomb in which Christ awaited Easter, its inhabitants are Christlike in awaiting the general Resurrection. Enclosure itself becomes the essence of imitation.

The imagery of the door leading to a paradisiacal interior immediately brings to mind John 10 : 9, Christ's identification of himself with the door through which all who would enter heaven must pass ("ego sum ostium"). In the drawing from St. Walburg, however, the image carries no connotation of judgment. To the contrary, the nun appears assured of salvation. Unlike the Wise and Foolish Virgins of Matthew 25 : 1 – 12, who awake from their slumber to face Christ's verdict, the nun at the center of the drawing does not rise to greet her heavenly bridegroom but falls asleep in his lap, like John the Evangelist, the virgin Apostle, at the Last Supper (John 13 : 23). The same image of contemplative repose served as the basis of the sculptural groups of Christ and St. John that, if not altogether exclusive to female houses, were especially popular among nuns (Fig. 95).[68] Enclosed in Christ's loving embrace, John listens to the secrets emanating from the heart of the Savior.

In the drawing, as in the sculptural group, sleep denotes, not sloth, but the tranquillity of mystical *otium*. If in the group of Christ and St. John the Apostle imbibes mystical secrets from the *Cor Salvatoris,* in the drawing, the nun has entered into its innermost chamber.[69] Its imagery would have recalled Song of Songs 5 : 2 ("I sleep, and my heart watcheth"), a commonplace in evocations of mystical rapture. A fourteenth-century treatise from the Dominican convent of Unterlinden in Colmar cites the passage in allegorizing the nuns' dormitory as the vigilant heart of the contemplative.[70] Even if only at a subliminal level, the nun who looked at the drawing of the soul asleep in Christ's arms in the chamber of the heart could have recalled this paradoxical expression of ecstasy.[71] The rest of chapter 5 in the Canticle provides a model of mystical dialogue, enacted in and around the door of a bedchamber.[72] To the bride's declaration, "I sleep, and my heart watcheth," the mystical bridegroom replies, "Open to me, my sister, my love, my dove, my undefiled: for my head is full of dew, and my locks of the drops of the night." The bride continues: "My beloved put his hand through the key hole, and my bowels were moved at his touch; I opened the bolt of the door to my beloved."[73] The drawing, however, does not illustrate this text literally: whereas in Song of Songs 5 : 6 the bride opens the door only to find that her beloved has departed, in the drawing, he has entered to consummate the mystical marriage.

The imagery of Song of Songs 5 provides the scriptural foundation for the allegorical architecture of the House of the Heart. Like any foundation, however, the underlying text remains invisible. Although extensive inscriptions crisscross the drawing, they give no verbal clue to the passage that authorizes the image. The draftswoman takes for granted that her audience is versed in Scripture, but more important than the "sources" per se were the conventions governing their interpretation. The nuns' knowledge of the sacred text was highly selective, stemming,

Fig. 95. Group of Christ and St. John, Antwerp, Mayer van den Bergh Museum.

not from firsthand knowledge of the Bible, but from devotional texts in the convent library that elaborated and ingrained its meanings.

The drawing of the Heart as a House spins out allusions in a web as intricate as that of the overlying inscriptions. The drawing elicits a reading in which every image summons up a chain of biblical sources, each of which elaborates others in turn. To the bridal imagery of the Song of Songs the artist adds a complementary reference from Revelation 14:4—the apocalyptic lamb who, sitting atop the aortalike chimney, turns back toward the 144,000 virgins. The heavenly maidens, led by a crowned figure who is probably St. Walburga herself, appear in abbreviated form, ensconced in the scroll that, like the lamb's banner, unfurls at the upper right corner of the drawing.

Like the Song of Songs, the Book of Revelation uses bridal imagery to speak of consummation and fulfillment, combining mystical and eschatological meanings in a manner reminiscent of the drawing. Once again, however, the key text is not the one cited or paraphrased in the accompanying scroll. Far more evocative of the drawing's imagery is Revelation 3 : 20: "Behold, I stand at the gate, and knock; if any man shall hear my voice, and open to me the door, I will come in to him and will sup with him, and he with me." Like Song of Songs 5 : 2, this text, together with subsequent verses, provides a scriptural foundation for much of the imagery in both drawings of the heart: the house, the altar, and other salient elements. Revelation 3 : 21 – 22 declares: "To him that shall overcome, I will give to sit with me in my throne: as I myself have overcome, and am set down with my Father in his throne. He that hath an ear, let him hear what the Spirit saith to the churches." The reference to Father, Son, and Holy Ghost in these verses accounts for the presence of the Trinity in both drawings. It also justifies the throne behind the altar in the drawing of the Eucharistic Banquet, an otherwise inexplicable piece of liturgical furniture. In effect, the image illustrates the reciprocal enthronement described in Revelation, first of Christ with his Father, then of the soul with them both. The cross-referencing of the Eucharist and its eschatological fulfillment is implicit in Revelation 3 : 20, which refers back to Matthew 26 : 29, where Christ, having just instituted the Eucharist at the Last Supper, declares to the Apostles: "And I say to you, I will not drink from henceforth of this fruit of the vine until that day when I shall drink it with you new in the kingdom of my Father." Both drawings extend the promise of eschatological fulfillment spelled out by the inscriptions, suggesting that through the Eucharist the nun can participate in Christ's sacrifice and be transformed in his image.

In combining allusions to Song of Songs 5 : 2 and Revelation 3 : 20, the draftswoman from St. Walburg made no arbitrary selection of texts. The two passages had already been wedded in patristic exegesis and in mystical poetry as early as the eleventh century.[74] A *Sammelhandschrift* in the library of St. Walburg, transcribed from a model provided by the Augustinian canons of Rebdorf, just outside Eichstätt, contains a text that treats the two interrelated passages.[75] Erroneously attributed to St. Bernard in its rubric ("Here begins the little book by Saint Bernard about the opening [or dilation] of the heart"), the text in fact constitutes a translation into Middle High German of portions of *De doctrina cordis,* a treatise written by Gerhard of Liège during the first half of the thirteenth century.[76] Addressed to a monastic audience, the treatise was widely disseminated, both in its original Latin and in various vernaculars.[77]

In typical scholastic fashion, Gerhard correlates the Seven Gifts of the Holy Spirit with the seven stages of mystical ascent. Most of his exposition bears little, if any, relation to the imagery of the heart as a house. Book III, chapter 2, however, in Latin entitled "De apertione cordis" (On the opening of the heart), begins by comparing the heart, first, to a book that should be opened and read, and then to a house: "It [the heart] is also a house, whose door should be opened to let in him who knocks there."[78] According to Gerhard, the beloved who asks admittance into the bedchamber in Canticles 5 is none other than Christ, who in Revelation 3 : 20 knocks on the door.[79] Commenting on these passages at great length—considering, for example, how quickly and how often one ought to knock—Gerhard asks, "With how much haste and pleasure, therefore, my most beloved friend, you ought to open to the knocking of Christ, your spouse, who knocks at the door of your heart with such a multitude of gifts."[80] After pondering many different tropological readings, he exhorts the bride of Christ to open her heart to prayer, her spirit to love, and her arms to an embrace.[81]

In the text as in the drawings Christ is the bridegroom who, having entered the heart, embraces the soul in its innermost chamber. The analogies extend further, however. The concluding section of book III, chapter 2, of *De doctrina cordis* describes union in eucharistic terms. After quoting John 19 : 34 ("But one of the soldiers pierced his side with a spear, and at once there came out blood and water"), Gerhard strings together scriptural passages to identify the door in Christ's heart with the wound in his side made by Longinus, through which, in turn, the sacraments are dispensed.[82] The door (and hence, the wound), are inter alia, the fissure in the rock in which the soul hides from the terror of the Lord (Isaiah 2 : 10), the rock of Horeb that provided the Israelites with water (Exodus 17 : 6), and the cleft in the rock in which the dove—that is, the soul—finds shelter (Canticles 2 : 14)—all conventional comparisons.[83] Coming full circle, Gerhard concludes by paraphrasing the same passages from Revelation and the Song of Songs with which he began: "Behold how Christ opened all his doors to you. Modestly, therefore, let your doors not be closed to him; shout 'to the door' [Revelation 3 : 20] and say 'open to me' [Song of Songs 5 : 2]."[84]

Even so short a summary of Gerhard's chapter illustrates how he enlarges on metaphors like those developed in the drawings from St. Walburg. It is tempting to identify Gerhard's treatise as their unequivocal source. But despite the rubric, which promises an elaboration on the theme of the heart as a house, the abridged translation that follows omits precisely the sections that correspond most faithfully to the drawings. And even if the nuns had gained access to the unabridged Latin original, probably only a few would have been able to read it.[85] There is no point in stretching the evidence in search of a neat explanation. Instead, the absent "source" points toward an altogether different solution, one that takes as its premise the equivalency of image and text and a more complex relationship of both the visual and the verbal to a shared set of scriptural and exegetical sources, mediated by traditions of devotional practice.

Freed from any obligation to root the images in a single source text, we, like the nuns, can approach them with the liberty and imagination that characterize monastic meditation. Far from being bound by exegetical conventions, the drawings from St. Walburg give them an unconventional twist. For example, commentators customarily interpreted the imagery of knocking in Revelation 3 : 20 in eucharistic terms: the door at which any man could knock, seeking entrance to the banquet, was identified with the side wound leading into Christ's heart. An anonymous devotional treatise from the St. Katharinenkloster in Nuremberg speaks of all Christ's wounds as doors to heaven: "Lord, open up the bloody door of your hand and your foot and draw us under the door of your perforated heart and side."[86] In similar fashion, Johannes Tauler paraphrases Revelation 3 : 20 in beseeching the soul "to knock with all devotion at the lovingly perforated heart and opened side of our Lord Jesus Christ."[87] In the library of St. Walburg itself, the unpublished treatise on the Eucharist, "Pone me ut signaculum super cor tuum," concurs in identifying Christ's wounds collectively with the apocalyptic door, then has the reader reply to Christ's knocking: "I will give him shelter and will listen attentively if he knocks; then I will open up to him and let him in."[88] In response to Christ's opening his heart for humanity, the nun opens hers for him.

By enclosing the eucharistic offering in the heart of the nuns, the drawings from St. Walburg allude to a comparable reciprocal opening. In contrast to the majority of texts in this tradition, however, they omit the motif of knocking per se and, in keeping with the situation of their audience, focus on the soul's enclosure in the house of the heart. They show the soul secure and at rest, supping at the eucharistic banquet.

In addition to eucharistic associations, the house of the heart carried eschatological and mystical connotations comparable to those developed in the drawing from St. Walburg. A Middle High German sermon for the feast of the Assumption of the Virgin invites its audience to imitate Mary: just as Christ's mother took him into the shrine of her heart—which doubles here as her womb—so too should nuns:

> And just as you [Mary] received our Lord Jesus Christ in your pure body and your heart, so should we also receive him with your help. He himself so instructs us and says: "I stand at the door and knock; if anyone hears my voice and opens the door, I will come in to him and eat with him." My beloved, our house is our heart, at whose door our Lord knocks. Just as he sends us his Holy Spirit to warn us that we should respond to his call with works, so he accompanies us to the table, and as David the prophet says, "He makes us drunk from the abundance of his house." How God makes people drunk can be seen in the affairs of the world; when people get drunk, they forget everything that previously troubled them.[89]

Like the nuns at St. Walburg, the anonymous preacher interprets the heart as a house in which the virtuous soul will join Christ in drinking "to its heart's content." Whereas the drawings gloss the eschatological banquet as eucharistic, the sermon glosses it as the reward for the good works that dull the soul to its worldly woes. Both interpretations, however, define the door as a secret entrance to the sanctum sanctorum, one through which only the spiritual elite are admitted.

Inherent in the concept of Christ inhabiting the devotee's heart, or the soul dwelling in the heart of the Savior, was a devotional dialogue, an intimate colloquy between Christ and the soul. By placing Christ and the soul side by side at the heart of each image, the drawings from St. Walburg define devotional dialogue as part of their subject matter. A Middle High German poem of the late thirteenth century known as "Gott und die Seele" illustrates the freedom with which spiritual authors elaborated the imagery of the Song of Songs in combination with that from Revelation 3 : 20 to give nuns models for an amorous colloquy with Christ.[90] In response to the soul's entreaty (lines 22–23)—"negel mich in die wunden dîn. / lêr mich stûdieren in dîn wunden," "nail me in your wounds; teach me to study in your wounds"—Christ replies:

> Ich oberstez guot und sumerwunne,
> ich klopfe an daz herze dîn,
> dîn friuntschaft mir daz niht verbunne,
> tuo ûf, mîn hort und lâ mich în.
> gedenke ich hân durch dich gelâzen
> wunn fröude und ouch mîns vater rîch,
> [und] hân dir gezöugt die rehten strâzen,
> dâ man phlît leben êwiclîch. . . .
>
> Zem gmahel hân ich dich erwelt
> und wil dich zuo mir ziehen,
> dîn herz dîn sêl mir wol gevelt,
> die welt die scholt du fliehen,

und pirc dich in daz herze mîn,
ez stêt al zît gên dir offen.

I, highest Good and summer joy,
I knock at your heart.
Your friendship shouldn't begrudge me that;
open up, my treasure, and let me in.
Remember, on your account I have left
bliss, joy, and also my Father's kingdom,
and have shown you the right road,
where one finds life eternally. . . .

As bride I have elected you
and will draw you to me.
Your heart, your soul please me well.
The world you should flee
and take shelter in my heart;
it always stands open for you.

(lines 28–35, 40–45)

Just below the surface of this seemingly simple text lies a wealth of references to the imagery of *Minnesang,* or vernacular love poetry. Still more important as a model, however, is the biblical Canticle, which, in addition to providing the framework of devotional dialogue, underlies specific passages. Among the echoes are reminiscences of Song of Songs 1 : 3 ("Draw me: we will run after thee") and 2 : 14 ("my dove in the clefts of the rock, in the hollow places of the wall"). Like the drawings from St. Walburg, the poem also takes up the motif of knocking from Revelation 3 : 20. The heart as the locus of union shifts constantly: in one stanza Christ seeks entrance to the heart of the soul; in the other, he invites the soul to take shelter in his own heart. This devotional exchange not only enhances the effect of intimate dialogue but also represents its ultimate object, the identity of one heart with the other.

In spite of their erotic imagery, amorous dialogues between Christ and the soul were illustrated from as early as the late thirteenth century and appear to have been widely distributed in convent libraries.[91] The most familiar of these texts, grouped under the rubric "Christus und die minnende Seele," "Christ and the loving soul," rearrange the shifting metaphorical imagery of the Song of Songs into a coherent narrative along the lines of a romance, with Christ and the soul as the hero and heroine.[92] By the fifteenth century, and probably much earlier, single sheets known as *Bilderbogen* condensed the narrative into a series of scenes resembling a page from a comic book (Fig. 96).[93] In the example reproduced here, the sole sheet

Fig. 96. *Christus und die minnende Seele,* Munich, Bayerische Staatsbibliothek, Einblatt III, 52[f].

that survives undamaged, each of twenty separate sections accompanies four lines of dialogue, much of it comprehensible only with the aid of the accompanying picture.[94] In this particular example the episodes most evocative of the drawings from Eichstätt are the first in the top row, in which Christ embraces the soul, and the scene immediately below it, in which the soul pierces Christ's heart with an arrow (a reference to Song of Songs 4:9).

The drawings of the mystical heart from St. Walburg represent, not "illustrations" of the iconographic and exegetical tradition rooted in Revelation 3:20 and Song of Songs 5:20, but an intuitive and imaginative reworking of the metaphors' scriptural foundations. Despite their extensive inscriptions, the drawings make no direct reference to the passages that authorize their imagery, a measure of both their freedom and the degree to which the artist could take familiarity with these texts for granted. No single passage or group of passages linked in exegesis serves as a univocal source. Instead, the devotional works that inform the drawings stand *pars pro toto* for the spiritual readings that would have informed the nuns' response to them, just as the drawings, in turn, focused and heightened their readings of exegetical and meditational texts. Imagery of the heart as the organ par excellence of subjective experience is omnipresent in late medieval devotional literature;[95] it was no more original to an author such as Gerhard of Liège than to the nuns of St. Walburg. The nuns hardly needed Gerhard's words or those of any other authority to approbate their use of it. Active as both readers and copyists of texts, they would have had no trouble taking the topos to heart. Whatever the differences in their forms of expression, the drawings from St. Walburg and the devotional literature from the convent's library draw on the same stereotypical imagery that for nuns and scholastics alike permitted, even sanctioned, descriptions of otherwise ineffable experience.

AN INTERIOR CASTLE

No matter how many texts and traditions one adduces, the images of the mystical heart from St. Walburg remain without match—an indication that they rely as much on the experience of the nuns who made them as on received conventions. The highly mediated topoi of exegetical and pastoral literature and the supposedly unmediated character of mysticism should not, however, be seen as mutually exclusive. That stereotypes not only preclude but also enable expression is the premise of the drawings from St. Walburg. Similarities between the drawings of the mystical heart, as well as other images from St. Walburg, and the imagery in the visions of nuns underscore the coalescence of example and experience in devotional practice.

Visionary texts describe the phenomena the images from St. Walburg were intended, at least in theory, both to describe and to configure. The visions were not, however, "sources" for the images, any more than the images were the inspiration for the texts.[96] Rather, the visions define a way of reading and seeing with which the nuns of St. Walburg would have been intimately acquainted. Only visionary literature presents a similar variety of images, combined with comparable freedom and imagination.

Few texts offer more analogies to the drawings from St. Walburg than the *Liber specialis gratiae,* which reports the visions of Mechthild of Hackeborn. If the heart is the dominant motif in Mechthild's religious imagination as represented in the *Liber,* then the house is the form it usually takes. Mechthild returns repeatedly to this image of interiority and, it might be added, "feminine" domesticity. In a vision the modern edition entitles "De Domo Cordis," one house encloses another:

> After this the Lord showed her the most beautiful home, extremely lofty and wide, in which she saw another little house made from cedar wood, its interior covered over entirely with a layer of magnificent silver, in whose center resided the Lord. She easily recognized this home as the heart of God, which she had seen many times in this form; truly the innermost little dwelling represented that soul which, just as cedar trees are beyond putrification, is immortal and eternal. The door of this little house was placed toward the east and had a golden bolt, from which hung a golden chain, extending to the heart of God, so that when the door was opened, the chain could be seen to move the heart of God. The door, she understood, designated the desire of the soul; the bolt, its will; the chain, the true desire of God, which always comes before the desire and will of the soul and stimulates and draws it to God.[97]

In this allegory of the mechanics of salvation, Mechthild describes a complex, shifting space. The outer shell represents the heart of God, the inner container, lined with incorruptible cedar, her own heart. But God also resides in the innermost space, so that Mechthild's heart both contains and is contained by the Deity. The bolt and chain on the door, a representation of prevenient grace, connect the two chambers and set the elaborate allegorical mechanism in motion.

In another vision, Christ invites Mechthild to join him in the bridal chamber of his heart. The vision opens, however, with Mechthild listening to a knocking within him, as if he were seeking entrance at the gate of her heart.

> She heard in the innermost reaches of the heart of God three knocks sounding. Because while wondering about this a great deal she desired to know what was meant

> by these blows, the Lord replied: "These three knocks denote three words that I address to the loving soul: and so the first is 'come,' that is, separation from all creatures; the second is 'into,' that is, faithfully just like the bride; the third is 'the chamber,' that is, the divine Heart." . . . and she entered the chamber of the heart of her Lord, in which abound and superabound profuse delights and joys, more of which no human heart could long for.[98]

Like the other texts to which the drawings from St. Walburg can be compared and on which it relies, Mechthild's vision draws on Revelation 3 : 20 as well as the Song of Songs. Her vision also supposes familiarity with the rite of the consecration of virgins (see Fig. 41 and Plate 7). The call to enter the bridal chamber, "Veni intra thalamum," recalls the invitation issued to the novice when she enters a monastic house, as does its systematic allegorical elaboration. In the vision, as in the drawings, the heart serves as an image of institutional as well as mystical withdrawal.

Mechthild's visions also employ the imagery of the exchange of hearts. Mechthild says to Christ, "If it please thee, I would make a delectable and seemly present to you of my heart."[99] Christ responds:

> "Thou may never give me a dearer or more delectable present than to make a little house of thy heart, in which I might delight and dwell. This house shall have but a window through which you may speak to men and send forth my gifts." By this she understood that her mouth should be but one window, with which she should minister God's word and doctrine and comfort those who came to her.[100]

Like Gerhard's treatise *De doctrina cordis,* Mechthild's vision offers tantalizing parallels to the imagery in the drawings. Mechthild compares her heart to a house and further describes it as having "only one window."[101] Here as elsewhere, however, the visual and the visionary parallel each other, without actually touching. In fact, Mechthild's vision focuses its allegorical attention on the window; the drawing, with its scrolls, focuses on the door. Despite a similar variety of imagery, Mechthild and the anonymous artist from St. Walburg draw very different conclusions.

Like Mechthild's visions, the images of the mystical heart from St. Walburg are multivalent in meaning. Their range of theological and exegetical references might seem to strain the limits of historical possibility, let alone the intellectual and literary capabilities often assumed typical of nuns.[102] But the recurrence of specific eschatological, eucharistic, and bridal themes in the drawings suggests that they give visual expression to systematic, if not programmatic, concerns: the longing for paradise; the desire for Christ, the mystical bridegroom; and intense eucharistic devotion—all hallmarks of female spirituality during the late Middle Ages.[103] The images from St. Walburg, however, are far more daring than these commonplaces might imply. In suggesting that God dwells in the heart of the devout believer, the drawings evoke God's birth in the soul or the heart, an idea rooted in patristic exegesis but elaborated most fully in German mysticism, above all by Master Eckhart.[104] Because the bodily chamber of the heart is like the womb, it suggests how the nun, like Mary, can take Christ into her own body and being; in meditations nuns were invited to imagine the newborn Christ Child sleeping in the cradle of their hearts.[105] The visions attributed to some religious women suggest that in a few cases spiritual pregnancy may have induced an autosuggestive simulation of its effects.[106] Far from trivializing the content of the drawings or suggesting that it represents little more than the sublimation of erotic fantasies, this element underscores the sophistication of their theological underpinnings. Their identification of the house of the heart with a womblike chamber, more than any other aspect of their imagery, transforms the erotic dalliance borrowed from the Song of Songs into a model of the ultimate bond and exemplary alliance between God and man or, in this case, woman: the Incarnation, initiated at the moment of Mary's miraculous impregnation by the Holy Spirit.

If we shrink from accepting what seems an outlandish interpretation, we might recall that the drawings of the heart from St. Walburg, though deeply rooted in traditional patterns of exegesis, are highly unconventional. Their extraordinary imagery finds its closest match, not in the devotional art of late medieval Catholicism, but in a Protestant altarpiece, commissioned in 1584 by the Elector August of Saxony from Lucas Cranach the Younger, and based closely on Luther's own reinterpretation of medieval materials (Figs. 97, 98).[107] Alongside the Fall of Man, the model of marriage deformed, the heart-shaped exterior of the altarpiece displays the Annunciation: the marriage between God and the Virgin that issued in the birth of Christ. Its interior—literally within the heart—reveals a crowded Crucifixion, an image that invites the worshiper not simply to contemplate the Passion but to take Christ into his own heart, just as Mary took Christ into hers.[108] Originally a third, smaller, image of the Trinity stood above the altar, with God the Father mourning over the body of the dead Christ much as Mary laments her Son in paintings of the Pietà.[109] Borrowing but reinterpreting the age-old image of God's birth in the soul, Luther employed a language of spiritual transformation (*Wandlung*) easily translated into the mechanics of Cranach's winged altar (or *Wandelaltar*):[110] "Therefore, if this birth is to be of use to us and transform (*wandeln*) our heart, we must impress the example of the Virgin in our heart . . . so that we too will become pregnant with the Holy Spirit and receive Christ spiritually." As the altar opened, its heart-shaped form was itself transformed, and so too, in theory, was the heart of the onlooker. In Luther's own terms, a spiritual pregnancy

Fig. 97. Lucas Cranach the Younger, altarpiece of the Incarnation and Passion in the form of a heart, 1584, exterior.

necessarily preceded a spiritual rebirth; the viewer could model himself or herself on the mourning figure of God the Father, who, as depicted in the uppermost panel, acted out a maternal role.

Although they intimate later imagery, the drawings from St. Walburg should not be imagined as anticipating the Pietist programs of late Reformation altarpieces or the high-minded sentiment of Counter-Reformation emblems. Yet the similarities between them and the devotional art of the two Christian confessions of the sixteenth century suggest that no medieval image of interiority proved more fertile than the house of the heart, even if in later incarnations its daring imagery

Fig. 98. Lucas Cranach the Younger, altarpiece of the Incarnation and Passion in the form of a heart, 1584, interior.

was often domesticated. The nuns of St. Walburg, inheritors of a rich tradition of their own, would have been intimately familiar with the drawings' essential and common conceit: the devotional dialogue between Christ and the soul imagined as an amorous exchange in the house of the heart, conceived as the dwelling of the soul as it strove for union with Christ.

The *Legenda maior* of Hedwig of Silesia, the thirteenth-century saint, describes her "archanum alloquium," or "secret dialogue," with Christ in analogous terms.[111] Hedwig, the legend reports, "desired the presence of God with her entire soul . . . so as to enjoy a secret dialogue with him, to enjoy his delightful love, to receive

Fig. 99. *Hedwig Codex,* Court Atelier of Ludwig I of Liegnitz and Brieg, Silesia, 1353, Malibu, Calif., Collection of the J. Paul Getty Museum, Ms. Ludwig XI 7 (83.MN.126), f. 46r, detail.

the power of his saving grace, and to taste the miraculous sweetness of his taste on the palate of her heart."[112] One of the many illustrations in the *Hedwig Codex* shows the Silesian saint as an exemplar of prayer, immured in an oratory whose roofline crenellations form a series of other diminutive chambers (Fig. 99). The text speaks of her servant Boguslaus of Schawoine, who fled after entering the room and seeing Hedwig ablaze with light as she went about her devotions.[113] In the illustration, however, he gazes transfixed, eyes agape, having thrown open the shutter in the door. By laying bare the interior, the illustration allow us to join Boguslaus in his act of visionary voyeurism, whereupon we see Hedwig, as he did:

> [Her] heart was like a flame; she was unable to rest for the love of God, whom she loved; she longed for the presence of her beloved, as the hart panteth after fountains of water . . . She continually awaited the coming of the Consoler, so that on his arrival and knocking at the gate of the heart she could quickly open the door.[114]

Like the illustrations in the vita of Hedwig, the images of the mystical heart from St. Walburg provided the community of nuns with exemplars of prayer and visionary immediacy. More important, however, they allowed the devotees to penetrate in spirit to the heart of a comparable experience, to pass from witnessing to participation. The drawings presented ready-made images of a secret place of mystical communion. Above all, they supplied images of interiority and spiritual refuge most befitting the cloistered nuns for whom they were intended.

5

NUNS' WORK

IN THE EARLY SIXTEENTH CENTURY, the Carthusian Johann Justus Landsperg (d. 1539) imagined a conversation between a monk and a Lutheran knight; after a long debate, the monk convinces the knight to return to the Catholic faith. To seal the conversion, the monk—clearly a stand-in for Landsperg himself—instructs his pupil in prayer, culminating in serial meditation on the life of Christ. The knight fears he will not be able to remember so complicated a set of devotions. Landsperg advises him:

> Begin with that which you are able to retain; write for yourself either in a list or a little booklet, which you may carry with you, until you are able to remember without it: or, if you do not know how to read, paint signs ("signa") for yourself whose significance you can infer.[1]

Landsperg, following a tradition that reaches back to Gregory the Great and beyond, defines devotional drawings as "signs" that spur the memory and the affections of those unable to rely on words alone.[2]

In trotting out this familiar apology for images—indeed, in applying it directly to small-scale devotional drawings—the Counter-Reformation Carthusian provides what seems an adequate explanation for *Nonnenarbeiten* such as the leaves from St. Walburg. Between the dictates of catechism and the realities of everyday conduct, however, lies the gulf dividing theory from practice. Devotional drawings were not used solely by those unable to read, nor did they serve simply as aides-mémoire, objects that lost their significance in the process of prayer. To the memory and the mind as the proper organs of piety, nuns and their advisers added the body: the eyes and the heart.

The lives of holy women testify vividly to the use of images as instruments of affective piety. The French anchoress Joanna Maria of Maillé, according to her confessor, constantly reviewed in her mind's eye ("ante oculos suae mentis assiduae versabantur") the sufferings of Christ, which she then had recorded in an image so as better to remember the Passion.[3] She also kept an image of the crucifix painted on parchment ("imaginem Crucifixi in pergameni depictam") tucked like a talisman between her breast and her garments.[4] The biographer of the Beguine Beatrice of Nazareth (before 1200–1268)—later a Cisterician nun—noted that

> day and night she wore on her breast a wooden cross, about a palm in length, tied tightly with a knotted string. . . . Besides this, she also carried tied to her arm another image of the Lord's cross, painted on a piece of parchment. A third one she painted on a piece of wood set before her when she was writing. . . . By means of the image of the cross she would keep impressed on her heart and memory whatever she feared forgetting.[5]

Similarly, the Dominican nun Margareta Ebner pressed to her heart every image of the crucifix she encountered, large and small, including a picture painted into a small prayer book, which she also laid under her head while she slept.[6] Reflection on the Passion impressed its image on the hearts of all these women, a process that became literal for the Umbrian tertiary Chiara of Montefalco (d. 1308): an autopsy after her death revealed images of the cross and the other *arma Christi* in her heart.[7] Letters of spiritual advice that the Dominican Venturino da Bergamo (1304–1346) addressed to nuns suggested graphically how to bond their bodies to Christ's: Venturino sealed his epistles with drawings of the *arma Christi,* enclosing, for good measure, scourges with which he had excoriated his own body, together with instructions on their use.[8] In this extension of the *imitatio Christi,* the image—Venturino's as well as Christ's—became flesh in the body of the nun.

No one advocated the use of small-scale drawings more skillfully or more self-consciously than Henry Suso, whose illustrated "autobiography" presents him as an adept in the use of images. In a passage that simultaneously describes and prescribes his practice, Suso's *Exemplar* recounts how he kept in his cell a picture of Holy Wisdom before which he prayed with "heartfelt desire" ("herzkliche begirde").[9] Suso also confesses that in the ardor of his devotion to the crucified Christ, he engraved the sacred monogram on his chest, an action then imitated by his "soul mate," Elsbeth Stagel, who, "in a good devotion, sewed this same name of Jesus in red silk onto a small piece of cloth in this form, IHS, which she herself intended to wear secretly."[10] A bleeding monogram inserted into the text of the earliest extant manuscript of *The Exemplar* does more than simply illustrate this passage; it identifies the corpus of Suso's writings with the corpus Christi in immediate, tangible fashion (Fig. 100). Painted on parchment, the oversize letters

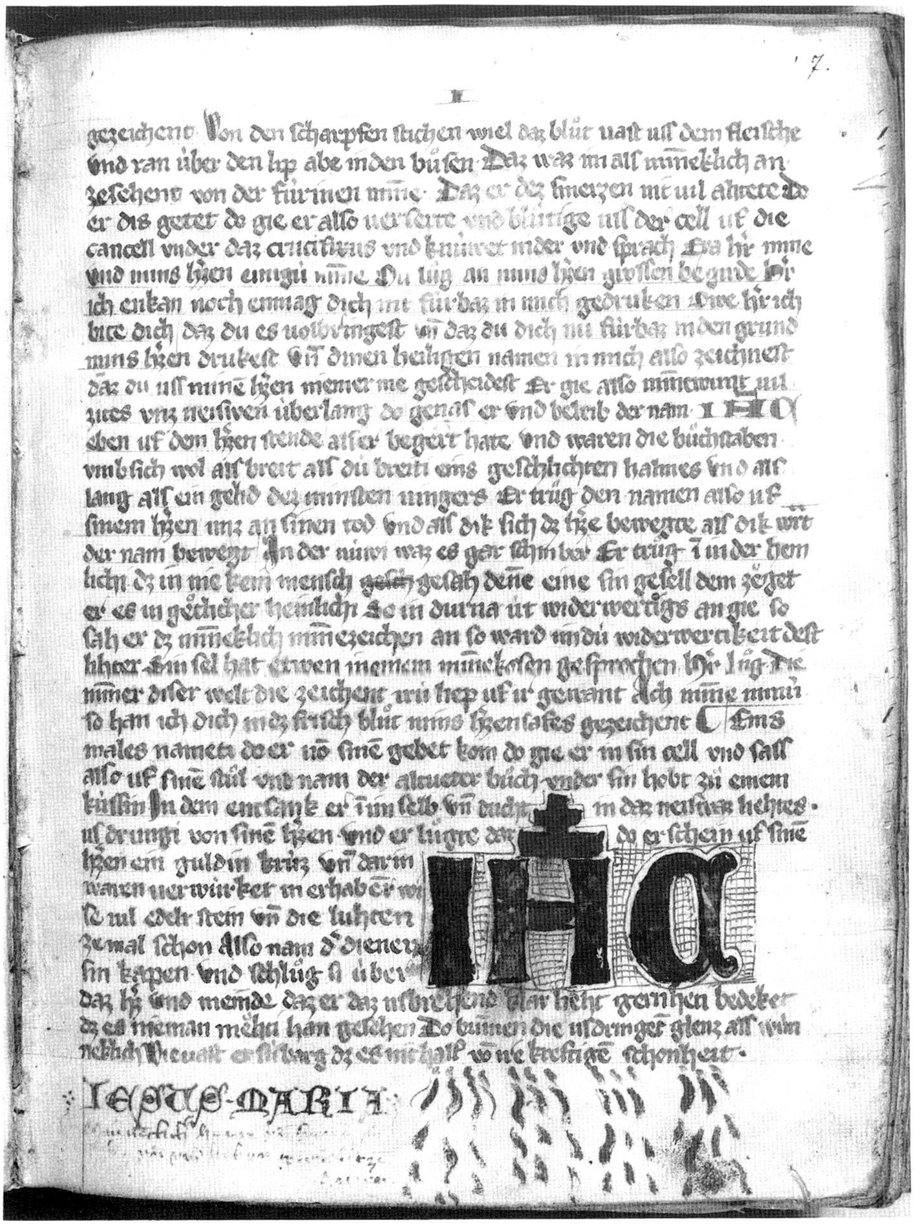

Fig. 100. The monogram of Jesus Christ incised on Suso's chest, Henry Suso, *The Exemplar,* Strasbourg, Bibliothèque Nationale, Ms. 2929, f. 7r.

give uncanny embodiment to the commonplace comparison of vellum and ink to the body and blood of Christ.[11] If at the Incarnation the Word became flesh, in Suso's writings, the flesh, his own included, patterns itself on the Word. As text becomes image, Suso's body becomes text, a reciprocity expressed in ideal form by the sacred monogram itself.

In the *cura monialium* images and texts served as indistinguishable and interchangeable instruments of imitation and edification. As the title of his work implies, Suso's account of Elsbeth's imitation encapsulates the complex circulation of images in this process of pastoral care. Stagel did not simply imitate Suso and, through him, Christ, by inscribing her own body in his image. Instead, she manufactured images for further distribution:

> From this same name [the sacred monogram] she made innumerably many names and brought it about that the servant [Suso] put them all over his bare breast. She would send them all over with a religious blessing to his spiritual children. She was informed by God: whoever thus wore his name and recited an Our Father daily for God's honor would be treated kindly by God, and God would give him his grace on his final journey.[12]

In an effort to define and delimit devotional response, Suso artfully crafts a representation of himself that includes its reception by others. First Stagel emulates Suso's imitation of Christ; then Suso reciprocates by emulating Stagel's effort to imitate him: Stagel acts as the exemplary reader of his text. Her reading, however, is not prescribed, but open-ended; she imitates her adviser by making herself a model for others, thereby initiating an unending sequence of response. Suso's exemplum ends with an invitation to the reader to continue this process of imitation enacted through images. Suso counsels that imitation is not to be understood as identification—an important lesson for nuns, who, in the view of their advisers, often took bodily asceticism to dangerous extremes.[13] Instead, Elsbeth's emulation of Suso translates his bodily mortification into a devotional exercise prescribed and performed through the reading and reproduction of a literary corpus. In this complex colloquy, images join texts as indispensable intermediaries in an interaction whose model-copy relationships extend from the images to the persons who make them.[14]

On its face no more than a simple edifying story, Suso's exemplum of Elsbeth Stagel's devotion to the sacred monogram defines the various roles of small-scale devotional drawings in the pastoral care and devotions of nuns. The leaves from St. Walburg operated similarly. No less self-conscious in their construction, they likewise make devotional response an intrinsic part of their subject matter. They served as aids to, and commentaries on, the act of devotion, spurs to memory and meditation. Yet they and other drawings also acted in far more personal ways. Worn as keepsakes and mementos, not only of Christ, but also of spiritual friends and exemplars, they were like relics, amulets, and talismans, protecting against ills seen and unseen. Exchanged or distributed as gifts to be kept close at hand, close to the heart, they served an affective piety so intense that they were thought of as leaving their imprint on body and soul. Handled, worn, caressed, and kissed, they functioned in ways far more immediate and tangible than devotional doctrine allowed. No wonder that so few comparable images survive; they were simply used up. Ephemeral yet effective, the drawings acquired their meaning in their manufacture and subsequent manipulation.

ORA ET LABORA: PRAYER AND WORK

As images made by and for nuns, the drawings from St. Walburg invite interpretation as autonomous expressions of female spirituality. Yet their independence of clerical oversight cannot be taken for granted, even if men had no hand in their making. In theory, any form of artistic or scribal activity in convents was subject to control, if only because virtually all supplies and artistic exemplars had to enter from outside. Like the writing of books, however, the making of images offered opportunities for independence and individual expression that clerics did their best to curtail. The explicit purpose of the handiwork the clergy encouraged, be it illumination or embroidery, was to foster discipline, quell idleness, and supply the church with the ornaments required for the celebration of the liturgy. All nuns' work, including the drawings from St. Walburg, directly or indirectly bears the imprint of this system of legislation and ecclesiastical oversight.

The regulations governing monastic handiwork were exacting. Dominican legislation went so far as to forbid nuns the possession of either pen and ink or needle and thread.[15] Cloistered women were not allowed to work alone, in the words of one set of directives, "ad angulos," "in the corners."[16] Free time, if not banned outright, was strictly delimited.[17] Even where women were active as scribes and illuminators, regulations sought to curtail excess production, not only to prevent commercial activity, but also to regulate reading. An anonymous friar, writing in the third quarter of the thirteenth century, stipulated that "female scribes should sit with the other laborers in the communal room, but they should not write other things as long as the convent has the necessary books."[18] A regime so strict allowed little room for the production of devotional images, let alone the physical or temporal space in which to conduct "private" devotions.

By statute, nuns' work served as no more than a substitute for the hard manual labor, mandated by the Rule, for which women were deemed unfit. In the late eleventh century, the nuns at Kloster Lippoldsberg in the Rhineland characterized their own handiwork in precisely these terms.[19] The Dominican constitutions for nuns defined their activities as an antidote to idleness, that "mother and nurturer of vices."[20] A friar elaborating these provisions remarked, "None shall be found idle, but should be occupied on behalf of the community in silence and in prayer."[21] Poor Clares received comparable advice: "The sisters and the servants should occupy themselves with useful, honorable work . . . under such supervision that they dispel idleness, for that is an enemy of the soul and also of the spirit of holy prayer and piety."[22] Never is there any mention of *otium,* the older monastic conception of contemplative leisure, let alone the notion that work itself might constitute a form of worship.[23]

To make such strictures memorable, perhaps even palatable, spiritual advisers saw to it that they were summarized, set to verse, displayed on tablets, and incorporated into prayer books.[24] The poem "Mea carissima," "My most beloved," written during the second half of the thirteenth century, exalts handiwork as the ideal expression of a woman's humility before God and service to the church:

dine hende svlen vlisic sin.	Your hands should be industrious
an den dienest der brŏdere din.	in the service of your brothers,
beide ze werke vnd andere swa.	both in toil and elsewhere.
swas si erbeite ane ga.	Whatever work they begin,
si sin siech oder gesvnt.	whether in sickness or in health,
so soltv in ze aller stunt.	you shall at all times help them
helften tragen ir arbeit.	shoulder their burden.
din dienest sol sin in bereit.	Your service shall be ready for them.
dine knú dv neige dicke.	Bend your knee often
mit menigem vf blicke.	with many upward glances
und danke gotte der gnaden.	and thank God for the grace
dc es er dich gerůhte enphahen.	that he deigned to receive you
vnd von der welte het gezogen.	and withdrew you from the world:
des soltu sine gůti loben.	for that you should praise his goodness.[25]

Exhorting his female reader to adorn her heart with paintings and wall hangings, allegorized as "lvteren gedencken," "honest thoughts," the anonymous author urges her to consider unceasing labor, not a bane, but a blessing: "so soltu ez denne behenken, / mit lvteren gedenken, / die gezemment ze vmbehange wol," "You should then bedeck it [your heart] with honest thoughts that are appropriate to hang there."[26] However ordinary such advice, its attitude toward handiwork

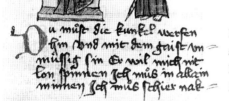

Fig. 101. Christ confiscating a distaff and spindle, *Die minnende Seele,* Karlsruhe, Badische Landesbibliothek, Ms. St. Georgen 89, f. 29v.

could not be taken for granted. The early-fifteenth-century verse dialogue "Die minnende Seele," probably written by a Beguine in or near Constance, has Christ admonish its reader: "Du můst die kunkel werfen hin, / Vnd mit dem geist vnmüßig sin" (You must set aside the distaff, and not be lackadaisical in spiritual things), to which the soul replies, "Er wil mich nit lon spinnen; / Ich muß in allain minnen. / Ich muß schier nakend gon, / Wenn ich nit tůches mag gehön" (He won't allow me to spin; I must love him alone. I must go completely naked, for I can't have any cloth).[27] The image of a woman so busy working or so fascinated by rich fabrics that she had no time for prayer would not have been lost on the women of Constance; the city had elaborate sumptuary laws and was a center of cloth trade and manufacture, in which women were active—witness the *Weberfresken,* or "weaving murals," in Constance in the so-called Haus zur Kunkel, "House of the Distaff," which show women at work spinning and weaving.[28] In this context the fabric, that is, the clothes that Christ urges the virtuous woman to cast aside, are not those that assure modesty but those that embody the worldly trappings she should discard to consummate her union with Christ. The illustration accompanying this passage in a copy both written and illustrated circa 1430 by nuns shows Christ confiscating the woman's distaff and spindle (Fig. 101).[29] As the anonymous author of "Mea carissima" defined it, however, *Nonnenarbeit* meant not simply manual labor but all the routines and rituals by which the devout nun made monastic virtues part of her mental fabric.

In the monastic legislation designed to inculcate humility and obedience, nuns' work was given little scope for religious, let alone artistic, expression. Yet we cannot assume that nuns never took a natural pride in their crafting. In the *Liber specialis gratiae,* Mechthild of Hackeborn compares the forethought an artist puts into her work with God's premeditation and predestination of the Virgin.[30] Other women surely saw in their work a means of preserving their own memory in addition to that of their patrons and forebears.[31] To the best of my knowledge, however, only a single surviving *Nonnenarbeit* indicates authorship, rescuing the name of the woman who made it from anonymity. Glued into the front cover of the pattern book for gold embroidery (*Goldbortenstickerei*) written in 1517 at St. Klara's in Nuremberg by Anna Neuperin, the drawing (Fig. 102) represents the Christ Child with the *arma Christi* surrounded by a floral border; it is inscribed "Dominus kindleín hat magdalenn lengen gemacht vnd gemalt," "Magdalena Lengen made and painted the little Christ Child."[32] In the introduction to the pattern book Anna Neuperin notes: "I often couldn't sleep when I was thinking how I wanted to make a model." She adds, "It troubles me that I didn't do it [i.e., compile the pattern book] in my youth when I would have been more skillful than some seventy years later, but my dear sisters wouldn't leave me in peace."[33] An unusual autobiographical touch, Anna Neuperin's words also suggest that in her old age she and her fellow nuns sought to codify a tradition that was in danger of dying out.

Between artistic expression, conceived in modern terms, and selfless anonymity, however, lies a wide array of other possibilities for creating and communicating meaning, few of them envisaged—or disallowed—by monastic legislation. In a context where prayer was imagined as an exercise for both body and mind, the manufacture of images could be an act of devotion. The Latin verb *operor* means "to keep busy," and this is the primary sense in which statutes understood manual labor. At the same time, however, it signified "to be engaged in worship," a meaning medieval monasticism took seriously.[34] In the handiwork of nuns, the two meanings converged: work itself was a form of worship.[35] The nun who made the devotional drawings from St. Walburg performed a service in both senses of the word. Dispensed to others, her drawings were gifts, but for their maker, as for their recipients, their circulation itself constituted a religious observance. As products of the nun's own labor, the drawings satisfied the requisite engagement in fruitful work; as instruments of prayer, they also fulfilled the requirements of worship. The drawings collapsed the dictates of the age-old Benedictine injunction *Ora et labora* into one.

The chronicle of St. Katharinental describes the intricate interweaving of work

Fig. 102. Christ Child with the *arma Christi,* Wolfenbüttel, Herzog-August Bibliothek, Ms. 57 Aug. 8°, front pastedown.

and prayer. After thirty years of exemplary service, the director of novices Diemůt von Lindow found herself uncertain how to pray during Advent: "And then one night, there happened what had never happened before: he [Christ] came and placed in her hand a rosary ['snůr,' literally 'cord'] that was bound together with red and green silk."[36] Diemůt, not knowing what to make of this, was instructed: "The red silk means the High Divinity, the green means the humanity of our Lord. The knotting together of the red and the green signifies that the two natures, divine and human, were unified in our Lady; you should pass this time with this [exercise] and should plait and unplait the cord."[37] Diemůt's devotion was requited on Christmas eve when, at midnight mass, she saw the Christ Child uplifted in the hands of the priest.[38]

In the devotions of nuns, prayers, visions, and meditational aids were no less intricately intertwined than the cords that Christ enjoins Diemůt to braid and

Fig. 103. The Virgin spinning in the Temple, Erfurt, ca. 1400, Staatliche Museen zu Berlin—Preußischer Kulturbesitz, Gemäldegalerie.

unbraid. The interest of this exemplum, however, lies, not in its timeworn allegory of the Incarnation as the interweaving of the human and the divine,[39] but in its description of prayer as an *imitatio Mariae.*[40] In unraveling, then reknotting the cord, Diemůt takes on the role of Christ's mother, in whom were conjoined the two natures of Christ.[41] Through her actions the nun can imagine herself taking the place of the Virgin as she spins in the Temple, as in a panel from Erfurt, dated about 1400, in which the thread that runs over the radiant homunculus in Mary's womb stands for the garment of her Son's flesh (Fig. 103).[42]

The Virgin Mary offered nuns the archetypal image of pious labor and prayer.[43] According to the chronicle of Kirchberg, the prioress Leugard recited a thousand Ave Marias as well as the Psalter each day as she worked, laboring like the Virgin with her spindle and thread.[44] Reading stories such as these, nuns could imagine themselves toiling alongside the Virgin in the Temple. In the course of the fif-

Fig. 104. The Virgin and her companions in the Temple, Cologne, ca. 1460, formerly Bottmingen, Sammlung Dr. Arthur Wilhelm.

teenth century, devotional images of the Virgin at a loom, many of them intended for nuns, became increasingly common, in both manuscripts and panel paintings.[45] A panel painting of the third quarter of the fifteenth century, probably from Cologne, portrays the Virgin working at her embroidery while her three female companions in the Temple either read, spin, or polish plate, all activities with which enclosed women could readily have identified (Fig. 104). By way of referring to her virginity, the speech scroll that unfurls to the Virgin's left cites Song of Songs 2 : 1 – 2: "Ego flos campi et lilium convallium. Sicut lilia inter spina sic amica mea inter filias," "I am the flower of the field, and the lily of the valleys. As the lily among thorns, so is my love among the daughters." An early-sixteenth-century panel, which may also come from Cologne, sets Mary in the foreground, either spinning (or perhaps making lace). One of the Virgin's handmaidens assists her; two others, to the right, weave, one on a large, upright loom, the other on a smaller handheld instrument in her lap (Fig. 105).[46] In the chapel at the rear, the Virgin appears a second time, kneeling at a prie-dieu before the high altar. As in the life of the nuns who most likely owned these images, prayer and work appear as complementary activities.

Fig. 105. Mary in the Temple, Cologne?, early sixteenth century, Riggisberg, Abegg-Stiftung.

According to the exempla collected in convent chronicles, the making of devotional images could itself stimulate visionary experience. For example, the Kirchberg chronicle reports that once, as Sister Leugard

> spun—for she would never come out of the workroom unless it was necessary—the most beautiful little lamb that ever was seen came to her, and with the pennant and the cross he was in all things just as one is accustomed to painting him in images. And the little lamb sat in her lap and took her little foot, and licked her on the hands and on the threads that she had spun at that very hour just as if the little lamb wished to please and to entertain her, and he continued to do that until she fell back in a window, and so she lay a long time in divine grace, as often and frequently happened to her.[47]

The Lamb's embrace of Leugard reenacts familiar passages from Scripture, specifically the Song of Songs and the account of the apocalyptic wedding banquet in

Fig. 106. The Lamb of God, Augsburg, Universitätsbibliothek, Ms. III.1.8° 56, front pastedown.

Revelation 19:9.[48] In referring, however, to the Agnus Dei "just as one is accustomed to painting him," the chronicle establishes a work of art as the benchmark of authenticity for visionary experience. In so doing, it associates Leugard's vision with its eschatological exemplar and legitimizes images as models for prayer. Images not only inspire visions but also, in turn, authenticate them.

The drawings from St. Walburg present images the female chroniclers trusted their readers could bring to mind—or take in hand. In the image of the Heart as a House, the apocalyptic lamb makes only a modest appearance; he sits atop the "chimney," or aorta, of the heart, cross and banner conflated into a single attribute (see Fig. 85 and Plate 12). In a drawing pasted into a prayer book from the Dominican convent of Medingen, from about 1462–70, however, he appears more prominently (Fig. 106).[49] The Lamb addresses the female viewer: "O du allerliebs swesterlein fůr her das lemblein," "O you, my most beloved little sister, bring the lamb here," to which is appended the beginning of the Agnus Dei from the Mass: "Agnus dei qui [tollit peccata mundi]." The life of Christina von Hane conveys the intense emotion with which cloistered women could invest such an image. As she lay in the infirmary on the feast of the Eleven Thousand Virgins (October 21), a priest brought her the sacrament in a pyx: "Inside the pyx she saw a sleeping lamb, and it had a little wreath on its head that was inscribed with golden letters: 'Agnus Dei, qui tollit peccata mundi.' "[50] Hosts were often imprinted with images, the Agnus Dei among them; when Christina received the Host, the image came to life: "Then the Lamb woke up and jumped quickly into the hand of the priest and reached toward me, as a manifestation of his desire."[51] In a vision such as this, our way of reading is reversed. Instead of interpreting the Lamb as a symbol of the Host, Christina sees the Host take on the living form of the Lamb.

As instruments of religious instruction, artistic and scribal activities were integral to monastic reform.[52] The nuns at the Katharinenkloster in Nuremberg were such assiduous copyists that the convent, besides compiling a vast library—over five hundred volumes, including many multiple exemplars—served as a clearinghouse for the devotional literature of Dominican convents in southwestern Germany.[53] In place of ordinances curtailing the copying or correction of books, the nuns enforced rules designed to ensure accuracy.[54] They also produced tapestries (and possibly prints as well), some for their own use, others for distribution to affiliated houses, male and female.[55] Among their customers or beneficiaries were the nuns of St. Walburg, who acquired, either by donation or direct commission, the *Ältere Walburga Teppich,* produced at the Katharinenkloster around 1465 (see Fig. 28).[56]

As incarnations of the Benedictine ideal of *ora et labora,* the drawings from St. Walburg testify to the efficacy of the reforms initiated at St. Walburg in 1456 by Bishop Johann III von Eych. The renewal of artistic activity was a concomitant of reform, both because of the increased emphasis on literacy and labor brought about by rehabilitation and because of the reformers' destruction of corrupt liturgical manuscripts, which had to be replaced by fresh, corrected copies. Following the reform of the Benedictine nunnery of Ebstorf in Saxony in 1469, the new prioress, Gertrude von dem Brake, together with the prior, Matthias von dem Knesebeck, systematically destroyed all the convent's liturgical manuscripts, replacing them, first with provisional books written out by the nuns and then with more lavishly decorated exemplars commissioned outside the convent. Of the older books, only a few fragments survive.[57] At Wienhausen in Saxony the second reform abbess, Susanna Pothstock, outfitted the choir with new liturgical books, altar implements, and processional banners, some commissioned from monks at nearby monasteries, others, according to the inventory, produced by the nuns themselves.[58] In 1491—eight years after the reform of the Dominican convent of the Holy Cross in Regensburg by the Katharinenkloster in Nuremberg—Agnes Volckamer of Nuremberg donated the funds for a new set of choir books in honor of her niece Magdalena Holtzschuerin, a novice. To the decoration the convent commissioned from Berthold Furtmeyer, the city's leading illuminator, a nun added several watercolors, one of which, inside the cover of the first volume, commemorates Magdalena's piety and Agnes's largesse.[59] According to Johannes Meyer, chronicler of the Dominican Observance in Germany, nuns in reformed convents throughout the Rhineland, among them those in Sélestat, Colmar, and Schönensteinbach, also transcribed and ornamented books for the celebration of the Divine Office.[60]

The liturgical books from St. Walburg, which have come down only as fragments, were probably the product of a similar revival of artistic and scribal activity in the wake of reform (see Figs. 15, 17–19, 22–24). Together with the drawings, the vernacular manuscripts in the library provide firsthand witness to the work in which the nuns engaged. The impulse and model for this activity probably came from the congregation of Marienberg bei Boppard in the Rhineland, some of whom were ordered to Eichstätt in 1456 to assist in the convent's reform. According to the *Confluvium historicum,* a compendium of documents related to the history of Marienberg gathered in 1772 by Conrad d'Hame, the nuns of Boppard were celebrated for their writing and their illumination:

> Around that time [the last quarter of the fifteenth century] the nuns of Marienberg were admired as much for their material possessions as for their spiritual life. The nuns distinguished themselves in particular by their elegant, accurate, and artful writing, with which, in addition to the spiritual exercises stipulated by the rule of the Bursfelde Congregation, they occupied themselves in the preparation of choral books. Some of these liturgical books were most elegantly written on parchment of the largest size and written and decorated with golden letters, initials, and figures. Some exist to this day, in one of which can be read at the end: this book was finished on the vigil of St. Matthew the Apostle [February 24], 1480, by two nuns of this convent whose names are inscribed in the book of life.[61]

The inscription states as succinctly as possible the significance of scribal activity, including illumination, for the process of reform: the nuns who wrote and decorated manuscripts ensured themselves places "in libro vitae," "in the book of life."

A letter at St. Walburg itself testifies to the renewal. It was sent on July 12, 1461, by Bishop Johann III von Eych to the Benedictine reformer Bernhard von Waging, who at the time resided at the convent of the Holy Cross in Bergen, only a few kilometers south of Eichstätt.[62] In it the bishop offers to send Bernhard and the abbess of Bergen two books belonging to St. Walburg, the first a treatise by the humanist Mapheus Vegius (d. 1458), perhaps his *Liber de perseverantia ad sorores eius Elisabeth et Monicam,* the other a book by the Franciscan Alvarez Pelayo

(d. 1350), conceivably his tract *De planctu ecclesiae*.[63] Although the library of St. Walburg no longer contains writings by either author, von Eych's letter testifies to the role of reform in encouraging the copying and exchange of manuscripts.

On their face, institutional programs of reform seem inherently at odds with the production of mystical drawings, let alone the practice of mysticism. Reform was predicated on conformity; it championed the ideals of discipline, obedience, and the renunciation of all forms of extravagance, devotional as well as material.[64] Nonetheless, the drawings from St. Walburg provided the nuns with the visual equivalent of a reformer's tract without forgoing mystical subject matter. In encouraging inwardness, they underscored the importance of the life of prayer in seclusion. In turn, their manufacture fulfilled the requirement that the nuns engage in labor that was sanctified through prayer. As the work of their own hands, the drawings expressed the nuns' own convictions. Like everything else in their lives, however, those convictions were shaped, if not controlled, by the concerns of ecclesiastical authorities. Sight and oversight, vision and supervision were not antithetical but went hand in hand.

THE CIRCULATION OF IMAGES

The term *Nonnenarbeit* insists on the distinctive character of the images manufactured by nuns. Yet *Nonnenarbeiten* also need to be considered from a complementary perspective—that of the nuns who used them. From this vantage point, the boundary separating works made by and for enclosed women proves less than exact. Loose-leaf images provide the physical equivalent of free-floating signifiers, their content changing with their context. A single-leaf drawing or print could serve successively or even simultaneously as an instrument of prayer, an indulgence image, and a pilgrimage token, to name but a few possible functions. Miniatures such as those that served the nuns of St. Walburg as models took on a different character once they were loosed from books and placed in textile frames that subjected them to manipulation independent of an accompanying text (see Fig. 12). Nuns embroidered objects figuratively as well as literally, quickly placing their own imprint on images originally destined for other audiences.

The Latin chronicle of the Poor Clares in Nuremberg—by its very nature a cumulative production—illustrates how nuns could tailor images to their own purposes.[65] Drawings fashioned by the nuns themselves sit side by side with prints imported into the convent. In the first column of one folio (Fig. 107) a drawing of God the Father and the Christ Child prefaces the obituary of Agnes of Hungary (d. 1344), co-founder of the Franciscan convent at Königsfelden in Switzerland,

Fig. 107. Latin chronicle of St. Klara, Nuremberg, Staatsarchiv, Reichstädt Nürnberg, Kloster St. Klara, Akten und Bände, Nr. 2, f. 68r.

while in the next column a single-leaf woodcut of an unidentified nun introduces a letter, dated 1309, in which the abbess Margaret records the convent's obligations to a benefactor, Helena Burckgrania.[66] Neither image has any obvious connection to the adjoining text; the upper portion of the drawing even obliterates a few lines of the obituary. Despite the apparent arbitrariness of the insertions, however, the images were not chosen at random; the chronicle could easily have been illustrated with images drawn directly on the page.[67] Placed in blank spaces and framed in thick bands of paint, the prints and drawings formed part of a deliberate plan of illustration. By pasting the loose-leaf images into the book, the nuns sought to preserve them, along with the adjoining documents, as objects of record.

The prints, drawings, and other small-scale images molded from materials as varied as tin, lead, and papier-mâché discovered in the 1950s at the Cistercian convent of Wienhausen in Saxony testify to an astonishing abundance of imagery throughout the cloister.[68] Many of these images, most notably the prints, must have been imported; they have been interpreted as indices of the place of mass-produced images in a broad-based, popular piety in which the nuns participated along with the laity at large.[69] A number of the images, however, most notably the drawings and miniatures that replicate monumental wall paintings and sculptural groups from the convent's inventory, must have been made exclusively for the convent's inhabitants. Only female artisans had access to the monumental models, and only they and their fellow nuns were in a position to comprehend their frame of reference, which extended the reach of cult images from the corporate spaces of the choir and cloister to the relative seclusion of individual cells.[70]

From the inventory of Wienhausen come a number of tiny Veronicas, together with an uncut sheet of eight identical icons. At first glance, the physical evidence suggests that these minuscule images were distributed to visitors as pilgrimage tokens or else as spiritual souvenirs (Fig. 108).[71] Yet small-scale images of the Veronica performed other functions as well. For example, in the Pontifical-Missal of William of Reichenau a tiny square of parchment bearing an image of the Holy Face has been glued into the margin opposite the text of the Canon (Fig. 109). The image served as an osculatory, to be kissed by the celebrant in lieu of the canon page Crucifixion, which explains why it is so badly abraded—but not why it had to be inserted rather than painted directly on the page.[72] Painted by the same artist responsible for the remaining decoration, it cannot be considered an addition or an afterthought. Although fixed in place, it has a separate support and, hence, an independent identity, allied to the concreteness of what it reproduces—the veil bearing Christ's visage—and, still more suggestively, to the reality of the Host, which, like the Holy Face, was considered more than merely a representation.

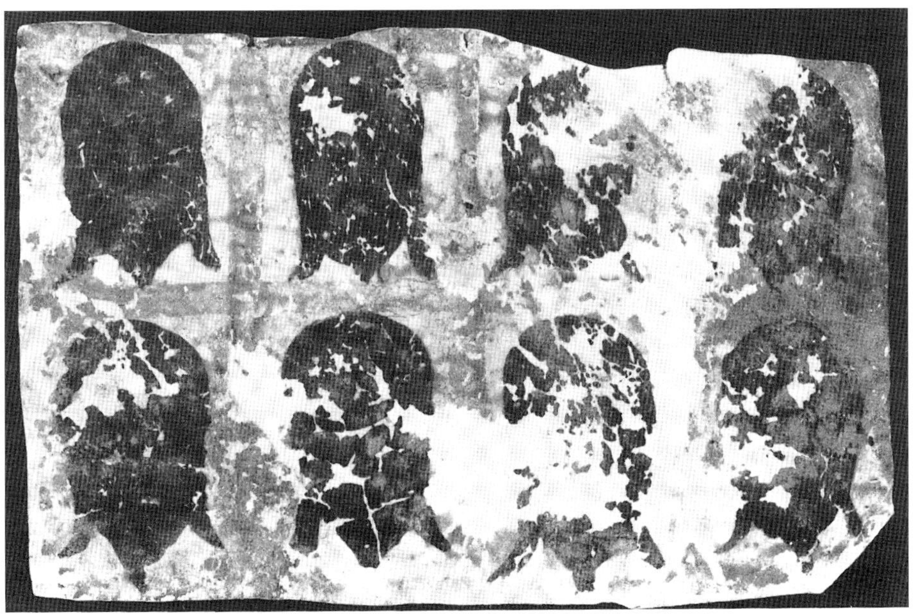

Fig. 108. Sheet of uncut images of the Veronica, Wienhausen.

Fig. 109. Veronica, Pontifical-Missal of William of Reichenau, Eichstätt, Diözesanarchiv, Ordinariatsbibliothek, Ms. 131, f. 107v.

Images such as the small-scale Veronicas from Wienhausen and Eichstätt need not, however, have been mass-produced for outsiders alone, whether priests or pilgrims. A reproduction of the Holy Face permitted nuns unable to journey to Rome an interior, proxy pilgrimage, especially on the feast in its honor, the second Sunday after Epiphany.[73] As an authentic likeness of Christ seen "face to face," an image of the Veronica gave nuns the experience of a female forebear of apostolic (if apocryphal) authority. The literature of female spirituality goes further, explicitly identifying the body of the female devotee as the medium through and in which Christ's body is reproduced. The vita of the thirteenth-century Beguine Elisabeth of Spalbeek reports of her stigmata that now the "illiterate man or woman can read, not in parchment or documents, but in the members and the body of this girl, as a vivid and unmistakable Veronica, a living image and an animated history of redemption, as if he or she were literate."[74] The female mystic, according to her biographer, does not merely simulate Christ's Passion; she becomes its authentic and charismatic reincarnation. She does so, however, by transforming herself into the likeness of an image. The *imitatio Christi* is transformed into the replication of a reproduction.

Images of the Holy Face appear to have been readily available to women in convents across Germany. According to the chronicle of the Dominican convent of Töß, a Holy Face stood in front of the chapter house, whence it spoke to the nun Anna Wansaseller as she prayed.[75] The chronicle specifies that the image "hung" ("hanget"), suggesting a panel rather than a mural. It also reports that the image incorporated inscriptions from the liturgy used to celebrate the Holy Face.[76] The image thus provided a verbal and visual basis for an interaction analogous to the visionary dialogues supposedly enacted before the Veronica by Gertrude the Great and Mechthild of Hackeborn, both nuns at the Cistercian convent of Helfta in Saxony. The meditation attributed to Gertrude incorporates references to penitence and indulgences—practices associated with pilgrimage—but nevertheless uses the image of the Veronica as the starting point for a more profound excursus on redemption. Playing on imagery of reproduction and simulation, the pious exercise defines the penitential process initiated by the image as the recovery of the *imago Dei,* identified as the splendor of the *facies Dei* reflected in the soul and an anticipation of the *visio Dei* face-to-face.[77] In Mechthild's *Liber specialis gratiae,* contemplation of the Veronica performs a similar function, expressed in more pedestrian terms: the text teaches the nuns to pray as many Paternosters as there are thousands of miles separating Helfta from Rome.[78] We can imagine how the Veronicas pasted into the front flyleaf of a Psalter (Fig. 110), dated around 1472, served as the starting point for a similar set of devotions. Although the image looks

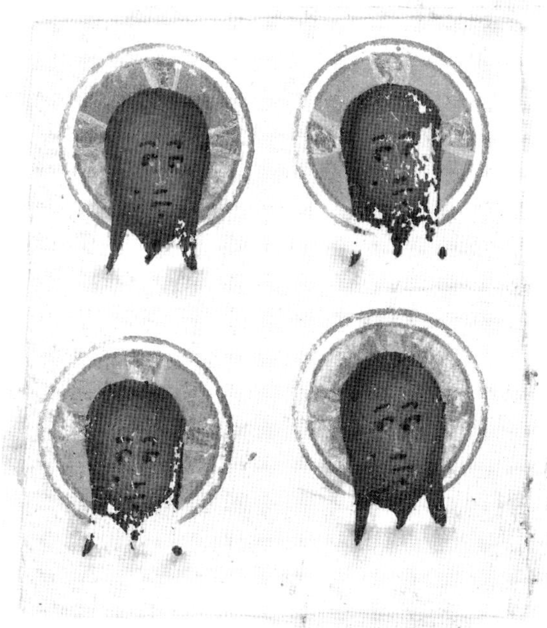

Fig. 110. Sheet of Veronicas, Psalter, Copenhagen, Det Kongelige Bibliothek, Ms. Thott 117, 8°, f. i verso.

like so many stamps awaiting distribution, the block of four faces indicates that such sheets were not always broken up. Extending the logic of the icon in a way that diminishes its power, even as it multiplies the original, the sheet suggests that several images of the same denomination might prove more efficacious than just one.

Not all images amassed or mass-produced by nuns directly served devotion. Cloistered women traditionally distributed loose-leaf images as gifts, some as amulets, others as keepsakes or tokens of affection. For example, on May 14, 1506, Katharina Pirckheimer the Elder (1476–after 1530), a nun at Kloster Geisenfeld near Nuremberg, sent her brother, Willibald, a charm in the form of an excerpt from the Gospel of St. John wrapped in *federkill,* "in a nutshell."[79] In a postscript she acknowledges her apprehension that her cosmopolitan brother might disdain her gift, adding: "I beg you not to despise it."[80] Whatever Pirckheimer thought of the charm, a traditional defense against demons and dangers of all kinds, he preserved it; it is housed, with his correspondence, in the Stadtbibliothek in Nuremberg (Fig. 111). Added to the transcription of John 1 : 1 – 14 is the account of the three Magi from Matthew 2 : 1 – 12, a charm for safe travel, and an invocation of the Trinity in Latin and Greek. At the center, an enigmatic diagram of the Triune Godhead inscribed "increatus pater, increatus filius, Sanctus spiritus increatus" provides a focal point for meditation.

Other images made by nuns were given as tokens of gratitude for donations.

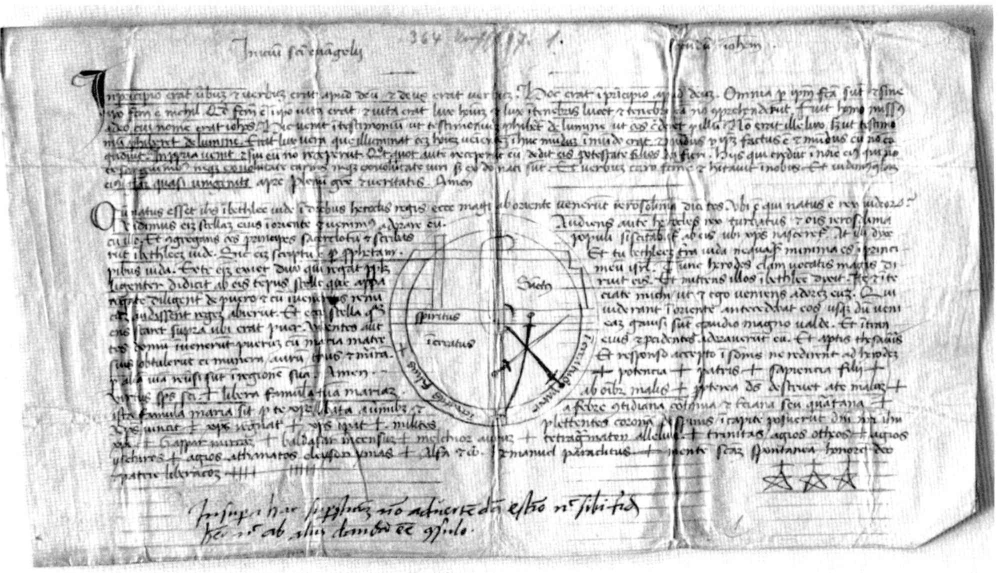

Fig. 111. Mystical diagram and charm, Nuremberg, Stadtbibliothek, Pirck. Umschlag 17, Blatt 1.

New Year's was the favorite time for the distribution of these visual mementos.[81] In an epistle written in her own hand—a personal touch, for normally she would have dictated her letters—Caritas Pirckheimer (1467–1532), the learned abbess of St. Klara's in Nuremberg, conveyed to the city architect Michael Behaim (1459–1511) her best wishes for the New Year (probably 1507).[82] She sealed her solicitation with a little figure of the Christ Child, which she characterized as a "dominus tecum," "Lord (be) with you." The title refers to the angelic salutation in Luke 1 : 28 ("et ingressus angelus ad eam dixit ave gratia plena Dominus tecum") as well as the etymology of Christ's name, Emmanuel, offered in Matthew 1 : 23 ("nomen eius Emmanuhel quod est interpretatum nobiscum Deus"). The words allow the recipient of the image to identify with the Virgin at the moment of the Annunciation.[83] With this image in hand, Behaim could, moreover, take literally Caritas's injunction to keep Christ in view at all times ("alle augenplick"). Added to the letter are a few sweets made by one of the nuns with lavender and other spices, in Caritas's words, to be used "to fortify your head."[84]

Herb candies and cookies were (and remain) traditional New Year's gifts—so much so that in an Alsatian woodcut of about 1470 that wishes the viewer "En gut jar," a box of sweets sits half open at Christ's feet (Fig. 112).[85] The statutes of the Poor Clares of Brixen, reformed in the mid fifteenth century by nuns from St.

Fig. 112. Infant Christ with a bird, New Year's greeting, woodcut, Schreiber 784, Paris, Bibliothèque Nationale, Cabinet des Estampes.

Klara in Nuremberg, explicitly legislates against such gifts, stating that the nuns should desist from "making and sending out into the world lebkuchen, spice cookies, doughnuts, hoods, bags, needles, ointment, sugar, rose water and schnaps, bleach and the like."[86] No matter how modest, such tokens reinforced the ties that bound the convent to its benefactors.[87] Caritas's present expressed her gratitude for Behaim's support; the prayers spoken on his behalf constituted a more substantial, if less tangible, offering that provided him an incentive to give yet again.[88] Not all nuns were so grateful, however; Anna Tucher (1430–1482), a member of the great Nuremberg patrician family, who became a nun at nearby Pillenreuth, wrote of Behaim, "Gott geb ihm ein verdorbenes Jahr, der mich macht zu einer Nonne," "May God give him who made me a nun a rotten year."[89]

The most extensive written evidence regarding *Nonnenarbeiten* comes from the convent of the Holy Cross at Bergen, a Benedictine house a few miles south of

Eichstätt with close ties to both St. Walburg and its episcopal reformers. No drawings and few manuscripts are extant from Bergen.[90] Altogether more unusual, however, are the letters to and from the nuns that bear vivid witness to their production of devotional images. Once again, the testimony comes from the correspondence of the far-flung Pirckheimer family, in this instance, the letters exchanged between Willibald and his sister Sabina (1482–1529), abbess of Bergen from 1521 to 1529.[91] The Pirckheimers had close ties to Eichstätt and the surrounding region: Willibald's father, Johannes, had been employed by the bishop William of Reichenau, with whom he had studied in Padua, and both Willibald and Sabina had been born in the city.[92] We think of Willibald Pirckheimer primarily as the dean of German humanists and the close friend of Albrecht Dürer. He had, however, a more cantankerous side, which surfaces in his correspondence with his sisters, seven of whom were nuns. As with his sisters, so too with his children: Pirckheimer's only son died shortly after birth, and three of his five daughters entered nunneries.[93] Some ten members of Pirckheimer's immediate family had entered convents of various orders in and around Nuremberg, a situation, by no means unusual, that suggests the social background of nuns in convents such as St. Walburg. Although by the late Middle Ages few, if any, of these houses were as aristocratic as they had been at their founding, most remained the preserve of the urban patriciate.[94]

Pirckheimer's sisters corresponded extensively with their brother, a reminder that nuns, even if removed from the world, remained in contact with it. Their letters are full of news, queries about friends and servants, gossip about the Peasants' War, complaints about monastic finance, casual pleasantries, quarrels (often about family matters), and substantive debates about such issues as theology and the status of convents, many of which were dissolved during the Reformation or converted into so-called *Damenstifte.* One letter, dated June 10, 1520, catches the sometimes sardonic tone of Pirckheimer's sisters. Rejecting a proffered gift of what she characterizes as pieces of rusty armor, Sabina writes:

> We thank you in any case for your goodwill and for offering them to us, but as we're completely unused to riding, we'd know of no other way of using them than for scraping pans . . . ;[95] sometimes a pajama is too rough for us, tender martyrs that we are. Our sister, the abbess of St. Klara [i.e., Caritas], gave us at our request a hair shirt in case we might need it; therefore keep your "armor" for yourself.[96]

Such sarcasm aside, Sabina clearly relied on her brother's goodwill for supplies and badgered him constantly to send materials for painting. As at St. Walburg and other convents, one nun served as *Malerin.* On August 9, 1524, Sabina thanks her brother for a variety of supplies, paper among them: "The medicine is good, also the paper; see to it that you send us a beautiful gold pigment. We want to try *aurum pigment;* never had it before."[97] Another letter, written early in the following year by Sabina's sister Euphemia (1486–1547), also a nun at Bergen (and, following her sister, the abbess as well), supplies more information. "Dear brother," Euphemia writes:

> I've written to you about a few things that the painter needs and ask you kindly to have them bought for us; no one else sends us anything worthwhile; what you don't send us here, we're unable to use; therefore we ask you to do us this favor, and whatever you spend or have spent our servant will pay, and whatever can't be had right away, you can have sent "auf das heiltum" [i.e., the second Friday after Easter, the day on which the *Reichskleinodien,* the imperial insignia, some of which doubled as relics, were displayed in Nuremberg]; perhaps we'll again have news, and the painter would gladly know how coppergreen is mixed so that it lasts. It's really beautiful when it's new, but once old, it tarnishes; what we otherwise receive from outside, that lasts much longer. She'd also like more brushes—she says she can't paint except with the brushes that you send here. She'd gladly return the favor with some embroidery, if she knew what you'd like. The mastic and silver leaf we'd like for [unclear in the original]; you know how to purchase it later, but we would like some very much now.[98]

The supplies apparently were sent; in a letter dated July 5, 1527, Sabina thanks her brother "for the apples and all the good you do for us; Sister Euphemia and the painter also thank you in all honesty." She adds that "the painter barely escaped the clutch of death; God has mercifully aided me in a great deal of adversity."[99]

Besides listing the articles the painter required, Sabina's letters give us a glimpse of the practice—and, more interesting, the functions—of painting in convents. The nuns depend utterly on the goodwill and cooperation of friends and patrons such as Pirckheimer to procure supplies. In addition to being a specialist eager to experiment with new techniques, the *Malerin* requests recipes for pigments so that she need no longer rely on outside sources.[100] The designation of one nun as the *Malerin* itself indicates that the production of images was an established part of the convent's spiritual and economic routine, and that the nun so designated, if not the only woman to try her hand at painting, held primary responsibility for this task. The stylistic uniformity of the drawings from St. Walburg suggests similar circumstances, for they too appear to be the work of a single hand.

Sabina's letters point to a lack of training and materials. Nevertheless, they provide more than an index of the nuns' deficiencies. Nuns sought skills because they could put them to good use, often in collaboration with their confessors. For ex-

Fig. 113. Meditational panel, Kloster Ribnitz, ca. 1530.

ample, at the convent of Poor Clares at Ribnitz, near Rostock, the abbess Dorothea commissioned from the confessor Lambrecht Slagghert a winged altarpiece for the nuns' choir, which he painted in 1530 with the help of three of the nuns, Anna van der Lů, Anna Bugghenhagen, and Cristina Bodins.[101] Slagghert reports that the nuns both prepared and gilded the panels. Two years later, a similar partnership produced a panel for the choir of the order's patron, St. Francis.[102]

None of these works survive, but a set of six early-sixteenth-century panels from Ribnitz suggests their appearance (Figs. 113, 114). Because of the small size of the panels, their unconventional selection of subjects, and a sequence that often ignores narrative progress, they probably never formed part of an altarpiece, serv-

Fig. 114. Meditational panel, Kloster Ribnitz, ca. 1530.

ing instead as devotional images in the nuns' cells or, conceivably, in individual prayer niches in the choir stalls.[103] In all likelihood the drawings from St. Walburg served a comparable function. Despite the difference in medium, the mode of manufacture may have been similar. Several subjects recur from one panel to another; the Resurrection alone appears in five of the six extant paintings.[104] The repetition of patterns suggests the recourse to models, including, but not limited to, prints.[105] Of these, at least one—the Christ Child with the chalice, God the Father, and the Holy Spirit—resembled the print used as a model for the roundel in the symbolic tapestry from St. Walburg (see Fig. 114; cf. Figs. 34–36).

Similar patterns of collaborative production can be traced at other houses. In

Nuremberg, for example, the nuns of the Katharinenkloster illuminated manuscripts for the friars, who, in turn, supplied them with bindings.[106] At least in theory, barter was required, for the selling of goods would have contravened the Rule.[107] There were exceptions: the chronicle of Wienhausen implies that in 1501 the nuns sold handicrafts, presumably embroidery, to purchase masonry for the restoration of the chapel of St. Anne.[108] In such exchanges, vestments and needlework provided the most common currency.[109] During its early days, the impoverished community of Dominican nuns at Oetenbach outside Zurich supported itself in part through painting, illumination, writing, and embroidery, which, according to the chronicle, brought in an income of 10 marks per annum.[110] Moreover, nuns manufacturing hangings and vestments participated by proxy in the liturgy or at least contributed to its celebration.

All these motivations, explicitly or implicitly stated, come together in a passage from a mid-thirteenth-century chronicle of the Dominican friars in Eisenach, in the Harz, that describes the circumstances under which the prior, Elger, count of Hohnstein, commissioned several altar cloths from his sister, a nun in the Dominican convent of Rohr bei Meinigen in Franconia.[111] The chronicler characterizes the unnamed nun as an industrious embroiderer who, despite her aristocratic ancestry, worked with her own hands ("operabatur manibus propriis illa"), making all that was necessary for the liturgy ("ad Dei cultum requirebantur"), specifically, an antependium and an altar cloth ("antependium cum linea et palla alteris"), to fulfill the requirements of the Rule ("ut Dei famula non esset ociosa"). Elger specified the form and figures to be included ("specificans ei formam et ymagines fiendas"); his sister's contribution consisted of her subtle skill and handiwork ("sue subtilitatis labore").[112]

The Pirckheimer correspondence testifies to a similar exchange. Sabina thanks her brother for a vestment he has sent to be decorated, adding an unexpected touch of humor: "We see that you had the vestment made according to your measurements; it is good and large, and when you become a priest and our confessor, it will be just right for you."[113] In a subsequent letter, she reports that "the vestment is already finished, as it has already been used for holy time [i.e., Easter]; there are beautiful figures of saints [literally, "götzen," or "idols"] on it, the likes of which we haven't had before; we'd like to grant them a place on our altars."[114] Several such vestments survive from St. Walburg, including the *Stifterkasula,* embroidered on Spanish silk and probably placed in the saint's tomb at the time of the reform in the mid fifteenth century, then removed in 1629, and another, dated 1527, of which only the portion embroidered by the nuns survives (Fig. 115).[115]

We take for granted the easy familiarity that characterizes the exchange be-

Fig. 115. Cope, Eichstätt, St. Walburg.

tween brother and sister, but even such intercourse was closely regulated and disparaged. For example, in 1362 Abbot Walter of the Benedictine monastery of Allerheiligen at Schaffhausen enjoined the sister house of St. Agnes "most earnestly and according to obedience that none of the women receive or hear, or send or give to people as offerings, books, letters, or precious objects."[116] Although they may rarely have been followed, Dominican directives also forbade nuns to provide friars with garments as a "special favor" ("favor specialis"). All superfluities were prohibited, including intricate stitching ("studiosae suturae"), belts, or girdles ("zonae"), and "signa cum serico," "signs with silk," apparently a reference to embroidery.[117] Personal, including devotional, items, however, were the stock-in-trade of exchanges between monks, friars, nuns, and their families. Preaching in 1414 to the Cistercian nuns of St. Nicholas "vor dem Stubentor" in Vienna on "das vbel der aigenschaft," "the evil of property," Nicholas of Dinkelsbuhl was scandalized to observe that

> some among you also take gifts or presents with the permission of your abbess, which your father or your mother, sister, brother, or one of your other good friends give or present to you, be it precious objects or cash or food or drink. And the things they are given, they use according to their own will. Moreover, the lay sisters who earn something with their handiwork use it, with permission of the abbess, according to their own whim and will. And some among you, whom it pleases, give presents, gifts, or precious objects to your father, mother, brother, sister, or others among your friends and thereby earn your keep, and do all that with permission of the abbess.[118]

In addition to providing a valuable source of income (especially for those nuns who wished to supplement their endowments), gift giving was the glue that bound the nuns to their friends, relatives, and patrons.

The Pirckheimer correspondence testifies vividly to this practice. In addition to unfinished vestments, Willibald sent prints to his sister, which she had colored by her painter before distributing them to the nuns, apparently in return for good behavior. In about 1520–21, before becoming abbess, Sabina writes, "We thank you very much for the little letter [in all likelihood a *Flugblatt,* or leaflet] that pleases us and gives us great joy; if we celebrate a church dedication, we will pray to God on your behalf, as we daily do."[119] Some five or six years later Sabina indicates that the *Malerin* would occasionally embellish such images: "The printed letters were not necessary; they're just fine when one can't have the others. In every respect I serve myself in a simple fashion;[120] give me those, and my painter colors them for me; then I don't have to buy any."[121] In a fleeting reference that implicates these simple images in Reformation debates over idolatry, she then adds, "Moreover, at the moment one can't find any saints to buy; they have been forbidden in these parts."[122]

Much like Elsbeth Stagel, Sabina distributed the images as gifts: "I often delight a nun with a little letter; when they work honestly, I give them one as a gift."[123] By honest work, Sabina probably meant embroidery, perhaps painting as well. In the *Klosterordnung,* or statutes, that he drew up for the convent at Bergen in 1458, Johann III von Eych, bishop of Eichstätt, also encouraged handiwork, but for different reasons: "On feast days they should cling to prayer the entire day, as much as necessity imposes, . . . but because as women they are not skilled at continually reading Holy Scripture, this [duty] can be converted into handiwork, so as to avoid idleness and gossip."[124] The bishop construed manual labor not only as a supplement but also as a substitute for prayer. More often, the injunction to silent work was taken to mean that the nuns should listen to pious readings.[125]

The nuns of Bergen, however, were not as unsophisticated as the bishop believed. At one point Sabina thanked her brother for a "little quarto," perhaps a Lutheran tract, noting that its "Saxon dialect doesn't bother us; we thank you kindly for it."[126] A further clue comes from Sabina's passing references to Willibald's close friend Albrecht Dürer. Writing on April 30, 1528, following the artist's death, Sabina consoles her brother: "I've been told that Dürer also has died, God be merciful to him. I'm especially sorry on your account that at your age you've been robbed of a good friend; we must, however, leave all things to God, who certainly knows how to deal justly."[127]

Clearly Dürer's fame had reached the convent at Bergen; conceivably some of the prints Pirckheimer sent were from his hand. The references to Dürer, however, are of more than anecdotal interest. Describing the vestments embroidered by her charges, Sabina, taking natural pride in their work, declares: "If we had our way, we'd like you and Dürer to see them."[128] We are not used to thinking of liturgical vestments as "high" art—nor, perhaps, were Dürer or Pirckheimer—but in the early sixteenth century the modern distinction between the "fine" and the "decorative" arts remained a novelty, at least in the North.

Still more striking is a passage, dated August 9, 1524, in which Sabina reveals not only that she herself paints for recreation, but also that she is aware of the disparity between her own skills and those of her *Malerin* and those of an artist like Dürer: "I have no recreation except painting; if I could only have Dürer for a fortnight so that he could instruct my painter."[129] Sabina's wish, however charming, marks the passing of an era. Whereas only a generation before, nuns might never have doubted the efficacy and adequacy of modest images such as single-leaf woodcuts or the drawings from Eichstätt, by 1525, on the eve of the Reformation, such images were suspect on both religious and aesthetic grounds. Religious imagery now had to be not only true but beautiful as well. In a word, it had to be "Art."[130]

None of Sabina's handiwork or that of her *Malerin* appears to have survived. Like the drawings from Eichstätt, however, it was probably a far cry from the stylish sophistication of Dürer's prints. Not that men were incapable of admiring the handiwork of their female contemporaries. In 1505 the prolific humanist and prior of the Benedictine monastery of Maria Laach, Johann Butzbach (1476–1526), dedicated a short tract, *Libellus de preclaris picture professoribus* (A little book on the famous practitioners of painting) to Gertrude Buchel, abbess of Rolandswerth (later Nonnenwerth) from 1507 to her death in 1543.[131] Butzbach compared her industry to that of her fellow nun Aleidis Roscop, to whom he dedicated a much longer treatise, *De illustribus seu studiosis doctisque mulieribus,* celebrating her skill as a Latinist.[132] For both works, Butzbach's immediate model appears to have been Boccaccio's *De claris mulieribus,* widely disseminated following its first printing in 1473.[133]

Butzbach was no Vasari, nor, for that matter, was he the first northerner to single out for special attention the trio of female artists chronicled in Pliny; that honor belongs to Christine de Pizan, who, like Butzbach, took Boccaccio as her source.[134] Butzbach's primary interest is neither aesthetics nor the history of art conceived as a history of style, but rather images as instruments of edification for their makers and their viewers. His booklet nonetheless marks a departure from medieval tradition. Despite his moralizing tone, the Benedictine prior dignifies the craft of painting by providing it with a historical lineage, classical as well as Christian. He also tailors his tract to his female audience by including among his list of worthies three women of antiquity: Tamyris, Irene, and Marcia, the same trio singled out from Pliny's *Natural History* by Boccaccio.[135] Whereas Marcia was celebrated for her portraits (including self-portraits produced with the aid of a mirror), Tamyris was famed for her effigies of what Butzbach calls false gods, "falsorum deorum dearumque," especially a painting of Diana of Ephesus.[136] In contrast, Gertrude devotes her ingenuity to depicting the "true God, Jesus Christ, and the effigy and deeds of his mother, the most glorious Virgin, and the most beautiful of womankind and the saints in the heavenly kingdom."[137] Most notable among the Christian counterparts to pagan idols are the icons of Christ and the Virgin, at least one of which, Butzbach reports, his fellow monk Veit of Moravia has witnessed firsthand in Prague.[138] To the ancient practitioners of painting, Butzbach contrasts Veronica, who, in holding her veil to Christ's face, collaborated in the making of the first *vera eikon,* an *acheiropoietos* that, unlike an idol, was not made by human hands.[139]

Butzbach's history of art leaves a woman such as Gertrude Buchel in a paradoxical position. Like the idols he is compelled to condemn, her work is handmade; it cannot claim miraculous origins or powers. At the same time, in singing her praises, he compromises the very humility he would have her handiwork exemplify. Illuminators of Boccaccio's *De claris mulieribus* solved the problem by depicting Tamyris painting, not an idol, but an icon of the Virgin and Child (Fig. 116). Butzbach's solution echoes a long Benedictine tradition: in contributing to liturgical performance, Gertrude's artistry serves the *opus Dei.*[140] Among her

Fig. 116. Tamyris painting an icon of the Virgin and Child, detail, Paris, Bibliothèque Nationale, Ms. fr. 12420, f. 86r.

accomplishments, Butzbach singles out her illumination of the choir books transcribed by his fellow monks Gerhard and Peter.[141] The convent's chronicle also credits her with having written and illuminated six choir books as well as several smaller compendia of prayers: "Before she was elected to be abbess, she wrote our six large parchment choir books that we still have, two graduals and four antiphonaries; she also painted with her own hand the large golden letters in these same books."[142] But what prompted Butzbach to write his tract in the first place was Gertrude's gift to him and his fellow monks of "little hearts of our most blessed Savior and Redeemer."[143] According to Butzbach, the hearts—most likely small drawings like those from Eichstätt—were conveyed to Maria Laach by Gertrude's confessor, Thomas von Wied, abbot of the monastery from 1512 to 1529.[144]

The liturgical manuscripts associated with Gertrude can no longer be traced.[145] To judge from a German translation of the Benedictine Rule for nuns of the Bursfelde Congregation, signed by Gertrude and dated 1497, Butzbach's praise outstripped her talents (Fig. 117).[146] The decoration consists solely of two brightly colored *fleuronné* initials. Butzbach nonetheless likened Gertrude to the "most subtle" of engravers, Israhel von Meckenem, a startling contrast to Sabina Pirckheimer's ready admission of Dürer's aesthetic superiority.[147] Even if Butzbach's encomium is little more than rhetorical exaggeration, his treatise, like Sabina's letters, points to a dramatic change in the standards by which images were evaluated. In setting Gertrude's painting and penmanship in a historical continuum, he ini-

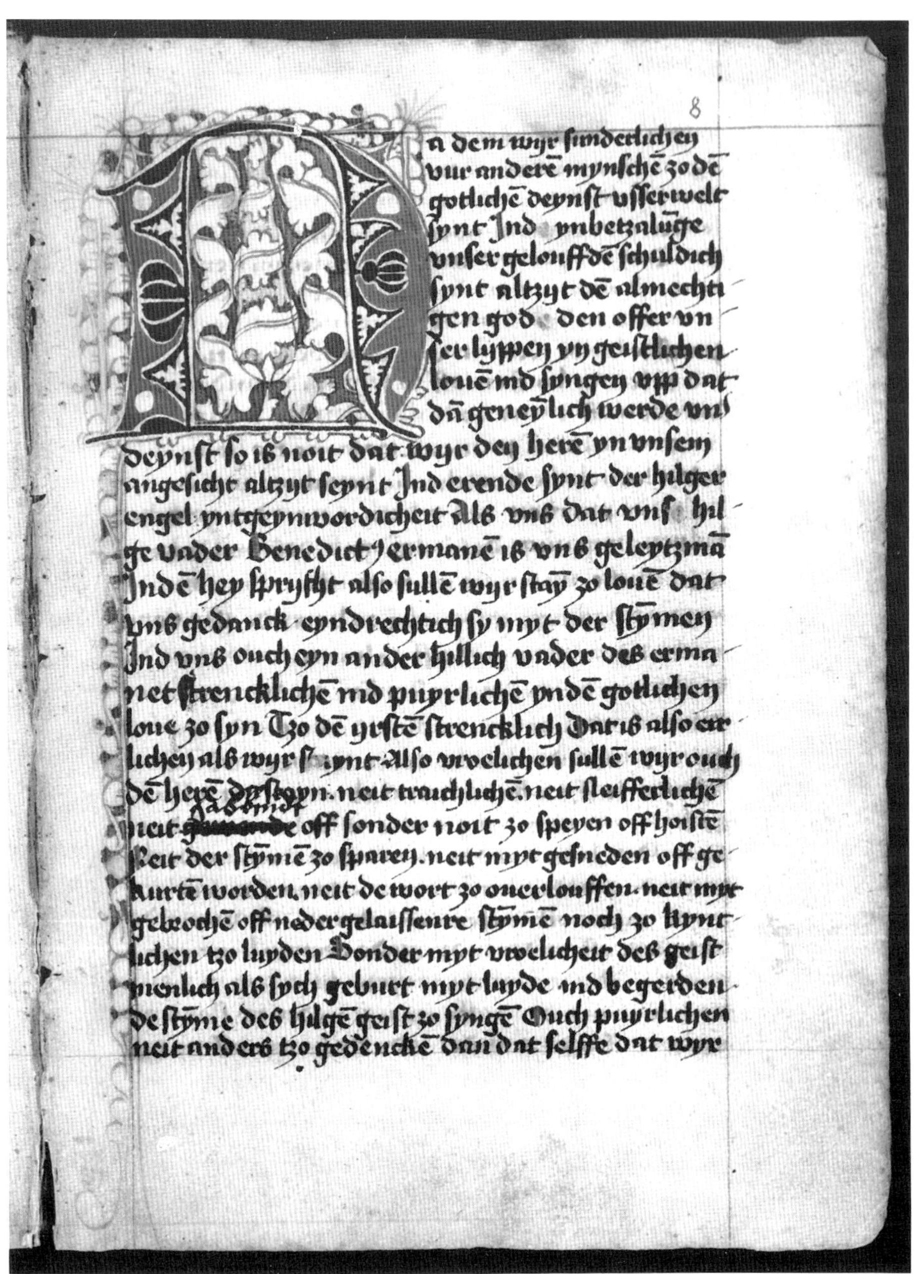

Fig. 117. Gertrude Buchel, Benedictine Rule, 1497, Staatsbibliothek zu Berlin—Preußischer Kulturbesitz, Ms. Germ. 4°555, f. 8r.

tiates the history of German art history by inserting the work of a woman into the discipline as we have come to define it, an account of the making of art extending from the past to the present. How ironic, then, that our own histories have found next to no place for women like Gertrude and her anonymous contemporaries.

Despite the Reformation and changing patterns of patronage and piety, the nuns of St. Walburg continued to produce manuscripts and devotional images well into the modern period. The account book for 1552–53 belonging to the abbess Margaretha von Seckendorf records payments for animal skins, presumably for parchment.[148] One of the convent's sixteenth-century prayer books includes a set of twenty-two initials historiated with prints cut to size and pasted in, including two representations of the Sacred Heart.[149] By the seventeenth century, the nuns had to provide their own liturgical books. To judge from their colophons, the gradual and antiphonary from St. Walburg occupied Maria Magdalena Hübschin for much of the last ten years of her life. Although salvaging scraps from medieval manuscripts may have been a means of saving time and money, it may also have provided visual reminders of the convent's tradition in the arts. Certainly if one wishes to find analogies for the borders in the drawings from St. Walburg, one need look no further than the fragments that survive, pasted into the later books.

In the seventeenth century, the nuns continued to copy liturgical books, embroider vestments, and produce devotional images, all despite the ravages of the Thirty Years' War. According to an eyewitness account in the convent's archives, in 1634, only three years after the church was rebuilt, Swedish troops ransacked the convent and tried to burn it to the ground. The Swedes seized the abbess Helena from her deathbed and took her, with several other nuns, to Regensburg to be held for ransom, which the nuns raised by pawning a silver lamp and a statue of the Madonna. Both the abbess and the Madonna were recovered; the lamp, however, was not.[150] Klara Staiger, prioress of the Augustinian nuns of Mariastein bei Eichstätt, who took refuge with her nuns at St. Walburg when their own convent was looted and then destroyed by Swedish troops in 1633–34, noted in her diary for February 9, 1637: "Sister Monica Fischerin (the *Malerin*) began with great trouble to make models and to paint little pictures, all of which handiwork also has been burned and destroyed."[151] As at the end of the Middle Ages, in the most troubled days of the early modern period the production of devotional drawings remained an indispensable part of the nuns' monastic routine.[152]

CONCLUSION: VISION VERSUS SUPERVISION

LIKE THE DRAWINGS AND CUTTINGS from St. Walburg, the art of female monasticism often survives only as an assortment of fragments. The indifference or even hostility of historians, more than the vicissitudes of time, has consigned much of it to oblivion or neglect. Often condemned as the naive expression of a supposedly unsophisticated spirituality, the material culture of convents has made little headway on the "high road" of art history, a fate that tells us more about the discipline than about the artifacts themselves.

As one of the few sets of small-scale, single-leaf devotional images that can be securely affiliated with a single hand or scriptorium, the drawings from St. Walburg invite contextual inquiry. If they nonetheless resist it, that is in part because they stand outside the aesthetic and stylistic categories that, from the Renaissance on, have defined art (and art history) as indifferent to function. Yet the drawings are not simply the poor relatives of other images, medieval or modern, such as woodcuts and emblems. They maintain their independence from mainstream artistic production in late medieval Franconia.

In the context of the abbey itself, the drawings from St. Walburg display a remarkable consistency, in the messages they convey and the strategies they employ to configure them. Less indicative of an individual idiom than a manner of expression shared by the draftswoman and her audience, the drawings participate in a common conventual mode. To this mode, the *Malerin* of St. Walburg gave her own inflection. Her art may have been unsophisticated technically, but artfulness was hardly its aim.

The principal characteristics of the *Malerin*'s style—including, but not limited to, unpolished technique, decorative and often repetitive patterning, and a general sweetness of sentiment—fit the common conception of "folk art." Under this rubric *Nonnenarbeiten* have been both celebrated and condemned. The term "folk art," however, is misleading (and in itself problematic). In content—not just iconography per se, but the entire apparatus of signification that the images set in motion—the drawings from St. Walburg prove anything but "popular." [1] On the contrary, in asserting religious privilege and exaltation, the majority are incontrovertibly exclusive, addressed and accessible only to initiates. They have little, if anything, in common with the images of "popular piety," itself an undifferentiated term not readily applicable to many categories of late medieval art, including devotional prints.[2]

The drawings from St. Walburg must be situated in an array of shifting attitudes and aspirations. Even as they draw on established conventions, they transfigure them. Their programmatic concerns play off the complex dialogue between corporate and individual experience. Moreover, they challenge some of the categories that dominate the debate over devotional imagery, not just for nuns, but for the laity at large. The ongoing argument over the characteristics of the *Andachtsbild* that sets text against image, private against public, original against imitation, or lay against monastic depends on terminology that would not have been meaningful to those for whom the imagery was made. For all their appeal to personal, even mystical, piety, the images from St. Walburg are rooted in references to the corporate experience of the cult, be it of the Eucharist or of relics. And, despite the textual evidence that must be invoked to explain them, the majority of the drawings cannot be conceived of as illustrations (not that illustration itself is a simple phenomenon). For none of the images has a defining source text. They incorporate inscriptions, without depicting their content; the involuted texts are integral to the images, without, however, explaining them. In the devotions inspired by the drawings, the meanings and memories of texts, together with associations codified by ritual, informed the process of viewing, just as the recollection of images structured the process of reading.

Without sufficient artistic comparanda, iconographic and stylistic analysis cannot account for the drawings from St. Walburg. Individually, the drawings are ingenious, even idiosyncratic; as a group, they are both unparalleled and unprecedented. More distinctive than their innovative imagery, however, is the consistency with which they self-consciously articulate and respond to the theme of the visual in the devotions of women. In addition to providing instruments of instruction, the drawings authorize themselves and, by extension, other works of art, as sources of religious authenticity independent of any miraculous origin. In the process, they craft an experiential practice of prayer in which the viewing of images complements the reading of texts as both the means and the end of devotional activity.

Seen in this light, the drawings come alive—not simply as documents that reflect religious life in a single late medieval convent community, but as icons of the nuns' religious vocation in all its complexity. The images testify unexpectedly to the community's complex visual culture, which at St. Walburg, as elsewhere, comprehended both the artifacts themselves and the conventions and rituals that governed how they were seen as well as how they were made. Integral to religious exercises that, in turn, were linked to the convent's liturgical and devotional life, the drawings underscore the systematic character of the convent's spiritual concerns and the extent to which images of all kinds participated in its devotional routines. They testify to the vital place of images in the full spectrum of the abbey's religious observances: from meditation, consecration, and the celebration of the sacraments to the cult of saints and the integration of prayer and work.

Through their compelling visual rhetoric, the drawings from St. Walburg champion the faculty of sight in ways a text, however inherently visual, never could.[3] Yet their appeal to the eye does not take the form of a pictorial illusion designed to conjure up the consciousness of an absent or illusory reality.[4] Anything but naturalistic in manner, the drawings nevertheless cultivate an aggressive immediacy of affect closely geared to their devotional context. As orchestrated by the drawings, the observance of prayer becomes literally a process of observing.

To our eyes, unaccustomed to seeing the world through the veil of visions, the drawings may appear obscure, perhaps even arcane. For the nuns of St. Walburg, however, they were hardly hermetic. The nuns dwelt on neither the occult nor the mysterious. The drawings gave them the means to achieve numinous transparency and presence, an immediate point of entry to a world that lay beyond ordinary experience. Not that the drawings can be conceived as scripts for visions, any more than the biographies of female visionaries can be regarded as eyewitness accounts or transcripts of experience. But we should not think of each drawing as a rebus, a visual puzzle whose symbolic correspondences we are to decode—the language of "this stands for that" or of "signifier and signified." If anything, the drawings, like much devotional imagery, are designed to collapse such distinctions, to the point of closing the gap between the self and their subject. Unlike signs, which are an index of absence, the drawings seek to establish a reciprocal presence, of Christ to the viewer and of the viewer to Christ, a mutual regard enacted by the imagery itself.

Devotional literature dictates that pleasure lies beyond, rather than in, the text, seducing the reader, even as it subscribes to the Augustinian notion that everything is to be used and nothing enjoyed—except God. By definition, the devotee seeks to transcend the word to reach the Logos itself. In contrast, postmodern theories of representation posit the limits of referentiality: symbols are unmasked as signs, metaphors as allegories. In visual terms, this mode of reading dictates that seeing is no longer believing. Nothing is "natural," let alone supernatural. Visual experience itself is translated into discourse; we no longer look at images but "read" them.[5] In this framework, it is argued, any appeal to the visual becomes suspect as an attempt to sanction a given account of experience over the discourses that might otherwise be seen as informing it. Subjected to scrutiny, the notions of sight and visibility are exposed as metaphors masking the illusion of truth:[6] so much so that the metaphor of "making visible," which until recently defined the project of feminist historians who sought to bring women into the historical "limelight," itself becomes suspect.[7]

In the study of devotional imagery, "vision" and "visual experience" are inescapable, if problematic, terms. As the study of *Andachtsbilder* has moved beyond the analysis of iconography to include the investigation of "the beholder's share," it has inevitably come to focus on the responses of medieval viewers.[8] From a postmodern perspective, however, any analysis that takes individual experience as its starting point seems outmoded, if not outdated.[9] Interiority itself—the very heart of the images from Eichstätt—along with other forms and vehicles of subjectivity and personal expression, whether authorship or intentionality, is decried as a myth.[10] At the very least, we are more inclined to view all forms of experience, including mysticism, as the outcome rather than the starting point of a complex cultural process and can more readily accept—as would, in fact, most medieval observers—that the visions of medieval nuns were highly mediated, screened through many a metaphorical veil.[11] The images put into their hands did not serve simply as points of departure for flights of devotional fancy; like all devotional imagery they controlled and channeled such flights along institutionally acceptable trajectories.

More than most phenomena, mysticism poses the problem of the respective roles of literary and religious tradition in the formation of experience.[12] Other than speaking in tongues—to employ the categories invoked by mystics themselves—the only alternatives are silence and the blinding light of interior illumination, in either case a dulling or even a negation of sensory experience.[13] In the realm of representation, however, there is no such thing as "raw" experience or the proverbial tabula rasa: whether visual or verbal, ocular or oral, conventions inevitably intervene to condition or compromise authenticity of expression. At the same time, however, conventional forms, mediated by institutional mechanisms, lend authority to experience, just as an eyewitness account confers an aura of authenticity on whatever it relates. In devotional practice, authenticity and authority were inextricably linked: the process of imitation required that the reader or viewer assimilate her experience to the forms, even the stereotypes, of a model.

Deceptively simple as it sounds, to interpret the drawings from St. Walburg on their own terms, we have to suspend our disbelief and adopt an alien conception of viewing, so that we see as we read rather than read as we see. The drawings belong to a culture in which sight had come to complement contemplation as an accepted avenue of insight and access to the divine.[14] Moreover, they open our eyes to another way of envisioning the history of sight itself. For all the recent interest in "visuality"—a historically and socially contingent conception of vision akin to Baxandall's notion of the "period eye"—the relation between medieval and modern modes of vision remains vexed, in large measure because, the history of optics and perspective aside, it remains virtually unexamined.[15] Focusing on the origins of modernity, historians as diverse in viewpoint as Norman Bryson, Martin Jay, and Robert Scribner use the Middle Ages as a foil for the modern constructions of visuality that form the subject of their own critiques.[16] According to Bryson, medieval images are essentially indistinguishable from texts and hence leave little room for questions of vision or viewer response. In his formulation, "Prior to the Renaissance neither the mosaic art of the South nor the glass-painting of the North radically questions the dispensation that had legitimated the image as a place of textual *relay*." Only the "expansion beyond the minimal schema" entailed by naturalism "precipitate[d] . . . a crisis in the [medieval] visual regime." [17] On closer inspection, however, Bryson's characterization of medieval images proves no less idealized than the naturalized notion of post-Renaissance art he sets out to deconstruct. Protestant reformers envisioned medieval images in exactly opposite terms: as illegitimate, even illicit, affronts to the authority of "sola scriptura," the word alone.[18]

Similarly problematic (and also linked to modern efforts to distinguish the modern from the medieval) are the accounts of "popular religion" offered by historians, such as Robert Scribner, who identify the visual element in late medieval spirituality with popular forms of piety. In so doing, they reiterate the rhetoric of reform, without, however, considering the consequences of their critique.[19] Their line of argument, echoing medieval theologians who maintained that women, in their reliance on images, gave vent to an innate corporeality and irrationality, implicitly depreciates the religious practices of women in which visual experience, much of it molded by images, played a central role.[20]

The visual culture of female monasticism need not, however, be defined in such pejorative terms. At issue is not women's nature but that of the institutions in which they lived, either by choice or by necessity. One cannot overlook the ways in which the conventions of female spirituality encouraged cloistered women to transfer their affections by way of sublimation to Christ as child or bridegroom.[21] The drawings from St. Walburg themselves explore both these possibilities. Far more important, though less familiar, are the complex conventions peculiar to the culture of female monasticism and the means by which women assimilated them until they became second nature. In this process of devotional discipline, objects such as the drawings from St. Walburg played an indispensable role, controlling as well as liberating the religious imagination. The larger, if not altogether determining, context was provided by the *cura monialium,* or the pastoral care of nuns.[22] Through its vast vernacular apparatus, embracing sermons, tracts, prayer manuals, and the liturgy, nuns were versed in a fixed body of texts, much of whose imagery they would have committed to memory. The edifying texts in the library of St. Walburg defined the context in which the nuns assimilated a fixed repertory of devotional protocols that governed their daily routine.

The devotional leaves from St. Walburg self-consciously manipulate these habits of worship, drawing on a reservoir of imagery, even as they reinforce and reshape it. They describe the mystical marriage less as the union than as the reunion of Christ with the soul. Remembrance (*recordatio*), defined along Augustinian lines as the recollection of archetypes implanted in the mind, becomes the model for meditation, with the heart (*cor*) as both its locus and goal.[23] In casting the heart as the focal point of union, the drawings define contemplation, not as an ecstatic exploration or ascetic ascent, but as an act of restoration and remembrance, a turning inward toward the depths of the soul.

The interrelation of sight and subjectivity forms one of the drawings' principal themes. Both subjects come together in the Song of Songs, the primary script for the devotional drama enacted by the nuns.[24] Given the complex place of the Song of Songs in medieval spirituality, we should be wary of reducing female piety to little more than the sublimation of sexual desire, if only because in so doing, we ape one of the marginalizing strategies employed by its least sympathetic medieval (and modern) critics.[25] Bridal mysticism both exploited and encouraged analogies between sexuality and spirituality by furnishing a model for the relationship between Christ and the nun and, no less important, for the liaison between the nuns and their spiritual advisers.[26] As Bernard McGinn has pointed out, however, "What is involved here," at least from the mystic's point of view, "is not so much the disguising of erotic language . . . as the full and direct use of certain forms of erotic expression for a different purpose—the transformation of all human desire in terms of what the mystic believes to be its true source."[27] Moreover, transformative erotic imagery was hardly unique to female spirituality; it was both supplied and shaped by a tradition of exegesis developed primarily by male mystics and commentators.[28] Although medieval interpreters never denied that the Song of Songs had a literal sense, nuns rarely, if ever, experienced this text as a unity unencumbered by commentary.[29] It came to them in snippets, embedded in exegesis, embroidered in homilies, or, most often, loud and clear, in liturgical song.[30] They developed their devotions in the framework provided by scriptural metaphors combined in complex and ever-changing catenae that interlinked images from texts as diverse as the Song of Songs and the Book of Revelation. By a process of inversion, what we regard as secondary or even tertiary readings served as the starting points for impressions that then shaped devotional experience. Rather than simply sublimate sexual desire, biblical bridal imagery enabled the expression of affective devotions in bodily terms.

In the drawings from St. Walburg the heart serves as an emblem of passion, the nun's as well as Christ's, to the point that the two can no longer be distinguished. This figure of union could be read as recapitulating a model of spiritual viewing defined in explicitly heterosexual terms, the penetrating glance piercing the vaginalike wound in Christ's flank (a play on the similarity of *vulnus,* "wound," and *vulva*).[31] The drawings, however, resist so reductive a reading.[32] Certainly they invite the onlooker's gaze, soliciting a kind of spiritual voyeurism. But the inspection they elicit does not conform to the "gaze" as feminist theory initially defined it, with the woman as the passive object of male surveillance and construction.[33] To begin with, as images made by and for women, the drawings posit a different conception of beholding, one in which what we regard as traditional roles are reversed. Even as the nun plays the part of the *sponsa Christi,* her active glance penetrates the body of Christ. If anything, the Savior's body—open, passive, suffering—is conceived in "feminine" terms.[34] Where we are inclined to read the opening in Christ's side as a fetish or an objectification of the body, nuns regarded it as an invitation to introspection, a literal looking inward. They likened the wound to the portal or entrance leading toward the womblike interior of his heart. The space opened up by the perforation supplied an enclosed "nest," "cleft," "house," or "womb" in which the soul could seek refuge and protection, all metaphors that emphasized the experience of enclosure, and all part of a much broader spectrum of imagery remarkable for its extraordinary lability.[35]

It is tempting to see in the drawings from St. Walburg a medieval response to the twentieth-century search for modes of representation particular to women, ways of seeing and experiencing the body that reject dominant paradigms. Identifying this project with the quest for "carnal knowing" and "embodied knowledge," Margaret Miles, echoing others, has called on us "to see and read the female body as the intimate reflection and articulation of women's subjective experience."[36] Yet to oppose a quintessentially female subjectivity to the objectifications of misogyny runs the risk of defining the difference between male and female in terms of a gendered distinction between body and soul. It also does violence to the history of Christian spirituality.[37] The doctrine of the Incarnation alone enjoins the opposite conclusion. In Christian theology and devotional practice, especially of the later Middle Ages, the flesh was not "scorned [or] the body marginalized in the project of a 'spiritual' journey."[38] So Manichean a formulation misreads the intensely somatic language of mainstream medieval spirituality, whether expressed in word or in image, from no later than the twelfth century onward. Fear of the flesh as the seat of death, decay, and sexuality informed Christian attitudes toward the body, especially the female body.[39] Yet as Caroline Bynum has argued, this identification not only constrained women but also permitted and ordained, perhaps for lack of an alternative, an imitation of Christ that women enacted in their flesh.[40] The path to salvation lay *through* the body, above all Christ's corpus embodied in the Host. In their emphasis on the Eucharist as the vehicle for union with Christ, the mystical bridegroom, the drawings from St. Walburg make an analogous argument.

In tracing the drawings from St. Walburg back to sources in orthodox piety and practice, we should not underestimate their unconventional, even nonconformist, character. Whether they can be considered the visual equivalent of the "écriture féminine" posited by Luce Irigaray and Julia Kristeva, however, remains an open question.[41] In transforming received traditions, visual or verbal, the drawings bear witness to the coexistence of habits of dependence and independence. They owe their creation less to the nuns' inability to produce or obtain conventional images than to their need to supplement art from "outside" with images that met their own special needs.[42]

The isolation of the community of St. Walburg, however, should not be exaggerated. Nuns were not insulated from the outside world, nor did that world leave them alone. The abbey's cuttings and tapestries, even if they survive only as scraps, testify to a continuous, if at times attenuated, tradition of production and patronage spanning at least three centuries. The dynamics of monastic reform testify to the give-and-take that characterizes convent patronage and piety. Benefactors such as the bishops of Eichstätt were generous, if not lavish, in their donations to the convent. The nuns, in turn, maintained a lively exchange with spiritual advisers and relatives. In this interchange, images played no small part, serving as tokens of esteem, affection, obligation, and, on occasion, indoctrination. Donations from episcopal patrons such as Johann III von Eych, William of Reichenau, and Christoph von Pappenheim created visible reminders of the mutual obligations established between the parties. The books from which the cuttings were taken not only sealed those bonds but also gave them substance and meaning. The bishop provided the nuns with priests and pastors; in return, the nuns prayed for the salvation of their benefactors. In all these ceremonies, the liturgical books dismembered in the modern period would have played an indispensable role.

The drawings from St. Walburg express a similar set of reciprocal relations. In elaborating the language of the liturgy, they redefine ecclesiastical imagery in forms appropriate to the nuns' situation and status. Much as we would like to interpret the drawings as affirmations of spiritual autonomy or even as evidence of resistance to prevailing norms of gender and authority, we cannot construe them as "self-representations" of female spirituality. Religious women did not see with "innocent" or uninformed eyes; on that ground alone we should forswear designating their drawings childlike and naive. Conditioned by the context in which they were made—above all, by the dictates of monastic reform and pastoral care—the drawings elaborate images injected into enclosure by male advisers. The claustration of nuns enforced autonomy without necessarily allowing independence; keeping out of sight did not preclude supervision.

On its face, an ancient abbey such as St. Walburg seems an unlikely place for the production of devotional drawings with a strong mystical tenor. We more readily associate the mendicant orders with the religiosity assumed to characterize the later Middle Ages: independent, personal, and subjective, with private devotion among its most characteristic expressions.[43] In this framework women, in particular mystics, visionaries, and quasi-religious women such as Beguines, are singled out for their "anti-institutional or a-institutional" tendencies.[44] As a radical expression of flight from the world, their ecstatic behavior exemplifies rejection of, and in some cases even resistance to, cultural norms. In a prophetic mode, female spirituality also provided seers with a platform from which they could criticize established politics and religion.[45]

Against this backdrop, orthodox accounts of late medieval monasticism typically paint a picture of decline and decay.[46] Yet introspective experience and organized religion were no more inherently at odds in the fifteenth century than they had been during the High Middle Ages, the period that witnessed the efflorescence of new monastic orders. In the context of monastic reform, the opposite often obtained (even as what was allowed and accepted as "mysticism" was itself redefined in keeping with a new emphasis on corporate, liturgical piety).[47] Under the aegis of reform, female spirituality did not by definition constitute a religious counterculture, nor, in evaluating its art, need we choose between resistance and repression, religious, political, or psychological.[48] In the words of Hans Robert Jauß, "How inappropriate and even misleading it is to judge the literature and art of this [i.e., the medieval] period *exclusively* according to the modern, i.e., categories of affirmation or negation of the existing order."[49] In contrast, the drawings from St. Walburg suggest the possibility of programmatic mysticism, a process of institutionalization that constituted part of their purpose. They both affirm and attest to the success of reform, at least at St. Walburg, and the vital role images played in realizing it.

Medieval nuns developed their distinctive visual culture within constraints that severely limited their agency. They and their images nevertheless came to exemplify the practical and experiential mysticism that established the benchmark for the lay spirituality of the later Middle Ages. In championing art as a vehicle for devotional experience, they both responded to and rejected traditions of pastoral care that regarded the visual arts either as a trap for the curious or as a concession to bodily, as opposed to intellectual, sight. Their experiences can hardly be characterized as "normal," but they nonetheless proved normative.

Produced on the cusp of the medieval and early modern eras, the drawings from St. Walburg invite interpretation as the culminating or concluding point in a long tradition of monastic exegesis and devotional practice. Viewed in these terms, the images inevitably exemplify either a denouement or decline, examples of what Huizinga so memorably called "ideas crystallizing into images."[50] Seen from our vantage point, they appear in a different, but no less linear, perspective, making up part of what so often is called the "background" of modernity. To comprehend the images from St. Walburg in either of these frameworks, however, is to insert them into a story of art in which they never played a part. Instead, we should take them on their own terms, as images with a raison d'être in the world of enclosure. The nuns took for granted that their images could serve as stepping stones on the path toward union with Christ, their mystical bridegroom. For us, they provide a less exalted, if no less unusual, pleasure: the unforeseen opportunity to see through the eyes of a community of Franconian nuns at the turn of the sixteenth century.

ABBREVIATIONS

AA.SS	J. Bollandus and G. Henschenius, *Acta sanctorum . . . editio novissima,* ed. J. Carnadet et al., Paris, 1863–.
CC.SL	*Corpus Christianorum: Series Latina*
CC.CM	*Corpus Christianorum: Continuatio Mediaevalis*
DS	*Dictionnaire de spiritualité,* Paris, 1937–.
LCI	*Lexikon der christlichen Ikonographie,* ed. E. Kirschbaum, 8 vols., Rome, 1968–76.
PL	*Patrologiae cursus completus: Series latina,* ed. J.-P. Migne, 221 vols., Paris, 1841–64.
RDK	*Reallexikon zur deutschen Kunstgeschichte,* ed. O. Schmidt et al., Stuttgart and Munich, 1937–.
^{2}VL	*Die deutsche Literatur des Mittelalters: Verfasserlexikon,* ed. K. Ruh et al., Berlin, 2d rev. ed., 1978–.

NOTES

Preface and Acknowledgments

1. For example, J. F. Hamburger, "Art, Enclosure, and the *Cura monialium:* Prolegomena in the Guise of a Postscript," *Gesta* 31 (1992): 108–34; P. Zimmer, *Die Funktion und Ausstattung des Altares auf der Nonnenempore: Beispiele zum Bildgebrauch in Frauenklöstern aus dem 13. bis 16. Jahrhundert,* Cologne, 1991; and R. Gilchrist, *Gender and Material Culture: The Archaeology of Religious Women,* London, 1994.

2. See J. F. Hamburger, "The Visual and the Visionary: The Changing Role of the Image in Late Medieval Monastic Devotions," *Viator* 20 (1989): 161–82; idem, *The Rothschild Canticles: Art and Mysticism in Flanders and the Rhineland ca. 1300,* New Haven, Conn., 1990; C. Frugoni, "Le mistiche, le visioni e l'iconographia: Rapporti ed influssi," in *Temi e problemi nella mistica femminile trecentesca,* Todi, 1983, 139–79; E. Vavra, "Bildmotiv und Frauenmystik: Funktion und Rezeption," in *Frauenmystik im Mittelalter;* D. Rigaux, "Dire la foi avec des images, un affaire de femmes?" in *La Religion de ma mère: Les Femmes et la transmission de la foi,* ed. J. Delumeau, Paris, 1992, 71–90; J. E. Ziegler, *Sculpture of Compassion: The Pietà and the Beguines in the Southern Low Countries, c. 1300–c. 1600,* Institute Historique Belge de Rome: Études d'Histoire de l'Art, 6, Brussels, 1992; P. Vandenbroeck, "Zwischen Selbsterniedrigung und Selbstvergottung: Bilderwelt und Selbstbild religiöser Frauen in den südlichen Niederländen: Eine erste Erkundigung," *De zeventiende eeuw* 5 (1989): 67–88; and idem, *Le Jardin clos de l'âme: L'Imaginaire des religieuses dans les Pays-Bas du Sud, depuis le 13e siècle,* Brussels, 1994.

3. M. R. Miles, *Image as Insight: Visual Understanding in Western Christianity and Secular Culture,* Boston, 1985, 64. The recent issue of *Arte Cristiana* 82 (1994) devoted in its entirety to "Vocazione artistica dei religiosi" contained no article on nuns as artists.

4. The notion of visual culture, introduced into art history and given wider currency by M. Baxandall, *Painting and Experience in Renaissance Italy,* Oxford, 1972, receives a new inflection, less closely allied with social history than with semiotics, in *Visual Culture: Images and Interpretations,* ed. N. Bryson, M. A. Holly, and K. Moxey, Hanover, N.H., 1994.

5. In its attention to visual culture, my approach differs from that of previous studies of individual female monastic houses, such as *Das Graduale von Sankt Katharinenthal: Kommentar zur Faksimile-Ausgabe des Graduale von Sankt Katharinenthal,* Lucerne, 1983; H. Appuhn, "Der Auferstandene und das heilige Blut zu Wienhausen," *Niederdeutsche Beiträge zur Kunstgeschichte* 1 (1961): 73–138; K. Hengevoss-Dürkop, *Skulptur und Frauenkloster: Studien zu Bildwerken der Zeit um 1300 aus Frauenklöstern des ehemaligen Fürstentums Lüneburg,* Artefact, 7, Berlin, 1994; A. Lindblom, *Kult och Konst i Vadstena Kloster,* Kungl. Vitterhets Historie och Antikvitets Aka-

demiens Handligar: Antivariska Serien, 14, Uppsala, 1965; and *Faszination eines Klosters: 750 Jahre Zisterzienerinnen-Abtei Lichtenthal,* ed. H. Siebenmorgen, Sigmaringen, 1995.

6. For periodization and the history of interiority, see D. Aers, "A Whisper in the Ear of Early Modernists; or, Reflections on Literary Critics Writing the 'History of the Subject,'" in *Culture and History, 1350–1600: Essays on English Communities, Identities, and Writing,* ed. D. Aers, Detroit, 1992, 177–202.

7. For one critique, see M. Bal and N. Bryson, "Semiotics and Art History," *Art Bulletin* 73 (1991): 174–208.

8. D. LaCapra, "Rethinking Intellectual History and Reading Texts," in *Rethinking Intellectual History: Texts, Contexts, Language,* Ithaca, N.Y., 1983, esp. 35.

9. Ibid., 64.

Introduction

1. For a brief discussion of the drawing, see F. O. Büttner, *Imitatio pietatis: Motive der christlichen Ikonographie als Modele der Verähnlichung,* Berlin, 1983, 150, 215, and fig. 162.

2. The measurements given in *Das Schnütgen-Museum: Eine Auswahl,* Cologne, 1968, are inaccurate; I am grateful to the director of the museum, Dr. H. Westermann-Angerhausen, for providing me with the correct dimensions.

3. The image evokes the popular and oft-illustrated story of St. Bernard from Conrad of Eberbach's *Exordium magnum Cisterciense,* II.7, which describes how a monk of Morimond witnessed Bernard embraced by an image of the crucified Christ. See B. P. McGuire, *The Difficult Saint,* Kalamazoo, Mich., 1991, esp. chap. 8.

4. See M. Pastoureau, "'Ceci est mon sang': Le Christianisme médiéval et la couleur rouge," in *Le Pressoir mystique: Actes du colloque de Recloses, 27 mai 1989,* ed. D. Alexandre-Bidon, Paris, 1990, 43–56; R. Suntrup, "Liturgische Farbendeutung im Mittelalter und in der frühen Neuzeit," in *Symbole des Alltags, Alltags der Symbole: Festschrift für Harry Kühnel zum 65. Geburtstag,* ed. G. Blaschitz et al., Graz, 1992, esp. 459–61; and C. Meier and R. Suntrup, "Zum Lexikon der Farbendeutung im Mittelalter: Einführung zu Gegenstand und Methoden sowie Probeartikel aus dem Farbbereich 'Rot,'" *Frühmittelalterliche Studien* 21 (1987): 390–478. N. Bériou, "De la lecture aux épousailles: Les Images dans la communication de la Parle de Dieu au XIIIe siècle," *Cristianesimo nella storia* 14 (1993), 546 n.25, cites a sermon that refers to a crucifix whose corpus was covered in blood.

5. For what little is known of Konrad, see D. Ladish-Grube, "Konrad von Eßlingen," ²VL, vol. V, 170.

6. For the convent and its history, see the exh. cat. *750 Jahre Dominikanerinnenkloster Adelhausen,* Freiburg, 1985.

7. For the precis of the sermon, see "Die Chronik der Anna von Munzingen," 189–91: "Das dritte die röte: wan die farwe sines blůtes wider verwetet vnd wider núweret das götlich bilde, das in die sele getruckt ist; das bilde mag der mensche nieme vertilgen, er kome in himelrich oder in helle. Wir tůnt aber dicke mit vnsern súnden als der des keysers schilt neme, vnd in truckte in die lachen, so wurde dz bilde vermasget vnd blibe doch an im selber, das wider verwet vnd wider firnisset die röti des blůtes." See also E. Krebs, "Die Mystik in Adelhausen: Eine vergleichende Studie über die 'Chronik' der Anna von Munzingen und die Thaumatographische Literatur des 13. und 14. Jahrhunderts als Beitrag zur Geschichte der Mystik im Predigerorden," in *Festgabe Heinrich Finke gewidmet,* Münster, 1904, 45–105; and W. Blank, "Anna von Munzingen," ²VL, vol. I, 365–66.

8. For the theological sources of such imagery, see R. Javalet, *Image et ressemblance au douzième siècle de saint Anselme à Alain de Lille,* 2 vols., Paris, 1967. For God as an artist, see F. Ohly,

"*Deus geometra:* Skizzen zur Geschichte einer Vorstellung von Gott," in *Tradition als historische Kraft: Festschrift Karl Hauck,* Berlin, 1982, 1–42.

9. For the mass production of imagery in Germany, aside from prints, see W. Krönig, "Rheinische Vesperbilder aus Leder und ihr Umkreis," *Wallraf-Richartz-Jahrbuch* 24 (1962): 98–101; *Meisterwerke massenhaft: Die Bildhauerwerkstatt des Niklaus Weckmann und die Malerei in Ulm um 1500,* Stuttgart, 1993; F. Arens, "Die ursprüngliche Verwendung gotischer Stein- und Tonmodel mit einem Verzeichnis der Model in mittelrheinische Museen," *Mainzer Zeitschrift: Mittelrheinisches Jahrbuch für Archäologie, Kunst und Geschichte* 66 (1971): 106–31; L. Saurma-Jeltsch, "Auftragsfertigung und Vorratsarbeit: Kriterien zu ihrer Unterscheidung am Beispiel der Werkstatt Diebold Laubers," *Unsere Kunstdenkmäler* 36 (1985): 302–9; and idem, "Buchmalerei in Serie: Zur Frühgeschichte der Vervielfältigungskunst," *Zeitschrift für Schweizerische Archäologie und Kunstgeschichte* 40 (1983): 128–35.

10. As noted by C. von Heusinger, "Studien zur oberrheinischen Buchmalerei und Graphik im Spätmittelalter," Ph.D. diss., Albert-Ludwigs-Universität, Freiburg, 1953, the terms *Nonnenarbeit* and *Nonnenmalerei* were coined by H. Wegener, *Beschreibendes Verzeichnis der deutschen Bilderhandschriften des späten Mittelalters in der Heidelberger Universitäts-Bibliothek,* Leipzig, 1927, and *Beschreibendes Verzeichnis der Miniaturen-Handschriften der preußischen Staatsbibliothek zu Berlin, V: Die deutschen Handschriften,* Leipzig, 1928.

11. As noted by N. H. Ott, *Rechtspraxis und Heilsgeschichte: Zu Überlieferung, Ikonographie und Gebrauchssituation des deutschen "Belial,"* Münchener Texte und Untersuchungen zur deutschen Literatur des Mittelalters, 80, Munich, 1983, 195–202 and 224–29, until recently notions of quality prevented any serious consideration of most illustrated German vernacular manuscripts. For the ways in which feminist criticism has led to a reevaluation of traditional aesthetic criteria, see the essays gathered in *Feminism and Tradition in Aesthetics,* ed. P. Z. Brand and C. Korsmeyer, University Park, Pa., 1995.

12. F. Wormald, "Some Popular Miniatures and Their Rich Relations," in *Miscellanea pro arte: Hermann Schnitzler zur Vollendung der 60. Lebensjahres,* Düsseldorf, 1965, 279–85. Pächt's remarks are included in his 1967 essay "Künstlerische Originalität und ikonographische Erneuerung," in idem, *Methodisches zur kunsthistorischen Praxis: Ausgewählte Schriften,* Munich, 1977, 153–64.

13. For the ugly and grotesque as signs of social stigma, see T. A. Heslop, "Romanesque Painting and Social Distinction: The Magi and the Shepherds," in *England in the Twelfth Century: Proceedings of the 1988 Harlaxton Symposium,* ed. D. Williams, Woodbridge, Suffolk, 1990, 137–52, and R. Mellinkoff, *Outcasts: Signs of Otherness in Northern European Art of the Late Middle Ages,* 2 vols., Berkeley and Los Angeles, 1993. For theological conceptions of ugliness, see P. Michel, *Formosa deformitas: Bewaltigungsformen des Häßlichen in mittelalterlichen Literatur,* Studien zur Germanistik, Anglistik und Komparatistik, 57, Bonn, 1976; and *Die nicht mehr schönen Künste: Grenzphänomene des Ästhetischen,* ed. H. R. Jauß, Poetik und Hermeneutik: Arbeitsergebnisse einer Forschungsgruppe, 3, Munich, 1968, esp. the contributions of Jauß and J. Taubes, both of whom build on E. Auerbach, "*Sermo humilis,*" *Romanische Forschungen* 64 (1952): 304–64. For comparable issues of decorum in representations of the Passion, see F. O. Büttner, "Das Christusbild auf niedrigster Stilhöhe: Ansichtigkeit und Körpersichtigkeit in narrativen Passionsdarstellungen der Jahrzehnte um 1500," *Wiener Jahrbuch für Kunstgeschichte* 46–47 (1993–94): 99–130 and 397–400.

14. For the literature on *Andachtsbilder,* see H. Belting, *Das Bild und sein Publikum im Mittelalter: Form und Funktion früher Bildtafeln der Passion,* Berlin, 1981; R. Haussherr, "Über die Christus-Johannes-Gruppen: Zum Problem 'Andachtsbilder' und deutsche Mystik," in *Beiträge zur Kunst des Mittelalters: Festschrift für Hans Wentzel zum 60. Geburtstag,* Berlin, 1974, 79–103; M. Schawe, "*Fasciculus myrrhae:* Pietà und Hoheslied," *Jahrbuch des Zentralinstituts für Kunstge-*

schichte 5–6 (1989): 161–212, nn.9–10; H. Appuhn, "Das private Andachtsbild: Ein Vorschlag zur kunstgeschichtlichen und volkskundlichen Terminologie," in *Museum und Kulturgeschichte: Festschrift für Wilhelm Hansen,* Münster, 1978, 289–92; and B. Schwering, "Ein Wort zur Terminologie," in *Das Kleine Andachtsbild,* Straelen, 1982, 7–10. For *Andacht* as defined in Middle High German texts, see K.-H. Göttert, "'Devotio-andâht': Frömmigkeitsbegriff und Darstellungsprinzip im legendarischen Erzählen des hohen Mittelalters," in *Zeiten und Formen in Sprache und Dichtung: Festschrift für Fritz Tschirch zum 70. Geburtstag,* ed. K.-H. Schirmer and B. Sowinski, Cologne, 1972.

15. See G. Gugitz, *Das Kleine Andachtsbild in den Österreichischen Gnadestätten in Darstellung, Verbreitung und Brauchtum nebst einer Ikonographie,* Vienna, 1950; E. Launert, "The Small *Andachtsbild:* A Little-Known Aspect of European Religious Art," *Connoisseur* 166 (1967): 164–69; M. Scharfe, *Evangelische Andachtsbilder: Studien zur Intention und Funktion des Bildes in der Frömmigkeitsgeschichte vornehmlich des schwäbischen Raumes,* Veröffentlichungen des Staatlichen Amtes für Denkmalpflege Stuttgart (Reihe C: Volkskunde, 5), Stuttgart, 1968; M. Brauneck, *Religiöse Volkskunst: Votivgaben, Andachtsbilder, Hinterglas, Rosenkranz, Amulette,* Cologne, 1978; G. Luther, *Sinnlichkeit und Heilserwartung: Lucas Cranachs Mariahilfbild und dessen Rezeption im Kleinen Andachtsbild und Bildvotive,* Marburg, 1978; *Klosterarbeiten aus dem Bodensee St. Gallen,* 1986; B. Rothemund, *Barocke Klosterarbeiten,* Autenried, 1982; M. T. Engels, *Das Kleine Andachtsbild: Prägedrucke und Stanzspitzenbilder des 19. Jahrhunderts,* Recklingshausen, 1983; and *"Gold, Perlen und Edel-Gestein . . .": Reliquienkult und Klosterarbeiten im deutschen Südwesten,* Freiburg, 1995.

16. Von Heusinger, 1959, 160, is not unsympathetic; nonetheless, his conclusions are typical. "Die Hände der Nonnen waren geschickt, sauber und fleißig; ihre Arbeiten sind teilweise sogar sehr reizvoll, entwicklungs-geschichtliche bleiben sie aber ohne Bedeutung. . . . Eine eigene typische Art wird ausgebildet, die keine künstlerischen Probleme kennt, keinen anderen Anspruch mehr stellt, als das durch die Lektüre mystischer Schriften schwämerische angeregte Bildbedürfnis der Nonne zu stillen." D. Freedberg, *The Power of Images: Studies in the History and Theory of Response,* Chicago, 1989, integrates such images into a general history of art; his examples, however, are later in date.

17. See H. Kämpf-Jansen, "Kitsch—oder ist die Antithese der Kunst weiblich?" in *Frauen-Bilder-Männer-Mythen: Kunsthistorische Beiträge,* ed. I. Barta, Berlin, 1987, 322–41; and S. Schade and S. Wenk, "Inszenierung des Sehens: Kunst, Geschichte und Geschlechterdifferenz," in *Genus: Zur Geschlechterdifferenz in den Kulturwissenschaften,* ed. H. Bußmann and R. Hof, Stuttgart, 1995, esp. 357–58.

18. Cf. the scathing comments of S. Beissel, "Religiöse Bilder für das katholische Volk," *Stimmen aus Maria Laach* 33 (1887): 456–72, and 58 (1900): 281–94, who blames the most egregious excesses on French, not German, Catholics. Beissel's condemnation formed part of a broader reaction against the proliferation of *Kleine Andachtsbilder,* discussed briefly by Scharfe, 62–64. For a less biased account of French devotional imagery in the nineteenth century, see J. Pirotte, "L'Imagerie de dévotion aux XIXe et XXe siècles et la société ecclésiale," in *L'Image et la production du sacré,* 233–49.

19. See W. Cohn, *Untersuchungen zur Geschichte des deutschen Einblattholzschnittes,* Studien zur deutschen Kunstgeschichte, 302, Strasbourg, 1934; and von Heusinger, 1953; the portions dealing with *Nonnenarbeiten* are epitomized in von Heusinger, "Spätmittelalterliche Buchmalerei in oberrheinischen Frauenklöstern," *Zeitschrift für die Geschichte des Oberrheins* 107 (1959): 136–60. Even A. Spamer, *Das Kleine Andachtsbild vom XIV. bis zum XX. Jahrhundert,* Munich, 1930, pays scant attention to medieval *Nonnenarbeiten,* in part because he sees them as little more than predecessors and analogues of prints. Spamer, however, did not yet know the largest surviving collection of *Nonnenarbeiten,* discovered at Kloster Wienhausen in 1953 and

documented by H. Appuhn and C. von Heusinger, "Der Fund kleiner Andachtsbilder des 13. bis 17. Jahrhunderts im Kloster Wienhausen," *Niederdeutsche Beiträge zur Kunstgeschichte* 4 (1965): 157–238; see also H. Appuhn, *Einführung in die Ikonographie der mittelalterlichen Kunst in Deutschland,* Darmstadt, 1985, 87.

20. For the "prehistory" of emblems, see K. J. Höltgen, "*Arbor, Scala,* und *Fons Vita:* Vorformen devotionaler Embleme in einer mittelenglischen Handschrift (B.M. Add. 37049)," in *Chaucer und seine Zeit: Symposium für Walter F. Schirmer,* Tübingen, 1968, 355–91; and T. W. Ross, "Five Fifteenth-Century 'Emblem' Verses from British Museum Additional Ms. 37049," *Speculum* 32 (1957): 274–82. F. Ohly, "Synagoge und Ecclesia: Typologisches in mittelalterlicher Dichtung," in *Judentum im Mittelalter: Beiträge zum christlich-jüdischen Gesprach,* Miscellanea mediaevalia, 4, Berlin, 1966, 369, once remarked with self-conscious hyperbole that "das Mittelalter endet erst bei Goethe." For the problems posed by periodization, see P. von Moos, "Gefahren des Mittelalterbegriffs: Diagnostische und präventative Aspekte," in *Modernes Mittelalter,* 33–63.

21. Bériou, 545, notes that, with the exception of the Crucifixion, references to images in thirteenth-century sermons are scarce.

Chapter 1

1. For the convent and the cult of St. Walburg, see A. Kirschmann, "Regesten des Klosters St. Walburg in Eichstätt," *Sammelblatt des historischen Vereins Eichstätt* 7 (1892): 38–64; *Die Abtei St. Walburg 1035–1935,* Eichstätt, 1935; *Zum 900jährigen Jubiläum der Abtei St. Walburg in Eichstätt: Historische Beiträge,* ed. K. Ried, Paderborn, 1935; H. Holzbauer, *Mittelalterliche Heiligenverehrung: Heilige Walpurgis,* Eichstätter Studien, NF 5, Kevelaer, 1972; and, for additional bibliography, M. Mengs, ed., *Schrifttum zum Leben und zur Verehrung der Heiligen Walburga († 779),* Eichstätt, 1979; *Aureatum Benedictinum: 1200 Jahre Benediktiner im Bistum Eichstätt,* Katalog zu einer Austellung aus Eichstätter Archiven und Bibliotheken, Eichstätt, 1979, 7–13; and A. Wendehorst, "Eichstätt," *Lexikon des Mittelalters,* vol. III, 1671–73.

2. R.D., "Religiös-Volkskundliches aus St. Walburg: Das volkstümliche Andachtsbild des 15. Jahrhundert," *Walburgis-Blätter* 24 (1936): 54–57.

3. Three of the drawings, the Eucharistic Banquet; the *Arbor virginis,* or Tree of the Virgin; and St. Barbara with the Virgin and Child, were included in *Klosterfrauenarbeiten: Kunsthandwerk aus bayerischen Frauenklöstern,* Munich, 1987, 9 and cat. no. 38, where they are said to have been produced when Ursula of Reichenau, sister of the bishop of Eichstätt, William of Reichenau, was abbess (1475–86). The stylistic evidence discussed in the course of this chapter, however, strongly suggests a somewhat later date.

4. For the "mass production" of devotional images, see Appuhn, 1985, 92.

5. Walburga and her brothers were one of several triads of saintly siblings compared to Mary Magdalene, Martha, and Lazarus; see F. Heinzemann and M. Köhler, *Der Magdalenenaltar des Lucas Moser in der gotischer Basilika Tiefenbronn,* Regensburg, 1994, 17.

6. A. Bauch, *Quellen zur Geschichte der Diözese Eichstätt I: Biographie der Gründerzeit,* Eichstätter Studien, NF 19, 2d ed., Regensburg, 1984.

7. For the dissemination of the cult, see Holzbauer; and *Heilige Walburga: Ihr Nachleben in der schriftliche Überlieferung,* Katalog zur Ausstellung anläßlich des 1200. Todestages, June–September 1979, Eichstätt, 1979.

8. For the privileges of canonesses in the German empire, see K. H. Schäfer, *Die Kanonissenstifter im deutschen Mittelalter: Ihre Entwicklung und innere Einrichtung im Zusammenhang mit dem altchristlichen Sanktimonialentum,* Kirchenrechtliche Abhandlungen, 43–44, reprinted Amsterdam, 1965; M. Parisse, "Les Chanoinesses dans l'Empire Germanique (IXe–XIe

siècle)," *Francia* 6 (1978): 107–28; idem, "Die Frauenstifte und Frauenklöster in Sachsen vom X. bis zur Mitte des XII. Jahrhunderts," in *Die Salier und das Reich,* Sigmaringen, 1991, vol. II, 465–501; and J. Siegwart, "Die Chorherren- und Chorfrauengemeinschaften in der deutschsprachigen Schweiz vom 6. Jahrhundert bis 1160," *Studia Friburgensia,* NF 30, Fribourg, 1962.

9. J. Schlecht, "Stiftungsbrief des Klosters St. Walburg," *Sammelblatt des historischen Vereins Eichstätt* 1 (1886): 29–37. For donor images commemorating monastic foundations, esp. in Bavaria, see C. Sauer, *Fundatio und Memoria: Stifter und Klostergründer im Bild 1100 bis 1350,* Veröffentlichungen des Max-Planck-Instituts für Geschichte, 109, Göttingen, 1993.

10. For the reform in Eichstätt, see "Versuch einer Conciliengeschichte des Bisthums Eichstätt," *Pastoralblatt des Bisthums Eichstätt* 1 (1854): 158–59; and F. Buchner, "Klosterverfassung und Klosterleben in St. Walburg vor der Säkularisation nach Klosterurkunden," in *Zum 900jährigen Jubiläum,* 27–39. I was unable to locate the source cited in L. Eckenstein, *Women under Monasticism: Chapters on Saint-Lore and Convent Life between A.D. 500 and A.D. 1500,* London, 1896, reprinted New York, 1963, 421.

11. For a description of the church and crypt as they appeared in 1611, see C. Häutle, "Die Reisen des Augsburgers Philipp Hainhofer nach Eichstädt, München und Regensburg in den Jahren 1611, 1612 und 1613," *Zeitschrift des historischen Vereins für Schwaben und Neuburg* 8 (1881): esp. 41.

12. For a nun's account of the Swedish assault, see *Walburgis-Blätter* 9 (1921–22): 4 and 20–22, reprinted in S. Hilpisch, *Aus deutschen Frauenklöstern,* Vienna, 1931, 132–35. For a detailed account of the building's history, see F. Mader, *Die Kunstdenkmäler von Mittelfranken I: Stadt Eichstätt,* Munich, 1924, 230–85; and A. Rauch, *Stadt Eichstätt,* Denkmäler in Bayern, vol. I.9, pt. 1, Munich, 1989, 156–63.

13. R.D., "Religiös-Volkskundliches aus St. Walburg."

14. Unable to enter enclosure, I had to content myself with the drawings the nuns could show me in the visitors' parlor.

15. See C. de Hamel, *Catalogue of Western Manuscripts and Miniatures,* Sotheby's, London, June 23, 1992, lot 32, where the drawing was attributed as follows: "Germany, probably Rhineland, second half of the fifteenth century."

16. According to E. Schleich, *Frommer Sinn und Lieblichkeit: Vom Zauber der "Schönen Arbeiten" in Altbayern,* Passau, 1973, 53.

17. For the secularization in Bavaria, see *Glanz und Ende der Alten Klöster: Säkularisation im bayerischen Oberland,* ed. J. Kirmeier and M. Treml, Veröffentlichungen zur Bayerischen Geschichte und Kultur, 21, Munich, 1991.

18. See G. Schnürer and J. M. Ritz, *Sankt Kümmernis und Volto Santo: Studien und Bilder,* Forschungen zur Volkskunde, 13–15, Düsseldorf, 1934.

19. St. Walburg, Ms. germ. 7, ff. 201r–206v, described in J. Lechner, *Die spätmittelalterliche Handschriftengeschichte der Benediktinerinnenabtei St. Walburg / Eichstätt (By.),* Münster, 1937, 59, and transcribed in idem, "Das Kloster St. Walburg und die Frühgeschichte der Kümmernisverehrung in Süddeutschland," in *Zum 900jährigen Jubiläum,* 40–60.

20. In addition to Schnürer and Ritz, see G. Schnürer, "Die Kümmernisbilder als Kopien des Volto Santo von Lucca," in *Die Görres-Gesellschaft 1876–1901: Denkschrift zur Feier ihres 25jähriges Bestehens nebst Jahresbericht für 1900,* ed. H. Cardanus, Cologne, 1901, 43–50; and J.-C. Schmitt, "Cendrillon crucifiée: À propos du *Volto Santo* de Lucques," in *Miracles, prodiges et merveilles au Moyen Âge,* Paris, 1995, 241–69. For the clothing of wonder-working images, see, in addition to Schmitt, R. C. Trexler, "Habiller et déshabiller les images: Esquisse d'une analyse," in *L'Image et la production du sacré,* 195–231; idem, "Der Heiligen neue Kleider: Eine analytische Skizze zur Be- und Entkleidung von Statuen," in *Gepeinigt, begehrt, vergessen,* 337–

64; and I. Schnell, *Das Problematik der Restaurierung von Gnadenbildern dargestellt am Beispiel des Villinger Nägelinskruzifixes,* Villingen, 1987, 15–20.

21. Barbara herself does this in the woodcut by Mair von Landshut dated 1499 (Schreiber cat. no. 1248-2), reproduced in R. S. Field, *German Single-Leaf Woodcuts before 1500: Anonymous Artists,* 4 vols., *The Illustrated Bartsch:* Supplement 161–64, New York, 1987–92, vol. 164, 312.

22. For the *Gnadenstuhl,* see S. J. Pearmann, "The Iconographic Development of the Cruciform Throne of Grace from the Twelfth to the Sixteenth Centuries," Ph.D. diss., Case Western Reserve University, Cleveland, 1974; and F. Boespflug, "The Compassion of God the Father in Western Art," *Cross Currents* 42 (1992–93): 487–503. For the glory of angels surrounding the Trinity, see K.-A. Wirth, "Engel," in RDK, vol. V, esp. 417–19 and fig. 52.

23. For the iconography of the family tree and its roots in imagery of the Holy Family, see P. Sheingorn, "The Holy Kinship: The Ascendancy of Matriliny in Sacred Genealogy of the Fifteenth Century," *Thought* 64 (1989): 268–86; and C. Klapish-Zuber, "The Genesis of the Family Tree," *I Tatti Studies: Essays in the Renaissance* 4 (1991): 105–30.

24. The smaller container might also represent one of the unguent jars implied by the Song of Songs and occasionally depicted in medieval art; see G. Cames, "Parfums et diadèmes: Le Cantique de Cantiques dans l'iconographie mariale romane," in *Miscellanea codicologica F. Masai dicata MCMLXXIX,* 2 vols., ed. P. Cockshaw, Ghent, 1979, 241–48.

25. As V. A. Kolve kindly reminded me, this scene recalls the extraordinary account of the marriage of Margery Kempe to God, in which Christ, who acts more as "best man" than as bridegroom, presents her to the Father. See *The Book of Margery Kempe,* trans. B. A. Windeatt, London, 1985, 122–25.

26. See the literature cited in note 19.

27. As far as I was able to determine, none of the drawings on paper bear watermarks.

28. *Chronik und Totenbuch des Klosters Wienhausen,* 28.

29. *Leben der Schwestern zu Töß,* 45, lines 29–30: "Wir hand och fil nach alle únser gůtten bild von ir; fil túscher bůcher hat sy gefrúmet." For further evidence of nuns as artists, see the material gathered in Chapter 5.

30. For good reproductions, see H. Appuhn, *Kloster Wienhausen,* Wienhausen, 1986, figs. 19–25.

31. The provenance, recorded by Spamer, 308, suggests that the drawing may have come from the convent of the Holy Cross, where in 1632 it was incorporated into an epitaph for the abbess, Katharina von Rogweil.

32. Acquired by private purchase and left to the university in 1927, the leaf has no provenance.

33. See K. Niebler, *Die Handschriften von St. Peter im Schwarzwald I.: Die Papierhandschriften,* Die Handschriften der Badischen Landesbibliothek in Karlsruhe, 10, Wiesbaden, 1969, 6–8; and *Das Vermächtnis der Abtei: 900 Jahre St. Peter auf dem Schwarzwald,* ed. H.-O. Mühleisen, Karlsruhe, 1993, 415.

34. For this and related iconography, see E. M. Vetter, *Die Kupferstiche zur Psalmodia Eucaristica des Melchor Prieto von 1622,* Spanische Forschungen der Görresgesellschaft, 2d ser., 15, Münster, 1972, 243–40; and F. Ohly, *Gesetz und Evangelium: Zur Typologie bei Luther und Lucas Cranach. Zum Blutstrahl der Gnade in der Kunst,* Schriftenreihe der Westfälischen Wilhelms-Universität Münster, NF 1, Münster, 1985, 48–81.

35. For a more detailed consideration of this issue, see Hamburger, 1992.

36. For the history of enclosure and varying judgments on its effectiveness, see P. Hofmeister, "Von den Nonnenklöstern," *Archiv für katholisches Kirchenrecht* 114 (1934): 3–96; G. Huyghe, *La Clôture des moniales des origines à la fin du XIIIe siècle: Étude historique et juridique,* Roubaix, 1944, who rely almost exclusively on statutes. For more nuanced evaluations, consult

R. Gazeau, "La Clôture des moniales au XIIe siècle en France," *Revue Mabillon* 63 (1979): 289–308; J. T. Schulenberg, "Strict Active Enclosure and Its Effects on the Female Monastic Experience (ca. 500–1100)," in *Medieval Religious Women I: Distant Echoes,* ed. J. A. Nichols and L. T. Shank, Kalamazoo, Mich., 1984, 51–86; J. Leclercq, "La Clôture: Points de repère historiques," *Collectanea Cisterciensia* 43 (1981): 366–77; and P. D. Johnson, *Equal in Monastic Profession: Religious Women in Medieval France,* Chicago, 1991, 150–63.

37. For the history and a catalogue of the library, see J. Lechner.

38. Spamer, 16–17.

39. Only H. Körner, *Der früheste deutsche Einblattholzschnitt,* Mittenwald, 1979, 27–28 and 42–46, acknowledges that the comparison of *Nonnenarbeiten* and prints cannot be pushed too far.

40. I here disagree with Körner, 77–83, who argues that the development of the single-leaf woodcut marks the dissolution of "aura" as defined by Walter Benjamin in his classic essay "The Work of Art in the Age of Mechanical Reproduction." For examples that support contrary conclusions, see J. F. Hamburger, "The *Liber miraculorum* of Unterlinden: An Icon in Its Convent Setting," in *The Sacred Image East and West,* 147–90; H. Dünninger, "Wahres Abbild: Bildwallfahrt und Gnadenbildkopie," in *Wallfahrt kennt keine Grenzen,* ed. L. Kriss-Rettenbeck and G. Möhler, Munich, 1984, 274–83; and the well-known case of the "Maria-Hilf" *Gnadenbild,* a copy of an original by Lucas Cranach that spawned countless copies, among them *Kleine Andachtsbilder,* a process documented in *Maria-Hilf: Ein Cranach-Bild und seine Wirkung,* Katalogreihe Marmelsteiner Kabinett, 13, Würzburg, 1994.

41. For the content of the inscription, see Chapter 4, pp. 146–47.

42. For prints preserved at Wienhausen, see Appuhn and von Heusinger; for the possibility of woodcuts produced at the Katharinenkloster in Nuremberg, see M. Weinberger, *Die Formschnitte der Katharinenklosters zu Nürnberg: Ein Versuch über die Geschichte der frühesten Nürnberger Holzschnitten,* Munich, 1925. For blocks from Söflingen in Ulm, see F. Falk, "Der älteste Formschnitt in seiner Beziehung zur Kirche," *Zeitschrift für christliche Kunst* 2 (1889): 232–34; and Körner, 30. In the convent of Bethany in Mechlin nuns produced prints and illustrated books; see M. Mauquoy-Hendrickx, "Une Dernière Hypothèse au sujet de 'Ecce panis angelorum' du couvent de Béthanie (Malines) portant le millésime 1467," *De gulden passer* 52 (1974): 177–89.

43. Of these, a number are reproduced in the pages of the *Walburgis-Blätter.* J. E. Weis-Liebersdorf, *Inkunabeln der Formschnitte in den Bibliotheken zu Eichstätt,* Einblattdrucke des fünfzehntes Jahrhunderts, 20, Strasbourg, 1910, does not include any of the prints from the abbey's collection.

44. See A. Rapp Buri and M. Stucky-Schnürer, "Klosterfleiß im Dienste der Gegenreformation: Die Bildteppiche von St. Johann bei Zabern in Elsaß," *Zeitschrift für die Geschichte des Oberrheins* 137, NF 98 (1989): esp. 312–14.

45. Based on comparison with the prints catalogued in Field; W. L. Schreiber, *Handbuch der Holz- und Metallschnitte des XV. Jahrhunderts,* 8 vols., Leipzig, 1926–30; and M. Lehrs, *Geschichte und kritischer Katalog des deutschen, niederländischen und französischen Kupferstichs im XV. Jahrhundert,* 9 vols., Vienna, 1908–34.

46. Reproduced in Spamer, 38, and described in E. Petzet, *Die deutschen Pergament-Handschriften Nr. 1–200 der Staatsbibliothek in München,* Munich, 1920, 188–91. The manuscript comes from the monastery of Benediktbeuren but was not necessarily produced there.

47. Cf., e.g., the left wing of the retable from the workshop of Daniel Mauch, now in Ulm, discussed in *Bildhauerei und Malerei vom 13. Jahrhundert bis 1600,* Kataloge des Ulmer Museums, 1, Ulm, 1981, cat. no. 128, 190–95, and in *Meisterwerke massenhaft,* 352–54 and fig. 507.

48. For the roots of this iconographic tradition, closely related to that of the Tree of Jesse,

see Hamburger, 1990, 89–92; M. Lingren-Fridell, "Der Stammbaum Mariä aus Anna und Joachim," *Marburger Jahrbuch für Kunstwissenschaft* 11–12 (1938–39): 289–307; and E. M. Vetter, "*Mulier amicta sole* und *Mater salvatoris,*" in *Speculum salutis,* Abtei Münsterschwarzach, 1995, esp. 57.

49. For the earliest extant example of the Virgin holding a crucifix, see Vetter, 1995, 59–60 and fig. 33.

50. See C. de Hamel, "Reflexions on the Trade in Books of Hours at Ghent and Bruges," in *Manuscripts in the Fifty Years after the Invention of Printing: Some Papers Presented at a Colloquium at the Warburg Institute on 12–13 March 1982,* London, 1983, 29–33.

51. For the artist, see *The Golden Age of Dutch Manuscript Painting,* intro. J. H. Marrow, ed. H. L. M. Defoer, A. S. Korteweg, and W. W. C. Wüstefeld, Stuttgart, 1989, 287–88 and 297–300; for this set of leaves, consult the London Sotheby's catalogue *Western Manuscripts and Miniatures,* December 5, 1994, lot 14, 18–19, where C. de Hamel argues that they were "certainly intended to be bound into a prayer book." That similar leaves were once commonplace devotional objects is suggested by the way in which they are represented in paintings, such as the *Portrait of a Young Man,* ca. 1450 (National Gallery, London) and the *Portrait of a Female Donor* (National Gallery of Art, Washington) both by Petrus Christus, reproduced in M. W. Ainsworth, *Petrus Christus: Renaissance Master of Bruges,* with contributions by M. P. J. Martens, New York, 1994, 133 and fig. 66.

52. See E. W. Bredt, *Der Handschriftenschmuck Augsburgs im 15. Jahrhundert,* Studien zur deutschen Kunstgeschichte, 15, Strasbourg, 1900; E. Steingräber, *Die kirchliche Buchmalerei Augsburgs um 1500,* Abhandlungen zur Geschichte der Stadt Augsburg: Schriftenreihe des Stadtarchivs Augsburg, 8, Augsburg and Basel, 1956; and O. Pächt, *Vita Sancti Simperti: Eine Handschrift für Maximilian I.,* Berlin, 1964; and R. Suckale, "Die Zeit der Gotik," in *Regensburger Buchmalerei von frühkarolingischer Zeit bis zum Ausgang des Mittelalters,* Munich, 1987, 58–102.

53. See H. Leporini, "Das Rankenornament in der Österreichischen und Süddeutschen Buchmalerei der Spätgotik und beginnenden Renaissance," *Buch und Schrift* 1 (1927): 9–39; and J. H. Marrow, "Two Newly Identified Leaves from the Missal of Johannes von Giltlingen: Notes on Late Fifteenth-Century Manuscript Illumination in Augsburg," *Anzeiger des Germanischen Nationalmuseums* (1984): 27–31.

54. The Pontifical-Missal of William of Reichenau is dated by an inscription on f. 3r: "Anno domini MCCCCLXVI reverendus in christo pater et dominus dominum Wilhelmus de Reichenaw . . . hunc librum missalem comparavit ac conscribi manducavit." For brief descriptions of the manuscript, see Mader, 631–35; *Caritas Pirckheimer 1467–1532: Kloster und Klosterleben in der Herausforderung der Zeit,* Munich, 1982, cat. no. 29, 52–53; and *Hl. Willibald, 787–1987: Künder des Glaubens, Pilger, Mönch, Bischof,* ed. B. Appel, E. Braun, and S. Hofmann, Eichstätt, 1987, 132–33. The missal merits a separate study, which I plan to publish elsewhere. For other fifteenth-century pontifical-missals from southwest Germany, see H. Tüchle, "Ein illuminiertes Pontifikalmissale aus dem Kloster Blaubeuron," *Ulm und Oberschwaben: Zeitschrift für Geschichte und Kunst* 42–43 (1978): 47–59.

55. See, most recently, F. Koreny, "A Colored Flower Study by Martin Schongauer and the Development of the Depiction of Nature from van der Weyden to Dürer," *Burlington Magazine* 133 (1991): 588–97.

56. See G. Dogaer, "Einfluss der Randverzierung der sogenannte Gent-Brügger Schule auf die deutsche Buchmalerei um 1500," in *Bibliothek-Buch-Geschichte: Kurt Koster zum 65. Geburtstag,* ed. G. Pflug, B. Eckert, and H. Friesenhahn, Frankfurt, 1977, 211–17.

57. See J. K. Eberlein, "Die bildliche Ausstattung des "Pontifikale-Gundekarianum," in *Das "Pontifikale Gundekarianum,"* vol. II, 39–83.

58. See R. Frankenberger and P. B. Rupp, *Wertvolle Handschriften und Einbände aus der ehe-*

maligen Oettingen-Wallersteinschen Bibliothek, Universitätsbibliothek Augsburg, Wiesbaden, 1987, pl. 19; and *Von der Augsburger Bibelhandschriften zu Bertolt Brecht: Zeugnisse der deutschen Literatur aus der Staats- und Stadtbibliothek und der Universitätsbibliothek Augsburg,* ed. H. Gier and J. Janota, Weißenhorn, 1991, cat. no. IV-20, 106, 108, and 110.

59. See J. F. Hamburger, "A *Liber precum* in Sélestat and the Development of the Illustrated Prayer Book in Germany," *Art Bulletin* 73 (1991): 209–36; G. Achten, *Das christliche Gebetbuch im Mittelalter: Andachts- und Stundenbücher in Handschrift und Frühdruck,* Berlin, 1987; J. M. Plotzek, *Andachtsbücher des Mittelalters aus Privatbesitz,* Cologne, 1937; P. Ochsenbein, "Deutschsprachige Privatgebetbücher vor 1400," in *Deutsche Handschriften 1100–1400,* Oxforder Kolloquium, 1985, ed. V. Honemann and N. F. Palmer, Tübingen, 1988, 379–98; and idem, "Stundenbücher," [2]VL, vol. IX, 468–72, where Ochsenbein notes that there are no more than around a hundred German Books of Hours from 1450 to 1530 and that of these only a small number contain elaborate decoration.

60. St. Walburg, Mss. Lat. 3–5, all approximately 55 × 41 cm., described in J. Lechner, 16–17.

61. According to J. Lechner, 16–18, all three volumes carry their original bindings, the earliest stamped 1622. The new set of liturgical books was probably prepared in conjunction with the renovation of the convent buildings, completed in 1631.

62. The fourteenth-century fragments consist almost entirely of gold initials with red penwork flourishes. The most elaborate have a baroque whimsy, incorporating large dragons whose exaggerated appendages extend to form all parts of the letter. The nuns, however, appear to have preserved only one historiated initial from this manuscript, a Resurrection (Eichstätt, Cod. S. Walburg, Lat. 4), p. 232.

63. The most extensive discussion of the group is still that of K. Holter, "Die Salzburg-Augsburger Werkstatt," in *Spätgotik in Salzburg: Die Malerei,* Salzburger Museum Carolino Augusteum: Jahresschrift, 17, Salzburg, 1972, 246–57. See also idem, "Die spätmittelalterliche Buchmalerei in Stift St. Florian," *Oberösterreichische Heimatblätter* 40 (1986): esp. 318–23; and idem, *Gotik in Steiermark,* Stift St. Lambrecht, 1978, 195–96 and fig. 70. To the manuscripts listed by Holter can be added a triptych of modern construction, sold recently at Sotheby's, London (*Western Manuscripts and Miniatures,* June 19, 1990, lot 61), whose wings are made up of late-fifteenth-century fragments from a manuscript produced by the workshop (kindly brought to my attention by Gerhardt Schmidt). From the diocese of Eichstätt comes a breviary (Sotheby's, London, November 26, 1975, Phillipps Ms. 841) written in 1487 for a nun, Veronika von Freudenberg, with decoration related to the workshop's style.

64. Of the manuscripts tabulated in the publications by Holter cited in the preceding note, the latest date to the first decade of the sixteenth century. For comments on connections between printing and the mass production of manuscripts in the later fifteenth century, see M. A. Rouse and R. H. Rouse, *Cartolai, Illuminators, and Printers in Fifteenth-Century Italy,* UCLA, University Research Library, Department of Special Collections Occasional Papers, 1, Los Angeles, 1988.

65. Reproduced in color in W. Neuhauser, "Vom Codex zum Computer, der Tradition und dem Fortschritt verplichtet: Die Innsbrucker Universitätsbibliothek," *Tirol: Immer einen Urlaub Wert,* Winter 1990/91, n.p. The manuscript is described fully in idem, *Katalog der Handschriften der Universitätsbibliothek Innsbruck,* Österreichische Akademie der Wissenschaften, Phil.-Hist. Kl., Denkschriften 192, Vienna, 1987, 86–93, where a good many closely related manuscripts are listed. For reproductions of selected examples of the Last Judgment opening the liturgy for Advent, see *Spätgotik in Salzburg:* cat. no. 295, fig. 102 (Salzburg, Universitätsbibliothek, cod. M III 12, f. 8r); and *Spätgotik in Salzburg,* fig. 46 (St. Florian, Cod. III/9, fol. 7r).

66. The workshop's close connections with the book trade are also consonant with the

precocious citation of printed models found in the Pontifical-Missal of William of Reichenau, discussed below.

67. For the cult of Willibald, see *H. Willibald, 787–1987.* For Christoph von Pappenheim, see J. Sax, *Die Bischöfe und Reichsfürsten von Eichstätt, 754–1806: Versuch einer Deutung ihres Waltens und Wirkens nach den neuesten Quellen zusammengestellt,* 2 vols., Landshut, 1884–85, vol. II, 425–30; and idem, *Geschichte des Hochstiftes und der Stadt Eichstätt,* Nuremberg, 1857, 200–203; see also S. Weinfurter et al., "Die Viten der Eichstätter Bischöfe im *Pontifikale Gundekarianum,*" in *Das "Pontifikale Gundekarianum,"* vol. II, 132–33.

68. The arms appear to be original—there is no evidence of overpainting—and, even if the initial and the fragment glued into the adjacent margin were cut from different manuscripts, the treatment of the faces, with their pursed lips and drooping eyelids, is the same. I am grateful to Herr Brun Appel of the Diözesanarchiv Eichstätt for bringing to my attention M. E. Dray, "Alte und neue Buchmalerei in St. Walburg, Eichstätt," *Sankt Wiborada: Ein Jahrbuch für Bücherfreunde* 3 (1936): esp. 65, where the coat of arms is identified. A Book of Hours (Eichstätt, Diözesanarchiv, Ordinariatsbibliothek, Ms. 132) painted for Christoph by Albrecht Glockendon demonstrates that in works commissioned for his own use the bishop's taste was very different: see *Hl. Willibald, 787–1987,* cat. no. D 1.7, 55 and 135–36; and B. Daentler, *Die Buchmalerei Albrecht Glockendons und die Rahmenornamentik der Dürernachfolge,* Munich, 1984.

69. See, e.g., G. Achten, "De gebedenboeken van de Cisterciënserinnenklosters Medingen en Wienhausen," in *Miscellanea Neerlandica,* vol. III, 173–88.

70. I was able to determine the dimensions of the following drawings (given in mm.):

St. Barbara with the Virgin and Child (135 × 88)
St. Kümmernis (74 × 63)
The *Arbor virginis* (201 × 121)
Symbolic Crucifixion (148 × 95)
The Eucharistic Banquet (103 × 86)
The Heart as a House (136 × 104)

71. St. Walburg, Ms. germ. 18, described by J. Lechner, 79. This drawing is also the only one whose verso is not blank, the writing having been added by the same scribe who wrote the rest of the book.

72. At least according to the evidence presently available. See A. Henry, *Biblia Pauperum: A Facsimile and Edition,* Ithaca, N.Y., 1987; the essays gathered in *Blockbücher des Mittelalters: Bilderfolgen als Lektüre,* Mainz, 1991; and the detailed discussion in N. F. Palmer, *Apokalypse, Ars moriendi, Biblia pauperum, Antichrist, Vom kranken Löwen, Kalendarium, Planetenbücher, Historia David: Die lateinisch-deutschen Blockbücher des Berlin-Breslauer Sammelbandes (Berlin, Staatliches Museen Preußischer Kulturbesitz, Kupferstichkabinett, Cim. 1, 2, 5, 7, 9, 10, 12),* Monumenta xylographica et typographica, 2, Munich, 1992, 23 and 46–47. My thanks to James Marrow, who first alerted me to the borrowings from the *Biblia pauperum* in the Pontifical-Missal of William of Reichenau.

73. See Henry, 113 and 115.

74. As noted by Marrow, 1984. Prints frequently served as models for the miniatures in German prayer books of the period; for several prestigious examples, see F. O. Büttner, "Die Illumination mittelalterlicher Andachtsbücher," in *Mittelalterliche Andachtsbücher: Psalterien-Stundenbücher-Gebetbücher, Zeugnisse europäischer Frömmigkeit,* ed. H.-P. Geh and G. Römer, Karlsruhe, 1992, esp. 52, 130, and 134–36 (cat. nos. 34 and 36). On occasion prints were actually pasted into manuscript books; see, e.g., A. Matthews, "The Use of Prints in the Hours of Charles d'Angoulême," *Print Quarterly* 3 (1986): 4–18; and the manuscripts from the library of

Hartmann Schedel, described in B. Hernad, *Die Graphik Sammlung der Humanistien Hartmann Schedel,* Munich, 1990.

75. *Die Eichstätter Bischofschronik des Grafen Wilhelm Werner von Zimmern,* Veröffentlichungen der Gesellschaft für Fränkische Geschichte, I. Reihe, Fränkische Chroniken, 3, ed. W. Kraft, Würzburg, 1956, 79: "Dan er gar ain fleyssigs aufmercken und grosse achtung het, das alles, so zu dem gotzdienst aufgericht, mit guter ordnung verpracht wurd, umb des willen er der priester mess und betbücher alle erneuwern und in den truck verfertigen liess." See also F. W. E. Roth, "Michael Renfer, ein Eichstätter Buchdrucker 1478–1494 und dessen Erzeugnisse: Eine Monographie," *Sammelblatt des historischen Vereins Eichstätt* 8 (1893): 1–40.

76. For humanism in Eichstätt, see M. Fink-Lang, *Untersuchungen zum Eichstätter Geistesleben im Zeitalter des Humanismus,* Eichstätter Beiträge: Abteilung Geschichte, 14, Regensburg, 1985; G. Gailhofer, "Der Humanist Albrecht von Eyb," *Sammelblatt des historischen Vereins Eichstätt* 42 (1927): 28–71; and K. Elm, "Monastische Reformen zwischen Humanismus und Reformation," in *900 Jahre Kloster Bursfelde: Reden und Vorträge zum Jubiläum 1993,* ed. L. Perlitt, Göttingen, 1995, 59–111. For its relation to William of Reichenau's patronage, see P. Crossley, "The Return to the Forest: Natural Architecture and the German Past in the Age of Dürer," in *Künstlerischer Austausch,* vol. II, 71–77.

77. Comparison of the drawings with devotional images printed in the Eichstätt region only underscores this point; for this material, see K. Haupt, "Mystik und Kunst in Augsburg und im östlichen Schwaben während des Spätmittelalters," *Zeitschrift des historischen Vereins für Schwaben* 59–60 (1969): 1–100.

78. R. Kroos, *Niedersächsische Bildstickereien des Mittelalters,* Berlin, 1970, 22, forecloses the possibility of meaningful stylistic comparisons between embroideries and paintings (and, by implication, tapestries and drawings): "Doch leider finden sich nirgends in oder aus ein und demselben Kloster gleichzeitig Stickereien und dazu Malereien, aus denen man eine über liebenswürdigen Dilettantismus hinausgehende Kunstübung erschließen könnte."

79. See A. Rapp Buri and M. Stucky-Schnürer, *"Zahm und wild": Basler und Straßburger Bildteppiche des 15. Jahrhunderts,* Mainz, 1990, 47–50.

80. See E. Schraut, *Stifterinnen und Künstlerinnen im mittelalterlichen Nürnberg,* Nuremberg, 1987; and idem, "Kunst im Frauenkloster: Überlegungen zu den Möglichkeiten der Frauen im mittelalterlichen Kunstbetrieb am Beispiel Nürnberg," in *Auf der Suche nach der Frau im Mittelalter: Fragen, Quellen, Antworten,* ed. B. Lundt, Munich, 1991, 81–114.

81. See *Die Abtei St. Walburg,* 103–13; Luitpold Herzog in Bayern, *Die Fränkische Bildwirkerei,* 2 vols., Munich, 1926, vol. I, 50–51 and 91–97, and vol. II, cat. nos. 59–66; L. von Wilckens, "Die Teppiche mit der Heiligen Walburga," *Studien und Mitteilungen zur Geschichte des Benediktiner-Ordens und seiner Zweige* 90 (1979): 81–96; and idem, *Die textilen Künste von der Spätantike bis um 1500,* Munich, 1991, 312.

82. See Luitpold Herzog in Bayern, vol. I, 91; and von Wilckens, 1979. The scenes from the older tapestry are reproduced in color in *Heilige Walburga: Leben und Wirken,* Eichstätt, 1979.

83. For the tapestries from St. Walburg, see, in addition to Luitpold Herzog in Bayern and von Wilckens, 1979, S. Durian-Ress, *Meisterwerke mittelalterliche Textilkunst aus dem Bayerischen Nationalmuseum: Auswahlkatalog,* Munich, 1986, who dates them all to ca. 1520. Their production, however, was more likely spread over a number of years. For Walburg von Absberg, see J. Schlecht, "Reihenfolge der Äbtissinnen des Klosters St. Walburg in Eichstätt," *Sammelblatt des historischen Vereins in Eichstätt* 7 (1892): esp. 41. A set of Dominican statutes, a treatise on confession, and a *Rituale* transcribed in 1487 by Conradus Seherlin, O.P., Eichstätt, confessor to the Dominican nuns at Maria Medingen, was in Walburga von Absberg's possession by the early sixteenth century, suggesting her wide-ranging contacts beyond her own order; see

H. Hilg, *Die mittelalterlichen Handschriften der Universitätsbibliothek Eichstätt,* Wiesbaden, 1984, 32 (Eichstätt, Universitätsbibliothek, Cod. st 109).

84. Only a single surviving tapestry associated with St. Walburg, the antependium (Fig. 34), discussed below, can be assigned an earlier date, and then only on the basis of style.

85. For the panels of SS. Lucia and Apollonia, see Durian-Ress, cat. no. 70, 180–82; for the portrait of Walburga as patron, cat. no. 68, 176–78.

86. Ibid., cat. nos. 70–71, 182–84.

87. The measurements given by Durian-Ress of the St. Apollonia are inaccurate; rather than 98.5 cm., the panel is ca. 89.7 cm. in height. My thanks to Dr. Birgitt Borkopp of the Department of Textiles at the Bayerisches Nationalmuseum for allowing me to examine the tapestries and for supplying this information.

88. B. Uhde Stahl, "Figürliche Buchmalereien in den spätmittelalterlichen Handschriften der Lüneburger Frauenklöster," *Niederdeutsche Beiträge zur Kunstgeschichte* 17 (1978): 25–60, compares manuscripts illuminated by nuns to decorated textiles; her conclusions, however, should be considered in light of the corrections offered by Achten, 1987b. For a reconstruction of a tapestry cartoon, see Rapp Buri and Stucky-Schnürer, 1990, 41–46.

89. Luitpold Herzog in Bayern, 92, defines these flowered grounds as the hallmark of the tapestries from St. Walburg.

90. Von Heusinger, 1953, argues that *Nonnenarbeiten* ceased to exist after 1500.

91. See Luitpold Herzog in Bayern, 93. Although preserved at the Bayerisches Nationalmuseum in Munich, the tapestry is not included in the partial catalogue prepared by Durian-Ress. An old exhibition label, kindly shown to me by Dr. Birgitt Borkopp, attributes the tapestry to the third quarter of the fifteenth century. It is rather unlikely, however, that the nuns would have had the wherewithal to manufacture the tapestry before 1469, when they imported the *Ältere Walburga Teppich* from Nuremberg, let alone before the abbey's reform in 1456.

92. Luitpold Herzog in Bayern suggests the Evangelist's eagle.

93. For other examples of this convention in medieval art, see W. Cahn, "Représentations de la parole," *Connaissance des arts* (November 1982): 82–89; I. Toiret, "La Parole incarnée: Voir la parole dans les images des XIIe et XIIIe siècle," *Médiévales* 22–23 (1994): 13–30; and S. Ringbom, "Rulle-Codex-Pratbulle: Om Boeken som Utsaga (Scroll-codex-balloon: About the book as statement)," *ICO: Iconographisk Post* (1994): 1–13.

94. For the iconography of the two infants, see H. Krause-Zimmer, *Die zwei Jesusknabe in der bildende Kunst,* 2d ed., Stuttgart, 1977.

95. Schreiber, cat. no. 811; see Field, vol. 163, 92. The tapestry workshop at St. Johann bei Zabern also used prints as models; see Rapp Buri and Stucky-Schnürer, 1989, 312–14.

96. See von Wilckens, 1991, 159–74; and A. M. Schmid, "Bemerkungen zu zwei spätmittelalterlichen Zeugdrücken aus dem Alpenraum," in *Artes minores: Dank an Werner Abegg,* ed. M. Stettler and M. Lemberg, Bern, 1973, 75–111, with additional bibliography.

97. My thanks to Dr. Birgitt Borkopp and the textile conservators at the Bayerisches Nationalmuseum, especially André Brutillot, for providing me with a tracing of the tapestry that allowed me to confirm the print's use as a cartoon.

98. As pointed out to me by M. Brutillot, only the stains left by the embroidery remain.

99. Although no longer clearly visible in the tapestry, the Hand of God once occupied the small oval area just beyond the periphery of the circle containing the Christ Child, now a small and relatively inchoate patch (and possibly a repair).

100. For Mechthild of Hackeborn, see K. Ruh, *Frauenmystik und Franziskanische Mystik der Frühzeit,* Geschichte der abendländischen Mystik, 2, Munich, 1993, 301–14; G. J. Lewis, F. Willaert, and M.-J. Govers, *Bibliographie zur deutschen Frauenmystik des Mittelalters mit einem Anhang zu Beatrijs van Nazareth und Hadewijch,* Bibliographien zur deutschen Literatur des

Mittelalters, 10, Berlin, 1989, 184–95; and A. M. Haas, "Mechthild von Hackeborn: Eine Form zisterziensischer Frauenfrömmigkeit," in idem, *Geistliches Mittelalter,* Fribourg, 1984, 373–91.

101. Mechthild of Hackeborn, 1875–77, 243–44 (bk. III, chap. 40): "in Missa vidit Dominum in altari in specie aquilae aureae, et agnovit quod sicut aquila habet volatum altissimum, ita et visum profundissimum, scilicet ad cor humile. Et videbatur sibi aquilam illam habere rostrum curvum et linguam nimis dulcem. Per rostrum significabantur eloquia Domini, quae per devotionem pungunt cor animae; per linguam vero, dulcedo figurabatur, quod sicut aquila semper quaerit dulcissimum in praeda, scilicet cor, ita Deus semper desiderat cor nostrum, ut illud in dulcedinem sibi offeramus."

102. For the image of the eagle in medieval literature, especially as a figure of the contemplative life, see P. Dinzelbacher, "Die mittelalterliche Adlersymbolik und Hadewijch," in idem, *Mittelalterliche Frauenmystik,* Paderborn, 1993, 188–204; A. Volfing, "The Authorship of John the Evangelist As Presented in Medieval German Sermons and Meisterlieder," *Oxford German Studies* 23 (1994): 1–44; and M. Wehrli-Johns, "Das Selbstverständnis des Predigerordens im Graduale von Katharinenthal: Ein Beitrag zur Deutung der Christus-Johannes-Gruppe," in *Contemplata aliis tradere: Studien zum Verhältnis von Literatur und Spiritualität,* ed. C. Brinker et al., Bern, 1995, 241–71.

103. See Hamburger, 1992. The library of St. Walburg included a short treatise by Silvester of Rebdorf on the evils of private property, dated 1438 and addressed to the nuns of Pulgarn in Oberösterreich (St. Walburg, Ms. germ. 7, ff. 146v–153v); see B. D. Haage and C. Stöllinger-Löser, "Privatbesitz im Ordensleben," ²VL, vol. VII, esp. 847–48, where additional manuscript copies are listed.

104. This officer's duties are described in the early constitutions, *Analecta sacri ordinis Fratrum Praedicatorum seu vetera ordinis monumenta,* vol. 3, Rome, 1897, 346: "Priorissa de consilio assignet duas sorores discretas et ordinis zelatrices que sint sollicite et intente circa gestus et facta sororum. et post completorium et de die eciam interdum claustrum et officinas cirvumeant," etc. For a German translation in a manuscript that belonged to the Katharinenkloster in Nuremberg, see A. Lee, *Materialien zum geisten Leben des späten fünfzehnten Jahrhunderts im Sankt Katharinenkloster zu Nürnberg, mit besonderer Berücksichtigung der Predigten Johannes Diemars,* Heidelberg, 1969, 79. According to the constitutions in *Analecta sacri ordinis,* 348, such a translation could not be carried out "sine licensia magistri vel prioris provincialis."

105. See Hamburger, 1992; and P. Zimmer, whose argument is epitomized in an article with the same title as her book *Die Funktion und Ausstattung des Altares auf der Nonnenempore,* in *Cistercienser Chronik* 99 (1992): 119–32.

106. See Hamburger, 1992, 109–11.

107. Johann III von Eych's account of the reform appears in B. Pez, *Bibliotheca Ascetica Antiquo-Nova,* Regensburg, 1725, vol. VIII, 651–70, reprinted (and slightly revised) in J. G. Süttner, "Reform des Klosters St. Walburg," *Pastoral-Blatt des Bisthums Eichstätt* 33 (1886). Regarding Johann III von Eych's reform efforts, *Die Eichstätter Bischofschronik,* 77, reports: "Sonst so gieng er nahend alle zeyt seyner regierung darmit umb wie er den geystlichen stand und besonder die priester in seynem bischtumb reformieren." For Marienberg bei Boppard, see P. Hofmeister, "Les Statuts du monastère des Bénédictines de Marienberg-lez-Boppard (1437)," *Revue Bénédictine* 46 (1934): 439–55; and the literature cited by P. Becker, "Rode, Johannes von Trier," ²VL, vol. II, 128–35.

108. See von Wilckens, 1979, 86; and *Die Eichstätter Bischofschronik,* 77: "Er ward in das kloster zu S. Walpurgen in die capellen S. Agnetis, die er von neuwen bauwen lassen, im auch ain ewigen jartag dahyn gestyfft, erlich zu den erden bestatet."

109. In this context, it is worth recalling that in Germany there was a long tradition of

incorporating single leaves such as those at Eichstätt into reliquaries; for an example of roughly the same date, see *Albrecht von Brandenburg, Kurfürst-Erzkanzler-Kardinal: Zum 500. Geburtstag eines deutschen Renaissancefürsten,* Mainz, 1990, fig. 20.

110. For the decoration of the altar, commissioned ca. 1500, see B. Mayer, "Die Schnitzfiguren des Gruftaltars von St. Walburg: Das Werk einer ostpreußischen Meister der Spätgotik?" *Historischer Verein Eichstätt: Sammelblatt* 87 (1994): 111–35.

111. See D. Schmidtke, *Studien zur dingallegorischen Erbauungsliteratur am Beispiel der Gartenallegorie,* Hermea NF 43, Tübingen, 1982, 400–405.

112. R. Metz, *La Consécration des vierges dans l'église romaine: Étude d'histoire de la liturgie,* Paris, 1954, 437, 439–40, and 442. In Saxon convents nuns atypically used conventional crowns; see H. Rüthing, "Die mittelalterliche Bibliothek des Zisterzienserinnenklosters Wöltingerode," in *Zisterzienische Spiritualität: Theologische Grundlagen, funktionale Vorraussetzungen und bildhafte Ausprägungen im Mittelalter,* 1. Himmelroder Kolloquium, Studien und Mitteilungen zur Geschichte des Benediktiner-Ordens und seiner Zweige: Ergängzungsband, 34, ed. C. Kasper and K. Schreiner, Ottobeuron, 1990, esp. 206.

113. For a related devotion, see W. Stammler, "Studien zur Geschichte der Mystik in Norddeutschland," in *Altdeutsche und altniederländische Mystik,* esp. 430.

114. For suckling as a metaphor of mystical union, see Hamburger, 1990, 78 and 82; for its roots in exegesis, consult H. Rahner, "'De Dominici pectoris fonte potavit,'" *Zeitschrift für katholische Theologie* 55 (1931): 103–8; and idem, "'Flumina de ventre Christi': Die patristische Auslegung von Joh. 7:37,38," *Biblia* 22 (1941): 269–302 and 367–401. For the imagery of the soul suckling at the breast of Jesus in twelfth-century texts, see C. W. Bynum, *Jesus as Mother: Studies in the Spirituality of the High Middle Ages,* Berkeley and Los Angeles, 1982, 110–69. Early modern examples are discussed by N. Pike, *Mystic Union: An Essay in the Phenomenology of Mysticism,* Ithaca, N.Y., 1992, 73–76.

115. See E. Panofsky, *Abbot Suger on the Abbey Church of St. Denis and Its Art Treasures,* ed. G. Panofsky-Soergel, 2d ed., Princeton, N.J., 1979, 10.

116. For the *imitatio Mariae* in female piety, see Hamburger, 1990, 88–104; M. Wehrli-Johns, "Haushälterin Gottes: Zur Mariennachfolge der Beginen," in *Maria, Abbild oder Vorbild? Zur Sozialgeschichte mittelalterliche Marienverehrung,* Tübingen, 1990, 146–67; and R. Hale, "*Imitatio Mariae:* Motherhood Motifs in Devotional Memoirs," *Mystics Quarterly* 16 (1990): 193–203. The study by G. Lüers, *Marienverehrung mittelalterliche Nonnen,* Munich, 1923, is disappointing.

117. My thanks to Del Kolve for providing this succinct formulation.

118. See the discussion of the Child in the Trinity, Chapter 4, p. 150. R. Berliner, "God Is Love," *Gazette des Beaux-Arts* 43 (1953): esp. 23, also defines the feminization and the infantilization of Christ as strategies for limiting the erotic suggestiveness of images depicting the love between Christ and the soul.

119. Metz, 442: "praesentantur ei a paranymphis duae primae virginis, ut prius, coram eo genuflexae."

120. Ibid., 439–40: "Tunc Pontifex accipiens annulum cum dextera sua, et dexteram manum virginis cum sinistra manu sua, et mittens annulum ipsum digito annulari dexterae manus virginis, desponsari illas Iesu Christo."

121. For the priesthood of Mary, see R. Laurentin, "Digne vesture au prestre souverain," *Revue du moyen âge latin* 4 (1948): 253–74; B. G. Lane, *The Altar and the Altarpiece: Sacramental Themes in Early Netherlandish Painting,* New York, 1984, 70–71; and K. Schreiner, *Maria: Jungfrau, Mutter, Herrscherin,* Vienna, 1994, 137–48.

122. Ordinariatsarchiv Eichstätt, Akt p. 33, transcribed in *Kloster Bergen bei Neuberg an der Donau und seine Fresken von Johann Wolfgang Baumgartner,* Kunst in Bayern und Schwaben, 3, ed.

B. Bushart et al., Weißenhorn, 1981, 37: "Sy sullen auch ir gewandt und pettgewandt und alle nottdurft also tragen und prachen nach geistlicher ordung und nicht nach köstlichait oder überflüssigkait, als dann die regel lernet." No less strict is the *ordo* addressed by Otto of Passau to the Poor Clares of Königsfelden, dated November 23, 1384, published in *Urkunden zur Schweizer Geschichte aus Österreichischen Archiven,* ed. R. Thommen, vol. II (1371–1410), Basel, 1890, cat. no. 184, esp. 179: "Die eptessin sol fliz han, wie krůslet tůchlin und wit hubtloch und enge rőkke und gevalten mentel und lang enge ermel und spizet schůh nach gesitlicher wiz gebessert wert, also so got und mir antwurten welle."

123. Mader, 277–78, fig. 210, notes that the figure was extensively restored in the eighteenth century.

124. Schreiber cat. nos. 824–25, reproduced in Field, vol. 163, 103, discussed briefly by Büttner, *Imitatio pietatis,* 129 and fig. 144, who, however, relates its imagery to depictions of the Coronation of the Virgin.

125. Metz, 448: "intraturae sponsi thalamum, occuratis cum gaudio."

126. Ibid., 452: "Oblatis hostiis, quaesumus, Domine, praesentibus famulabus tuis perseverantiam perpetuae virginitatis accomoda; ut apertis ianuis, summi Regis adventu regnum coelestum cum laetitia mereantur intrare."

127. Ibid., 453: "Deus, qui habitaculum tuum in corde pudico fundasti."

128. Hamburger, 1990, 52–55.

129. Pez, vol. VIII, 657: "suntque sine macula ac signati in frontibus suis sequuntur Agnum, quocunque ierit."

130. Metz, 444: "Te invocamus, Domine sancte, Pater omnipotens, aeterne Deus, super has famulas tuas, quae tibi voverunt pura mente, mundoque corde servire; ut eas sociare digneris inter illos centum quadraginta quatuor millia, qui virgines permanserunt, et se cum mulieribus non coinquinaverunt."

131. Ibid., 455: "Post haec virgines consecratae revertuntur ad portam monasterii, ubi Pontifex eas coram se genuflexas praesentat Abbatissae similiter genuflexae."

132. See Gertrude of Helfta, 1967; and idem, 1989. For additional literature on Gertrude, see Bynum, 1982, 170–262; Lewis, Willaert, and Govers, 196–218; and K. Ruh, 1993, 296–97.

133. Gertrude of Helfta, 1967, 102, lines 124–28: "Sancta Maria, mater regis agni, sponsi virginum, eia introduc me mundo corde et corpore ad filii tui Iesu contubernium. Omnes sancti angeli et archangeli, aia obtinete mihi puritate angelica introire thalamum Iesu sponsi mei." The translation is from Gertrude of Helfta, 1989, 45.

Chapter 2

1. See E. Wilkens, *The Rose-Garden Game: The Symbolic Background to the European Prayer-Beads,* London, 1969.

2. See E. M. Vetter, *Maria im Rosenhag,* Düsseldorf, 1956; and Stammler, "Studien zur Geschichte der Mystik in Norddeutschland," in *Altdeutsche und altniederländische Mystik,* 410–12.

3. See E. Auerbach, "Gloria passionis," in *Literary Language and Its Public in Late Latin Antiquity and in the Middle Ages,* trans. R. Manheim, intro. J. M. Ziolkowski, Princeton, N.J., 1993, 67–81.

4. See Hamburger, 1990, 70–72; also F. Ohly, *Hohelied-Studien: Grundzüge einer Geschichte der Hoheliedauslegung des Abendlandes bis um 1200,* Wiesbaden, 1958, 143–46.

5. For this complex of imagery, see F. Ohly, *Süsse Nagel der Passion: Ein Beitrag zur theologischen Semantik,* Saecvla spiritalia, 21, Baden-Baden, 1989, esp. 413–36.

6. See P. Dronke, "The Song of Songs and the Medieval Love Lyric," *The Bible and Medieval Culture,* Mediaevalia Lovaniensia 1/7, Louvain, 1979, 236–62; J. Brückmann and J. Couchman, "Du *Cantique des cantiques* aux *Carmina Burana:* Amour sacré et amour érotique," in *L'Érotisme au Moyen Âge: Études présentées au Troisième colloque de l'Institut d'études médiévales,* ed. B. Roy, Montreal, 1977, 37–50; R. Herde, "Das Hohelied in der lateinischen Literatur des Mittelalters bis zum 12. Jahrhundert," *Münchener Beiträge zur Mediävistik und Renaissance,* Forschungen 3, Spoleto, 1968, 957–1073; E. A. Matter, *The Voice of My Beloved: The Song of Songs in Western Medieval Christianity,* Philadelphia, 1990, esp. chap. 7; and the important qualifications added by A. W. Astell, *The Song of Songs in the Middle Ages,* Ithaca, N.Y., 1990, esp. 106 and 137.

7. Act II, scene ii, line 185.

8. I draw this apt opposition from B. Newman, "*La mystique courtoise:* Thirteenth-Century Beguines and the Art of Love," in *From Virile Woman to WomanChrist: Studies in Medieval Religion and Literature,* Philadelphia, 1995, esp. 140.

9. *John Donne: Poetry and Prose,* ed. F. J. Warnke, New York, 1967, 45, lines 71–72.

10. For an exploration of this issue in the context of German mystical literature, see A. M. Haas, "'Trage Leiden geduldiglich': Die Einstellung der deutschen Mystik zum Leiden," in idem, *Gottleiden-Gottlieben: Zur volkssprachlichen Mystik im Mittelalter,* Frankfurt, 1989, 127–52.

11. In addition to Michel, see A. M. Haas, "Sinn und Tragweite von Heinrich Seuses Passionsmystik," in *Die Passion Christi,* 94–112.

12. *Sermones de Vetere Testamento,* CC.SL, 41, ed. C. Lambot, Turnhout, 1961, no. 27.6: "Pendebat in cruce deformis; sed deformitas illius pulchritudo nostra erat."

13. See A. M. Haas and K. Ruh, "Seuse, Heinrich," ²VL, vol. VIII, 1109–29.

14. See E. Colledge and J. C. Marler, "Mystical Pictures in the Suso *Exemplar,* Ms. Strasbourg 2929," *Archivum Fratrum Praedicatorum* 54 (1984): 293–354; J. F. Hamburger, "The Use of Images in the Pastoral Care of Nuns: The Case of Heinrich Suso and the Dominicans," *Art Bulletin* 71 (1989): 20–46; and U. Weymann, *Die Seusesche Mystik und ihre Wirkung auf die bildende Kunst,* Berlin, 1939, 37–40.

15. *Henry Suso: The Exemplar, with Two German Sermons,* trans. and ed. F. Tobin, intro. B. McGinn, New York, 1989, 106. For the original German, see *Heinrich Seuse: Deutsche Schriften,* 64, lines 9–16: "und betútend die wissen rosen sin luterkeit und die roten rosen sin gedultekeit in menigvalitigem liden, daz er muͤz erliden. Und als der guldin sinwel ring, den man den heiligen umb daz hobt pfliget ze malene, als der bezeichent der roͤselohte ring menigvalitkeit dez lidens, daz die lieben gotesfrúnde muͤssent tragen, die wil sú noch in der zit mit ritterlicher uͤbung got dienend sind."

16. For Suso as a "knight," see M. Bindschedler, "Seuses Begriff der Ritterschaft," in *Heinrich Seuse: Studien zum 600. Todestag 1366–1966,* ed. E. M. Filthaut, Cologne, 1966, 233–40; for the imagery of athletic asceticism, see C. Eisler, "The Athlete of Virtue: The Iconography of Asceticism," in *De artibus opuscula xl: Essays in Honor of Erwin Panofsky,* ed. M. Meiss, 2 vols., New York, 1961, vol. I, 82–97.

17. For the varied functions of flower imagery in late medieval devotional painting, see, in addition to Wilkens, T. D. Kaufmann and V. R. Kaufmann, "The Sanctification of Nature: Observations on the Origins of Trompe l'Oeil in Netherlandish Book Painting of the Fifteenth and Sixteenth Centuries," *J. Paul Getty Museum Journal* 19 (1991): 43–64; D. Freedburg, "The Origins and Rise of the Flemish Madonnas in Flower Garlands: Decoration and Devotion," *Münchener Jahrbuch der bildenden Kunst,* 3d ser., 32 (1981): 115–50; K. McDonald, "*Et verbum caro factum est:* The Prayer-Book of Michelino da Besozzo," in *Medieval Texts and Images: Studies of Manuscripts from the Middle Ages,* ed. M. M. Manion and B. J. Muir, New York, 1991, 201–6; and R. L. Falkenburg, *The Fruit of Devotion: Mysticism and the Imagery of Love in Flemish Paintings*

of the Virgin and Child, 1450–1550, Oculi, 5, trans. S. Herman, Amsterdam and Philadelphia, 1994.

18. The various impressions and states, Schreiber cat. nos. 778–79, are listed in Field, vol. 163, 52–53. Further discussion is provided by *Einblattholzschnitte des XV. Jahrhunderts aus dem Kupferstichkabinett Basel,* Basel, 1994, 70. For the ostentatious display of the penis in medieval and Renaissance art, see L. Steinberg, *The Sexuality of Christ in Renaissance Art and in Modern Oblivion,* New York, 1983.

19. Reproduced and described in Spamer, pl. 8, fig. 1, without further discussion.

20. See R. Suckale, "*Arma Christi:* Überlegungen zur Zeichenhaftigkeit mittelalterlicher Andachtsbilder," *Städel-Jahrbuch* 6 (1977): 177–208; and D. Arasse, *Le Détail: Pour une histoire reproché de la peinture,* Paris, 1992, 52–78. As noted by C. W. Bynum, *The Resurrection of the Body in Western Christianity, 200–1336,* New York, 1995, 314 n.129, the fragmented representation of Christ's tortured body curiously contradicts the corporeal integrity of his "impassive and impassible" saints.

21. For the history of rosary devotions, see S. Ringbom, "*Maria in sole* and the Virgin of the Rosary," *Journal of the Warburg and Courtauld Institutes* 25 (1962): 326–30; J.-C. Schmitt, "La Confrérie du Rosaire de Colmar (1485): Textes de fondation, 'exempla' en allemand d'Alain de la Roche, liste des prêcheurs et des soeurs dominicaines," *Archivum Fratrum Praedicatorum* 40 (1970): 97–124; *500 Jahre Rosenkranz 1475 Köln 1975: Kunst und Frömmigkeit im Spätmittelalter und ihr Weiterleben,* Cologne, 1975; and A. Winston, "Tracing the Origins of the Rosary," *Speculum* 68 (1993): 619–36, with additional bibliography.

22. For the print, Schreiber cat. no. 1129, dated 1485, see Field, vol. 164, 163. For the sculpture in Nuremberg, see *Der Englishe Gruss des Veit Stoss zu St. Lorenz in Nürnberg,* Bayerische Landesamt für Denkmalpflege: Arbeitsheft, 16, Munich, 1983.

23. Adamantly opposed to rosary devotions, Luther chose as his own device a black cross set against a red heart enclosed in a white rose, a symbol of the saving power of faith selected in self-conscious opposition to the Marian cult at the heart of rosary rites, reproduced and discussed in *Martin Luther und die Reformation in Deutschland, Ausstellung zum 500. Geburtstag Martin Luthers,* Nuremberg, 1983, 378. For further discussion, see D. Koepplin, " 'Kommet her zu mir alle': Das tröstliche Bild des Gekreuzigten nach dem Verständnis Luthers," in *Martin Luther und die Reformation in Deutschland: Vorträge zur Ausstellung im Germanischen Nationalmuseum, Nürnberg, 1983,* ed. K. Löcher, Schriften des Vereins für Reformationsgeschichte, 194, 153–99. My thanks to Joseph Koerner for bringing this material to my attention.

24. See A. Schnyder, *Die Ursulabruderschaften des Spätmittelalters: Ein Beitrag zur Erforschung der deutschsprachigen religiösen Literatur des 15. Jahrhunderts,* Sprache und Dichtung, 34, Bern, 1986, 412–13; idem, "Die geistliche Padstube: Eine spätmittelalterliche Andachtsübung," *Zeitschrift für deutsches Altertum und deutsche Literatur* 113 (1984): 146–57; and T. Lentes, "Die Gewände der Heiligen: Ein Diskussionsbeitrag zum Verhältnis von Gebet, Bild und Imagination," in *Hagiographie und Kunst: Der Heiligenkult in Schrift, Bild und Architektur,* ed. G. Kerscher, Berlin, 1993, 120–51.

25. For the legend and its sources, see H. G. Richert, ed., "Vom Mönch und den Rosenkränzen," in *Marienlegenden aus dem Alten Passional,* Altdeutsche Textbibliothek, 64, Tübingen, 1965, 115–30; for the church and its decoration, which included paintings by Dürer and Grünewald, see K. Beck, *Das Dominikanerkloster in Frankfurt am Main,* Frankfurt, 1977.

26. AA.SS March III, esp. 737: "Nam cum esset sex annorum, quasi suae praenuntia sanctitatis, cum puellis sibi coaevis flores colligens, illos non sibi sed imaginibus Sanctorum repraesentabat; ferraque rosarum, quae sibi afferebantur, imagini Virginis gloriosae benigne offerebat."

27. Also discussed by Lentes, fig. 1.

28. H. Meersseman, "Les Frères prêcheurs et le mouvement dévot en Flandre au XIIIe s.,"

Archivum Fratrum praedicatorum 18 (1948): esp. 86 n. 44: "délivrer pour le doit de relief ung chapeau de roses ou de violettes ou d'autres verdures selon la saison, le quel chapeau sera offert et posé sur le chief Nostre Dame en la chapelle que l'on dist à la Treille."

29. See *Sieben bisher unveröffentlichte Traktate und Lektionen,* ed. P. Strauch, Schriften aus der Gottesfreund-Literatur, 1, Halle, 1927, 1–21; and G. Steer, "Merswin, Rulwin," ²VL, vol. VI, 420–42, esp. 432–33.

30. "Lebensbeschreibung der sel. Christina von Retters," *Archiv für mittelrheinische Kirchengeschichte* 17–18 (1965–66): vol. 17, 230: "yn der roge sache [sie] yn eynem geistlichyn gesicht daz aller lyeblichstes kyntgyn Jesus vor yr vff dem stoille gayn spellen vnd waden yn den aller suberlichtsten roißen, die vff erden noch ye geworden. Iß waren keyn yrdeschyn roißen, sie waren hemelsche; . . . Da sache sie aber daz zarte aller suberlichstes kyntgen stayn vor dem elter yn eyner wegen, vnd iß was gedecket myt eym dechelach van roißen, vnd vff eynem yecklichyn blaytde der roißen stontde geschrebyn: 'pater noster,' vnd iß hait eyn crantze vf sym heubt van XII gar schonen roißen, vnd got gaiffe yre so verstayn, daz iß waren die czwolff funffzich pater noster, die sie dem kynde Jesu gesprochyn haitte." For additional bibliography on Christina, see Lewis, Willaert, and Govers, 236–37; and K. Kösters, "Christina von Hane," ²VL, vol. I, 1225–28.

31. Nuremberg, Stadtbibliothek, Ms. Cent. VI 43ᵇ, ff. 83v–92v. For an edition and commentary, see J. F. Hamburger, "*Von Jhesus pettlein* (On the little bed of Jesus): Pictorial Piety in an Unpublished Letter of Spiritual Advice from the Katharinenkloster in Nuremberg," forthcoming.

32. "*Jhesus* der jünckfrawen *Maria* sun der wünniglich schön wolriechend rosenstock sey dein trost der dir dein hercz stetiglich erfrewen müß vnd auch dein kürczweil für dy zeitlichen vnd kürcz hy in diser falschen welt, vnd dein erster amplick so du auff steest vnd dar vntter spaciren geest, vnd dye rosenpletter in das körblein dein herczen list dy der rosenstock cristus in der angst seins leydens gerertt hatt do er am olperg knÿet vnd do er das creucz auff trug." For the symbolism of the bed, see Hamburger, 1990, 76 and 106–16; and K. Lerchner, *Lectulus floridus: Zur Bedeutung des Bettes in Literatur und Handschriftenillustrationen des Mittelalters,* Pictura et poesis, 6, Cologne, 1993.

33. Falkenburg, 43 and fig. 49, reproduces a plate from *Die geestelicke boomgaert* (The spiritual orchard), in which the soul gathers flowers, roses among them, in the garden of Gethsemane. Suso employs similar imagery; see *Heinrich Seuse,* 54★ and 61★.

34. P. M. Halm, "Die Madonna mit dem Rosenstrauch im Bayerischen Nationalmuseum," *Münchener Jahrbuch für bildenden Kunst* 9 (1921): 3–12.

35. See L. Gnädinger, "Rosenwunden: Des Angelus Silesius, 'Die Psyche begehrt ein Bienelein auff den Wunden Jesu zu seyn,' (Heilige Seelenlust II,52)," in *Deutsche Baroklyrik: Gedichtinterpretationen von Spee bis Haller,* ed. M. Bircher and A. M. Haas, Bern and Munich, 1973, esp. 110–14.

36. See W. Passarge, *Das deutsche Vesperbild im Mittelalter,* Deutsche Beiträge zur Kunstwissenschaft, 1, Cologne, 1924; and F. C. Schneider, *Die mittelalterlichen deutschen Typen und Vorformen des Vesperbildes,* Rendsburg, 1933.

37. For the joyful Pietà, see E. Reiners-Ernst, *Das freudvolle Vesperbild und die Anfänge der Pietà-Vorstellung,* Munich, 1939, a theme inexplicably omitted by J. Svenberg, "The Gothic Smile," in *Künstlerischer Austausch,* vol. II, 357–70.

38. For the *Liebestod* in *Minnesang* as well as mystical thought, see A. M. Haas, "Mystik oder Erotik: Dialektik von Tod und Leben in Gottfried's *Tristan,*" and "Mors Mystica," both in *Todesbilder im Mittelalter: Fakten und Hinweise in der deutschen Literatur,* Darmstadt, 1989, 139–74 and 222–32, with extensive bibliography.

39. For this motif, see W. Krönig, *Rheinische Vesperbilder,* Mönchengladbach, 1967, 18–19.

Cf. the rose prominently displayed between the two kneeling donors immediately beneath the *sudarium* in the wall plaque from Brombach, second quarter of the fourteenth century, now in the Liebieghaus, Frankfurt, reproduced and discussed with related representations by A. Legner, "Das Bronnbacher Wanddenkmal im Liebieghaus," in *Kurt Bauch zum 70. Geburtstag von seinen Schülern,* Berlin, 1970, esp. 33–35.

40. As noted by Büttner, 1983, 47–55. For the example illustrated in Fig. 57, see J. H. Oliver, *Gothic Manuscript Illumination in the Diocese of Liège (c. 1250–c. 1330),* 2 vols., Corpus of Illuminated Manuscripts from the Low Countries, Louvain, 1990.

41. See C. W. Dutschke, *Guide to Medieval and Renaissance Manuscripts in the Huntington Library,* 2 vols., San Marino, Calif., 1989, vol. 1, with a discussion of the prints on 225–27; and P. E. Webber, *A Late Medieval Devotional Anthology from Salzburg ("Nonnberg Passion": Huntington Library HM 195) Commentary and Edition,* Göppingen Arbeiten zur Germanistik, 531, Göppingen, 1990, 77–78. For a closely related vernacular prayer book with a series of Passion scenes printed directly on its pages (Munich, Staatsbibliothek Cgm. 105), see B. Weiske, "Bilder und Gebete vom Leben und Leiden Christi: Zu einem Zyklus im Gebetbuch des Johannes von Indersdorf für Frau Elisabeth Ebran," in *Die Passion Christi,* esp. 118–21. For other prayer books illustrated with prints, F. O. Schuppisser, "Copper Engravings of 'Mass Production' Illustrating Netherlandish Prayer Manuscripts," in *Master and Miniatures: Proceedings of the Congress on Medieval Manuscript Illumination in the Northern Netherlands (Utrecht, 10–13 December 1990),* ed. K. van der Horst and J.-C. Klamt, Dornspijk, 1991, 389–400; and P. E. Webber, "*Denuo ad fontes:* Un(der)studied Analogues of Previously Reported Visual and Textual Material in *Vita Christi* Devotional Cycles," in *Miscellanea Neerlandica,* vol. I, 465–77, with additional bibliography.

42. Webber, 78: "Schreib in mein hertz die gedachtnüz deiner pittern angst vnd mater vnd besunder die vnwerd vnd smachait in deiner ellenden vankchnusß die du durich meinen willen geliten hast; mach ledig mein arme sel von den panden der sund, Vnd behuet sy hinfur von der ewigen vankchnusß. Gib zu betrachten meiner sel dein groz leyden, dein pleutuergissen daß du vergossen hast in der gayslung, in der chronung, Vnd an dem heyligen chreutz, Da dein heyliger leichnam versert ward vnd dein vnschildigß hertz verbundt. Hilff meiner chrankchen sel vnd gib ir eryzney auß deinem verwuntten hertzen daß sy chom in das wesen," etc. For Johannes, see B. D. Haage, "Johannes von Indersdorf," [2]VL, vol. IV, 647–51.

43. "Ne abscondas faciem tuam a me in die tribulationis meae, inclina ad me aurem tuam in quacumque die invocavero velociter exaudi me."

44. For the motif of Christ reciprocating the gaze of the viewer, see J. H. Marrow, "'In desen speigell': A New Form of *Memento mori* in Fifteenth-Century Netherlandish Art," in *Essays in Northern European Art Presented to Egbert Haverkamp-Begemann,* ed. A.-M. Logan, Doornspijk, 1983, 154–63.

45. See *Il Libro della Beata Angela da Foligno,* 466: "Pone hoc speculum ante oculos tuos et stude cum tot te de ista oratione habere, quia ipse pro te oravit, non pro seipso."

46. Cf. the evocation of the Agony in the Garden in Aelred of Rievaulx's letter of spiritual advice to his sister, *De inclusione inclusarum,* chap. 31, lines 1110–11, in *Opera Omnia,* CC.CM 1, ed. A. Hoste and C. H. Talbot, Turnhout, 1971, 669: "Noli dormire cum Petro, ne merearis audire: Sic non potuisti una hora uigilare mecum?"

47. See, for example, the engraving of the Agony in the Garden by the Master of the Berlin Passion, reproduced in Hernad, fig. 30.

48. See G. Schiller, *The Iconography of Christian Art,* vol. II, *The Passion of Jesus Christ,* trans. J. Seligman, Greenwich, Conn., 1972, 48–51; M. Bartmuss, *Die Entwicklung der Gethsemane-Darstellung bis um 1400,* Halle, 1935; and J. Thüner, "Öelberg," LCI, vol. III, 342–49.

49. See O. (Schmucki) von Rieden, "Das Leiden Christi im Leben des heiligen Franziskus von Assisi: Eine quellenvergleichende Untersuchung im Lichte der zeitgenössischen Passionsfrömmigkeit," *Collectanea Fransiscana* 30 (1960): 5–30, 129–45, 241–63, and 353–97; idem, *The Stigmata of St. Francis of Assisi: A Critical Investigation in the Light of Thirteenth-Century Sources,* trans. C. F. Connors, St. Bonaventure, N.Y., 1991; and S. da Campagnola, *L'angelo del sesto sigillo e l'"alter Christus": Genesi e sviluppo di due temi francescani nei secoli XIII–XIV,* Rome, 1971. For representations of Francis as the *alter Christus,* see H. van Os, "St. Francis of Assisi as a Second Christ in Early Italian Painting," in idem, *Studies in Early Tuscan Painting,* London, 1992, 203–32.

50. For the iconography of St. Francis, see, most recently, C. Frugoni, *Francesco e l'invenzione delle stimmate: Una storia per parole e immagini fino a Bonaventura e Giotto,* Turin, 1993. Reports of the stigmatization were subject to skepticism that was met, in part, through an appeal to the testimony, miraculous or otherwise, of images; see A. Vauchez, "Les Stigmates de saint François et leurs détracteurs dans les derniers siècles du Moyen Âge," *Mélanges d'archéologie et d'histoire* 80 (1968): 595–625.

51. Explored by J. Fleming, *From Bonaventure to Bellini: An Essay in Franciscan Exegesis,* Princeton, N.J., 1982, esp. 32–74.

52. On the parallel between Francis at Alverna and Christ on the Mount of Olives, which has virtually escaped notice, see H. Feld, *Der Ikonoklasmus des Westens,* Studies in the History of Christian Thought, 41, Leiden, 1990, 73–79; and Frugoni, 321–24 and pls. 11–12. The seal of the Franciscan province of Strasbourg, reproduced in *Alemania Franciscana Antiqua* 3 (1957), 44, depicts the Agony in the Garden, together with an inscription that paraphrases Luke 22:42: "verumtamen pater non mea volunta apostoli dormiunt."

53. See K. Kruger, *Der frühe Bildkult des Franziskus in Italien: Gestalt- und Funktionswandel des Tafelbildes im 13. und 14. Jahrhundert,* Berlin, 1992, esp. 149–72.

54. Büttner, 1983, 51, 255, and fig. 38, with additional bibliography. The same motif is sometimes incorporated into epitaphs; see, e.g., the tomb of Canon Jean de Wastine, ca. 1433, in the cathedral of Tournai, reproduced in *Notre-Dame, the Cathedral of Tournai: The Visitor's Guidebook,* Tournai: Art et histoire, 10, Tournai, 1994, 15, in which the canon kneels in prayer at the gate of the garden of Gethsemane.

55. For this phenomenon, see M. Camille, *The Gothic Idol: Ideology and Image-Making in Medieval Art,* Cambridge, 1989; for iconoclastic tendencies in the German-speaking world during the fifteenth century, see J. Rohls, "'. . . unser Knie beugen wir doch nicht mehr': Bilderverbot und bildende Kunst im Zeitalter der Reformation," *Zeitschrift für Theologie und Kirche* 81 (1984): 322–51; H. Bredekamp, *Kunst als Medium sozialer Konflikte: Bilderkämpfe von der Spätantike bis zur Hussitenrevolution,* Frankfurt, 1975, esp. pt. III; Feld, 85–104; S. Michalski, *The Reformation and the Visual Arts: The Protestant Image Question in Western and Eastern Europe,* London, 1993; and N. Schnitzler, *Ikonoklasmus-Bildersturm: Theologischer Bilderstreit und ikonoklastisches Handeln während des 15. und 16. Jahrhunderts,* Munich, 1996.

56. See D. Munk, *Die Ölberg-Darstellung in der Monumentalplastiks Sud-Deutschlands,* Tübingen, 1968. The arcade above the door opening onto the cloister of the cathedral in Eichstätt, reproduced in Mader, 172, incorporates a reproduction of an Agony in the Garden, ca. 1425, of which the original is now in the Bayerisches Nationalmuseum, Munich. Set into the tracery of the lintel and facing out into the cloister, it identifies the enclosed space as the garden of Gethsemane.

57. Ms. 241, described by L. Hunkeler, "Ein Chorwochenbüchlein aus dem Engelberger Frauenkloster," in *Angelomontana: Blätter aus der Geschichte von Engelberg: Jubiläumsgabe für Abt Leodegar II.,* Gossau and St. Gall, 1914, esp. 186. For mystical literature from Engelberg, see

K. Ruh, "Deutsche Literatur im Benediktinerinnenkloster St. Andreas in Engelberg," in idem, *Kleine Schriften II: Scholastik und Mystik im Spätmittelalter,* Berlin, 1984, 275–95.

58. For the commemoration of the Agony in the Garden on Holy Thursday, see L. A. Veit, *Volksfrommes Brauchtum und Kirche im deutschen Mittelalter,* Freiburg, 1936, 169. The texts gathered by D. Schmidtke, 16–17, 40, 56–58, and 405–6, under the rubric "Rosegarten des Leidens Christi" associate each of Christ's three petitions at Gethsemane with a rosebush.

59. See P. Ochsenbein, *Das Grosse Gebet der Eidgenossen: Überlieferung, Text, Form und Gehalt,* Bibliotheca Germanica, 29, Bern, 1989. In the Latin life of Angela of Foligno, her biographer uses similar, if not identical, terminology to refer to bodily, mental, and supernatural prayer; see *Il Libro della Beata Angela da Foligno,* 638: "Triplex schola orationis . . . est enim oratio corporalis, mentalis et supernaturalis."

60. Hence Hunkeler's bewilderment, 186, as to what the nun might have meant by the term "threefold": "Was damit gemeint ist, konnte ich nich ermitteln."

61. Ibid.: "und zeichnet das dů únser her got uf dem berg bettet, und er denn blůtigen schweiß schwiczt, das er dů dristen ab sinem gebett gieng und er trost sůcht an sinen lieben jungren und er kein trost an inen fand, und sond zu dem ersten únsren her got bitten und ermanen als des we und schmerczes so er an sinem heilgen höpt je erleid, das er sich erbarmi úber alle die höpter in der cristenheit. Zů dem andren mal so söllend wir únsren her got ermanen als des we und der müdi so er an sinen heilgen glideren je erleid die ällÿ verserd waren von dem höpt biß uf die füß, das nút ganczes an im was, das er sich erbarmi über ällÿ die glieder der heilgen cristenheit. Zů dem tritten so sollen wir únsren her got ermanen aller der angst und not in die sin heilige sel ie kam, das er sich erbarmi úber all glůbig selen."

62. Reproduced and described in ibid., 178 and 185.

63. *Leben der Schwestern zu Töß,* 33: "als únser her Jhesus Christus bettet uff dem berg." For the question of authorship, see K. Grubmüller, "Die Viten der Schwestern von Töss und Elsbeth Stagel: Überlieferung und literarische Einheit," *Zeitschrift für deutsches Altertum und Literatur* 98 (1969): 171–204; and B. Stoll, "Die theologischen Denkfiguren bei Elsbeth Stagel und ihren Mitschwestern," in *Denkmodelle von Frauen im Mittelalter,* Dokimion, 15, ed. B. W. Acklin Zimmermann, Fribourg, 1994, 149–72.

64. *Leben der Schwestern zu Töß,* 33–34: "das erst der ellendikait so sin zartes hertz hat, do er sich verzech aller menschen gesellschaft, und in allen sinen nötten unbehulfen von allen creaturen wolt sin; das ander der grossen nott so sin ellendes hertz hat, do er gieng uss dem schirm sins himelschlichen vatters in allen den unmilten úblen gewalt siner figenden; das drit, das er gieng uss dem trost des hailgen gaistes, also das sin martter und liden kam uff das aller hőchst."

65. Bonaventure, *Legenda maior S. Francisci Assiensis,* Florence, 1941, 107: "quod sicut Christus fuerat imitatus in actibus vitae, sic conformis ei esse deberet in afflictionibus et doloribus passionis, antequam ex hoc mundo transiret."

66. Ludolf of Saxony, *Vita Jesu Christi,* 4 vols., Paris, 1870, vol. IV, 469–79. For an exhaustive treatment of Ludolf's sources, see W. Baier, *Untersuchungen zu den Passionsbetrachtungen in der Vita Christi des Ludolfs von Sachsen,* 3 vols., Analecta Carthusiana, 44, Salzburg, 1977.

67. For another extended set of meditations on the Agony in the Garden in which prayer postures are specified, see the "Grosse Gebet der Eidgenossen," analyzed by Ochsenbein, esp. 62–68, first recorded in the sixteenth century but based on earlier models.

68. Both postures, with reference to Christ's words at Gethsemane, are referred to in the treatise on prayer by Peter the Chanter as his fourth and fifth modes; see R. C. Trexler, *The Christian at Prayer: An Illustrated Manual Attributed to Peter the Chanter,* Medieval and Renaissance Texts and Studies, 44, Binghamton, N.Y., 1978, 187–88; and idem, "Legitimating Prayer Gestures in the Twelfth Century: The *De penetentia* of Peter the Chanter," *History and Anthropology* 1 (1984): 97–126.

69. Ludolf of Saxony, vol. IV, 473: "Vigilate, attente, oculis mentis et corporis, et orate, devote, verbis cordis et oris."

70. Ibid., 471: "et positus genibus, procidit in faciem suam, super terram, ut humilitatem mentis ostenderet habitu corporis, et orebat corde."

71. Part of a larger practice, for which see J.-C. Schmitt, *La Raison des gestes dans l'occident médiévale,* Paris, 1991.

72. M. Harrsen, *Cursus Sanctae Mariae: A Thirteenth-Century Manuscript, now M. 739 in the Pierpont Morgan Library,* New York, 1937.

73. See Thüner, "Öelberg," LCI, vol. III, 342–49

74. Ochsenbein, esp. 203–12. M. Barth, "Die Haltung beim Gebet in elsässischen Dominikanerinnenklöstern des 15. und 16. Jahrhunderts," *Archiv für elsässische Kirchengeschichte* 13 (1938): 141–48, also inventories prayer gestures prescribed in the rubrics of German-language prayer books, none of which, however, corresponds to the prayer customs I describe here.

75. See E. Plüss, *Dürers Darstellungen Christi am Ölberg,* Zurich, 1954; also Büttner, 1993–94, 115–16.

76. Not that monks and friars did not employ them as well, although there is far less evidence that they did. See, e.g., W. Hood, "St. Dominic's Manners of Praying: Gestures in Fra Angelico's Frescoes at S. Marco," *Art Bulletin* 68 (1986): 195–206; and idem, *Fra Angelico at S. Marco,* London, 1993, 245, who discusses the fresco of the Agony in the Garden at San Marco as an exemplum of prayer and meditation.

77. See W. Fries, "Kirche und Kloster zu St. Katharina in Nürnberg," *Mitteilungen des Vereins für Geschichte der Stadt Nürnberg* 25 (1924): esp. 91, who, however, does not speculate on the function of the two murals.

78. Staatsbibliothek zu Berlin—Preußischer Kulturbesitz, Ms. germ. oct. 17, ff. 18r–18v: "Wen du bist jn betrübnis vnd angst, so val nider für das Bild der angst vnsers herren an dem ölleberg vnd sprich den Psalm [50]: 'Miserere,' do mit beger vergebung der sünden, durch dü du solliches verschuldet hest," transcribed by Barth, 1938, 145.

79. For prayer of this kind, see Barth, ibid.; and P. Ochsenbein, "Beten 'mit zertanen armen': Ein alteidgenössischer Brauch," *Schweiz: Archiv für Volkskunde* 75 (1979): 129–72.

80. Barth, 1938, esp. 145: "Wenn du bist jn betrübnis, so gang für das bild vnser lieben frowen vnd knuwe nider vnd sprich ein Salve Regina vnd denn diß gebet stonde krucz wiß: 'Stand vf du rein küsche maget Maria.' "

81. See J. E. Ziegler and W. Simons, "Phenomenal Religion in the Thirteenth Century and Its Image: Elisabeth of Spalbeek and the Passion Cult," in *Women in the Church,* Studies in Church History, 27, ed. W. J. Sheils and D. Woods, Oxford, 1990, 117–26; and Simons, "Reading a Saint's Body: Rapture and Bodily Movement in the *Vitae* of Thirteenth-Century Beguines," in *Framing Medieval Bodies,* ed. S. Kay and M. Rubin, Manchester, 1994, 10–23.

82. "Vita venerabilis Lukardis," 327–28 (chap. XXXV).

83. For Marienwerder's life of Dorothy of Montau, see P. Hörner, *Dorothea von Montau: Überlieferung—Interpretation,* Information und Interpretation: Arbeiten zu älteren germanische, deutsche und nordischen Sprachen und Literaturen, 7, Frankfurt, 1993. For additional bibliography, see A. Triller, "Marienwerder, Johannes," [2]VL, vol. VI, 56–61; and Lewis, Willaert, and Govers, 263–75.

84. R. Kieckhefer, *Unquiet Souls: Fourteenth-Century Saints and Their Religious Milieu,* Chicago, 1984, 117.

85. *Vita Dorotheae Montoviensis Magistri Johannis Marienwerder,* ed. H. Westphal and A. Triller, Forschungen und Quellen zur Kirchen- und Kulturgeschichte Ostdeutschlands, 1, Cologne and Graz, 1964, 69: "Solebat eciam noctis tempore hoc frequenter agere, quod brachia in modum crucis extendit et sic stando ad lassitudinem se afflixit. Post hoc ponens se ad parietem

quasi ad crucem se affixit, cuius brachia aliquando clavis, aliquando foraminibus digitis intrusis sustentabantur."

86. Ibid.: "Unde in memoriam trine oracionis Domini Ihesu in monte Oliveti tres solebat exercere venias. Primam fecit geniculando manus extendens crucifixe, et hec vocabatur ab ea genuum venia (scil. knyvenie). Secundam fecit geniculando manibus coniunctus et in celum erectis, sicut salvator depingitur orans in monte Oliveti. Terciam fecit procidendo in faciem manibus extensis in modum crucis, et hec nominabatur ab ea venia crucis (scil. cruczvenie)."

87. Bériou, 552, cites another instance, exceptional in her words, of a thirteenth-century author, Peter Comestor, appealing to images (in this case, of the Nativity) as supplements to the authority of Scripture.

88. For another comparison of a prayerful attitude to the pose of a figure in a painting, see S. Tugwell, "The Nine Ways of Prayer of St. Dominic: A Textual Study and Critical Edition," *Medieval Studies* 47 (1985): 1–24, 47, and 108, cited with further commentary by A. D. Hedeman, "Roger van der Weyden's Escorial Crucifixion and Carthusian Devotional Practice," in *The Sacred Image East and West,* esp. 197.

89. Dresden, Kupferstichkabinett der Staatlichen Kunstsammlungen, Hs. A 71a, ff. 7v–9v, described by F. O. Schuppisser, "Schauen mit dem Augen des Herzens: Zur Methodik der spätmittelalterlichen Passionsmeditation, besonders in der *Devotio moderna* und bei den Augustinern," in *Die Passion Christi,* 174–76, who does not, however, affiliate it with the tradition of devotions I have reconstructed here.

90. Ibid.: "Primo ipsum Christum in sua ymagine ante oculos ponere, tamquam Christum corporaliter videat."

91. As noted by Schuppisser, 176–84.

92. Ibid., 175 n. 23.

93. Ibid., 175: "Secundo gracias agere. Tercio compati. Quarto sibi oracionem formare, secundum membrum in quo meditatur. Quinto exemplum vite sue accipere, prout Christus in vita sua docuit et monstravit."

94. Karlsruhe, Badische Landesbibliothek, Ms. Donaueschingen 437, f. 74r, formerly Donaueschingen, Hofbibliothek Ms. 437. See Büttner, 1983, 54–55, 213, and fig. 41; von Heusinger, 1953, 103 and 144–49; and *Bewahrtes Kulturerbe— "Unberechenbare Zinsen": Katalog zur Austellung der vom Land Baden-Württemberg erworbenen Handschriften der Fürstlich Fürstembergischen Hofbibliothek,* ed. F. Heinzer, Stuttgart and Karlsruhe, 1993, 118–19. The miniature, one of forty-three, accompanies the fifteenth of twenty-five prayers for Tuesday, "ferya tercia" in a set of seven, one for each day of the week, which as a whole make up an extended meditation on the lives of Christ and the Virgin.

95. See H. Degering, *Kurzer Verzeichnis der germanischen Handschriften der Preußischer Staatsbibliothek, II, Die Handschriften in Oktavoformat,* Mitteilungen aus der Preußischer Staatsbibliothek, 9, Leipzig, 1932, reprinted Graz, 1970, 23–25; Wegener, 1928, 65; and Büttner, 1983, 51 and 208.

96. G. Hoppeler, "Ein Erbauungs- und Andachtsbuch aus dem Dominikanerinnenkloster Ötenbach in Zürich vom Jahre 1436," *Zeitschrift für Schweizerische Kirchengeschichte* 18 (1924): esp. 214: "O milter herre Jesu Criste, als du an dem Öliberg fúr mich und alle menschen in der aller grősten not, in dinem andechtigen gebette blůtigen sweis hett geswitzet, der angste und note erman ich dich herre und bitten dich, das du mir gebest, das ich in der gedechtnusse des selben dines heiligen lidens enzúndet und also inbrustig werde, das ich har inne erwerbe fúr dinen plutigen sweis andehtige tråhen, di mir ab wåschen alle min sunde und mich behůten wellest nu und ewenclich vor allem úbel."

97. In the prayer book in Berlin, ff. 3v–18v, the accompanying rubric and prayer (the first

of eight for the liturgical hours) refer at the outset to Christ's eucharistic sacrifice: "Dis gebet kumet von dem öleberg vnd wart einem heiligen einsidel geoffenbart. Der erste complet [Compline]: O süsser ihesus christus des lebenden gottes sun unser erlöser, ich danke dir wie gar getruwe bistu uns gewesen, wie erbarmherczelich hestu vns besorget do du vns geben hest den köstlichen schatz dines heiligen libes vnd blůtes."

98. "Die Chronik von Anna von Munzingen," 161: "Da sprach ein styme zů ir: 'Das ich nacket vnd blos stůnd an dem crutz durch dinen willen, des machtu mir niena mit als wol gedancken als da mit, dz du dich beroubest dines eignen wilen.' "

99. Ibid., 185. "Die bettete sunderlich gerne vnseres Herren marter. Vnd zů einem male, do stůnd si vor eime crúcifixe vnd bettete gar ernst, vnd vnser Herre der neiget sich ab dem crútze gen ir. Vnd si sprach: 'O we Herre, dis verdiente ich nie vmb dich, vnd enbin sin nút wirdig.' . . . Vnd darnach gie si als grosse betrübde an, vnd leit als vil, das si, das duchte das es ir vnmúglich were, keine wile ze lidende. Vnd forchte, das ir Gotte vergessen hette, vnd bat vnsern Herren von allem irem hertzen vnd mit maingem trähene, das er ir die leidunge abnäme, vnd dett das gar dicke, vnd sunderlich zů einem male nach metti. Da lag si in dem cappittel in dem rechten core an ir andacht, vnd bat vnsern herren gar erstlich, das er ir die lidunge abneme, vnd weinde hertzeklich. Also was ir wie ir hertze gar wite wurde, vnd ein gross liechte kam in si, vnd vnßer Herre kam mit dem liechte, vnd stůnd fúr si mit allen den wundem, so er je enpfieng vnd sprach zů ir: 'Owe, machtu nút enwenig durch minen willen geliden?' Vnd nam si bi der hant vnd sprach zů ir: 'Sich mine frúsche wunden vnd lůg was ich durch dinen willen erlitten han.' Vnd sprach aber: 'Da was dich ze liden anegat, das soltu getulteklich liden. Wann ich bin mit dir vnd wil mit dir sin in allen dinen arbeiten, vnd wil dich niemer gelan.' Vnd si sprach: 'Herre ich will yemer me gerne durch dinen willen liden wz mich joch anegat.' "

100. E. Duffy, "Devotion to the Crucifix and Related Images in England on the Eve of the Reformation," in *Bilder und Bildersturm,* esp. 31, overemphasizes the differences between pre- and post-Reformation attitudes on this score.

101. *St. Benedict's Rule for Monasteries,* trans. L. J. Doyle, Collegeville, Minn., 1948, 1.

102. Ibid., 6.

103. *Analecta sacri ordinis Fratrum Praedicatorum seu vetera ordinis monumenta,* vol. 3, 342: "propriam voluntatem deserere pro voluntate maiorum, voluntariam obedienciam in omnibus observare."

104. M. Straganz, "Die ältesten Statuten des Klarissenklosters zu Brixen (Tirol)," *Franziskanische Studien* 6 (1919): esp. 152: "alle ding sollen mit ordnung vnter euch beschehen, . . . die in inen soll mer vnd förderlicher den in andern vnd weltlichen menschen gehalten werden, do wider aber der geistlich mensch, der durch sein aigen willen sunder andacht oder werck von der gemain sich abzeucht, oft vil vnordnung pringt vnd also sich von got entpfrömdet. . . . das gehorsam pesser [ist] den kein opfer, vnd ein klein zymlich gut werck in gehorsam volpracht werder ist den vil grosser ander gutter werck auß aygmen furnemen."

105. H. Menhardt, "Nikolaus von Dinkelsbühls deutsche Predigt vom Eigentum in Kloster," *Zeitschrift für deutsche Philologie des Mittelalters* 73 (1954): 1–39, 268–91, and 74 (1955): 36–41, esp. vol. 73, 24: "vnd die selben ding, die ir also gegeben sind, die nůczt si nach alem irem willen."

106. For self-mortification in medieval monasticism, see G. Constable, *Attitudes towards Self-Inflicted Suffering in the Middle Ages,* Ninth Stephen J. Brademas, Sr., Lecture, Brookline, Mass., 1982; and, for a case study involving one convent, Hamburger, 1995.

107. For similar admonitions, see Hamburger, 1995; Haas, 1985; and O. Langer, " 'We ist ein gut wort, weist ein gnadenrichez wort': Zur Spiritualität der Dominikanerinnen im Spätmittelalter," in *Lerne leiden: Leidensbewältigung in der Mystik,* ed. W. Böhme, Karlsruhe, 1985, 21–34.

108. *Heinrich Seuses Horologium Sapientiae,* 478 ("Quam utile sit servo dei in hoc mundo multas sustinere tribulationes") and 499 ("Quomodo verus Christi discipulus debet se configurare passionibus ipsius").

109. Ibid., 492: "ad rosiferas passiones tuas, o flos campi et rosa sine spina, aeterna sapientia, summo cum desiderio rursus cordis oculos retorquemus."

110. Ibid., 487: "Si tribulationes non affligerent, tribulationes appellari non valerent."

111. Ibid., 486: "Accede et fiducialiter dic ad ipsum: 'Pater mi, non mea sed tua voluntas fiat.'"

112. See K. Ruh, *Meister Eckhart: Theologe, Prediger, Mystiker,* Munich, 1989, 114–35.

113. *Meister Eckhart: Sermons and Treatises,* trans. M. O'C. Walshe, Longmead, Dorset, 1987, vol. III, 69–71.

114. For the vast and growing bibliography on Gertrude, see Lewis, Willaert, and Govers, 196–223.

115. See K. Ruh, "Gertrud von Helfta: Ein neues Gertrud-Bild," *Zeitschrift für deutsches Altertum und deutsche Literatur* 121 (1992): 1–20. For obedience as a theme in the works by Gertrude's associates, see J. Lanczkowski, "Gertrude die Große von Helfta: Mystik des Gehorsams," in *Religiöse Frauenbewegung,* 153–64; and C. Eliass, *Die Frau ist die Quelle der Weisheit: Weibliches Selbstverständnis in der Frauenmystik des 12. und 13. Jahrhunderts,* Frauen in Geschichte und Gesellschaft, 28, Pfaffenweiler, 1995, 161–63.

116. Gertrude of Helfta, 1978, 208 (bk. IV, chap. 22): "Ut scilicet frequentius mente revolvas cum gratitudine et compassione anxietatem illam qua ego Creator tuus et Dominus in agonia constitutus prolixus oravi, dum prae nimietate anxietatis desiderii et amoris, sanguineo sudore faciem terrae irrigavi; et omnia opera tua omniaque circa te agenda mihi commendes in unione subjectionis illius qua ego in eadem oratione dixi ad patrem: 'Pater, non mea sed tu voluntas fiat.' Et sic omnia prospera et adversa suscipias in illo amore quo ego tibi omnia immitto ad salutem. Prospera igitur suscipias cum gratitudine, in unione illius amore quo ego amator tuus fragilitati tuae condescendens ea tibi procuro, ut per ea discas aeternam prosperitatem cogitando sperare."

117. Ibid.: "Hinc ista proposuit per hebdomadam illam legere orationem quamdam per quam singula membra salutaret, scilicet: 'Salvete delicata membra,' etc. Quod Domino multum persensit complacere. Unde et nos idem facere non pigeat, ut consimilem beatudinem consequi mereamur."

118. Gertude of Helfta, 1978, 228 (bk. IV, chap. 23).

119. Ibid.

120. Ibid.: "Tunc divinitus inspirata, legit vice omnium membrorum suorum CCXXV vicibus illud evangelium: 'Non mea sed tua voluntas fiat,' amantissime Jesu."

Chapter 3

1. See G. Lüers, *Die Sprache der deutschen Mystik des Mittelalters im Werke der Mechthild von Magdeburg,* Munich, 1926, 275; Rudolf von Bieberach, *Die siben strassen zu got: Die hochalemannische Übertragung nach der Handschrift Einsiedeln 278,* Spicilegium Bonaventurianum, 6, ed. M. Schmidt, Florence, 1969, 163–67; and Ludolf of Saxony, vol. IV, 473: "Oratio enim est elevatio mentis in Deum."

2. Augustine, *In Iohannis Evangelium Tractatus CXXIV,* CC.SL, vol. 36, ed. D. R. Willems, Turnhout, 1954, 132, lines 14–15 (Tractatus XIII, pt. 4).

3. *St. Benedict's Rule for Monasteries,* 21.

4. See W. Cahn, "Ascending to and Descending from Heaven: Ladder Themes in Early

Medieval Art," in *Santi e demoni nell'Alto Medioevo occidentale (secc. V–XI), 7–13 aprile 1988,* Settimane di studio del Centro italiano di studi sull'alto medioevo, 36, Spoleto, 1989, 697–724.

5. *St. Benedict's Rule for Monasteries,* 21–22.

6. See, e.g., the text attributed to Augustine, PL 40, 698: "Quattuor gradus posuit crucis. Non ergo laboriosae sunt hae scalae: quatuor gradus habent et perducunt ad coelum," etc. Numerous pertinent passages are gathered in *Altdeutsche Predigten,* ed. A. E. Schönbach, 3 vols., Graz, 1886–91, vol. II, 177–89, supplemented by R. L. Füglister, *Das lebende Kreuz: Ikonographische-ikonologische Untersuchung der Herkunft und Entwicklung einer spätmittelalterlichen Bildidee und ihrer Verwurzelung im Wort,* Einsiedeln, 1964.

7. G. B. Ladner, "St. Gregory of Nyssa and St. Augustine on the Symbolism of the Cross," in *Images and Ideas in the Middle Ages: Selected Studies in History and Art,* Storia e Litteratura, 155, 2 vols., Rome, 1983, vol. II, 197–208.

8. For the *compassio* of the Virgin in late medieval art and spirituality, see O. G. von Simson, "*Compassio* and *Co-redemptio* in Roger van der Weyden's *Descent from the Cross,*" *Art Bulletin* 35 (1953): 9–16; E. von Witzleben, "Compassio," *Lexikon der Marienkunde,* Regensburg, 1967, vol. I, 1179–86; M. Barth, "Zur Herz-Mariä-Verehrung des deutschen Mittelalters," *Zeitschrift für Aszese und Mystik* 4 (1929): 193–219; E. Wimmer, *Maria im Leid: Die Mater dolorosa insbesondere in der deutschen Literatur und Frömmigkeit des Mittelalters,* Würzburg, 1968; S. Sticca, *The Planctus Mariae in the Dramatic Tradition of the Middle Ages,* trans. J. R. Berrigan, Athens, Ga., 1988; Büttner, 1983, 63–131; C. M. Schuler, "The Sword of Compassion: Images of the Sorrowing Virgin in Late Medieval and Renaissance Art," Ph.D. diss., Columbia University, New York, 1987; and G. Satzinger and H.-M. Ziegeler, "Marienklagen und Pietà," in *Die Passion Christi,* 241–76.

9. For the wound of love, see A. Cabaussut, "Blessure d'amour," DS, vol. I, cols. 1724–29.

10. For allegorical images of the Crucifixion, see Füglister; and P. Verdier, "Un Monument inédit de l'art mosan du XIIe siècle: La Crucifixion symbolique de la Walters Art Gallery," *Revue belge d'archéologie et d'histoire de l'art* 30 (1961): 115–71.

11. See Hamburger, 1990, 75; K. Berg, "Une Iconographie peu connue du crucifiement," *Cahiers archéologiques* 9 (1957): 319–28; R.-J. Hesbert, *Le Problème de la transfixion du Christ dans les traditions biblique, patristique, iconographique, liturgique et musicale,* Paris, 1940; and N. Morgan, "Longinus and the Sacred Heart," *Wiener Jahrbuch für Kunstgeschichte* (*Beiträge zur mittelalterliche Kunst: Festschrift Gerhard Schmidt*) 46–47 (1993–94): 507–18 and 817–20.

12. For a catalogue and description of known examples, see H. Kraft, *Die Bildallegorie der Kreuzigung Christi durch die Tugenden,* Frankfurt, 1976.

13. For the Regensburg lectionary, see M. Parkes, *The Manuscripts of Keble College Oxford,* London, 1979, 227–47 and pl. X; and H. M. Barth, "Liebe verwundet durch Liebe: Das Kreuzigungsbild des Regensburger Lektionars als Zeugnis mittelalterlicher Passionsfrömmigkeit," *Beiträge zur Geschichte des Bistums Regensburg* 17 (1983): 229–68.

14. For the interrelated themes of ascent and descent in Bernard's writings, see J. Leclercq, "Le Mystère de l'Ascension dans les sermons de S. Bernard," *Collectanea Ordinis Cisterciensium Reformatorum* 15 (1953): 81–88; and B. McGinn, "Resurrection and Ascension in the Christology of the Early Cistercians," *Cîteaux: Commentarii Cistercienses* 30 (1970): esp. 10–16.

15. Sermon 60, "De Ascensione Domini," in *S. Bernardi Opera,* Rome, 1970, vol. VI/1, 291, lines 12–13: "Descendit autem dictum est, non 'cecedit'; quia qui cadit, sine gradu ruit; qui autem descendit, gradatim pedem ponit."

16. Ibid., lines 14–25: "Sunt autem gradus in descendendo, et sunt in ascendendo. Et in descendendo primus quidem gradus est a summo coelo usque ad carnem; secundus, usque ad

crucem; tertius, usque ad mortem. . . . Vidimus descensum, videamus et ascensum. Sed et ille quoque triplex est, et eius primus gradus gloria resurrectionis; secundus potestas iudicii, tertius, concessus ad dexteram Patris. Et de morte quidem meruit resurrectionem de cruce iudicii potestatem, ut quoniam in illa iniuste iudicatus est, de illa iustam obtineret iudicis censuram, ipso post resurrectionem dicente: 'Data est mihi omnis potestas in caelo et in terra.' "

17. Ibid., 292, lines 4–6: "Hac ascensione nihil sublimius, hoc honore nihil gloriosius dici potest aut excogitari. Sic per incarnationis suae mysterium descendit et ascendit Dominus, relinquens nobis exemplum, ut sequamur vestigia eius."

18. Cf. Astell, 102, who notes that "paradoxically, for Bernard the way down is the way up."

19. Both formulations are those of McGinn, 1979, 11 and 22.

20. For instances of the Psalm cited as an image of mystical ascent, see Walter Hilton, *The Scale of Perfection,* ed. J. P. H. Clark and R. Dorward, New York, 1991, 223 and 308 n. 89.

21. E.g., the rungs do not correspond to the twelve degrees of humility spelled out in the Benedictine Rule; see *St. Benedict's Rule for Monasteries,* chap. 7, 22–29.

22. For the term *gelassenheit* in Middle High German mystical texts, see L. Völker, *Die Terminologie der mystischen Bereitschaft in Meister Eckharts deutschen Predigten und Traktaten,* Tübingen, 1964, 80–91; idem, " 'Gelassenheit': Zur Entstehung des Wortes in der Sprache Meister Eckharts und seiner Überlieferung in der nacheckhartschen Mystik bis Jacob Böhme," in *"Getempert und gemischet" für Wolfgang Mohr zum 65. Geburtstag von seiner Tübinger Schülern,* ed. F. Hundsnurscher and U. Müller, Göppinger Arbeiten zur Germanistik, 65, Göppingen, 1972, 281–312; H. R. Gehring, "The Language of Mysticism in South German Dominican Chronicles of the Fourteenth Century," Ph.D. diss., University of Michigan, Ann Arbor, 1957, 181–84; and L. Gnädinger, *Johannes Tauler: Lebenswelt und mystische Lehre,* Munich, 1993, 272–86.

23. See Kieckhefer, chap. 3.

24. See E. Bertaud and A. Rayez, "Échelle spirituelle," DS, vol. IV, 62–86; J. O'Reilly, *Studies in the Iconography of the Virtues and Vices in the Middle Ages,* New York, 1988, 349–59; R. Schleier, *Tabula Cebetis, oder "Spiegel des Menschlichen Lebens darin Tugent unt untugent abgemalet ist": Studien zur Rezeption einer antiken Bildbeschreibung im 16. und 17. Jahrhundert,* Berlin, 1973; Hamburger, 1990, 49, 58, 65–66, 93, and 148; and C. Heck's forthcoming monograph on the iconography of the ladder in the Middle Ages. F. Ohly, *Metaphern für die Sündenstufen und die Gegenwirkungen der Gnade,* Rheinische-Westfälische Akademie der Wissenschaften; Geisteswissenschaften: Vorträge G 302, Düsseldorf, 1990; and G. Müller, "Gradualismus: Eine Vorstudie zur altdeutschen Literaturgeschichte," *Deutsche Vierteljahrschrift für Literaturwissenschaft und Geistesgeschichte* 2 (1924): 681–720, discuss other metaphors for spiritual ascent and descent.

25. Herrad of Hohenbourg, *Hortus deliciarum,* Studies of the Warburg Institute, 36, 2 vols., ed. R. Green et al., London, 1979, vol. II, 352–53: "Quindecim autem gradus texuntur et per quindecim ramos caritatis celestia petuntur. Unde et in Templo Domini ad sanctuarium XVcim gradibus ascendebatur, quia scandens in hac scala ad celestis templi sanctuarium Christum sublevatur." See also J. M. Willeumier-Schalij, *Dat Boec der Minnen: Die Rede von den 15 Graden,* Leiden, 1946.

26. See C. Fischer, "Bonaventure (Saint): Apocryphes," DS, vol. I, 1847. The tract remains unedited.

27. See Höltgen; Wormald; T. W. Ross, "Five Fifteenth-Century 'Emblem' Verses from British Museum Additional Ms. 37049," *Speculum* 32 (1957): 274–82; and, for a partial facsimile of the manuscript, J. Hogg, *An Illustrated Yorkshire Carthusian Religious Miscellany, British Library London Additional MS. 37049,* vol. III, *The Illustrations,* Analecta Cartusiana, 95, Salzburg, 1981. A *Sammelhandschrift* from the Benedictine convent of Heiningen bei Goslar, pub-

lished by W. Stammler, *Frau Welt: Eine mittelalterliche Allegorie,* Freiburger Universitätsreden, NF 23, Freiburg, 1959, 58–60, pls. XIV–XV, also incorporates an array of ladder imagery.

28. See P. Heitz, *Einblattdrucke des 15. Jahrhunderts,* 23, Strasbourg, 1911, cat. no. 10; Schreiber, vol. IV, 1927, cat. no. 1861, 45; and *Blockbücher des Mittelalters: Bilderfolgen als Lekturen,* Mainz, 1991, cat. no. 43d, 183 and 186. I am grateful to Christian Heck for bringing this image to my attention.

29. A. Schramm, *Der Bilderschmuck der Frühdrucke,* vol. II, Leipzig, 1920, fig. 698. Once again, I am indebted to Christian Heck for this image.

30. In the print the inscription just above the head of the woman reads, in part: "Ich wirt aufsteygen in den palmen vmb daz daz ich sein frucht erlang."

31. For the iconography and interpretation of this verse, see Hamburger, 1992, 35–42.

32. B. Newman, "Flaws in the Golden Bowl: Gender and Spiritual Formation in the Twelfth Century," *Traditio* 45 (1989–90): 111–46.

33. See, e.g., Ambrosius Autpertus, *Ambrosii Autperti opera,* CC.CM 27B, ed. R. Weber, Turnhout, 1975 (Sermo de adsumptione sanctae Mariae, part 10, lines 7–9 [pp. 1033–34]): "O uere inquam, gloriosa Mariae humilitas, quae porta paradisi efficitur, scala caeli constituitur! Facta est certe humilitas Mariae scala caelestis, per quam descendit Deus ad terras." See also *Sancti Petri Damiani Sermones,* CC.CM 57, ed. J. Lucchesi, Turnhout, 1983 (Sermon 46), line 244: "scala caelestis per quam supernus rex humilatus ad ima descendit, et homo qui prostratus iacebat, ad superna exaltus ascendit."

34. "Es ist viel davon gechrieben, wie der mensch soll vergottet werden, da haben sie leytern gemacht, daran man gen hymel steyge und viel solchs dings, Es ist aber eytel partecken werck"; quoted by G. Seebass, *Die Himmelsleiter des hl. Bonaventura von Lukas Cranach d.Ä.: Zur Reformation eines Holzschnitts,* Sitzungsberichte der Heidelberger Akademie der Wissenschaften, Phil.-Hist. Kl. 1985/4, Heidelberg, 1985, 50. For a nuanced assessment of Luther's changing attitude toward images and their role in Christian worship, see Michalski, 1–42.

35. From the vast literature, see the following selected studies: Ohly, 1985; S. Urbach, "Eine unbekannte Darstellung von *Sündenfall und Erlösung* in Budapest und das Weiterleben des Cranachschen Rechtfertigungsbildes," *Niederdeutsche Beiträge zur Kunstgeschichte* 28 (1989): 33–63; and, more generally, J. Wirth, "Le Dogme en image: Luther et l'iconographie," *Revue de l'Art* 52 (1981): 9–24; and Michalski.

36. For the alterations, see, in addition to Seebass, Koepplin, esp. 180–81. The medieval mystical tradition reasserts itself in Pietist tracts and their illustrations; see, e.g., the remarkable image of Christ's body as a ladder, its rungs inscribed with virtues, reproduced by H.-J. Schrader, "Le Christ dans le coeur de ses fidèles: Quelques aspects 'poétiques' de la christologie du piétisme," in *Le Christ entre orthodoxie et lumières: Actes du colloque tenu à Genève en août 1993,* ed. M.-C. Pitassi, Histoire des idées et critique littéraire, 332, Geneva, 1994, esp. 62–63 and 76. M. Warnke, *Cranachs Luther: Entwurfe für ein Image,* Frankfurt, 1984, comments on the recasting of medieval iconographic schema to suit Protestant purposes.

37. On this theme in female mysticism, see E. Ross, "'She Wept and Cried Right Loud for Sorrow and for Pain': Suffering, the Spiritual Journey, and Women's Experience in Late Medieval Mysticism," in *Maps of Flesh and Light: The Religious Experience of Medieval Women Mystics,* ed. U. Wiethaus, Syracuse, 1993, 45–59.

38. Cited by Kieckhefer, 109. The imagery of mounting a ladder to enter into the wounds of Christ recurs in Jesuit devotional imagery of the seventeenth century; see, e.g., the images reproduced by E. M. Vetter, "'Dei famulam amplecti videbatur': Zur Darstellung des hl. Franziskus mit dem Gekreuzigten," in idem, 1995, 201–14, esp. figs. 10–11.

39. See, most recently, F. Avril and N. Reynaud, *Les Manuscrits à peintures en France, 1440–1520,* Paris, 1993, 236–37, fig. 128, with additional bibliography.

40. For comparable instances in devotional poetry, see S. Stanbury, "The Virgin's Gaze: Spectacle and Transgression in Middle English Lyrics of the Passion," *PMLA* 106 (1991): 1083–93. A double miniature in the *Rothschild Canticles* (New Haven, Beinecke Rare Book and Manuscript Library, Yale University, Ms. 404, ff. 18v–19r), a devotional miscellany compiled for a nun in French Flanders ca. 1300, posits a similar pattern. As the Sponsa thrusts her spear into Christ's side, she points to her eye, identifying her action as an enactment of Song of Songs 4: 9: "Thou hast wounded my heart, my sister, my spouse, thou hast wounded my heart with one of thy eyes." See Hamburger, 1990, 72–77 and pl. 5.

41. One occasionally finds a similar conceit in Dutch manuscripts of the period; see, e.g., the *Hours of Margaret Uutenham,* private collection, United States, reproduced in *The Golden Age of Dutch Manuscript Painting,* 233 and 251–52.

42. See V. Gurevitch, "Observations on the Iconography of the Wound in Christ's Side," *Journal of the Warburg and Courtauld Institutes* 20 (1957): 358–62.

43. Maggs, *European Bulletin,* 18, cat. no. 68, 39, reproduced in color on the inside of the front cover (where it is inaccurately identified as no. 67).

44. The scroll reads: "Vulneraverat caritas christi cor eius et gestabat verba eius in visceribus quia sagittas acutus." For Augustine with his heart pierced by an arrow, see Hamburger, 1990, fig. 137 (Paris, Bibliothèque Nationale, Ms. fr. 17115, f. 156r); and *Manuscripta pretiosa & incunabulae illuminatae: Auswahl aus den Sammlungen der Lippischen Landesbibliothek Detmold und der Erzbischöflichen Akademischen Bibliothek Paderborn,* Auswahl- und Austellungskataloge der Lippischen Landesbibliothek Detmold, 33, ed. D. Hellfaier, Detmold, 1995, 33–35 (Paderborn, Erzbischöfliche Akademische Bibliothek, Ms. Ba 3, f. 163r).

45. Reproduced in color in *Glanz alter Buchkunst: Mittelalterliche Handschriften der Staatsbibliothek Preußischer Kulturbesitz Berlin,* Wiesbaden, 1988, 202–3. For an earlier image of Augustine pierced by the arrow of divine love, see Hamburger, 1990, 74 and fig. 137; for the metaphor of the piercing glance, see R. H. Cline, "Heart and Eyes," *Romance Philology* 25 (1971–72): 263–97.

46. Hamburger, 1990, 48–49.

47. See "Das Wienhausen Liederbuch," ed. P. Alpers, *Jahrbuch des Vereins für Niederdeutsche Sprachforschung* 60–70 (1943–47): esp. 33–34; and the studies by W. Lipphardt, "Die liturgische Funktion deutscher Kirchenlieder in den Klöstern Niedersächsischer Zisterzienserinnen des Mittelalters," *Zeitschrift für katholische Theologie* 94 (1972): 158–98; "Niederdeutsche Reimgedichte und Lieder des 14. Jahrhunderts in den mittelalterlichen Orationalien der Zisterzienserinnen von Medingen und Wienhausen," *Niederdeutsches Jahrbuch* 95 (1972): 66–131; summarized in "Medinger Gebetbücher," ²VL, vol. V, 277–80, to which now should be added Achten, 1987b.

48. Of the twenty-six stanzas, I quote stanzas 4, 6–8, and 10 here.

49. See Kraft, 65–76; also H. Traver, *The Four Daughters of God,* Philadelphia, 1907.

50. Cf. also the allegory of Charity included in a tract published by K. Reider, "Mystischer Traktat aus dem Kloster Unterlinden zu Colmar i. Els.," *Zeitschrift für hochdeutsche Mundarten* 1 (1900): esp. 84–85.

51. "Das Wienhausen Liederbuch," 33, stanzas 13 and 21–23.

52. For this motif and its allegorical elaboration in conjunction with images of the Pietà, see Schawe.

53. PL 204, 511–18, trans. D. N. Bell, *Baldwin of Ford: Spiritual Treatises,* 2 vols., Kalamazoo, Mich., 1986, vol. II, 74–84.

54. See, e.g., the sermon by Bonaventure cited by M. Rubin, *Corpus Christi: The Eucharist in Late Medieval Culture,* Cambridge, England, 1990, 27: "Et ratione istius unionis dicit Christus animae gustanti dulcendinem sacramenti eucharistiae et amoris. Pone me ut signaculum, cari-

tatis et benevolentiae, super cor tuum . . . ut signaculum super brachium tuum . . . quia fortis est ut mors dilectio."

55. See Hogg, 27; and M. C. Spalding, *The Middle English Charters of Christ,* Bryn Mawr, Pa., 1914.

56. For examples, see the sources conveniently gathered in S. Ringler, *Viten- und Offenbarungsliteratur in Frauenklöstern des Mittelalters: Quellen und Studien,* Münchener Texte und Untersuchungen zur deutschen Literatur des Mittelalters, 72, Zurich and Munich, 1980, 275–76.

57. In addition to J. Lechner, see S. Krämer, *Handschriftenerbe des deutschen Mittelalters,* Mittelalterliche Bibliothekskataloge Deutschland und der Schweiz: Ergänzungsband 1, 3 vols., Munich, 1989, vol. I, 199–200.

58. The canons of Rebdorf, who participated in the pastoral care of the nuns at St. Walburg and provided them with manuscript exemplars, were active in disseminating Tauler's work; see J. G. Mayer, "Tauler in der Bibliothek der Laienbrüder von Rebdorf," in *Überlieferungsgeschichtliche Editionen und Studien zur deutschen Literatur des Mittelalters,* ed. K. Kunze, J. G. Mayer, and B. Schnell, Tübingen, 1989, 365–90.

59. St. Walburg, Ms. germ. 4, ff. 1–138r, described by J. Lechner, 31. I am grateful to Dr. Karin Schneider of the Staatsbibliothek in Munich for confirming that no other manuscripts of this unidentified text appear to be extant.

60. St. Walburg, Ms. germ. 4, f. 1r: "Dyse wort sind geschriben in dem puech der lieb. Die spricht xps zu seiner prawt vnd sprechen zu teucz also: leg mich als ein zaichen uff dein hercz."

61. Ibid.: "In dissen wortten [Song of Songs 8 : 6] vermant xps die sel, wen er gegenwürtig pey ir in dem sacrament ist, das sy denn ingedenck sey seiner grosser lieb, die er Jr beweist hat Besunder in seinem leiden."

62. As does another short treatise on the same passage found in a fifteenth-century Alsatian devotional compendium, almost certainly from a convent in Strasbourg (Staatsbibliothek zu Berlin—Preußischer Kulturbesitz, Ms. germ. 4° 149, ff. 125r–127r), which begins, "Pone me ut singnaculum [*sic*] super cor tuum. Zů tusche lege mich als ain minne zeichen uf den hertzen . . . (f. 125v) So ir nit anders müget so sullent ir sin bilde durch vwer hertze selen vnd ougen drucken."

63. Ibid., f. 2v: "ir augen habt ein fleyssiges auff sehen, Das nichs da sey, Das dem herr nit entgee, Vnd secht in so lieplich an, das der herr sprech, verwunt hastu mein hercz mit einen deiner augen swester meine."

64. Ibid.: "Yr oren hört fleissigklichen die gepot des herren, vnd sein redt vnd seine lieppliche wort, besunder hört die lieplichen stym als geschriben in dem püechlein Der lieb canticorum. Da spricht der herr, stee auff mein frewntin mein schonne, vnd kum mein taub in die höller Der stein. Aber spricht er nechen dich zu mir mein frewntin wann nun ist vergangen der winter."

65. In addition to the studies by Bynum, see K. Richstätter, *Die Herz-Jesu-Verehrung des deutschen Mittelalters,* Regensburg, 1924; and G. Schreiber, "Mittelalterliche Passionsmystik und Frömmigkeit: Der älteste Herz-Jesu-Hymnus," *Theologische Quartalschrift* 122 (1941): 32–44 and 107–23.

66. A conflation spelled out in Master E.S.'s engraving *Christ Child in the Heart,* dated 1467 (Lehrs, 51), which shows the Christ Child, surrounded by the *arma Christi,* standing in his own heart but also bears the inscription "wer Iesus in sinem herczen tret dem ist alle zit die ewig froed beraeit," reproduced, together with a manuscript copy (Stuttgart, Württembergische Landesbibliothek, Ms. brev. 12, f. 14v), in Büttner, 1992, 52–53 and figs. 17–18.

67. An echo of Proverbs 3 : 3: "Let not loyalty and faithfulness forsake you; bind them around your neck, write them on the tablet of your heart." Exegetes such as Augustine elaborated the Pauline image, arguing that God wrote on the heart of the soul with the finger of the Holy

Spirit; see, e.g., Augustine, *Enarrationes in Psalmos, CI–CL,* CC.SL., 40, Turnhout, 1961, 1696 (commenting on Psalm 118:33–34), "... sancto Spiritu tamquam digito Dei in mente datur, et in cordibus scribitur," cited by F. Ohly, "Cor amantis non augustum: Vom wohnen im Herzen," in *Gedenkschrift für William Foerste,* ed. D. Hofmann, Niederdeutsche Studien, 18, Cologne, 1970, 460–61 n. 14. From imagery such as this derives the apt use of heart-shaped prayer books, such as those recorded in two devotional portraits by the Master of St. Gudule, one in the Metropolitan Museum, New York, the other in the National Gallery, London, both reproduced in G. Bauman, *Early Flemish Portraits, 1425–1525,* New York, n.d., 40, reprinted from the *Metropolitan Museum of Art Bulletin* (Spring, 1986).

68. St. Walburg, Ms. germ. 4, f. 138r: "vnd mein kreucz sol auch dein wallstecken sein hie in dissem ellendt, daran du wallen solt in das vaterlandt, vnd denn will ich dein gekreuczigter lieb haber, dein gemachel vnd das pettlen sein, dar ynn du ewiglich mit grossen frewden rwen solt vnd mich deinen liebhaber lieben on mittel."

69. For the rose as a symbol of *amor vulnerans,* see St. Katharinenthal, 262, with additional bibliography.

70. The heart pierced by the glance of the beloved is an ancient topos; see H. Kolb, *Der Begriff der Minne und das Entstehen der höfischen Lyrik,* Tübingen, 1958, 18–38; and Cline, who, however, underestimates the importance of the tradition of commentary on Song of Songs 4:9. In the Middle Ages, as in antiquity, sight was a metaphor for enlightenment. Significant studies include H. Blumenberg, "Light as a Metaphor for Truth at the Preliminary Stage of Philosophical Concept Formation," in *Modernity and the Hegemony of Vision,* 30–62; J. Koch, "Über die Lichtsymbolik im Bereich der Philosophie und der Mystik des Mittelalters," *Studium Generale* 13 (1960): 653–70; E. Beer, "Mystik des Lichts in der Kunst des Abendlands," *Mystik und Wissenschaftlichkeit,* Universität Bern: Kulturhistorische Vorlesungen, ed. A. Mercier, Frankfurt, 1970–71, 81–106; M. Schmidt, "'Das lieht ist vernúnftekeit': Zur Mystik Mechthilds von Magdeburg (ca. 1208–ca. 1282)," in *Gottes Nähe: Religiöse Erfarhrung in Mystik und Offenbarung: Festschrift zum 65. Geburtstag von Josef Sudbrack S.J.,* ed. P. Imhof, Würzburg, 1990, 48–61; and idem, "Das Auge als Symbol der Erleuchtung bei Ephräm und Parallelen in der Mystik des Mittelalters," *Oriens Christianus* 68 (1984): 27–57.

71. See G. Schleusener-Eicholtz, *Das Auge im Mittelalter,* Münstersche Mittelalter-Schriften, 35, 2 vols., Munich, 1985, 787–97. Cistercian exegetes were especially fond of the passage; see K. Ruh, "Die Augen der Liebe bei Wilhelm von St. Thierry," *Theologische Zeitschrift* 45 (1989): 103–14; and B. McGinn, *The Growth of Mysticism: Gregory the Great through the Twelfth Century,* New York, 1994, 180, 233, 303, 345, and 354.

72. In addition to Hamburger, 1990, 162–67, see Cline, 286–87, who connects Christian conceptions of insight to an indwelling of Christ in the heart; Kolb, 18–39; and W. Gewehr, "Der Topos 'Auge des Herzens': Versuch einer Deutung durch die scholastische Erkenntnistheorie," *Deutsche Vierteljahrschrift für Literatur und Geistesgeschichte* 49 (1972): 626–49. M. Miles, "Vision: The Eye of the Body and the Eye of the Mind in Saint Augustine's *De Trinitate* and *Confessions,*" *Journal of Religion* 63 (1983): 125–42, argues that Augustine extrapolated his theory of spiritual vision from his understanding of physical sight.

73. PL 175, 976A: "Oculus carnis videtur mundus, et ea quae sunt in mundo. Oculo rationis animus, et ea quae sunt in animo. Oculo contemplationis Deus, et ea quae est in Deo. Oculo carnis videt homo quae sunt extra se; oculo rationis quae sunt in se; oculo contemplationis quae sunt intra se et supra se," quoted by A. Solignac, "Oculus," DS, vol. XI, esp. 598.

74. Bonaventure, 1964, 213: "Si autem quaeras, quomodo haec fiant, interroga gratiam, non doctrinam; desiderium, non intellectum; gemitum orationis, non studium; lectionis sponsum, non magistrum; deum non hominem; caliginem, non claritatem; non lucem, sed ignem totaliter inflammantem et in deum excessivis unctionibus et ardentissimis affectionibus transferentem." English translation from Bonaventure, 1955–56, vol. II, 101.

75. P. Saenger, "Books of Hours and the Reading Habits of the Later Middle Ages," in *The Culture of Print: Power and the Uses of Print in Early Modern Europe,* ed. R. Chartier, trans. L. G. Cochrane, New York, 1989, 141–73.

76. For an overview of the literature on illustrated prayer books, see Achten, 1987a; and Hamburger, 1991.

77. See, most recently, H.-J. Schiewer, "Die beiden Sankt Johannsen, ein dominikanischer Johannes-Libellus und das literarische Leben im Bodenseeraum um 1300," *Oxford German Studies* 22 (1993): 21–54. For references in the chronicle of St. Katharinenthal to the example illustrated here, see *Das "St. Katharinthaler Schwesternbuch,"* 190, 201, 261, 288, and 299

78. On the relationship between loving and looking in medieval narrative, see A. C. Spearing, *The Medieval Poet as Voyeur: Looking and Listening in Medieval Love Narratives,* Cambridge, England, 1993, esp. 1–25.

79. In addition to Hamburger, 1990, esp. 162–67, see S. Ringbom, "Devotional Images and Imaginative Devotions: Notes on the Place of Art in Later Medieval Piety," *Gazette des Beaux-Arts,* 6th ser., 73 (1969): 159–70; and H. L. Kessler, "'Facies bibliothecae revelata': Carolingian Art as Spiritual Seeing," in *Testo e immagine,* vol. II, 534–94.

80. For the topos in Dominican convent chronicles, see Haussherr; and Ringler, 285–86. For vision itself as a form of dialogue or exchange, see F. Ohly, "Gebärden der Liebe zwischen Gott und Mensch im St. Trudperter Hohelied," *Literaturwissenschaftliches Jahrbuch* 43 (1993): 9–31. According to A. Vauchez, "L'Image vivante: Quelques réflexions sur les fonctions des représentations iconographiques dans le domaine religieux en Occident aux derniers siècles du Moyen Âge," in *Arme und Reiche: Studien aus der Geschichte der Gesellschaft und der Kultur. Bronislaw Geremek zum 60. Geburtstag gewidmet,* Warsaw, 1992, esp. 235–36, the earliest account of an animated image in the medieval West, a vision of a miraculous crucifix reported by Rupert of Deutz in his commentary on the Song of Songs, is attributed to a woman.

81. For the history of the convent of Weiler, see S. Uhrle, *Das Dominikanerinnenkloster Weiler bei Esslingen (1230–1571/92),* Veröffentlichungen der Kommission für Geschichtliche Landeskunde in Baden-Württemberg, Reihe B: Forschungen, 49, Stuttgart, 1968. For the convent's chronicle, see "Mystisches Leben in dem Dominikanerinnenkloster Weiler," esp. 77: "Zu einem mal saz sie bey irem pett, da hört sie ein stimm die sprach: 'du solt in den chor gen.' Da sie da hin ein kom, da sahe sie unsern herrn hoch sweben ob dem altar. Zehant da ward sie auf gezogen an daz crewtz und süßlich ward sie ümgeben von got an sel und an leib, und sprach zu ir: "ich wil allweg mit dir sein und du mit mir, und will mich von dir nymmer gescheyden." The passage vaguely recalls Song of Songs 6:2: "ego dilecto meo et dilectus meus mihi."

82. See Hamburger, 1989b.

83. For the first phenomenon, see J.-C. Schmitt, "Rituels de l'image et récits de vision," in *Testo e immagine,* vol. II, 419–62. For an example of the second, see Vauchez.

84. For the visions of John the Evangelist as understood by medieval theologians, see W. Kamlah, *Apokalypse und Geschichtstheologie: Die mittelalterliche Auslegung der Apokalypse vor Joachim von Fiore,* Historische Studien, 285, Berlin, 1935; for illustrations of the Book of Revelation as allegories and reenactments of spiritual sight, see Kessler. For depictions of John as the visionary Evangelist, see J. O'Reilly, "St. John as a Figure of the Contemplative Life: Text and Image in the Art of the Anglo-Saxon Benedictine Reform," in *St. Dunstan: His Life, Times, and Cult,* ed. N. Ramsey, M. Sparks, and T. Tatton-Brown, Woodbridge, Suffolk, 1992; H. Buchthal, "A Byzantine Miniature of the Fourth Evangelist and Its Relatives," *Dumbarton Oaks Papers* 15 (1961): 127–39; W. Weisbach, "Die Darstellungen der Inspiration auf mittelalterlichen Evangelistenbildern," *Rivista di Archeologia Cristiana* 16 (1939): 101–27; and C. Nordenfalk, "Der inspirierte Evangelist," *Wiener Jahrbuch für Kunstgeschichte* 36 (1983): 175–90.

85. For Elisabeth of Schönau, see Bertaud and Rayez, 70; for a more general discussion, consult P. Dinzelbacher, "Die Offenbarungen der hl. Elisabeth von Schönau: Bildwelt, Erleb-

nisweise und Zeittypisches," in Dinzelbacher, 1993, 78–101; and A. L. Clark, *Elisabeth of Schönau: A Twelfth-Century Visionary,* Philadelphia, 1992.

86. See E. Beer, "Die Buchkunst des Graduale von St. Katharinenthal," in *Das Graduale von Sankt Katharinenthal: Kommentarband zur Faksimile-Ausgabe,* Lucerne, 1983; and A. Knoepfli, *Die Kunstdenkmäler des Kantons Thurgau, IV: Das Kloster St. Katharinenthal,* Basel, 1989, 170–79.

87. "Vita venerabilis Lukardis," 341–42: "et ecce vidit de corde suo scalam auream erectam et eius summitatem cacumen caeli attingentem; in cuius summitate vidit Christum dilectum suum innixum scalae et ad se inclinatum ac amabili visu se dulciter intuentem. Cuius visus dulcedinem quotiens memoriae postea retulit, totiens sibi consolationem mirabilem asseruit innovari. Vidi quoque gradus iam dictae scalae diversarum gemmarum ornatos decore, per quos angelos Dei descendentes vidit ac etiam ascendentes." On Lukardis, see, most recently, A. M. Kleinberg, *Prophets in Their Own Country: Living Saints and the Making of Sainthood in the Later Middle Ages,* Chicago, 1992, 99–125.

88. See C. Meier, *Gemma spiritalis: Methode und Gebrauch der Edelsteinallegorie vom frühen Christentum bis im 18. Jahrhundert,* Münstersche Mittelalter-Schriften, 34, Munich, 1977; U. Engelen, *Die Edelsteine in der deutschen Dichtung des 12. und 13. Jahrhunderts,* Münstersche Mittelalter-Schriften, 27, Munich, 1978; and U. Henze, "Edelsteinallegorese im Lichte mittelalterliche Bild- und Reliquienverehrung," *Zeitschrift für Kunstgeschichte* 54 (1991): 428–51.

89. Lukardis of Weimar, 341–42: "Scio, dilectissima, scio quia de valle lacrimarum disponis ad me ascensiones in corde tuo nunc votis, nunc sanctis meditationibus et desideriis, nunc orationibus, nunc patientia et incommodorum passionibus, quibus in me affectuose ascendis et mi tibi adtrahis et in amplexus tuae devotionis me dulciter stringis. Haec est scala, quam vides, habens duo latera aurea, cuius unum latus dextrum est aurea et ardens caritas; quam geris erga me Deum tuum; alterum latus sinistrum est aurea ardens caritas, quam geris erga proximum tuum. Gradus scalae, quod vides tanto decore ornatos, sunt vota tua et sancta desideria, orationes et bona opera et passionum diversa incommoda, quae patienter passa es et passura. Angelos vides per hos gradus descendentes, ut haec omnia diligenter colligant. Vides eos ascendentes, ut haec omnia collecta mihi fideliter et integraliter offerant totius humani generis pro salute. Et sicut per hanc scalam saepius trahor ad te, sic per eandem de valle miseriae cito ad me traheris in aeterna requie et gloria mecum perenniter regnatura."

90. Bonaventure, 1964, 182.

91. Lukardis of Weimar, 341–42.

92. In addition to the literature cited in note 9, see J. O'Reilly, "Early Medieval Text and Image: The Wounded and Exalted Christ," *Peritia* 6–7 (1987–88): 72–118.

93. See M. Schmidt, "Mechthild von Hackeborn," [2]VL, vol. VI, esp. 256–60.

94. See Bynum, 1982, 170–262.

95. As noted by Schmidt.

96. Mechthild of Hackeborn, 1875–77, vol. II, 62 (bk. I, chap. 19).

97. See, e.g., Ruh, 1993, 312, who observes of Mechthild's visions: "diese Äußerungen ihrer Frömmigkeit, die Herz-Jesu-Spiritualität mit ihren kindlich-künstlichen Verbildlichungen überhaupt, sind nicht dazu angetan, Mechthild zur Leitfigur eines verinnerlichten Christentums zu machen. . . . Wer den *Liber specialis gratiae* im Zusammenhang liest, dem fällt es schwer, Mechthilds zwar reiche, aber intellektuell durchsetzte geistige Vorstellungswelt, ihre ausschweifenden Allegoresen und technischen Phantasien, endlich ihre theologischen Versteigenheiten gegen ein kirchlich geläutertes Frömmigkeitsbildeinzutauschen." For a more sympathetic assessment, see Haas, 1984, 373–91.

98. See, e.g., the material gathered by A. Sauvy, *Le Miroir du cœur: Quatre siècles d'images*

savantes et populaires, Paris, 1989. I am grateful to François Boespflug, O.P., for bringing this book to my attention.

99. Mechthild of Hackeborn, 1875–77, vol. II, 195–96 (bk. III, chap. 1): "Virgo Christi cum praesentiam Dilecti sui die quadam non sentiret, et multum desideraret, videbatur sibi quasi stare Dominum coram se, et apertum est cor eius velut janua, et visum est ei quid illud intraret quasi magnam domum, habentem pavimentum aureum. Et domus erat rotunda, significans aeternitatem Dei; et Dominus stabat in medio domus, et anima cum eo, multa ad invicem colloquentes. Dum ergo cantaretur ad Missam: *et tibi reddetur votum in Jerusalem,* cogitabat illa quanta vota sancti obtulisset Domino in hoc saeculo. . . . Et vidit beatam Virginem sibi a dextris stantem, dantem sibi annulum aureum, quem statim Domino obtulit, et Dominus gratanter accipiens digiti suo imposuit. Tunc illa intra se desiderans dicebat: 'O si fieri posset ut tibi ipse annulum suum daret in signum desponsationis!' . . . Ad quam Dominus: 'Do tibi annulum septem lapidibus insignitum, quos potes rememorari in septem articulis digiti tui.' "

100. Ibid., 196–97: "In primo articulo potes recordari amoris divini, qui me de sinu Patris inclinans, triginta tribus annis multis laboribus te quaerendo fecit servire. Et cum tempus instatet nuptiarum, proprio amore cordis mei venditus in pretium convivii, meipsum in panem et carnem et poculum dedi. . . . In septimo, memor eris qualiter thalamum crucis sum ingressus," etc.

101. Ibid., 197: "Memor eris qualiter thalamum crucis sum ingressus; et sicut sponsi vestes suas dant histrionibus, ita vestimenta mea dedi militibus, et corpus meum crucifixoribus. Deinde extendi brachia mea per durissimos clavos in tuos amplexus suaves, tibi cantans in thalamo amoris septem cantilenas mirae suavitatis plenas. Post haec cor meum ad introeundum tibi aperui, cum somnum amoris tecum moriens in cruce cepi."

102. Ibid., 197.

103. Ibid., 197–98 (bk. III, chap. 2): "In Missa quadam audivit Dominus sibi dicentem: 'Eamus in desertum interiorem.' Statim per longam viam sibi visum est cum Domino ire, quasi ulnis eum complexans, et haec verba dicens: 'Laudo te in tua aeternitate, immensitate, pulchritudine, veritate, justitia,' etc. Deinde pervenientes in magnam solitudinem quae erat locus magnae amoenitatis, arboribus ex utraque parte consitus ad modum tecti supernis conclusis. Et pavimentum erat viridissimum, floribus plenum, ubi residet Dominus. Et anima in specie ovis perambulabat pascua illa, habens in collo catenulam aureis et argenteis circulis consitam, quae processit de corde Domini, significans amorem Dei et proximi, sine quo nemo Deo poterit adhaerere. Tunc anima desiderans laudare Deum dicebat: 'O amantissime, doce me laudare te.' Qui Dominus: 'Respice cor meum.' Et ecce rosa pulcherrima habens quinque folia exivit de corde dei totum pectus eius cooperiens. Et ait Dominus: 'Lauda me in quinque sensibus meis, qui significatur per hanc rosam.' Et intellexit quod Deum laudare deberet, pro visu amabili quo semper respicit hominem."

Chapter 4

1. Field, vol. III, 76–89 (Schreiber cat. nos. 796–808.1) reproduces extant woodcuts of the subject. For specific examples, see Richstätter; Hernad, 166–67 and 176–79; A. Nägele, "Das verwunderte Herz: Ein altes Herzjesubild in einer Münchener Handschrift vom Jahr 1429," *Sankt Wiborada* 6 (1939); 56–61; M. Hartig, "Das deutsche Herz-Jesu Bild," *Das Münster* 2 (1948): 76–99; J. Schnelbögl, "Die Reichskleinodien in Nürnberg 1424–1523," *Mitteilungen des Vereins für Geschichte der Stadt Nürnberg* 51 (1962): 78–159; A. Bühler, "Die Heilige Lanze: Ein ikonographischer Beitrag zur Geschichte der deutschen Reichskleinodien," *Das Münster* 16 (1963): 85–116; N. Niedermeier, "Die Herzsymbolik in der Volksfrömmigkeit des Mittel-

alters," *Bayerisches Jahrbuch für Volkskunde* (1968): 58–64; and D. Alexandre-Bidon, "Le Cœur du Christ au pressoir mystique: Le Cas de céramiques du Beauvaisis au début du XVIe siècle," in *Le Pressoir mystique: Actes du colloque de Recloses, 27 mai 1989,* ed. D. Alexandre-Bidon, Paris, 1990, 155–70, with additional bibliography.

2. J. Wirth's assertion that in late medieval devotions the heart of Jesus was a spiritual, not a corporeal entity (*L'Image et la production du sacré,* 20 and 158) cannot be maintained in light of the textual evidence, e.g., Mechthild of Hackeborn (1875–77), 203–4 (bk. III, chap. 6). He joins those theologians who condemn the cult of the corporeal heart as an "error" and ascribe its corruption to women. As the focal point of incarnational piety, the heart of Jesus was, by definition, a bodily as well as a spiritual organ.

3. Similar images are discussed by Schmidtke, 400–402.

4. For the motif of the dog at the door—but open, not closed—see I. Ragusa, "*Terror demonum* and *terror inimicorum:* The Two Lions of the Throne of Solomon and the Open Door of Paradise," *Zeitschrift für Kunstgeschichte* 40 (1977): 93–114; and A. C. Esmeijer, "The Open Door and the Heavenly Vision: Political and Spiritual Elements in the Programme of Decoration of Schwarzrheindorf," in *Polyanthea: Essays on Art and Literature in Honor of William Sebastian Heckscher,* The Hague, 1993, 43–56.

5. See Büttner, 1983, 124–31; and P. Verdier, *Le Couronnement de la Vierge: Les Origins et les premiers développements d'un thème iconographique,* Montreal, 1980, figs. 74a–b.

6. See *I Fioretti di San Francesco,* intro. N. Fabretti, commentary E. Silber, Turin, 1981, 177 and 263; and *Das Leben des hl. Franz von Assisi nach der Legenda Maior des Bonaventura illustriert mit den Miniaturen der Sibilla von Bondorf,* with an afterword by Sister A. Lagier, O.S.C., Freiburg, 1988. For other manuscripts closely related in style, see von Heusinger, 1953, 96–106 and 195–208; and *Clara und Franciscus von Assisi: Eine spätmittelalterliche alemannische Legende der Magdalena Steimerin,* trans. F. A. Schmitt, Constance, 1959, with an afterword by C. von Heusinger.

7. In *Bonaventuras Legenda Sancti Francisci,* D. Brett-Evans identifies Sibilla von Bondorf as the translator, a claim refuted by K. Ruh, "Sibilla von Bondorf," [2]VL, vol. VIII, 1134–35, who, in "Konrad von Bondorf," [2]VL, vol. V, 141–45, suggests that Konrad, possibly a relative of Sibilla's, was the author.

8. For the adjoining text, see *Bonaventuras Legenda Sancti Francisci,* 96.

9. See P. Dinzelbacher and K. Ruh, "Magdalena von Freiburg," [2]VL, vol. V, 1117–21; and, for the manuscript now in Karlsruhe, the summary descriptions in K. A. Barack, *Die Handschriften der Fürstlich-Fürstembergischen Hofbibliothek zu Donaueschingen,* Tübingen, 1865, 240; and von Heusinger, 1953, 143.

10. Karlsruhe, Badische Landesbibliothek, Ms. Donaueschingen 298, 64v: "Der geist des heiligen gottes ret zuo minen geist vnd sprach, 'schrib mir dz pater noster in dz selterli vnd verwirk die selben wort in dz pater noster.' vnd ich hőr si als gern als die engelsche zit vnd lob gesang. DEO GRATIAS." Kate Greenspan has completed a partial edition, commentary, and translation of the text, which will appear in *Magdalena of Freiburg: Selections from Her Vitae and Meditative Works,* Binghamton, N.Y. In the meantime, consult K. Greenspan, "A Medieval Iconographic Vernacular," in *So Rich a Tapestry: The Sister Arts and Cultural Studies,* ed. A. Hurley and K. Greenspan, Lewisburg, Pa., 1995, 200–215. I am grateful to Kate Greenspan for bringing her essay to my attention.

11. For the image of the heart as God's altar, see K. Ruh, *Bonaventura deutsch: Ein Beitrag zur deutschen Franziskaner-Mystik und -Scholastik,* Bern, 1956, 215 n. 1.

12. See F. Rapp, "Le Prière dans les monastères de Dominicaines observantes en Alsace au XVe siècle," *La Mystique rhénane: Colloque de Strasbourg, 16–19 mai 1961,* Paris, 1963, 207–18; and P. Ochsenbein, "Deutschsprachige Privatgebetbücher vor 1400," in *Deutsche Handschriften*

1100–1400, Oxforder Kolloquium, 1985, ed. V. Honemann and N. F. Palmer, Tübingen, 1988, 379–98.

13. In addition to A. Vauchez, "Dévotion eucharistique et union mystique chez les saintes de la fin du Moyen Âge," in *Les Laïcs au Moyen Âge: Pratiques et expériences religieuses,* Paris, 1987, 259–64, see the studies by C. W. Bynum, "Woman Mystics and Eucharistic Devotion in the Thirteenth Century," in idem, *Fragmentation and Redemption: Essays on Gender and the Human Body in Medieval Religion,* New York, 1991, 119–50; and idem, 1982, 170–262. For the context of the cult of *Corpus Christi,* consult Rubin; and C. M. A. Caspers, *De Eucharistische Vroomheid en het Feest van Sacramentsdag in de Nederlanden tijdens de Late Middeleeuwen,* Miscellanea Neerlandica, 5, Louvain, 1992.

14. For the relation between "private" devotions and the rituals of cult in the context of convents, see S. Hilpisch, "Chorgebet und Frömmigkeit im Spätmittelalter," in *Heilige Überlieferung: Auschnitte aus der Geschichte des Mönchtums und des heiligen Kultes (Festschrift für Ildefonsus Herwegen),* ed. O. Casel, Münster, 1938, 262–84; and U. Küsters, *Der verschlossene Garten: Volkssprachliche Hohelied-Auslegung und monastische Lebensform im 12. Jahrhundert,* Studia Humaniora, 2, Düsseldorf, 1985, esp. 282–88.

15. Revelation 19:9 was itself the common subject of both illustration and visionary experience; see Hamburger, 1990, 47–55; and P. Dinzelbacher, "Das Christusbild der heiligen Lutgard von Tongeren im Rahmen der Frauenmystik und Bildkunst des 12. und 13. Jahrhunderts," in Dinzelbacher, 1993, 136–87.

16. See Hamburger, 1992; and Zimmer.

17. *Die Offenbarungen der Adelheid Langmann: Klosterfrau zu Engelthal,* Quellen und Forschungen zur Sprach- und Kulturgeschichte der germanischen Völker, 26, ed. P. Strauch, Strasbourg, 1878, 18: "doch enpfing erz und wart sein herz als lauter als die sunne und daz kindelein spilt in im." Greenspan, 206, compares the heart reproduced in Fig. 88 to a monstrance.

18. C. Henriquez, *Quinque prudentes virgines,* Antwerp, 1630, esp. 274: "Ita ut frequenter a refectorio salutaris Eucharistiae transiret ad dormitorium spirituale, in quo, a sensibus corporeis alienata, inter Sponsi sui brachia quiete felicissima sopietur." Translation from *Lives of Ida of Nivelles, Lutgard, and Alice the Leper,* trans. M. Cawley, Lafayette, Oreg., 1987, 86.

19. "Leben heiliger alemannischer Frauen des Mittelalters V: Die Nonnen von St. Katarinental bei Dieszenhofen," ed. A. Birlinger, *Alemannia* 15 (1887): esp. 167: "si hatt ein gewohnheit wenn der couent vnsern herren empfieng, do stůnd si in einen stůl, das si in wolgesehen maht vnd ze einem mål, do ward si in grosser andaht vnd empfing der couent vnsern herren. vnd do so ir hercz genczlich mit got vereinde vnd vnsern herren ansah, do sprach der zů ir vsser des priesters handen in der form der oflaten: sich mich an vnd sich mich begirlich an, won du solt min gőtlich antlút eweklich schǒwen nach alles dines herczen girde."

20. See Hamburger, 1992.

21. See C. W. Bynum, *Holy Feast and Holy Fast: The Religious Significance of Food to Medieval Women,* Berkeley and Los Angeles, 1987, esp. 257.

22. Ibid. For the concept of spiritual communion, see S. Grosse, *Heilsungewißheit und Scrupulositas im späten Mittelalter: Studien zu Johannes Gerson und Gattungen der Frömmigkeitstheologie seiner Zeit,* Beiträge zur historischen Theologie, 85, Tübingen, 1994, 212–14. As pointed out by B. W. Acklin Zimmermann, *Gott im Denken Berühren: Die theologischen Implikationen der Nonnenviten,* Dokimion, 14, Fribourg, 1993, esp. 90–106, although theologians of the High Middle Ages accepted the notion of spiritual communion, they accorded it a less prominent place in their writings than the female authors of the convent chronicles.

23. "Aufzeichnungen über das mystische Leben der Nonnen von Kirchberg," 120–21: "Sie begert auch, das ir got zu erkennen geb, ob es muglich wer, das ein mensch unsern herrn mocht enpfahen geistlich als werlich als der prister ob dem altar in der messe. Da antwurt ir unser herr,

und sprach: 'Es gen vil luet ze mess von einer guten gewonheit. Die enphahen teil nach ir begird. Aber dem ich meinen leichnam und mein plut gab zu einer speiss und ze einem tranck geistlich in sein sel, als werlich ich mich gib got und mensch dem prister ob dem altar. Das ist als ein auss genomen genad.' . . . Und doch het sie als gross begird unsers herrn leichnam ze enpfahen dick zu dem altar, das sie unser herr trost, und sprach zu ir: 'So du zu dem altar geest, so enpfahest du nicht, das du da sihest, sunder das gelaubest.' . . . und [er] sprach: 'Gin auff und tu auf den munt deiner begird. *Hoc est corpus meum.*' Mit den selben wort enpfant sie gotes als werlich in irr selle in aller sussikeit und genad, als sine in zu alter enpfing."

24. The image of the heart as an altar at which the soul joins Christ in a spiritual union persisted into the eighteenth century, as, e.g., in the Pietist tract by J. H. Reitz, *Histoire der Wiedergebohrnen,* Idstein, 1716; Schrader, 64 n. 39, notes that in this tract, one who received the word of God in his soul ascended to heaven, whereupon his heart became a temple: "Herz zum Tempel, darin der Herr Jesus das Abendmahl mit ihm hielte."

25. For the comparable illustrations in the various manuscripts and printed editions, see A. M. Diethelm, *Durch sin selbs unerstorben vichlichkeit hin zuo grosser loblichen heilikeit: Körperlichkeit in der Vita Heinrich Seuses,* Deutsche Literatur von den Anfängen bis 1700, 1, Bern, 1987, 178–79.

26. See S. Gohr, "Anna Selbdritt," in *Die Gottesmutter: Marienbild im Rheinland und Westfalen,* 2 vols., ed. L. Küppers, Recklinghausen, 1971, vol. II, 243–54; *Interpreting Cultural Symbols: St. Anne in Late Medieval Society,* ed. K. M. Ashley and P. Sheingorn, Athens, Ga., 1991; and *Heilige Anna, groete Moeder: De cultus van de Heilige Moeder Anna en haar familie in de Nederlanden en aangrenzende streken,* Uden, 1992.

27. Mader, 284 and fig. 214.

28. De Hamel.

29. For the infant Christ in representations of the Trinity, see K. A. Wirth, "Zur religiösen Herzenemblematik des 18. Jahrhunderts: Ein Bildzyklus in Mindelheim, seine Quelle und seine Deutung," *Jahrbuch des Vereins für Augsburger Bistumsgeschichte* 9 (1975): 221–71, figs. 6a–6c.

30. For the theme of "mother mysticism," see Hale; and Klapisch-Zuber, 1985.

31. See P. Kern, *Trinität, Maria, Inkarnation: Studien zur Thematik der deutschen Dichtung des späteren Mittelalters,* Philologische Studien und Quellen, 55, Berlin, 1971, esp. 128–38.

32. See G. Radler, *Die Schreinmadonna "Vierge ouvrante" von den bernhardinischen Anfängen bis zur Frauenmystik im Deutschordensland mit beschreibendem Katalog,* Frankfurter Fundamente der Kunstgeschichte, 6, Frankfurt, 1990, esp. 75–122; *800 Jahre Deutsche Orden,* Nuremberg, 1990, 39–42 and 119–20; and R. Kroos, "'Gotes tabernakel': Zur Funktion und Interpretation von Schreinmadonnen," *Zeitschrift für Schweizerische Archeologie und Kunstgeschichte* 43 (1986): 58–64.

33. Kern, 137.

34. For the *imitatio Mariae,* see Hamburger, 1990, 88–104.

35. See F. Ohly, "Du bist mein, ich bin dein, du in mir, ich in dir, ich du, du ich," *Kritische Bewahrung: Beiträge zur deutschen Philologie. Festschrift für Werner Schröder zum 60. Geburtstag,* ed. E.-J. Schmidt, Berlin, 1974, 371–415; and Matter, 192.

36. The cross-referencing between the sacred and the secular, common in the fifteenth century, is elucidated by L. Patterson, "Ambiguity and Interpretation: A Fifteenth-Century Reading of *Troilus and Criseyde,*" in *Negotiating the Past: The Historical Understanding of Medieval Literature,* Madison, Wis., 1987, 115–53.

37. See R. Lewinsohn, *Histoire entière du cœur: Érotisme, symbolisme, chirurgie, physiologie, psychologie,* Hamburg, 1959; also T. A. Campbell, *The Religion of the Heart: A Study of European Religious Life in the Seventeenth and Eighteenth Centuries,* Columbia, S.C., 1991; and *Herz: Das menschliche Herz—der herzliche Mensch,* Dresden, 1995. For theories of meditation of the vari-

ous confessions, see K. Erdei, *Auf dem Wege zu sich selbst: Die Meditation im 16. Jahrhundert. Eine funktionsanalytische Gattungsbeschreibung,* Wolfenbüttler Abhandlungen zur Renaissanceforschung, 8, Wiesbaden, 1990.

38. For Protestant, especially Pietist, examples, see Scharfe, 273–81; Schrader; and J. Harasimowicz, "'Scriptura sui ipsius interpres': Protestantische Bild-Wort-Sprache des 16. und 17. Jahrhunderts," in *Text und Bild, Bild und Text: DFG-Symposion 1988,* Germanistische Symposien: Berichtsbände, 11, Stuttgart, 1990, 262–82, esp. fig. 135.

39. See *Martin Luther und die Reformation in Deutschland,* 378.

40. Catalogued by M. Mauquoy-Hendrickx, *Les Estampes des Wierix conservées au Cabinet des Estampes de la Bibliothèque Royale Albert Ier: Catalogue raisonné,* 3 vols., Brussels, 1978, vol. I, 68–79 (cat. nos. 429–46). Sauvy; and K.-A. Wirth, "Religiöse Herzenemblematik," in *Das Herz,* vol. II, 65–105, describe Wierix's series and its variants in extensive, if not exhaustive, detail. For adaptations of Wierix's heart emblems, Protestant and Catholic, see Vandenbroeck, pl. 44; C. Opsomer-Halleux, *Trésors manuscrits de l'Université de Liège,* Liège, 1989, 43; I. Rosell, "Hjäj tats Skola: Vägen till Enheten met Gud (The school of the heart: The road to union with God)," *ICO: Iconographisk Post* (1992): 14–32; H. von Achen, "Det Invortis Menniske: Barokkens hjertesymbolikk i glassmaleriene fra Norddal kirke," in *Balansepunketet: Sunnmöres eldste historie, ca. 800–1660,* Ålesund, 1994, 420–30.

41. To judge from a reproduction in their pastoral newsletter, *Walburgis-Blätter* 24 (1936): 19, the nuns of St. Walburg owned a later German edition of one of these tracts, most likely *Daß Gott Zugeeignete Hertz, IESV des Fridsamen SALOMONIS Königlicher Thron,* Augsburg, 1630. Belser Wissenschaftlicher Dienst, Wildberg, is preparing a microfiche edition of the abbey's early modern holdings, the most extensive of their kind in Germany, to appear as *Edition St. Walburg: FrauenklosterBibliothek 17.–19. Jahrhundert.*

42. Neither Sauvy, Wirth, nor Lewinsohn deals effectively with medieval antecedents for the emblematic imagery of the heart. For studies tracing continuities between other forms of late medieval devotional imagery and baroque emblems, see Vetter, 1972; Schawe; and Höltgen.

43. An eighth drawing, originally on f. 275r, is missing. See Spamer, 16–17, who, however, incorrectly gives the date 1534.

44. For the manuscript in Munich, see Schmidtke, 58 (cat. no. 38b). For Fridolin, see N. Paulus, "Der Franziskaner Stephan Fridolin: Ein Nürnberger Prediger des ausgehenden Mittelalters," *Historisch-politische Blätter* 113 (1894): 465–83; F. Landmann, "Zum Predigtwesen der Straßburger Franziskanerprovinz in der letzten Zeit des Mittelalters," *Franziskanische Studien* 15 (1928): esp. 322–29; and U. Schmidt, *P. Stephan Fridolin: Ein Franziskanerpater des ausgehenden Mittelalters,* Munich, 1911, esp. 103–24.

45. The transcriptions given by Spamer, 11–12, are inaccurate.

46. See P. Heitz, *Neujahrswünsche des XV. Jahrhunderts,* Strasbourg, 1909; also K. H. Schreyl, *Der graphische Neujahrsgruß aus Nürnberg,* Nuremberg, 1979.

47. See O. Schade, "Klopfan: Ein Beitrag zur Geschichte der Neujahrsfeier," *Weimarisches Jahrbuch für deutsche Sprache, Litteratur und Kunst* 2 (1855): 75–147; F. J. Mone, "Neujahrswünsche," *Anzeiger für Kunde der teutschen Vorzeit* 7 (1838): 553–57; and H. Moser, "Zur Geschichte der Klöpfelnachtbräuche: Ihrer Formen und ihrer Deutungen," *Bayerisches Jahrbuch für Volkskunde* (1951): 121–40. For additional literature, consult A. Holtdorf, "Klopfan," ²VL, vol. IV, 122–25.

48. For a comparable approach to devotional imagery of an earlier period, see B. Raw, "What Do We Mean by the Source of a Picture?" in *England in the Eleventh Century: Proceedings of the 1990 Harlaxton Symposium,* ed. C. Hicks, Stamford, England, 1992, 285–300.

49. For sketches toward a history of the commonplace and its elaboration, see, in addition to G. Bauer, *Claustrum animae: Untersuchungen zur Geschichte der Metapher vom Herzen als Kloster,*

Munich, 1973; Ohly, 1970, 454–76; idem, "Haus als Metapher," *Reallexikon für Antike und Christentum* 13 (1986): 905–1063; H. Flasche, "Similitudo templi (Zur Geschichte einer Metapher)," *Deutsche Vierteljahrschrift* 23 (1949): 81–125; Küsters, 278–82; and the studies gathered in *Das Herz,* especially A. Walzer, "Das Herz im christlichen Glauben," vol. I, 63–106; and H. Rüdiger, "Die Metapher vom Herzen in der Literatur," vol. III, 87–134.

50. For medieval concepts of "edification," see A. Schoenen, "Aedificatio: Zum Verständnis eines Glaubenswortes in Kult und Schrift," *Enkainia: Festschrift Abtei Maria Laach,* Maria Laach, 1956, 14–29; and R. Schulmeister, *Aedificatio und imitatio: Studien zur intentionalen Poetik der Legende und Kunstlegende,* Hamburg, 1971.

51. For medieval texts that build on this metaphorical foundation, see R. D. Cornelius, *The Figurative Castle: A Study in the Medieval Allegory of the Edifice with Especial Reference to Religious Writings,* Bryn Mawr, Pa., 1930.

52. For the debate on how nuns both recorded and read sermons, see the literature cited by K. Schneider, "Felix Fabri als Prediger," in *Festschrift Walter Haug und Burghart Wachinger,* Tübingen, 1994, esp. 468.

53. For the literature on this set of sermons, see W. Frühwald, "St. Georgener Prediger," [2]VL, vol. II, 1207–13; K. Ruh, "Deutsche Predigtbücher des Mittelalters," *Vestigia Bibliae* 3 (1981): esp. 21–23; and K. O. Seidel, "Die St. Georgener Predigten und ihre Mitüberlieferung," in *Die deutsche Predigt im Mittelalter: Internationales Symposium am Fachbereich Germanistik der Freien Universität Berlin vom 3.–6. Oktober 1989,* ed. V. Mertens and J.-H. Schiewer, Tübingen, 1992, 18–30.

54. K. Rieder, *Das sogennante St. Georgender Prediger aus der Freiburger und der Karlsruher Handschrift herausgegeben,* Deutsche Texte des Mittelalters, 10, Berlin, 1908, 240, line 11: " 'Unsers herren wort sol in úrem hertzen wonen.' "

55. Ibid., 244, line 5: "Sant Paulus sprichet: 'ir sint ain tempel Gottes und ain hus.' " The same passage is incorporated into Sermon 34, ibid., 84, lines 10–11: "Nu sont wir únserm herren ain tempel und ain hus machen, da sin wandlung und sin wesen inne si. dis tempel sol sin únser herze."

56. Ibid., 74, lines 9–15: "si sont daz hus beraiten, so der herre kome, daz er es schoͤn vinde und wol berait. dis hus is únser hertze; daz sont wir beraiten, swenn únser herre kome, daz er es schoͤn vinde. daz únser hertze si únsers herren hus, daz sprichet er selbe: 'min vatter hât mir dis hus geben ze ainem rehten erbe.' dis hus sont wir beraiten. intrúwen, wir sont die súnde us fúrben und die untugend der súnden. und denne sont wir es zieren mit tugendlichen werchen und sont únser hertze reht bluͦmen mit tugendlichen gedâͤnken."

57. The same sentiments inform a Franciscan sermon attributed to an otherwise unknown Father Sigmund and preserved in a single mid-fifteenth-century manuscript from the Dominican convent of Unterlinden (Colmar, Bibliothèque de la Ville, Ms. 210, 93r–114v), published by K. Ruh, assisted by D. Ladisch-Grube and J. Brecht, *Franziskanisches Schrifttum im deutschen Mittelalter,* 2 vols., Munich, 1985, vol. 2, esp. 102, lines 55–58: "Ach min kind, tů im din herz vff mit gantzer begird, so hastu in wenn du wilt, du bedarfft nit verr löffen, er stot vor der túr dines herzen vnd alle mol so klopft er an, ob du in wellest in losen."

58. Blumenberg, 38.

59. Bauer, 1973; idem, "Herzklosterallegorien," [2]VL, vol. III, 1153–69; and K. Ruh, "Das geistliche Haus," [2]VL, vol. II, 1162–63.

60. See B. Bischoff, "Eine frühmittelalterliche Allegorie: 1. De domo Domini. 2. De camera Christi (Achtes Jahrhundert)," in *Anecdota Novissima: Texte des vierten bis sechzehnten Jahrhunderts,* Quellen und Untersuchungen zur lateinischen Philologie des Mittelalters, 7, Stuttgart, 1984, 85–90.

61. G. Oury, "Le *De claustro animae* de Jean, prieur de Saint-Jean-des-Vignes," *Revue d'ascetique et de mystique* 40 (1964): 427–42.

62. For the copy from Rebdorf (Munich, Staatsbibliothek, Clm. 509, ff. 364r–365v), see E. Weidenhiller, *Untersuchungen zur deutschsprachigen Literatur des späten Mittelalters nach den Handschriften der Bayerischen Staatsbibliothek,* Münchener Texte und Untersuchungen zur deutschen Literatur des Mittelalters, 10, Munich, 1965, 140–41. For Rebdorf and reform, see K. Schreiner, "Gebildete Analphabeten? Spätmittelalterliche Laienbrüder als Leser und Schreiber wissensvermittelnder und frömmigkeitsbildender Literatur," in *Wissensliteratur im Mittelalter und in der frühen Neuzeit: Bedingungen, Typen, Publikum, Sprache,* Wissensliteratur im Mittelalter: Schriften des Sonderforschungsbereichs, 226, Würzburg/Eichstätt, 13, ed. H. Brunner and N. R. Wolf, Wiesbaden, 1993, esp. 316–18; and J. Höcherl, *Rebdorfs Kanoniker der Windesheimer Zeit 1458–1853,* Eichstätt, 1992 (= *Historischer Verein Eichstätt: Sammelblatt* 85 [1992]).

63. Nuremberg, Stadtbibliothek, Ms. Cent. VI, 43[e], ff. 196v–197r, dated 1454: "Nu merck von eim geistlichen closter, wie und wo mit du daz in dir pawen vnd machen solt nach sant Bernharts ler." And "Ein fridsam hercz ist ein geistlich closter, dorynnen got selber der apt ist." For yet another example, dated 1407, see W. Stammler, *Prosa der deutschen Gotik: Eine Stilgeschichte in Texten,* Berlin, 1933, cat. no. 28, 50.

64. Ibid: "Gelossenheit ist die kirch, Andacht ist der kor, Übung ist der kreuczgang, Gedechtnuß des tods ist der kirchhoff . . . kewscheit ist daz sloffhaus." The construction of the allegory varied according to the gender of the audience: in contrast to nuns, monks would have read that God is the abbot and discernment, the prior ("Ain fridsam hercz ist ain gaistlich closter in dem got selber apt ist. Beschaidenhait ist prior dar jn"). I quote Ms. 101 in the Eis collection in Heidelberg, late fourteenth century, published by G. Eis, "Zwei unbekannte Handschriften der Allegorie vom Seelenkloster," *Leuvense Bijdragen* 53 (1964): 148–53. Ignoring the currency of the image among monks as well as nuns, F. Rapp, "Zur Spiritualität in elsässischen Frauenklöstern am Ende des Mittelalters," in *Frauenmystik im Mittelalter,* 360, concludes on a gratuitously pejorative note: "Mit dem Thema der Wohnung des Herrn in Innersten des Menschen wird eher gespielt, als daß es vertieft wird. Das Emblematische überwächst gewissermaßen den Gedanken, statt ihn zu enwickeln. . . . Dies alles sieht sich wie eine hübsche Stickerei an."

65. For an overview, with additional bibliography, see Hamburger, 1992. The three doors hence serve a function very different from that of the three windows of the anchoress's cell described in such detail in the early-thirteenth-century *Ancrene Wisse,* discussed by L. Georgianna, *The Solitary Self: Individuality in the Ancrene Wisse,* Cambridge, Mass., 1981, 59–65.

66. J. Meyer, *Buch der Reformacio Predigerordens,* Quellen und Forschungen zur Geschichte des Dominikanerordens in Deutschland, 2–3, ed. B. M. Reichert, Leipzig, 1908–9, 74 (bk. III, chap. 14): "Ich beschlüss mich alle tag in druy sloss: Daz erst sloss ist daz rayn, luter, megtlich hertz der edlen junckfrowen Marien für alle an vechtung des bösen gaistes. Daz II sloss ist daz gütig hertz unsers lieben heren Jesus Christus für alle an vechtung ds libs . . . Daz III sloss ist daz hailig grab, da verbirg ich mich zů unserm heren vor der welt und vor allen schedlichen creaturen."

67. Meyer was familiar with these provisions at first hand. His *Ämterbuch,* a "Book of Offices" modeled on Humbert of Romans's *Instructiones de officiis ordinis,* spells them out in exhaustive detail, mandating specifically that "dz inwendig tor sol haben drü schlösse und drige schlussel." There remains no edition of this text, although segments were published in "Die Chronik von Anna von Munzingen," 196–206. My transcription follows University of Indiana, Lilly Library, Ricketts Ms. 198, ca. 1455, from the Katharinenkloster in Nuremberg; see *A Catalog of Selected Illuminated Manuscripts in the Lilly Library, Indiana University* [= *The Indiana University Bookman* 17 (1988)]: 69–75.

68. See Schiewer.

69. For the imagery of St. John drinking from Christ's heart, see H. Rahner, "De Dominici pectoris fonte potavit," *Zeitschrift für katholische Theologie* 55 (1931): 103–8; and idem, "Flumina de ventre Christi: Die patristische Auslegung von Joh. 7:37–38," *Biblia* 22 (1941): 269–302 and 367–401.

70. See K. Rieder, "Mystischer Traktat aus dem Kloster Unterlinden zu Colmar i. Els.," *Zeitschrift für hochdeutschen Mundarten* 1 (1900): esp. 87: "derselbe dormetor zu Unterlinden sol sin ein gedultiges herze. . . . Da kumest du erst in ein jubiliren und mag dir danne zumal nicht bas gesin, danne alzo inwendige mit got dich vereinen. Danne so mach öch sprechen: 'ego dormio et cor meum vigilat,' eich slaffe, aber doch min herze wachet mit meinem geminten."

71. In the Middle Ages, the passage was only occasionally illustrated; for instances, see H. Buchthal, "A Byzantine Miniature of the Fourth Evangelist and Its Relatives," *Dumbarton Oaks Papers* 15 (1961): 127–39; B. Todic, "*Anapeson:* Iconographie et signification du thème," *Byzantion* 64 (1994): 134–65; and Hogg, 40, who reproduces London, British Library, Ms. Add. 37049, f. 30v.

72. McGinn, 1994, 144–46.

73. For the rare medieval illustrations of this passage, see Hamburger, 1990, 148; J. A. Endres, *Das S. Jacobsportal in Regensburg und Honorius Augustodunensis,* Kempten, 1903, 33–34; and S. Ringbom, "Filippo Lippis New Yorker Doppelporträt: Eine Deutung der Fenstersymbolik," *Zeitschrift für Kunstgeschichte* 48 (1985): 133–37.

74. See the sources cited in Ohly, 1986, 1004–5; the poem attributed to Peter Damian, "Quis est hic qui pulsat ad ostium?" discussed by McGinn, 1994, 144–45; P. Dronke, "The Song of Songs and the Medieval Love Lyric," in *The Bible and Medieval Culture,* Mediaevalia Lovaniensia, I/7, ed. P. Lourdaux and D. Verhelst, Louvain, 1979, 236–62; and Astell, 155–58, who discusses the fourteenth-century Italian poem "Vndo pi dore." The two passages continue to be combined in the emblematic tradition discussed by Sauvy.

75. St. Walburg, Ms. germ. 7, ff. 65r–78r, transcribed from Munich, Bayerische Staatsbibliothek, Cgm. 447, ff. 122r–144r, which is described in K. Schneider, *Die deutschen Handschriften der Bayerischen Staatsbibliothek München, Cgm. 351–500,* Catalogus codicum manu scriptorum Bibliothecae Monacensis, vol. V, pt. 3, Wiesbaden, 1973, 292–93.

76. The rubric reads, "Hie vachet an da puchlein saint bernharcz von der offnung des herczens." The manuscript from St. Walburg is one of at least five known to contain the Middle High German version, either in part or in its entirety; see Schneider, 292–93.

77. See A. Wilmart, "Gérard de Liège: Un Traité inédit de l'amour de Dieu," *Revue d'ascetique et de mystique* 12 (1931): 349–430; and G. Hendrix, "Handschriften en in handschrift bewaarde vertalingen van het aan Gerard van Luik toegeschreven traktaat *De doctrina cordis,*" *Ons geestelijk Erf* 51 (1977): 146–68. The text remains unedited; I consulted one of the rare printed copies of the 1506 edition (Stuttgart, Württembergische Landesbibliothek, Theol. oct. 14.461), described in G. Hendrix, "Drukgeschiedenis van het Traktaat *De doctrina cordis,*" *Archives et bibliothèques de Belgique* 49 (1978): 224–39. For additional literature, see V. Honemann, "Gerhard von Lüttich," [2]VL, vol. II, 1233–35; and P. Dinzelbacher, ed., *Wörterbuch der Mystik,* Stuttgart, 1989, 186.

78. "Von der offnung des herczen hab wir willen zw sagen. Das hercz ist als an puch, das auff gethon soll werden zw lesen" and "Es ist auch als ein hawß, des dore auff gethon soll werden ein zw laßen den, der da an klopfft."

79. "canti. 5 aperi michi soror mea, amica mea, immaculata mea. hec vox est dilecti pulsantis ut legitur in canti. et in apocalipsi 3 Ego sto ad ostium et pulso et cetera."

80. "Quanta ergo festinatio et leticia o amica carissima debes aperire sponso tuo christo pulsanti qui cum tanta donorum multitudine pulsat ad ostium cordis tui."

81. "Aperi michi cor tuum ad orationem, . . . spiritum ad amorem; brachia ad amplexus."

82. See Chapter 3, note 11.

83. Cf., e.g., their use by Suso, discussed by Bühlmann, 185–88.

84. "Ecce quomodo omnia ostia sua christus tibi aperuit. Verecundum ergo sit tibi ostia tua ei non aperire clamanti ad ostium et dicenti aperi michi et cetera."

85. This is not to underestimate the Latinity of some nuns but simply to recognize that in late-fifteenth-century German convents, literacy essentially meant vernacular literacy. See P. Ochsenbein, "Latein und Deutsch im Alltag oberrheinischer Dominikanerinnenklöster des Spätmittelalters," in *Latein und Volkssprache,* 42–51, with additional bibliography. There were, of course, notable exceptions, with Caritas Pirckheimer only the most celebrated.

86. J. Werlin, "Zwei mystische Traktate aus dem Nürnberger Sankt Katharinenkloster: Texte aus der Sammlung Eis," *Neuphilologische Mitteilungen* 64/3 (1963): esp. 299: "Herr schliuss vff die blůtigen tuͤr diner hend vnd diner fuͤss vnd zier vͤns under dem tǒr dins vffgetǎnen herczen vnd siten."

87. See, e.g., a sermon by Tauler, "Dixit Jhesus discipulus suis," in *Die Predigten Taulers aus der Engelberger und der Freiburger Handschrift sowie aus Schmidts Abschriften der ehemaligen Straßburger Handschriften,* ed. F. Vetter, Berlin, 1910, 284, lines 19–21: "mit aller andacht klopfen vor dem minneklichen uf getanem herzen und uf geschlossener siten unsers herren Jhesu Christi." Spamer, 16–17, discusses this motif but, as in the rest of his book, with the emphasis on the postmedieval examples.

88. St. Walburg, Ms. Germ. 4, f. 2r: "ich will im die herberg geben vnd will fleissigklich hören wenn er anklopft, So will ich im auff thon vnd ein lassen."

89. *Altdeutsche Predigten,* vol. I, p. 342, line 40–p. 343, line 10: "und als sie unsern herrin Jhesum Christum intphing in irn reinen lichnam und ir herze, also sul wir in ouch entphan mit irre helft. er manet uns selbe und spricht: 'ego sto ad hostium et pulso. si quis aperuerit mihi, intrabo ad eum et cenabo cum eo,' 'ich ste zu der tůre, und clophe,' spricht er; swer mir uf tut, zu dem gen ich und ezze mit ime. Liebn, unser hus ist unser herze da unser herre got zu clophit, so er sinen heiligen geist uns sendet, daz er uns mane, ist daz wir die manunge mit den werkin irvůllen, so get er mit uns zu tische, und als her David der propheta spricht: 'inebriabit nos ab ubertate domus sue.' 'er machit uns trůnkin von der genůchsam sines hůses.' wie got die lůte trunkin mache, daz sůl wir merkin bi weltlichen dingen, so die lůte trunkin werden, so vorgezzin si allis des da sie vor ê warin bekummert." The motif of the *imitatio Mariae* is introduced by a citation from Song of Songs 1 : 3 (342, lines 35–39): " 'trahe me post te, curremus in odorem unguentorum tuorum.' 'zůch uns nach dir,' sul wir sprechen, daz wir loufen in dem smacke und in dem růche diner salbin. der salben růch und smack ist die othmůticheit und die kůscheit und andere tůginliche werk die an ir warn, die wir nimmer můgin gehabn, sie enzieh uns nach."

90. *Die Erlösung mit einer Auswahl geistlicher Dichtungen,* Bibliothek der gesammten deutschen National-Literatur, 37, ed. K. Bartsch, Quedlinburg, 1858, reprinted Amsterdam, 1966, xxxv and 214–16 (after a fifteenth-century manuscript, Nuremberg, Stadtbibliothek, Ms. Cent. VII 19 in 12°).

91. See Hamburger, 1990, 70–87.

92. See *Christus und die minnende Seele: Zwei mittelalterliche mystische Gedichte. Im Anhang ein Prosadisput verwandten Inhaltes. Untersuchungen und Texte,* Germanistische Abhandlungen, 29, ed. R. Banz, Breslau, 1908; H. Rosenfeld, "Der mittelalterliche Bilderbogen," *Zeitschrift für deutsches Altertum und deutsche Literatur* 85 (1954–55): 66–75; idem, "Christus und die minnende Seele," [2]VL, vol. I, 1235–37; W. Williams-Krapp, "Bilderbogen-Mystik: Zu 'Christus und die minnende Seele' mit Editionen der Mainzer Überlieferung," in *Überlieferungsgeschichtliche Editionen und Studien zur deutschen Literatur des Mittelalters: Kurt Ruh zum 75. Geburtstag,* Texte und Textegeschichte, 31, ed. K. Künze, Tübingen, 1989, 350–64; and, for a related

work, L. Wolff, "Jesu Gespräch mit der treuen Seele nach einer Helmstedter Handschrift des 14. Jahrhunderts," in *Festschrift für Gerhard Cordes zum 65. Geburtstag,* 2 vols., ed. F. Debus and J. Hartig, Neumünster, 1973, vol. II, 249–54.

93. A comparison made by D. Kunzle, *The Early Comic Strip: Narrative Strips and Picture Stories in the European Broadsheet from c. 1450 to 1825,* Berkeley and Los Angeles, 1973, 22–23, who provides an English translation of the texts.

94. As noted by Williams-Krapp, 1989, 350, an inversion that can have the effect of reducing the text to an "illustration" of the image.

95. See S. B. Spitzlei, *Erfahrungsraum Herz: Zur Mystik des Zisterzienserinnenklosters Helfta im 13. Jahrhundert,* Mystik in Geschichte und Gegenwart: Text und Untersuchungen (Abteilung I: Christliche Mystik, 9), Stuttgart–Bad Cannstatt, 1991, esp. 90–97, who, however, concentrates on theology and Scripture without adequate consideration of the mediating role of sermons and devotional literature.

96. For the complex relationship between art and visions, see Hamburger, 1989b; and P. Dinzelbacher, *Christliche Mystik im Abendland,* Paderborn, 1994, 429–40, both with additional bibliography.

97. Mechthild of Hackeborn, 1875–77, 61–62 (bk. I, chap. 19): "Post haec ostendit ei Dominus pulcherimam domum excelsam et amplam nimis; intra quam aliam vidit domunculam factam ex lignis cedrinis, interius laminis argenteis valde splendidis coopertam, in cujus medio Dominus residebat. Hanc domum Cor Dei esse bene recognovit, quia multoties ipsum tali viderat forma; domuncula vero interior animam illam figurabat quae, sicut ligna cedrina imputribilia sunt, immortalis est et aeterna. Hujus domunculae janua erat ad Orientem posita, habens pessulum aureum, in quo aurea catenula pendebat, tendens in Cor Dei, uta ut cum janua aperiretur, catenula illa Cor Dei commovere videretur. Per januam intellexit designari desiderium animae; per pessulum, ejus voluntatem; per catenulam vero Dei desiderium, quod semper animae desiderium et voluntatem praevenit et excitat et trahit ad Deum."

98. Ibid., 157–58 (bk. II, chap. 20): "Audivit in intimis divini cordis quasi tres pulsus sonantes. Quod dum illa multum admirans, scire cuperet quid per tales pulsus notaretur, Dominus respondit: 'Tres isti pulsus tria denotant verba quibus animam alloquor amantem: primus itaque, est *veni,* scilicet secendo ab omnibus creaturis; secundus est, *intra,* videlicet fidenter tamquam sponsa; tertius est, *thalamum,* id est, Cor divinum.' . . . et intret thalamum Cordis sui divini, in quo abundat et superbundat copia totius delectationis et beatitudinis, quam nunquam cor poterit humanum exoptare."

99. Ibid., 178: "Eia praecordialis dilecte mi, utinam de corde meo delectabilissimum et tibi decentissimum tibi xenium facere possem." A late-fifteenth-century woodcut from Ulm depicts a monk offering up his heart in a similar manner: Christ implores, "Sun, gib mir din hercz den ich lieb hab. dem läß ich sträff nit ab," to which the sinner, paraphrasing Song of Songs 1 : 3, replies, "O herr, das will ich, das beger ich darumbe so soltu ziehen mich." R. S. Field, *Fifteenth-Century Woodcuts and Metalcuts from the National Gallery of Art,* Washington, n.d., cat. no. 266, describes the print; for a brief discussion of its imagery, see C. Harbison, "The Sexuality of Christ in the Early Sixteenth Century in Germany," in *A Tribute to Robert A. Koch: Studies in the Northern Renaissance,* Princeton, N.J., 1994, esp. 73–74.

100. Mechthild of Hackeborn, 1885–87, 178: "'Nullum delectabilius atque mihi carius xenium mihi poteris exhibere, quam si domunculam inde mihi facias, in qua sine intermissione habitem et delecter. Haec domus unam tantum fenestram habeat, per quam hominibus loquar et dona mea distribuam.' Haec fenestram os suum esse intellexit, per quam verbum Dei ad se venientibus per doctrinam seu consolationem deberet ministrare." Ruh, 1993, 325, comments briefly on this passage, but only to compare it pejoratively with Gertrude of Helfta's imagery of the heart.

101. For related imagery, see Ohly, 1986, 988–1007; and C. Gottlieb, *The Window in Art from the Window of God to the Vanity of Man: A Survey of Window Symbolism in Western Painting,* New York, 1981, esp. 172–88.

102. E. Schraut, "Zum Bildungsstand fränkischer Zisterzienserinnenkonvente," *Württembergisch Franken* 71 (1988): 42–67, appraises the education of Cistercian nuns in Franconia.

103. See Hamburger, 1990; and Bynum, 1987.

104. For the patristic sources of the mystical tradition, see H. Rahner, "Die Gottesgeburt: Die Lehre der Kirchenväter von der Geburt Christi im Herzen der Gläubigen," *Zeitschrift für katholische Theologie* 59 (1935): 333–418.

105. For the heart as a cradle, see Lentes, 129–35. Some medieval texts actually compare the womb to a chamber in a house; see, e.g., *Le Propriétaire des choses,* cited by M. Rubin, "The Person in the Form: Medieval Challenges to Bodily 'Order,'" in *Framing Medieval Bodies,* esp. 110; or the tradition of exegesis of Luke 10:38 (Intravit in quoddam castellum) discussed by J. Mann, "Allegorical Architecture in Medieval Literature," *Medium Aevum* 53 (1994): 191–210, who notes: "The exegetes read the biblical text as an allegory of Jesus' entry into Mary's womb" (198). For texts that more generally compare the body to a house or castle and the senses to the wardens that guard it, see Cornelius, 20–36.

106. For this phenomenon, see P. Dinzelbacher, *Heilige oder Hexen: Schicksale auffäliger Frauen in Mittelalter und Frühneuzeit,* Zurich, 1995, 186–92; and his forthcoming article announced there, 311, "Die Gottesgeburt in der Seele und im Körper: Von der somatischen Konsequenz einer theologischen Metapher."

107. Reproduced in *Martin Luther und die Reformation in Deutschland,* 373–74, with additional bibliography; and Koepplin, esp. 171.

108. For Luther's understanding of Marian devotion, see E. Iserloh, "Die Verehrung Mariens und der Heiligen in der Sicht Martin Luthers," in *Ecclesia militans: Studien zur Konzilien- und Reformationsgeschichte,* 2, ed. W. Brandmüller et al., Paderborn, 1988, 109–15; and R. Schimmelpfennig, *Die Geschichte der Marienverehrung im deutschen Protestantismus,* Paderborn, 1952.

109. The panel, now in the Staatliche Kunstsammlungen in Dresden, is reproduced and discussed in Koepplin, 173, fig. 13.

110. Koepplin: "Desshalb wenn diese Geburt uns soll zu Nutze kommen und das Herz wandeln soll, müssen wir das Exempel der Jungfrau in unser herz bilden. . . . Also werden auch wir schwanger vom Heiligen Geist und empfangen Christum geistlich."

111. J. Gottschalk, "Die älteste Bilderhandschrift mit den Quellen zum Leben der hl. Hedwig, im Auftrag des Herzogs Ludwig I. von Liegnitz und Brieg im Jahre 1353 vollendet," *Aachener Kunstblätter* 34 (1967): 61–161; and A. von Euw and J. M. Plotzek, *Die Handschriften der Sammlung Ludwig,* 4 vols., Cologne, 1982, vol. III, 78–81.

112. *Der Hedwigs-Codex von 1353: Sammlung Ludwig,* ed. W. Braunfels et al., Berlin, 1972, 89: "spiritu et animo semper se conabatur Domino exhibere presentem et dilecti miri modo consolantis et consolari scientis presenciam totis affectabat precordiis, ut archano eius potiretur alloquio, amoris frueretur dulcedine et salutaris effectum preciperet gracie degustaretque cordis palato mirande suavitatis ipsius saporem."

113. Ibid., 90–91.

114. Ibid., 89: "Ardens erat cor eius, unde nec quiescere poterat pre amore Dei, quem amabat et desiderabat habere presentem, quemadmodum desiderat cervus ad fontes aquarum. . . . prestolando Consolatoris adventum, ut venienti et pulsanti ad ianuam cordis celeriter aperiret."

Chapter 5

1. J. J. Landsperg, *Opera Omnia,* 5 vols., Monserrat, 1890, vol. IV, esp. 76: "Ab eo quod retinere potes incipe, aut in schedula tibi vel libello, quem tecum feras, conscribe, donec absque libello retinere possis: vel si non scias legere, signa tibi, quo quid significent intelligas, depinge." See also J. Greven, *Die Kölner Karthäuser und die Anfänge der katholischen Reform in Deutschland,* Katholisches Leben und Kämpfen im Zeitalter der Glaubensspaltung, 6, Münster, 1935, 27–42.

2. For the Gregorian dictum, see L. Duggan, "Was Art Really the 'Book of the Illiterate'?" *Word and Image* 5 (1989): 227–51; and, with emphasis on fifteenth- and sixteenth-century Germany, H. Lülfing, "Pro lectione pictura est," in *Buch-Bibliothek-Leser: Festschrift für Horst Kunze zum 60. Geburtstag,* Berlin, 1969, 567–82. For the dictum in the context of Gregory's own thought and time, see C. Chazelle, "Pictures, Books, and the Illiterate: Pope Gregory's Letters to Serenus of Marseilles," *Word and Image* 6 (1990): 138–53. Landsperg conceivably refers to the practice of using signs as mnemonic devices, for which see M. J. Carruthers, *The Book of Memory: A Study of Memory in Medieval Culture,* Cambridge, England, 1990; however, his use of the verb "depingo," together with the context of the passage, which refers explicitly to Passion meditations, suggests that he may just as well have had narrative illustrations or other images of the Passion in mind.

3. AA.SS March, vol. III, 741: "In operibus istis occupata exterius, non minus ardebat sua caritas interius, Deum enim in omnibus et super omnia diligebat. Plagae Christi et mors salutifera; crux sancta, decorata pretioso sanguine filii summi Regis; sputa, clavi, lancea, livor, caro rubea, acetum et spongia et corona spinea; sel, arundo, ante oculos suae mentis assiduae versabantur: et in pergameno haec omnia depingi fecit, ut ceteros excitaret ad memoriam Passionis. . . . Certe a iuventute sua usque ad senectutem et senium Christi mors et passio gloriosa erat praesens suae menti." For Joanna see also A. Vauchez, "Une 'Sainte Femme' du Val-de-Loire à l'époque de la guerre de cent ans: Jeann-Marie de Maillé (1331–1414)," *Revue d'Histoire de l'Église de France* 70 (1984): 96–105; and idem, "Influences Franciscaines et réseaux aristocratiques dans le val du Loire: autour de la Bienheureuse Jeanne-Marie de Maillé (1331–1414)," in *Mouvements Franciscains et Société Française XIIe–XXe siècles,* Paris, 1984, 95–105.

4. AA.SS March, vol. III, 734: "Et ut cordi suo Passionis Dominicae memoria insigeretur, imaginem Crucifixi in pergameni depictam, inter pectus et tunicam absconditam, et aliquando in manibus elevatum, deportabat."

5. *Vita Beatricis: De Autobiografie van de Z. Beatrijs van Tienen O.Cist., 1200–1268,* ed. L. Reypens and J. van Mierlo, Studiën en textuitgaven van *Ons Geestelijk Erf,* 15, Antwerp, 1964, 56–57 (bk. I, chap. 14): "Crucem quippe ligneam, unius palmi longitudinis, nodoso funiculo sibi stricte colligatam, die noctuque gestabat in pectore; cui tytulum dominice passionis, horrorem extremi iudicii, iudicisque seueritatem inscripserat, et cetera que iugitur proponebat in memoria retinere. Aliud nichilominus dominice crucis signaculum, in pargameni cedula depictum, etiam gestabat in brachio colligatum; tercium, quoque coram se, cum scribendi vacabat officio, depictum habebat in assere; quatenus ad quecumque loca se diuerteret, aut quidquid operis extrinsecus actitaret: omnis oblivionis effugata caligine, per dominice crucis signaculum, id, de cuius amissione timebat, impressum cordi suo in memoria firmiter retineret." R. De Ganck, *Beatrice of Nazareth in Her Context,* Cistercian Studies Series, 121, Kalamazoo, Mich., 1991, 254, whose translation I use, discusses this passage in the context of Beguine devotions, as does J. H. Oliver, " 'Je pecherise renc grasces a vos': Some French Devotional Texts in Beguine Psalters," in *Medieval Codicology, Iconography, Literature, and Translation: Studies for Keith Val Sinclair,* ed. P. Monks and D. Owen, Leiden, 1994, esp. 259.

6. *Margareta Ebner und Heinrich von Nördlingen,* p. 20, line 26–p. 21, line 3: "dar zuo het ich ain büechlin, da was auch ain herre an dem criucz. daz schob ich haimlich in den bousen also

offenz, und wa ich gieng, so druckt ich ez an min hercz mit grosser fräude und mit unmessiger gnaud. und as ich dann schlauffen wolt, so nam ich den herren, den an dem büechlin, und let in under min antlütcz."

7. See AA.SS. August III, 673 and 685, an episode discussed by P. Camporesi, *The Incorruptible Flesh: Bodily Mutation and Mortification in Religion and Folklore,* trans. T. Croft-Murray and H. Elsom, Cambridge, England, 1988, 3–6; and by K. Park, "The Criminal and the Saintly Body: Autopsy and Dissection in Renaissance Italy," *Renaissance Quarterly* 47 (1994): 1–33.

8. A. Grion, "La 'Legenda' del B. Venturino da Bergamo secondo il testo inedito del codice di Cividale," *Bergomum* 50 (1956): esp. 102. "In fine, vero, depingebat inferius manu propria omnia insignia passionis: scilicet crucem, clavos, coronam spineam, lanceam, spongiam cum situla, columpnam cum scuticis, scalam et martellum, atque tenaculas." For further discussion of this passage, see Hamburger, 1995.

9. *Heinrich Seuse,* 103: "Daz minneklich bilde fůrt er mit ime, die wil er ze schůl fůr, und sast es fúr sich in siner celle venster und blikt es an lieplich mit herzklicher begirde. Er braht es wider hein und verwurkt es in die capell mit minneklicher meinunge."

10. Ibid., 154: "in einem gůten andacht do nate si den selben namen Jesus mit roter siden uf ein kleines tůchli in diser gestalt: IHS, den si ir selben wolte heinlich tragen"; translation from *Henry Suso,* 173–74. The discussion of this passage in U. Weymann, *Die Seusesche Mystik und ihre Wirkung auf die bildende Kunst,* Berlin, 1938, is inadequate. For the history of the cult to Christ's name, see P. R. Biasiotto, *History of the Development of Devotion to the Holy Name, with a Supplement,* St. Bonaventure, N.Y., 1943.

11. See D. Richter, "Die Allegorie der Pergamentbearbeitung: Beziehungen zwischen handwerklichen Vorgängen und der geistlichen Bildersprache des Mittelalters," in *Fachliteratur des Mittelalters: Festschrift für Gerhard Eis,* ed. G. Keil, R. Rudolf, W. Schmitt, and H. J. Vermeer, Stuttgart, 1968, 83–92.

12. *Heinrich Seuse,* 155: "Und machete do dez selben namen glich unzallichen vil namen und schůf, daz der diener die namen alle uf din herz bloss leit und sú mit einem gőtlichen segen sinen geischlichen kinden hin und her sante. Und ir ward kund getan von gote: wer den namen also bi im trůge und im teglich ze eren ein Pater noster sprech, dem wőlte got hie gůtlich tůn und wőlti in begnaden an siner junsten hinvart." Translation, with slight changes, from *Henry Suso,* 173–74.

13. See Hamburger, 1995, with additional bibliography.

14. As I have elaborated elsewhere; see Hamburger, 1989a. For a fuller discussion of this passage and its accompanying illustration in *The Exemplar,* see my essay "'For Every Tree Is Known by Its Fruit': Devotional Rhetoric and the Reception of Seuse's *Exemplar,*" forthcoming in *Christ among the Medieval Dominicans,* ed. K. Emery and J. Wawrykow, Notre Dame, Ind., 1997.

15. E. Ritzinger and H. C. Scheeben, "Beiträge zur Geschichte der Teutonia in der zweiten Hälfte des 13. Jahrhunderts," *Archiv der Deutschen Dominikaner* 3 (1941): 20: "Item cistas et clausuras, sive de clave fixa sive aliquo artificio factas, sororibus habere non licet. Sed quia hanc praetendunt causam, quia res suas perdunt, unde turbationes in conventibus saepe fiunt, et propter hoc clausurae sint ipsis necessariae, hanc occasionem amputans ordino, ut, si res parvulae sint, utpote acus, fila, penna, cedula et huiusmodi tolluntur, moneat priorissa, quod reddantur, vel a vino abstineant, quae non reddiderint."

16. Ibid., 37: "Consutrices similter operentur in communi laborerio nec divertant ad angulos." Cf. the instructions delivered by Frederik van Heilo to nuns of the Windesheim congregation in his pastoral letter *Epistola contra pluralitatem confessorum et de regime sororum,* unedited but published in part by J. J. Prins, *Frederik van Heilo en zijn Schriften,* Amsterdam, 1866, 59–60: "singulares semper suspecte sunt et que angulos querunt."

17. Ritzinger and Scheeben, 38: "Poterit autem pars sabbati concedi, praesertim post nonam, sororibus, ut vacent a communi opere pro suis necessitatibus expendiendis. Sed tamen haec interpolatio operibus inutilibus minime concedatur."

18. Ibid., 37–38: "Scriptrices sedeant cum aliis laborantibus in communi domo, sed hae non scribant aliis, donec conventus habeat libros necessarios."

19. Kroos, 160: "Sed quia opus manuum quod sanctus Benedictus in regula viris precepit, nos mulieris pro peccatis nostris incarcerate, implere non possumus, illud quod de opere manuum sanctus Jeronimus sanctimonialibus precepit, libenti animo in quantum possumus, adimplere promittimus."

20. *Analecta Sacri Ordinis Fratrum Praedicatorum,* 346: "quia ociositas inimica est anime et mater et nutrix vitiorum, nullus sit ociosa." The passage continues: "Sed dilegenter observetur ut exceptis illis horis et temporibus quibus oracioni vel officio vel alii occupationi necessarie debent intendere: operibus manuum ad utilitatem communem omnes attente insistant."

21. Ritzinger and Scheeben, 37: "nulla inveniatur otiosa, sed operetur quaelibet pro communitate in silentio et oratione."

22. "Die Regensburger Klarissenregel," 9, lines 26–29: "Aber die swestern und die servicial die suln sich uben an nuzzer, und an erberre arbeit, . . . under sogetaner fursihtekeit, daz sie die muzekeit vertriben, diu da ist ein vint der sele, und doch den geist heiliges gebetes und andacht."

23. For the concept of *otium,* see J. Leclercq, *Otia monastica: Études sur le vocabulaire de la contemplation au Moyen Âge,* Studia Anselmiana, 51, Rome, 1963.

24. A prayer book from the house of the sisters of Mary Magdalene in Erfurt, dated 1497, provides fascinating evidence of this process. Published by A. Zumkeller, "Vom geistlichen Leben im Erfurter Weißfrauenkloster am Vorabend der Reformation nach einer neu aufgefundenen handschriftlichen Quelle," in *Reformatio ecclesiae: Beiträge zu kirchlichen Reformbemühungen von der alten Kirche bis zur Neuzeit. Festschrift für Erwin Iserloh,* ed. R. Bäumer, Paderborn, 1980, esp. 253–54, the book contains a series of texts spelling out the duties and virtues of a reformed nun explicitly identified as having been excerpted from "tabula de institutione religiosorum et proficere volencium," presumably catechismal tablets of the kind discussed by H. Boockmann, "Über Schrifttafeln in spätmittelalterlichen deutschen Kirchen," *Deutsches Archiv für Erforschung des Mittelalters* 40 (1984): 210–24.

25. Known from a single manuscript (Zurich, Zentralbibliothek, Ms. C 76 [290], ff. 147v–149r); see W. Wackernagel, "Geistliches Lehrgedicht aus dem zwölften Jahrhundert," *Altdeutsche Blätter* 1 (1836): 343–47; and, for the revised date, K. Ruh, "Mea carissima," [2]VL, vol. II, 1174–76.

26. Cf. "Das Wienhausen Liederbuch," 28: "Virtutis ad preludium / fit artis nobis studium. / wol ome, de de scrifft vorstan, / concordes federe. / Quo sine stat in ocio / claustralis heu devocio, / nicht leren is ovel dan / ergo kyrie." A variant of these verses was copied onto the flyleaf of a manuscript from the Cistercian convent of Wöltingerode, Wolfenbüttel Cod. Guelf. 498 Helmst.; Rüthing, 215–16, erroneously assumes that they must have originated there. For other texts that allegorize the activity of spinning, see K. Schneider, "Der geistliche Spinnrocken," [2]VL, vol. II, 1174–76.

27. For the *Weberfresken,* see P. Ketsch, *Frauen im Mittelalter: Frauenarbeit im Mittelalter, Quellen und Materialien,* Geschichtsdidaktik: Studien, Materialien, 14, Düsseldorf, 1983, 170–73 (who erroneously reports that the paintings have been destroyed); L. Ettmüller, "Die Freskobilder zu Konstanz," *Mittheilungen der Antiquarischen Gesellschaft in Zürich* 15 (1966): 223–42; and *Ritter—Heilige—Fabelwesen: Wandmalerei in Konstanz von der Gotik bis zur Renaissance,* ed. P. Wollkopf, Konstanzer Museumsjournal, Constance, 1988, 105–6 and pls. 19–20. For women in textile trades, see K. Wesoly, "Die weibliche Bevölkerungsanteil im spätmittelalterlichen und

frühneuzeitlichen Städten und die Betätigung von Frauen in zünftigen Handwerk (insbesondere am Mittel- und Oberrhein)," *Zeitschrift für die Geschichte des Oberrheins* NF 89 (1990): 69–117; M. Wensky, *Die Stellung der Frau in der stadtkölnischen Wirtschaft im Spätmittelalter,* Quellen und Darstellungen zur hansischen Geschichte, NF 26, Cologne, 1980; and M. C. Howell, *Women, Production, and Patriarchy in Late Medieval Cities,* Chicago, 1986. For nuns as producers of textiles, see R. Parker, *The Subversive Stitch: Embroidery and the Making of the Feminine,* New York, 1989, 42–43; J. Bumke, *Courtly Culture: Literature and Society in the High Middle Ages,* trans. T. Dunlop, Berkeley and Los Angeles, 1991, 339–40; and G. Rehm, *Die Schwestern vom gemeinsamen Leben im nordwestlichen Deutschland. Untersuchungen zur Geschichte der Devotio moderna und des weiblichen Religiosentums,* Berliner Historische Studien, 11 (Ordensstudien, 5), Berlin, 1985, 230–45.

28. Quoted from the manuscript in Karlsruhe, Badische Landesbibliothek, Ms. St. Georgen 89, ff. 29v–30r.

29. For the other manuscripts and their illustrations, see *Christus und die minnende Seele.*

30. Mechthild of Hackeborn, 1875–77, 99 (bk. I, chap. 29): "Sicut enim artifex qui mirificum opus facere decrevit, magno studio praemeditatur, et in delectatione cordis sui praeimaginatur: sic veneranda Trinitas delectabatur, et gaudebat quia me talem imaginem facere volebat, in qua totius sapientiae et bonitatis sua artificium elegantissime appareret."

31. For women's manufacture of textiles as memorial images in the ritual commemoration of the dead, see H. Wunder, "'Gewirkte Geschichte,' Gedenken und 'Handarbeit': Überlegungen zum Tradieren von Geschichte im Mittelalter und zu seinem Wandel am Beginn der Neuzeit," in *Modernes Mittelalter,* 324–54.

32. For a brief description, see O. von Heinemann, *Die Handschriften der Herzoglichen Bibliothek zu Wolfenbüttel: Zweite Abteilung. Die Augusteischen Handschriften,* 5, Wolfenbüttel, 1903, 88. That the inscription is not a signature per se but an addition intended to commemorate the artist cannot be ruled out. Manuscript illumination signed by nuns, while rare, is less infrequent; see, e.g., W. A. Schulze, "Margarete Rorer, eine Freiburger Buchmalerin," *Freiburger Diözesan-Archiv* 103 (1983): 335–38.

33. "ich hab meinen schlof oft dar durch geprochen wen ich gedocht wie ich je einem model wolt machen" (f. 1v) . . . "es mich rewt dz ich es nit in meinem jugent hab thu do ich geschiter wer geweßen den noch lxx jaren so wolten mir mein lieb swest[ern] doch auch kein rw lasen."

34. See H. Dedler, "Vom Sinn der Arbeit nach der Regel des heiligen Benedikt," in *Benedictus: Der Vater des Abendlandes, 547–1947,* ed. H. S. Brechter, Munich, 1947, 103–18; and J. van Engen, "Theophilus Presbyter and Rupert of Deutz: The Manual Arts and Benedictine Theology in the Early Twelfth Century," *Viator* 11 (1980): 147–63.

35. Ziegler, 95–113, also emphasizes the importance of manual labor as a constitutive element in the devotions and devotional imagery of religious women.

36. For the text, see *Das "St. Katharinentaler Schwesternbuch,"* 117: "Vnd do in einer nacht ward, do was ir vor wie neiswas zů ir keme vnd gab ir ein snůr in ir hand, die was mit roten vnd grůner syden zemen geflohten"; for Diemůt, see 233.

37. Ibid.: "Die rot sid betút die hohen gotheit; die grů betůtet die mentschheit ýnsers herren. Das die rot vnd grůnn sid zemen sind geflohten, das ist, das die zwv natur, gőtlich vnd mentschlich natur, verainet ward in ýnser fröwen. Da mit solt du dis zit vmb gän vnd solt die schnůr flehten vnd entflehten." For a commentary on the symbolism of this particular passage, see *Das "St. Katharinentaler Schwesternbuch,"* 234–35; and for a no less corporeal image of manual labor, see *Das Leben der Schwestern zu Töß,* 52, a passage in which Adelhait von Frauenberg is described as weaving a dress for the infant Jesus with her veins.

38. *Das "St. Katharinentaler Schwesternbuch,"* 117: "An dem heiligen tag ze winnehten do

was si in grosser gnäd. Vnd in der ersten mess, die sang brůder Cůrat sålig von Lindöw, do der v̈nsern herren vffhůb, do sah si, das sin hend guldin wären, vnd sah, das sich die oflat verwandlet in das aller schönst kindli, das ie gesehen ward."

39. This topos, rooted in patristic exegesis, was familiar to nuns from Middle High German devotional poetry; see Kern, 189–220.

40. See M. Wehrli-Johns, "Haushälterin Gottes: Zur Mariennachfolge der Beginen," in *Maria, Abbild oder Vorbild? Zur Sozialgeschichte mittelalterlicher Marienverehrung,* ed. H. Röckelein, C. Opitz, and D. R. Bauer, Tübingen, 1990, 147–67, with further bibliography.

41. See R. L. Wyss, "Die Handarbeiten der Maria: Eine ikonographische Studie unter Berücksichtigung der Techniken," in *Artes minores: Dank an Werner Abegg,* ed. M. Stettler and M. Lemberg, Bern, 1973, 113–88; and G. M. Gibson, "The Thread of Life in the Hand of the Virgin," in *Equally in God's Image: Women in the Middle Ages,* ed. J. B. Holloway, C. S. Wright, and J. Bechtold, New York, 1990, 46–54.

42. See E. Behrens, "Zur *Maria am Spinnrocken* im Deutschen Museum," *Berliner Museen: Berichte aus den preußischen Kunstsammlungen* 59 (1938): 84–86; H. Rosenau, "A Study in the Iconography of the Incarnation," *Burlington Magazine* 85 (1944): 176–79; and G. M. Lechner, *Maria gravida: Zum Schwangerschaftsmotive in der bildenden Kunst,* Münchener Kunsthistorische Abhandlungen, 9, Munich, 1991, 446 and fig. 212.

43. For texts extolling the Virgin's handiwork, see Kroos, 158–60.

44. "Aufzeichnungen über das mystische Leben der Nonnen von Kirchberg," 138: "Dar zu sprach sie alle tage tausent Ave Maria, und einen psalter sprach sie auch alle tage ob dem wercke."

45. Wyss reproduces numerous examples. See also H. van Os, "Mary as Seamstress," in *Studies in Early Tuscan Painting,* London, 1992, 277–86; O. F. M. Meinardus, "Zur 'strickenden Madonna' oder 'Die Darbringung der Leidenswerkzeuge' des Meister Bertram," *Idea: Jahrbuch der Hamburger Kunsthalle* 7 (1988): 15–22; and C. Gerhardt, "Die Karitas webt die Einheit der Kirche: Der ungenähte Rock Christi in Otfrids von Weißenburg 'Evangelienbuch' (IV, 28.29)," in *Der Heilige Rock zu Trier: Studien zur Geschichte und Verehrung der Tunika Christi,* ed. E. Avetz et al., Trier, 1995, 877–913. For images of a later date, see J. F. Moffitt, "Mary as a 'Prophetic Seamstress' in Siglo de Oro Sevillian Painting," *Wallraf-Richartz-Jahrbuch* 54 (1993): 141–62.

46. For a longer description, see Wyss, 125–28, fig. 11.

47. "Aufzeichnungen über das mystische Leben der Nonnen von Kirchberg," 138: "Und eins mals, da sie span, wann sie kom auss dem werckhauss nymmer an not, da kom das aller schönste lemlein, das je gesehen ward, und was aller dinge in dem pilde mit dem vannen und mit dem creücz, als man es pflieget ze malen. Und sas ir in die schoss, und das lemlein nam sein pfötlein, und sluck sie an die hende und an den vaden, den sie gespunen hete ze der selben stunde rechte in der weise, als ir das lemlein chürzveil und freüde wolte machen, und das treib es als lange, piss sie hinder sich in ein fenster vil und also lage sie lange weil in göttlicher genade, als ir vil und dicke geschach."

48. Both sources would have been familiar from any number of sources, among them, the vitae of female mystics; see Chapter 4, note 15.

49. K. Schneider, *Deutsche mittelalterliche Handschriften der Universitätsbibliothek Augsburg: Die Signaturgruppen Cod. I.3 und Cod. II.1,* Wiesbaden, 1988, 674–83 and pl. 8.

50. "Lebensbeschreibung der sel. Christina von Retters," vol. 17, 249: "da sach sie vbyn yn der boißyn eyn lemgyn slaiffyn, vnd iß hait eyn crentzgyn vff synem heubt, daz was vmbschrebyn myt gulden bustabyn: 'Agnus dei, qui tollit peccata mundi.' "

51. Ibid.: "Zo haynt entwacht das lemgyn vnd sprancke snel yn das prysters hant vnd strebete zo myr, als syne begert zo myr stontde."

52. For the visual arts, see E. Michael, "Bildstickereien aus Kloster Lüne als Ausdruck der

Reform des 15. Jahrhunderts," *Die Diözese Hildesheim in Vergangenheit und Gegenwart* 53 (1985): 633–78; and J. Hamburger, "Texts vs. Images, or the Reformation of History: The Literature of Female Spirituality from an Art Historian's Perspective," forthcoming. For the production of manuscripts, see W. Williams-Krapp, "Ordensreform und Literatur im 15. Jahrhundert," *Jahrbuch der Oswald von Wolkenstein-Gesellschaft* 4 (1986): 41–51; idem, "Frauenmystik und Ordensreform im 15. Jahrhundert," *Literarische Interessenbildung im Mittelalter,* DFG-Symposion 1991, ed. J. Heinzle, Stuttgart, 1993, 301–13; idem, "Observanzbewegungen, monastische Spiritualität und geistliche Literatur im 15. Jahrhundert," *Internationales Archiv für Sozialgeschichte der deutschen Literatur* 20 (1995): 1–15; and G. Stamm, "Klosterreform und Buchproduktion: Das Werk der Schreib- und Lesemeisterin Regula," in *Faszination eines Klosters,* 63–70. See also E. König, "New Perspectives on the History of Mainz Printing: A Fresh Look at Illuminated Manuscripts," in *Printing the Written Word: The Social History of Books, circa 1450–1520,* ed. S. Hindman, Ithaca, N.Y., 1991, 143–73; and K. Holter, "Der Einfluß der Melker Reform auf das klösterliche Buchwesen in Österreich," in *Klösterliche Sachkultur des Spätmittelalters: Internationaler Kongress Krems an der Donau 18. bis. 21. September 1978,* ed. H. M. Appelt, Veröffentlichungen des Instituts für mittelalterliche Realienkunde Österreichs, 3 (Österreichische Akademie der Wissenschaften, Phil.-Hist. Kl., Sitzungsberichte, 367), Vienna, 1980, 305–20.

53. See K. Schneider, "Die Bibliothek des Katharinenklosters in Nürnberg und die städtische Gesellschaft," in *Studien zum städtischen Bildungswesen des späten Mittelalters und der frühen Neuzeit,* Abhandlungen der Akademie der Wissenschaften in Göttingen, Phil.-Hist. Kl., 3. Folge, 137, Göttingen, 1983, 70–82; and idem, "Beziehungen zwischen den Dominikanerinnenklöstern Nürnberg und Altenhohenau im ausgehenden Mittelalter: Neue Handschriftenfunde," in *Würzburger Prosastudien II,* Medium Aevum: Philologische Studien, 31, Munich, 1975, 211–18.

54. See Stammler, 1933, 11 ("Vom Abschreiben deutscher Bücher"; Nuremberg, Stadtbibliothek, Ms. Cent. VI 85, 148b–149a): "Es ist zu wißen und zu mercken, daz die teutschen buch gar ser und gar vast gefelschet und geswecht werdent mit dem schreiben. . . . Und darumb sol man sie, wenn man diß oder ein anders abschreiben wil, gar wol laßen corrigiren, aun auch pessern, daz man iht betrogen werd, wann die synne swer und tapfer und auch trefflichen seint."

55. Although Weinberger, 11, exaggerates the evidence for printmaking at the convent, the possibility cannot be ruled out. The nuns also illuminated manuscripts for the Dominican friars in Nuremberg; see Schraut, 58.

56. See von Wilckens, 1979.

57. See C. Borchling, "Litterarisches und geistiges Leben in Kloster Ebstorf am Ausgange des Mittelalters," *Zeitschrift des Historischen Vereins für Niedersachsen* (1905): esp. 389–92; and B. Uhde-Stahl, "Drei Miniaturen aus den ehemaligen Klöstern Lüne und Ebstorf," *Niederdeutsche Beiträge zur Kunstgeschichte* 15 (1976): 63–70. For the library at Ebstorf, much of it a direct byproduct of the reform, see R. Giermann and H. Härtel, *Handschriften des Klosters Ebstorf,* Mittelalterliche Handschriften in Niedersachsen, 10, Wiesbaden, 1994.

58. *Chronik und Totenbuch des Klosters Wienhausen,* 26–28: "Was betrifft die Sachen, Zieraht und Kleider, so diese Gottselige Äbtißen an das Kloster gebracht, ist es auch nach einhallt der Briefe und Verzeichniße folgendes. . . . Die besten Fahnen hat sie wieder erneuren und durch eine ihrer Jungfern auffs neue bemahlen laßen. Sie hat auch zu Gottes Ehren viele Bücher bey das Kloster gebracht, deren etliche von den Brüdern in Hilden, etliche in Zell etliche von ihren Jungfrauen im Kloster sind geschrieben worden." For nuns as patrons, see Hamburger, 1992; and V. Kessel, "Frauen als Auftraggeberinnen von illuminierten liturgischen Handschriften," in *Liturgie und Frauenfrage: Ein Beitrag zur Frauenforschung aus liturgiewissenschaftlicher Sicht,* Pietas Liturgica, 7, ed. T. Berger and A. Gerhards, St. Ottilien, 1990, 195–209.

59. See L. Kurras, in E. Kistner and R. Kistner, Buch- und Kunstantiquariat, *200 Seltene Bücher und Karten* (Antiquariatskatalog 76 zur 20. Stuttgarter Antiquariatsmesse 1981), cat. no. 88, pls. I and III–IV; and idem, "Ein Bildzeugnis der Reformtätigkeit des Nürnberger Katharinenklosters für Regensburg," *Mitteilungen des Vereins für Geschichte der Stadt Nürnberg* 68 (1981): 293–96.

60. Meyer, vol. III, 11: "Es koment och vil erlicher jungkfrowen us der welt in dis closter [Schönensteinbach] . . . und swöster Lucardis, schaffnerin und dar zů schryberin der mess bücher, gradal, antifüer, lecte bücher und ander bücher des chores"; vol. III, 42 [Colmar, St. Catherine's]: "Die IV swöster heiss Magtdalena Franckengrünerin; dise swöster hat under ander ir arbait dem closter wol gehulfen mit schriben, besunder mit den schönen bücher des cors by dem götlichen dienst; sy ward dar nach erte supriorin in sant Gertdruten closter zů Köln, als man es reformiert anno domini MCCCCLXVI"; vol. III, 50 [Sélestat]: "die vierd swöster Margretha Merin, underschaffnerin, cirkerin und an wol geschickte swöster zů malen, schriben und wor zů man ir bedorfft." For Meyer's attitude toward art and its place in reform, see J. Hamburger, forthcoming.

61. Trier, Stadtbibliothek, Ms. 1693, p. 396, cited by G. Kentenich, "Die Mattheiser Klosterreform im 15. Jahrhundert und die Kunst," *Trierische Chronik* 4 (1908): 100–102, but transcribed here after a microfilm of the original kindly sent to me by Dr. Nolden of the Stadtbibliothek in Trier: "Circa hac quoque tempora [1482] in spiritualibus, et temporalibus, et sanctimonia praestantes, plurimum etiam excellerunt in elegante, accurata, et artificiosa scriptura; et enim extra exercitia spiritualia sese iuxta Constitutiones S. Congregationis Bursfeldensis occupabant in conscribendis libris Choralibus, quorum aliqui in maxima forma membranea elegantıssıme cum deauratus litteris initialibus, et figuris exarati et picti hodiedum adhuc existunt, in quorum uno in fine annotatum legitur: anno 1480 feria sexta ipso die vigiliae S. Matthiae Apstoli finitus est iste liber per duas moniales professas huius monasterii, quarum nomina in libro vitae sint adscripta."

62. The letter reads, in part: "Intelleximus scripta vestra et quantum ad librum Vegii, si de manu illa, uti presumimus, satis cognoscitis et domine Abbatisse pariter videre placeat, gratis habemus, ut sibi communicetur, alioquin sororibus ad S. Walburgam restitui faceremus. De Allauaro autem, quia codex magnus est, si volueritis, libenter ipsum ad eas mitteremus, quinymmo novum habemus scriptum, sed nondum correctum. Et pro temporis deductione, si solacium appeteretis huiuscemodi, essemus contenti utrumque destinare et ad legendum et ad corrigendum." For a full account of the letter and its manuscript sources, see J. Lechner, 4–8. For Bernhard von Waging, see M. Grabmann, "Die Erklärung des Bernhard von Waging O.S.B. zum Schlusskapitel von Bonaventuras *Itinerarium mentis in Deum,*" *Franziskanische Studien* 8 (1921): 125–35; and P. Wilpert, "Bernhard von Waging: Reformer vor der Reformation," in *Festgabe für seine Königliche Hoheit Kronprinz Rupprecht von Bayern,* Munich and Parsing, 1953, 260–76.

63. Both titles proposed by J. Lechner, 7.

64. For Benedictine reform in fifteenth-century Germany, see P. Becker, "Benediktinische Reformbewegungen im Spätmittelalter: Ansätze, Entwicklungen, Auswirkungen," in *Untersuchungen zu Kloster und Stift,* Veröffentlichungen des Max-Planck-Instituts für Geschichte, 68 (Studien zur Germania Sacra, 14), ed. K. Elm, Göttingen, 1980, 167–87; and idem, "Erstrebte und erreichte Ziele benediktinischer Reformen im Spätmittelalter," in *Reformbemühungen und Observanzbestrebungen im spätmittelalterlichen Ordenswesen,* Berliner Historische Studien, 14 (Ordenstudien, 6), ed. K. Elm, Berlin, 1989, 23–34, both with additional bibliography. See also D. Mertens, "Riforma monastica e potere temporale nella Germania sud-occidentale prima della Riforma," in *Struttere ecclesiastiche in Italia e in Germania prima della Riforma,* Annali dell'Istituto storico italo-germanico, 16, ed. P. Prodi and P. Johanek, Bologna, 1984, 171–206.

65. See *Caritas Pirckheimer,* 98.

66. For Agnes of Hungary, see E. Maurer, *Das Kloster Königsfelden,* Die Kunstdenkmäler des Kantons Aargau, 3, Basel, 1954; K. Ruh, "Agnes von Ungarn und Luitgart von Wittichen: Zwei Klostergründerinnen des frühen 14. Jahrhunderts," in *Philologische Untersuchungen gewidmet Elfriede Stutz zum 65. Geburtstag,* ed. A. Ebenbauer, Philologica Germanica, 7, Vienna, 1984, 374–91; and idem, *Meister Ekhart,* 114–35.

67. As noted by Webber, 5, the prints that serve as illustrations to the prayers in the devotional anthology from Nonnberg are printed directly on the vellum of the manuscript.

68. See Appuhn and von Heusinger; and, for a somewhat fuller inventory, J. Bühring and K. Maier, *Die Kunstdenkmale des Landkreises Celle im Regierungsbezirk Lüneburg,* Die Kunstdenkmale des Landes Niedersachsen, 34, 2 vols., Hannover, 1972, vol. I, 135–42.

69. See the various studies by Appuhn.

70. For this group of images, see Hengevoss-Dürkop, 121–39.

71. Appuhn and von Heusinger, 199–200, describe the images from Wienhausen. For more general discussions of devotion to the Veronica, see K. Gould, *The Psalter and Hours of Yolande de Soissons,* Cambridge, Mass., 1978, 81–94; F. Lewis, "The Veronica: Image, Legend, and Viewer," in *England in the Thirteenth Century: Proceedings of the 1984 Harlaxton Symposium,* ed. W. Ormond, Woodbridge, Suffolk, 100–106; and E. Kuryluk, *Veronica and Her Cloth: History, Symbolism, and Structure of a "True" Image,* Cambridge, Mass., 1991.

72. The osculatory is pasted in opposite the following rubrics and texts from the Canon: "*hic datur benedictio in missa solemni pontificis.* 'Pax + domini sit + semper vo + biscum.' *Hic mittet particulam in calicem dicem:* 'Fiat hec comixtio corporis et sanguinis domini nostri ihesu christi omnibus accipientibus salus in vitam eternam.' " A similar Veronica was inserted into the *Missale itineratium,* 1485, f. 74r, now in Solothurn (Ms. S 485), described in A. Schönherr, *Die mittelalterlichen Handschriften der Zentralbibliothek Solothurn,* Solothurn, 1964, 76–77.

73. For the liturgy of the feast, S. Corbin de Mangoux, "Les Offices de la Sainte Face," *Bulletin des Études Portugaises* NS 11 (1947): 1–65; for the phenomenon of proxy pilgrimage, R. Röhricht and H. Meisner, *Deutsche Pilgerreisen nach dem heiligen Lande,* Berlin, 1880, 278–96; D. Huschenbrett, " 'Von laden und ynselen': Literarische und geistliche Meerfahrten nach Palästina im späten Mittelalter," in *Wissensorganisierende und wissensvermittelnde Literatur im Mittelalter: Perspektiven ihrer Erforschung, Kolloquium 5.–7. Dezember 1985,* ed. N. R. Wolf, Wissensliteratur im Mittelalter, 1, Wiesbaden, 1987, 187–207; and N. Miedema, " 'Geestelike rijckdom': Over pelgrims reizen en aflaten in de Middeleeuwen," in *Een school spierinkjes: Kleine opstellen over Middelnederlandse artes-literatur,* ed. W. P. Gerritsen, A. van Gijs, and O. S. H. Lie, Middeleeuwse studies en bronnen, 26, Hilversum, 1991, 123–26. During the reforms carried out in 1453 under the supervision of Nicholas of Cues, nuns at the Benedictine abbey of Rijnsburg in the Netherlands were absolved of their oaths to go on lengthy pilgrimages (with the exception of those to Rome and Santiago da Compostela); see M. Hüffer, *Die Reformen in der Abtei Rijnsburg im 15. Jahrhundert,* Vorreformationsgeschichtliche Forschungen, 13, Münster, 1937, 84.

74. Quoted and translated by W. Simons, "Reading a Saint's Body: Rapture and Bodily Movement in the *Vitae* of Thirteenth-Century Beguines," in *Framing Medieval Bodies,* esp. 11.

75. *Das Leben der Schwestern zu Töß,* 46: "Nun hat su die gewonheit das sy gar dik bettet vor dem antlút das vor dem capitel hus hanget."

76. Ibid., 46–47: "das selb gebet das da by geschriben stat: 'Salve summe deitatis'; und so sy an den vers kam in dem stat: 'Te saluto milies,' Ich grůss dich tusent stund, so naigt sy ir hobt gar andåchtiklichen, und sprach sy dik mit begirigem hertzen." For the liturgy of the Veronica, see Corbin.

77. Gertrude of Helfta, 1978, vol. IV, 99–105 (bk. IV, chap. 7). The extended meditation

attributed to Gertrude deserves a more detailed analysis, which I plan to publish in the proceedings of the conference on the Holy Face, to be held at the Bibliotheca Hertziana, Rome, and the Villa Spelman, Florence, in May 1996. Here I cite only the beginning and end of Gertrude's exposition: "In dominica 'Omnis terra,' dum sero, more fidelium Romae imaginem amantissimae facei Domini videre desiderantium, per confessionem spiritualem se praepararet, et inde ex recordatione peccatorum suorum sibi deformata videretur, processit ad pedes Domini Jesu, eamdem deformitatem depositura, petens a Domino remissionem omnium peccatorum. . . . Hinc beginissimus Dominus, propria dulcedine placatus, benedicta manu sua dabat benedictionem cum his verbis: 'Omnes qui desiderio amoris mei attracti frequentant memoriam visionis faciei meae, illis ego ex virtute humanitatis meae imprimo vivificum splendorem meae divinitatis, cujus claritas eo interius jugiter perlustret et faciet in aeterna gloria prae caeteris in speciali similitudine faciei meae omnem caelestem curiam irradiare.' "

78. Mechthild of Hackeborn, 1885–87, 31 and 34 (bk. I, chap. 10): "Ad excitandam devotionem fidelium in veneratione reverendissimae imaginis Domini nostri Jesu Christi, Dominica *Omnis terra* quando Romae agitur festum Ostensionis ejusdem imaginis, data est sibi talis visio. . . . Haec Dei ancilla docuerat Sorores ut spirituali devotione Romam ad diem qua ostenditur Facies Domini tenderent, legendo tot Pater noster quot milliaria inter Romam et ipsum locum essent. Quo cum pervenissent, summo Pontifici, Deo scilicet, omnia peccata sua in oratione confiterentur, accipientes ab eo remissionem omnium peccatorum, et sic in Dominica sumentes corpus Domini. Hora qua eis liberius vacaret ad orandum, cum oratione quam ad hoc dictaverat, reverendam Christi Imaginem suppliciter adorarent. Quod sum Sorores fecissent, supradicta visio eidem est demonstrata."

79. For charms of this kind, see A. Franz, *Die kirchlichen Benediktionen im Mittelalter,* 2 vols., Freiburg, 1909, vol. II, 57 and 229; and K. Schreiner, "Volkstümliche Bibelmagie und volkssprachliche Bibellektüre: Theologische und soziale Probleme mittelalterlicher Laienfrömmigkeit," in *Volksreligion im hohen und späten Mittelalter,* Quellen und Forschungen aus dem Gebiet der Geschichte, NF 13, ed. P. Dinzelbacher and D. R. Bauer, Paderborn, 1990, esp. 346–49.

80. "Ich schick dir ain Ew[angelium] Sant Johannes in ainem federkil, wöllest dir est nit verschmahen lassen." See *Willibald Pirckheimers Briefwechsel,* Veröffentlichungen der Kommission zur Erforschung der Geschichte der Reformation und Gegenreformation: Humanistenbriefe, 4, ed. E. Reicke, Munich, 1940, vol. I, 367.

81. See Heitz; Schreyl, *Der graphische Neujahrsgruß aus Nürnberg;* and Field, vol. 163, cat. nos. 47–73.

82. See *Caritas Pirckheimer,* with additional bibliography.

83. For Marian exegesis on the "Dominus tecum," see Kern, esp. 108–12 and 128–38.

84. See J. Pfanner, ed., *Briefe von, an und über Caritas Pirckheimer (aus den Jahren 1498–1530),* Caritas Pirckheimer: Quellensammlung, 3, Landshut, 1966, 112 (letter 51): "wunsch ich euch vil tausent guter seliger gesunter und gluckseliger newr jar, in denen der edel dominus tecum all augenplick in ewr sel pey euch und mit euch sey durch sein gnad. . . . schick E.w. auch ein kleines figurlein des dominus tecum zu einem angedenken unßer freuntschaft und ein wenig zuckertefelein mit lavendel und andern guten speciebus hab ich E. w. mein schwester laßen machen zu kreftigung ewrs haubts."

85. See Field, vol. 163, no. 58 (Schreiber cat. no. 784); Heitz, pl. 12; and *Caritas Pirckheimer,* 123–24 (cat. no. 128).

86. Straganz, 160: "do sollchs gancz abgelefgt, zu machen vnd auß zu senden in die welt leckuchen, pfeferzelten, krapfen, hauben, peutel, nadel, pain schmir, zucker, rosat vnd geprent wasser, tuch pleichen vnd der gleichen."

87. See Hamburger, 1995.

88. In 1496 Behaim also received New Year's greetings from his niece, the Dominican nun

Brigitte Holzschuher: "Jesus Christus . . . mit allem Trost, Freud und Seligkeit . . . wünsch und begehr ich Dir aus Grund meines Herzens, zu einem guten seligen gnadenreichen neuen Jahr"; quoted from Schreyl, 12.

89. Ibid., 12. For Anna Tucher's dates, see J. G. Biedermann, *Geschlechtsregister des hochadelichen Patriciats zu Nürnberg,* Nuremberg, 1748, reprinted Neustadt an der Aisch, 1982, Table D/VII. I am grateful to Deborah Rose-Lefmann for bringing this book to my attention.

90. Krämer, 81, cites a thirteenth-century Psalter as the only extant manuscript known to have belonged at one point to the convent's library; but according to E. Steingräber, "Ein illuminiertes fränkisches Psalterium des 13. Jahrhunderts," *Anzeiger des Germanischen Nationalmuseums* (1963): 23–27, it might have been produced in, or at least for, Komburg. Not mentioned in Krämer is a breviary (Bamberg, Diözesanmuseum) that belonged to Caritas Pirckheimer the Younger (1503–after 1554), a nun at Bergen, published by P. Weißenberger, "Ein Brevier der Charitas Pirckheimer aus dem Kloster Bergen bei Neuburg," *Zeitschrift für bayerische Kirchengeschichte* 18 (1948–49): 81–88. For the history of the convent, see also J. Heider, "Das Benediktinerinnenkloster Bergen und sein Archiv," *Neuburger Kollektaneenblatt: Jahresschrift des Heimatvereins Neuburg/Donau* 117 (1964) [= *Das Benediktinerinnenkloster Bergen und seine Urkunden*]: 7–17.

91. "Briefe der Aebtissin Sabina."

92. See H. Flachendecker, "Die Familie Pirckheimer in Eichstätt," *Sammelband des Historischen Vereins Eichstätt* 80 (1987): 138–46.

93. For a family tree and list of Pirckheimer's relatives and their monastic affiliations, see *Caritas Pirckheimer,* 49 and 162.

94. For the state of research, see E. Koch, "Entry into Convents and the Position on the Marriage Market of Noble Women in the Late Middle Ages," in *Marriage and Social Mobility in the Late Middle Ages,* Handelingen van het Colloquium gehouden te Gent op 18 April 1988, ed. W. Prevenier, Ghent, 1989, 50–68, with bibliography.

95. "Briefe der Aebtissin Sabina," 530–531 (letter 2): "Du hast uns vergangener zeit geschrieben eines oder zweier rostiger Panzer halb, danken wir dir dennoch, daß du so gutwillig bist und uns die willst lassen widerfaren, die wil wir aber der reiterei ganz ungewont sein, westen wir si nit anderst denn sie pfannen zu segen zu nützen, legen uns den geist nit als hert, ist uns oft ein schlafrock zu rauh, als zart martrer sein wir. unser schwester abtissen zu sant Claren hat uns mit härem tuch für ein gute notdurft versehen auf unser begeren darum behalt deine panzer selber."

96. I have not been able to make sense of the phrase "legen uns den geist nit als hert," which the editor, Lochner, says is "unverständlich."

97. "Briefe der Aebtissin Sabina," 533 (letter 3): "die erznei ist recht, auch das papier, ker fleiß an daß du uns ein schöns gemalens gold zu wenden bringst, *aurum pigment* wollen wir versuchen, habens vor nie gehabt."

98. Ibid., 536 (letter 5): "ich hab dir etliche ding angeschrieben, die die malerin bedarf, bitt dich freundlich, laß uns es kauffen, es schicht uns sonst niemand nichts guts, was du nit herschichst, das können wir nit nutzen, darum bitten wir dich, du wollst uns damit zu willen werden, und was du ausgibst oder ausgeben hast, soll unser knecht bezalen, und was jetzt nit so bald mag sein, magstu etwa auf das heiltum zu wegen bringen, haben wir veilleicht wieder botschaft, und die malerin west gern wie man den spangrün anmachet, daß er belieb, er ist wol schön wenn er neu ist, aber in das alter wird er gar unsauber, was man aber sonst herein schenkt, das bliebt veil länger, auch hett sie gern mer pensel, sie meint, sie könn nit malen dann mit den penseln die du herschickst, sie thät dir gern auch ein dienst mit sticken, wenn sie west was dir ebens wär, den mastir und die silberglätt wollen wir zu einem braun zug, weißtu ihn darnach zu kaufen, aber dasselb hätten wir jetzt gar gern." According to the editor, "zu einem braun

zug" is incomprehensible. The passage appears to refer to some kind of pigment or technique, perhaps outlining.

99. Ibid., 558 (letter 15): "ich dank dir gar treulich um die ambran äpfel und alles gut das du uns thust, auch schwester Eufemia und die malerin danken dir gar treulich. es ist die malerin dem tod kaum entrunnen, gott hat mir in veil widerwärtigkeit als genädiglich geholfen."

100. The recipes sought by Sabina were hardly state secrets, even if they remained mysteries to the nuns at Bergen. The formulas for both "spangrün" and "auripigment," the former a green dye derived from copper acetate, the latter a false gold or yellow, appear in the oldest extant collection of color recipes in German (Innsbruck, Universitätsbibliothek 355); see E. Ploß, *Ein Buch von alten Farben: Technologie der Textilfarben im Mittelalter mit einem Anhang auf die festen Farben,* Heidelberg, 1962: auripigment, 82, 94; grünspan, 82. For other fourteenth- and fifteenth-century recipes for *grünspan,* see E. Ploß, "Studien zu den deutschen Maler- und Farberbüchern des Mittelalters: Ein Beitrag zur deutschen Altertumskunde und Wortforschung," Ph.D. diss., Ludwig-Maximilian Universität, Munich, 1952, 172, 178. Compiled at the Dominican convent of St. Katharina in Nuremberg during the second half of the fifteenth century, the manual guided the nuns in producing dyes for use in the manufacture not only of tapestries, but also of printed textiles and, possibly, woodcuts.

101. See *Die Chroniken des Klosters Ribnitz,* 170–71: "Item in desser tydt unse gnedighe moder froychen Dorothea heft ghesyren laten dat Maryen bilde, dat uppe ereme kore steyt achter ofte by deme sacramente, myt twen flogelen. Darinne stån II apostel alse sunte Thomas, welker er gnaden apostel, unde sunte Mathias, de froychen Ursula apostel ys, und an der anderen syden buten steyt sunte Ursulen bylde, welken beyde flogel unde lede der tafelen hebben bereth vnd vorguldet III susteren, alse suster Anna van der Lů, suster Anna Bugghenhagen unde suster Cristina Bodins. De bilde heft gemahlet broder Lambrecht Slagghert, bichvader, unde am avende Martini gheendiget." See also the brief excerpts incorporated into the second edition of F. Schlie, *Die Kunst- und Geschichts-Denkmäler des Grossherzogthums Mecklenburg-Schwerin,* 2d ed., vol. I, Schwerin, 1898, 363–66.

102. *Die Chroniken des Klosters Ribnitz,* 172: "Anno domini MV^C XXXII. jegen dat fest Francisci ys gesettet dat grote sunte Franciscus bylde up dat chor, dartho unse gnedige moder unde abbatissa froychen Dorothea gaff dat golt unde froychen Ursula, vicaria, lede dat golt althosamen unde de susteren, besundergen Anna van der Lů unde Christina Bodins makeden dat fundament unde broder Lambrecht Slagghert, bichtvader, gaff dartho alle verwe unde målde dat ganze breet."

103. As proposed by C. Gerhardt, "Meditationsbilder aus dem ehemaligen Klarissenkloster Ribnitz (Bez. Rostock, DDR)," *Trierer theologische Zeitschrift* 98 (1989): 95–112. Similar sets of panels, with less unusual subject matter, survive from the Cistercian convent of the Holy Cross in Rostock; see F. Schlie, *Die Kunst- und Geschichts-Denkmäler des Grossherzogthums Mecklenburg-Schwerin,* vol. I, Schwerin, 1896, 223–28; K. Hegner, *Mittelalterliche Kunst II: Kleinkunst, Kunsthandwerk,* Schwerin, 1983; and idem, *Kleinbildwerke des Mittelalters in den Frauenklöstern des Bistums Schwerins, vornehmlich im Zisterzienserinnenkloster zum Heiligen Kreuz in Rostock und im Klarissenkloster Ribnitz,* Leipzig, 1994. For *Gebetsnischen,* see, e.g., the early modern set installed in the nuns' choir at St. Clare's in Brixen, reproduced in K. Gruber, "Das Brixner Klarissenkloster im 13. Jahrhundert: Kunst im Klarissenkloster," *Der Schlern* 59 (1985): 459–86.

104. See Gerhardt, figs. 1–2 and 4–6.

105. Ibid., 105–6.

106. See K. Fischer, *Die Buchmalerei in den beiden Dominikanerklöstern Nürnbergs,* Nuremberg, 1928; and Schraut.

107. See, e.g., the stipulations of a council in Magdeburg, dated ca. 1383–1403, reproduced

by Kroos, 160: "Prohibemus etiam Monialibus . . . aliquod artificium, vel manuum suarum opus exerceat causa lucri, seu negotii cujuscunque"; see also "Die Regensburger Klarissenregel," 10, lines 1–4: "so sol daz flizeclichen werden behutet, daz niht von der ursache solicher arbeit oder lones, daz si enphahent umb die arbeit den swestern zu gange daz gesuhte der gitekeit oder eigensheft dekeines dinges."

108. *Chronik und Totenbuch des Klosters Wienhausen,* 39: "Die Capelle St. Anne hat man auch wieder eingeweihet und neue Privilegia und Freiheiten zur Ehre der Mutter Mariae dabey erhalten. Die Steine womit besagte Capelle überlegt, hat man vor die Handarbeit der Jungfrn. zuwege gebracht."

109. In return for daily masses said by the friars, the Dominican nuns of Frankfurt agreed by formal contract in 1688 to supplement an annual payment of 1,000 florins by ironing the vestments and making candles, provided the friars supplied them with the necessary wax; see K. Beck, *Das Dominikanerkloster in Frankfurt am Main,* Frankfurt, 1977, 46–47.

110. H. Zeller-Werdmüller and J. Bachthold, ed., "Die Stiftung des Klosters Oetenbach und das Leben der seiligen Schwestern daselbst, aus der Nürnberger Handschrift," *Zürcher Taschenbuch* NF 12 (1889): 230–31: "Es kament auch mit ir drei junkfrawen, der kond eine schreiben und luminieren, die andre malen, die dritt würken in der dicht das beste werk, das man finden mocht. Also schribent si und ander swester, dass von luminieren und von schreiben alle jar aus der schreibstuben gieng X mark."

111. See Kroos, 160.

112. Ibid., 23 and 160.

113. "Briefe der Aebtissin Sabina," 528–29 (letter 1): "Wir sehen das meßgewand datur an, du habst es nach dir lassen machen, ist je ratlich und groß, wenn du ein pfaff wirst und unser beichvater, wird es dir gerecht sein."

114. Ibid., 530–31 (letter 2): "Das meßgewand ist schon fertig, daß man es die heilige zeit hat braucht, es sein schön götzen darauf, dergleichen wie wir vor nit haben, möchten ihnen aber wol ein statt vergönnen in unsern ältern." Sabina may use the term "götzen" ironically by way of teasing her brother, who at about the time her letter was written had gone over to the Protestant party in Nuremberg.

115. See Mader, 272.

116. Frauenfelder, 111: "gar ernstlich und bi Gehorsami, dass enkaini der Frowen Buch, Tavellen, Brief, Klainot als Boten enphahe ald höre, sende oder an Lüt schrib oder geb." The passage comes from the first *ordo* issued by Abbot Walter, dated March 17, 1362.

117. Ritzinger and Scheeben, 37–38: "Fratribus vero si de gratia committantur nec aliqua quaeratur, quasi habens ad illum fratrum, cuius vestis consuenda est, favorem specialem; nec ipsa invocet auxilium aliarum sed, sicut dictum est, per certas et communes haec et omnia expediantur. Non fiant studiosae suturae in vestibus fratrum, vel zonae aut signa cum serico, sed expediantur, sicut citius fieri potest." Cf. the language of the visitation report cited by Kroos, 160 (no. 12): "Precipimus etiam . . . nec clenodia faciant secularia, que vantitatem aliquam vel levitatem ostendant, sed simplicia de lino operentur, que et utilia sint accipientibus et religionem in eis commendent et exhibeant que fecerunt, cirotecas non habeant seculares."

118. Menhardt, 268–69, lines 8–19: "Auch ein yede vnder euch, die von vrlaub irer abbteszinn gab nimpt oder schanckung, die ir gebent oder schenckent ir vater oder ir muͤter, swester, pruͤder oder ir ander guͤ frewnt, es sey von clainat oder von phennigen oder von essen oder von trincken, und die selben ding, die ir also gegeben sind, die nüczt sy noch allem irem willen. Auch die daigen frawen, die etwas gewinnent mit irer arbait, als mit nen oder mit ander arbait, dasselb nuczent si vnd nyessens von vrlaub irer abbtessinn nach irem aigen wolgeuallen vnd willen. Auch ein yede vnder euch, der es geuellt, die gibt irem vater, muͤter, pruͤder, swester

oder andern iren frewnten schanckung, gab oder clainat, wein oder prot, vnd den dirnen iren lon, vnd das tuet die alles von vrlaub der abtessinn."

119. "Briefe der Aebtissin Sabina," 529 (letter 1): "wir danken dir hoch und groß um die brieflein, die uns gross erfreut und wolgefallen; wenn wir ein kirchweih ausrichten, wollen wir dein gen got gedenken, als wir täglich thun."

120. The editor argues that the original, "Karkheit," should not be corrected to "Kargheit," "poverty" or "parsimony," and suggests instead "Krankheit," "illness," which, however, makes no sense in context. "Karkheit," however, can still be read as "parsimony" and is perfectly in keeping with the sense of the following passage, "bedarf ichs nit kaufen," in which parsimony is Sabina's theme.

121. Ibid., 556 (letter 14): "der druckten brief hat es kein not, es sind die auch gut, wenn man die andern nit kann haben, ich richt mich allenthalben nach der karkheit an, schenk sie hin, streicht mirs mein malerin aus, bedarf ichs nit kaufen."

122. Ibid.: "dazu findt man jetzt kein heilig zu kaufen, man hat ihnen das land verboten." The nuns were aware of Luther's teachings, if only because, in addition to prints, Pirckheimer appears to have sent them a copy of his writings; see 528–29 (letter 1).

123. Ibid, 556: "Ich erfreu oft eine mit einem brieflein, wenn sie erlich arbeiten schenk ich ihnens."

124. Ordinariatsarchiv Eichstätt, Akt p 33, transcribed in *Kloster Bergen bei Neuburg,* 36: "Aber an den feirtagen so sullen sie den ganczen tag, als vil ine dann notdurft verhengt, anliegen dem gebet, . . . aber darumb, daz die frawen als geschickt not sind, stättig die heilig geschrift zu lesen, so mag das verwandelt werden werd in arbait der hend, damit müssichgeen vermiten werd und unnücze wort."

125. See the commentary on the constitutions of the Dominican Order published by T. V. Kern, "Die Reformation des Katharinenklosters zu Nürnberg im Jahre 1428," *Jahresbericht des Historischen Vereins in Mittelfranken* 31 (1863): esp. 20: "vnd wann die statuten sagend: 'ir sullend mit sweigen arbeiten,' daz ir daz dester leichter haltend, so sullen do selbst in dem arbeit haufz gelesen werden vigily mit IX leczen von den, die dar zu gnad haben, vnd die andern all sweigen."

126. "Briefe der Aebtissin Sabina," 529 (letter 1). The reference is to a "little quarto" in Saxon dialect: "die quaterlein haben wir noch nit gelesen, irrt uns die sächsisch sprach nicht, danken dir gar freundlich darum."

127. Ibid., 560 (letter 17): "Man hat mir gesagt, daß der thürer auch gestorben ist, Gott sei ihm gnädig, ist mir leid sonderlich um euch, daß ihr in eurem alter als eins guten freunds beraubt seid, wir müssen es aber alles gott befehlen, der weiß den sachen wol recht zu thun."

128. Ibid., 530 (letter 2): "wenn es mit wünschen zugieng, wollten wir gern, daß du und der Dürer si sollten sehen."

129. Ibid., 532–33 (letter 3): "ich hab kein kurzweil denn malen, wenn ich nur den thürer ein xiiii tag het, daß er mir mein malerin unterwies."

130. Cf. the remarks of Belting, 1990, esp. chap. 20.

131. For Butzbach and Maria Laach, see B. Resmini, *Die Benediktinerabtei Maria Laach,* Germania Sacra, NF 31, Erzbistum Trier, 7, Berlin, 1993, 71–74 and 419–21; and idem, "Der Laacher Prior Johann Butzbach und der Humanismus rheinischer Benediktinerabteien," in *Ecclesia Lacensis: Beiträge aus Anlaß der Wiederbesiedlung der Abtei Maria Laach durch Benediktiner aus Beuron vor 100 Jahren am 25. November 1892 und der Gründung des Klosters durch Pfalzgraf Heinrich II. von Laach vor 900 Jahren 1093,* ed. E. von Severus, Münster, 1993, 111–35. There remains no adequate edition of Butzbach's treatise, first published by A. Schultz, "Johannes Butzbach's 'Libellus de preclaris picture professoribus' aus der Bonnenser Handschrift veröffentlicht," *Jahr-*

bücher für Kunstwissenschaft, ed. A. von Zahn, 2 (1869): 60–72. Johannes Butzbach, *Libellus de praeclaris picturae professoribus (mit der Urschrift in Nachbildung),* ed. O. Pelka, Heidelberg, 1952, provides a facsimile and transcription of the sole surviving manuscript (Bonn, Universitätsbibliothek, Ms. S. 356, ff. 131r–138v) together with a German translation that, as noted by A. Beriger, *Johannes Butzbach Odeporicon (eine Autobiographie aus dem Jahre 1506): Zweisprachige Ausgabe,* Weinheim, 1991, 49 and 57–58, is not free of errors. For further commentary, see W. Waetzoldt, *Deutsche Kunsthistoriker,* 2 vols., Leipzig, 1921 and 1924, vol. I, 13–14; and J. L. Koerner, *The Moment of Self-Portraiture in German Renaissance Art,* Chicago, 1993, 123–26.

132. Beriger, 49 and 57–60; and Butzbach, 27: "Nam alterum Alleydis sororis tue doctissime, alterum tue industrie est." In a letter to Roscop, dated October 31, 1506, published by N. N. Floss, "Die Kloster Rolandswerth," *Annalen des historischen Vereins für den Niederländen insbesondere die alte Erzdiözese Köln* 19 (1868): 76–219, esp. 150–51, Butzbach asks that she send him several Latin poems she has written on St. Scholastica and the image of the crucifix: "Ceterum intelligo nonnulla de beata Scholastica ac imagine crucifixi vos composuisse carmina, que mihi excopiari destinarique desidero."

133. For early editions of Boccaccio, see F. S. Borroni, "L'incisione al servizio del Boccaccio nei secoli XV e XVI," *Annali della Scuola Normale di Pisa,* Classe di Lettere e Filosofia, 7, Pisa, 1977, 595–734, cited by G. Schweikhart, "Boccaccios *De claris mulieribus* und die Selbstdarstellungen von Malerinnen im 16. Jahrhundert," *Der Künstler über sich in seinem Werk: Internationales Symposium der Bibliotheca Hertziana Rom 1989,* ed. M. Winner, Weinheim, 1992, 114 n. 7, who, however, omits Butzbach from his account of Boccaccio's reception in the sixteenth century. As a listing of virtuous women, Butzbach's letter belongs to the genre of such catalogues, for which see G. McLeod, *Virtue and Venom: Catalogues of Women from Antiquity to the Renaissance,* Ann Arbor, Mich., 1991.

134. See S. Hindman, "The Roles of the Author and the Artist in the Procedure of Illuminating Late Medieval Texts," in *Text and Image,* Acta, 10, Binghamton, N.Y., 1983, esp. 51–53. I was unable to consult C. Schöll-Glass, *Aspekte der Antikenrezeption in Frankreich und Flandern im fünfzehnten Jahrhundert: Die Illustration der "Epistre Othea" von Christine de Pizan,* Hamburg, 1987.

135. Schultz, Beriger, and Butzbach's editor, Pelka, all assume Butzbach drew directly on Pliny.

136. Butzbach, 29.

137. Ibid.: "sed veri dei domini nostri Ihesu Christi et effigiem et gesta matrisque eius glorisissime virginis Marie pulcherrimum specimen mulierum ac sanctorum cum illis in celesto regno." For the manner in which Butzbach accommodated his interest in classical sources to the Christian context in which he worked, in part under pressures produced by the Bursfeld reform, see Resmini, 105, 223, and 228.

138. Ibid., 36: "Quarum quidem ymaginum quedam Rhome ostenditur, quedam vero in monte divi Wentzeslai martiris apud civitatem pragensem in Bohemia reservatur, que quottannis populo ostenditur, quam et frater Vittus moravus, donatus noster se ibidem vidisse affirmat."

139. Ibid.: "Qui idem salvator noster Ihesus Christus cum ad mortem duceretur, petenti Veronice sui vultus effigem velamini illius impressit."

140. For this tradition, see van Engen.

141. Butzbach, 27: "Que ubi ingenio et arte manibusve tuis virgineis mirifice fabrefacta accepissemus quanto cunctos tum gaudio affecerint, hic calamus noster studulus haud satis digne enarrare valet, sed his paruulis delectatos exeniis non multo post maiori artis tue monumento quasi miraculo quodam stupefactos reddidisti, dum grandiori usa cothurno ymaginatis apicibus libros chorales mira quadam subtilitate pulcherrime adornavisti, quos fratris Gerhardus

scilicet de Fredis et Petrus de Wyda nunc plebanus in Crufft studioso exaravere calamo." Butzbach also mentions the monk Henry of Maria Laach, "Cuius multe in libris choralibus capitales extant littere foliatis, ymaginibus et flosculis amenissimis depicte"; see Butzbach, 37.

142. Floss, 143: "Diese hat, ehe sey zur Ehrw. frawen Elegirt, geschriben Unsere 6 große pergaments Chorböcher die wir noch haben, 2 graduale Und 4 Antifonaria. hat auch mit ihrer eigener Handt gemahlt die große goldene Litteren in denselben böchern."

143. Butzbach, 27: "corcula scilicet benignissimi salvatoris et redemptoris nostri."

144. H. Heinen, "Beiträge zur Geschichte des Klosters Rolandswerth (Nonnenwerth)," *Annalen des historischen Vereins für den Niederrhein insbesondere die alte Erzdiöceze Köln* 128 (1936): esp. 35, comments briefly on this passage, without, however, citing his source. For Thomas Wied, see J. Wegeler, *Das Kloster Laach: Geschichte und Urkunden-Buch. Ein Beitrag zur Spezial-Geschichte der Rheinlande,* Bonn, 1854, 53; also Beriger, 300–301.

145. See Krämer, 691.

146. For a summary description, see H. Degering, *Kurzes Verzeichnis der germanischen Handschriften der preußischen Staatsbibliothek,* Leipzig, 1926, reprinted Graz, 1970, vol. II, 96. The Latin colophon is on f. 143v: "finitus et completus est liber iste per me sororem girdrudus buchel pro stellam monialem Insule rolandi anni domini Milesimo quadragintesimo nonagesimo septimo in vigilia mathie apostoli [= February 24, 1497]. Oretis dominum deum pro me." I am grateful to Dr. Peter Jörg Becker for supplying me with this information.

147. Butzbach, 37: "In arte sculpendi Israel, civis bucoliensis, iam subtilissimus predicatur, ast te in arte pigendi ingeniosissimam cuncti mirantur."

148. F. Mader, "Das Haushaltungsbuch der Aebtissen Margaretha von Seckendorf zu St. Walburg in den Jahren 1552/53," *Sammelblatt des historischen Vereins Eichstätt* 50–51 (1935–36): esp. 83. For nuns as artists in the early modern period, see P. Bonnet, "La Pratique des arts dans les couvents de femmes au XVIIe siècle," *Bibliothèque de l'École des Chartes* 147 (1989): 433–72.

149. See J. Lechner, 81. The representations of the "Herz Jesu" occur on ff. 270r and 289v.

150. See Hilpisch, 132–35: "Frau Äbtissen Helena . . . wurde sie selbst, so todschwach sie immer war, mit anderen Klosterfrauen als Geisel nach Regensburg fortgeschleppt und allda gefangen gehalten, bis ein großes Lösegeld erlegt worden, welches aufzubringen eine schöne große silberne Ampel und ein Frauenbild mußte versetzt werden, deren das Letztere widerum eingelöst worden, das Erstere aber von ihren Besitzern nicht mehr konnte zurückerhalten werden."

151. O. Fina, "Walburgis-Verehrung und Frömmigkeit in der Barockzeit: Nach Tagebucheintragungen der Mariasteiner Priorin Clara Staiger," *Studien und Mitteilungen zur Geschichte des Benediktiner-Ordens und seiner Zweige* 90 (1979): 97–120; and *Klara Staigers Tagebuch: Aufzeichnungen während des Dreißigjährigen Krieges im Kloster Mariastein bei Eichstätt,* ed. O. Fina, Regensburg, 1981, 210: "Montag den 9 hat schwester Monica Fischerin mit grosser müehe anfangen muster machen und bildtle maln, zue welchem handwerch auch alles verprunnen und verkhummen geweßen." According to J. Schlecht, "Beiträge zur Kunstgeschichte der Stadt Eichstätt," *Sammelblatt des historischen Vereins Eichstätt* 14 (1899): 32–69, portions of the library of Mariastein, including images painted after "ältere Vorlagen," were sold in 1898 in Berlin by the book dealer J. U. Stargardt and described in his catalogue no. 187. I have been unable to trace this catalogue or any of the manuscripts.

152. Evidence for the tradition at other houses extends into the seventeenth century; see, e.g., the letter, illustrated by an emblematic image of the heart, written by the Sicilian nun Maria Crocifissa, edited by L. Sciascia, *Della cose di Sicilia: Testi inediti o rari,* vol. 3, Palermo, 1984, 87–94. I am grateful to M. P. Di Bella for bringing this publication to my attention.

Conclusion

1. As noted by Ott, 200, the term *Volkskunst,* applied to most illustrated vernacular manuscripts, "trifft doch die Rezipienten dieser Handschriften keineswegs."

2. For some problems with the term, see L. E. Boyle, "Popular Piety in the Middle Ages: What is Popular?" *Florilegium* 4 (1982): 184–93; and the essays collected in *Volkskultur des europäischen Spätmittelalters,* Böblinger Forum, 1, ed. P. Dinzelbacher and H.-D. Mück, Stuttgart, 1987; and *Volksreligion im hohen und späten Mittelalter.* For the bibliography, see H.-J. Gilomen, "Volkskultur und Exempla Forschung," in *Modernes Mittelalter,* 165–208.

3. In insisting on the distinct character of vision, I mean to imply, not that visual experience is ahistorical, akin to the physiological processes of perception, but simply that visual images elicit responses different from those elicited by texts and that historically, these differences have been significant to a wide range of observers. My approach here differs from that of theorists such as M. Bal, "Visual Poetics: Reading with the Other Art," in *Theory between the Disciplines: Authority / Vision / Politics,* ed. M. Kreiswirth and M. A. Cheetham, Ann Arbor, Mich., 1990, esp. 136, who, despite her disclaimers, is less interested in defining distinct modes of visual experience than in making "such characteristics of visual analysis as perspective and vantage point . . . work for literary analysis." Bal speaks of "the specific contribution *each* discipline could make . . . to the theoretical and practical developments within the other" (135), but then adds within the ellipsis, "through semiotics," thereby reducing all disciplines to branches of a single master method that inherently translates visual experience into discursive terms.

4. For this practice and the devotional tradition that informed it, see J. H. Marrow, "Symbol and Meaning in Northern European Art of the Late Middle Ages and Early Renaissance," *Simiolus* 16 (1986): 150–72; C. Harbison, "Visions and Meditations in Early Flemish Painting," *Simiolus* 15 (1985): 87–118; and D. Despres, *Ghostly Sights: Visual Meditation in Late-Medieval Literature,* Norman, Okla., 1989.

5. S. Alpers, "No Telling, with Tiepolo," in *Sight and Insight: Essays on Art and Culture in Honour of E. H. Gombrich at Eighty-five,* ed. J. Onians, London, 1994, esp. 329, makes much the same point: "For all the interest in it at the moment, what is loosely and expansively called visuality is under suspicion. Pictures . . . have been replaced by an assemblage of signs and idols deconstructing the practices and the institutions of what was previously considered and made as art. When the text is expanded to include the entirety of culture construed as a text . . . then the aesthetic and the difference between picture and text is no longer of much interest."

6. Cf. the discussion of the "metaphor of visibility as literal transparency" in J. W. Scott, "The Evidence of Experience," *Critical Inquiry* 17 (1991): esp. 775–76: "In this conceptualization, the visible is privileged; writing is then put at its service. Seeing is the origin of knowledge. Writing is reproduction, transmission—the communication of knowledge gained through (visual, visceral) experience."

7. Witness the ungenerous critique of C. W. Bynum's pioneering work in K. Biddick, "Genders, Bodies, Borders: Technologies of the Visible," *Speculum* 68 (1993): 389–418.

8. See Marrow, 1986; Belting, 1990; and Freedberg.

9. Cf., e.g., the remarks of W. Haug, "Gottfrieds von Straßburg '*Tristan*': Sexueller Sündenfall oder erotische Utopie," in idem, *Strukturen als Schlüssel zur Welt: Kleine Schriften zur Erzählliteratur des Mittelalters,* Tübingen, 1989, esp. 610; also Scott, esp. 797: "*Experience* is not a word we can do without, although . . . it is tempting to abandon it altogether."

10. See, e.g., K. Moxey, "Hieronymus Bosch and the 'World Upside Down': The Case of *The Garden of Earthly Delights,*" in *Visual Culture,* 104–40, who quotes Foucault: "The contemporary critic is abandoning the great myth of interiority" (106).

11. See S. Beckwith, *Christ's Body: Identity, Culture, and Society in Late Medieval Writings,*

New York, 1993, esp. 7–21. For medieval theories on the formation of what medieval theologians termed "cognitio affectiva et experimentalis," see P. Miquel, *Le Vocabulaire latin de l'expérience spirituelle dans la tradition monastique et canoniale de 1050 à 1250,* Théologie historique, 79, Paris, 1989; U. Köpf, *Religiöse Erfahrung in der Theologie Bernhards von Clairvaux,* Beiträge zur historischen Theologie, 61, Tübingen, 1980; W. Haug, "Grundformen religiöser Erfahrung als epochale Positionen: Vom frühmittelalterlichen Analogiemodell zum hoch- und spätmittelalterlichen Differenzmodell," in *Religiöse Erfahrung: Historische Modelle in christlicher Tradition,* ed. W. Haug and D. Mieth, Munich, 1992, 75–108; and, in the same volume, O. Langer, "Zum Begriff der Erfahrung in der mittelalterlichen Frauenmystik," 229–46. For a nuanced analysis of the range of meanings associated with the term "experience" in medieval texts, see B. Stock, "Experience, Praxis, Work, and Planning in Bernard of Clairvaux: Observations on the *Sermones in Cantica,*" in *The Cultural Context of Medieval Learning: Proceedings of the First International Colloquium on Philosophy, Science, and Theology in the Middle Ages, September, 1973,* Boston Studies in the Philosophy of Science, 26, Dordrecht, 1975, 219–68; and idem, 1994.

12. For a wide-ranging philosophical discussion of the status of "experience" in mystical expression, see S. T. Katz, "Language, Epistemology, and Mysticism," in *Mysticism and Philosophical Analysis,* ed. S. T. Katz, New York, 1978, 22–74; idem, "The 'Conservative' Character of Mystical Experience," in *Mysticism and Religious Traditions,* ed. S. T. Katz, New York, 1983, 3–60; and idem, "Mystical Speech and Mystical Meaning," in *Mysticism and Language,* 3–41. Katz's position, which works from the premise that no experience, including ostensibly "ineffable" mystical phenomena, is unmediated, has been challenged by, among others, A. N. Perovich, Jr., "Mysticism and the Philosophy of Science," *Journal of Religion* 65 (1985): 63–82; D. Evans, "Can Philosophers Limit What Mystics Can Do? A Critique of Steven Katz," *Religious Studies* 25 (1989): 53–60; and W. Proudfoot, *Religious Experience,* Berkeley and Los Angeles, 1985, 119–54. See also the exchange by Katz, S. B. King, and H. Smith in the pages of the *Journal of the American Academy of Religion* 55 (1987): 553–65, and 56 (1988): 257–79 and 751–61. B. McGinn, "Theoretical Foundations: The Modern Study of Mysticism," in *The Foundations of Mysticism,* New York, 1994, esp. 321–24, supplies a sage review of this debate, its implications, and its place in the historiography of mysticism. I am greatly indebted to Prof. McGinn for bringing much of this material to my attention.

13. For this debate as it relates specifically to German mysticism, see P. Dinzelbacher's review of Ringler (1980), *Zeitschrift für deutsches Altertum und deutsche Literatur* 111 (1982): 63–71; and idem, "Zur Interpretation erlebnismystischer Texte des Mittelalters," *Zeitschrift für deutsches Altertum und deutsche Literatur* 117 (1988): 1–23, expanded in Dinzelbacher, 1993, 304–31; also U. Peters, *Religiöse Erfahrung als literarisches Faktum: Zur Vorgeschichte und Genese frauenmystischer Texte des 13. und 14. Jahrhunderts,* Hermea: Germanistische Forschungen, NF 56, Tübingen, 1988; together with the review by U. Küsters and O. Langer, *Arbitrium: Zeitschrift für Rezensionen zur germanistischen Literaturwissenschaft* 1 (1991): 36–41. J. Quint, "Mystik und Sprache: Ihr Verhältnis zueinander insbesondere in der spekulativen Mystik Meister Eckharts," *Deutsche Vierteljahrschrift* 27 (1953): 48–76, remains a touchstone, but for more recent discussion, see the work of A. M. Haas, *Sermo mysticus: Studien zu Theologie und Sprache der deutschen Mystik,* Dokimion, 4, Fribourg, 1979; idem, "Was ist Mystik?" in *Abendländische Mystik im Mittelalter: Symposion Kloster Engelberg 1984,* ed. K. Ruh, Germanistische Symposien Berichtsbände, 7, Stuttgart, 1986, 319–41; and *Das "Einig Ein": Studien zu Theorie und Sprache der deutschen Mystik,* Dokimion, 6, ed. A. M. Haas and H. Stirnimann, Fribourg, 1980.

14. For discussions of this development, see Donat de Chapeaurouge, *"Das Auge ist ein Herr, das Ohr ein Knecht": Der Weg von der mittelalterlichen zur Abstrakten Malerei,* Wiesbaden, 1983; and J.-C. Schmitt, "Écriture et image: Les Avatars médiévaux du modèle grégorien," in *Théories*

et pratiques de l'écriture au Moyen Âge: Actes du colloque Palais du Luxembourg-Sénat, 5 et 6 mars 1987, ed. E. Baumgartner and C. Marchello-Nizia, Paris, 1988, 119–54, both of whom, however, emphasize the role of "popular" piety at the expense of monastic spirituality. For allegories of spiritual seeing encoded in early medieval images, see Kessler; O'Reilly, 1987–88; and C. Hahn, "Purification, Sacred Action, and the Vision of God: Viewing Medieval Narratives," *Word and Image* 5 (1989): 71–84.

15. Histories of "visuality" focus on the origins of modernity; see, e.g., the essays gathered in *Modernity and the Hegemony of Vision,* ed. D. M. Levin, Berkeley and Los Angeles, 1993; and *Vision and Visuality,* Dia Art Foundation Discussion in Contemporary Culture, 2, ed. H. Foster, Seattle, 1988. M. Jay, *Downcast Eyes: The Denigration of Vision in Twentieth-Century French Thought,* Berkeley and Los Angeles, 1994, 21–82, offers no exception to this rule.

16. See N. Bryson, *Word and Image: French Painting of the Ancien Régime,* 2d ed., New York, 1983, 1–4 (on the stained-glass windows of Canterbury cathedral); idem, *Vision and Painting: The Logic of the Gaze,* New Haven, Conn., 1983, esp. chap. 5, "The Gaze and the Glance"; and R. Scribner, "Vom Sakralbild zur sinnlichen Schau: Sinnliche Wahrnehmung und das Visuelle bei der Objektivierung des Frauenkörpers in Deutschland im 16. Jahrhundert," in *Gepeinigt, begehrt, vergessen,* 309–36.

17. Bryson, *Word and Image,* 96–98.

18. The attitudes of the Reformers both evolved and varied greatly; see, most recently, C. M. Eire, *War against the Idols: The Reformation of Worship from Erasmus to Calvin,* Cambridge, England, 1986; the essays gathered in *Bilder und Bildersturm;* and Michalski, who notes that for Luther, "art is a medium that lacks its own inherent sacrality . . . language was the 'sword of the spirit': that is, a medium capable of absolutely unmistakable meaning. Art, on the other hand, was a much more ambiguous sign, which could conceal some unrecognized error" (38).

19. See, e.g., the following essays by R. Scribner: "Popular Piety and Modes of Visual Perception in Late-Medieval and Reformation Germany," *Journal of Religious History* 15 (1989): 448–69; "Zur Wahrnehmung des Heiligen in Deutschland am Ende des Mittelalters," in *Das Mittelalter: Unsere fremde Vergangenheit,* ed. J. Kuolt et al., Stuttgart, 1990, 241–67; and "Das Visuelle in der Volksfrömmigkeit," in *Bilder und Bildersturm,* 9–20. Scribner overestimates the *Bildlosigkeit* of late medieval mysticism; he also overlooks the extent to which traditions that he identifies as "popular" characterized the culture as a whole. The problem lies in assuming that what Scribner identifies as a "sacramental" mode of vision is inherently popular. For alternative approaches, see Hamburger, 1989b; and V. Reinburg, "Hearing Lay People's Prayer," in *Culture and Identity in Early Modern Europe (1500–1800): Essays in Honor of Natalie Zemon Davis,* ed. B. B. Diefendorf and C. Hesse, Ann Arbor, Mich., 1993, 19–39. M. Jay, "Scopic Regimes of Modernity," in *Vision and Visuality,* 3–27, also encourages consideration of what he calls "visual subcultures."

20. For some of the stereotypes associated with women, see M.-T. d'Alvernay, "Comment les théologiens et les philosophes voient la femme," *Cahiers de civilisation médiévale* 20 (1977): 105–29; E. McLaughlin, "Equality of Souls, Inequality of Sexes: Woman in Medieval Theology," in *Religion and Sexism: Images of Women in the Jewish and Christian Traditions,* ed. R. R. Reuther, New York, 1974, 213–66; E. Robertson, *Early English Devotional Prose and the Female Audience,* Knoxville, Tenn., 1990, esp. 32–43; and C. W. Bynum, "The Female Body and Religious Practice," in idem, 1991, 181–238.

21. Of the various considerations of this topic, A. Vergote, *Guilt and Desire: Religious Attitudes and Their Pathological Derivatives,* trans. H. M. Wood, New Haven, Conn., 1988, is among the most sensitive to issues of context.

22. As first argued by H. Grundmann, *Religiöse Bewegungen im Mittelalter: Untersuchungen über*

die geschichtlichen Zusammenhänge zwischen Ketzerei, den Bettelorden und der religiösen Frauenbewegungen im 12. und 13. Jahrhundert und über die geschichtlichen Grundlagen der deutschen Mystik, 1935, reprinted Darmstadt, 1977. See also idem, "Die Frauen und die Literatur im Mittelalter," *Archiv für Kulturgeschichte* 26 (1936): 129–61.

23. See most recently Carruthers; see also S. Huot, "Inventional Mnemonics, Reading, and Prayer: A Reply to Mary Carruthers," *Connotations* 3 (1993–94): 103–9; and the introductory chapter of V. A. Kolve, *Chaucer and the Imagery of Narrative: The First Five Canterbury Tales,* Stanford, Calif., 1984, 9–58.

24. See U. Köpf, "Bernhard von Clairvaux in der Frauenmystik," in *Frauenmystik im Mittelalter,* 48–77; and Matter, 138–42. As Bynum, 1982, points out, female mysticism was not "characterized primarily or universally by the use of bridal images" (171). This, however, did not prevent others from casting it in those terms.

25. See, e.g., U. Wiethaus, "Sexuality, Gender, and the Body in Late Medieval Women's Spirituality," *Journal of Feminist Studies in Religion* 7 (1991): 35–52; but the marginalizing strategy is particularly pronounced in the older literature on the psychoanalysis of visions, e.g, O. Pfister, "Hysterie und Mystik bei Margaretha Ebner (1291–1351)," *Zentralblatt für Psychoanalyse* 1 (1911): 468–85, an essay that has itself been subjected to analysis; see W. Beutin, "Hysterie und Mystik: Zur Mittelalter-Rezeption der frühen Psychoanalyse. Die 'Offenbarungen' der Nonne Margarete Ebner (ca. 1291–1351), gedeutet durch den Zürcher Pfarrer und Analytiker Oskar Pfister," in *Mittelalter-Rezeption: Medien, Politik, Ideologie, Ökonomie. Gesammelte Vorträge des 4. Internationalen-Symposions zur Mittelalter-Rezeption an der Universität Lausanne, 1989,* Göppinger Arbeiten zur Germanistik, 55, ed. I. von Burg, Göppingen, 1991, 11–26. See also A. Vergote, "Visions et apparitions: Approches psychoanalytiques," *Revue théologique de Louvain* 22 (1991): 202–25. Other problematic contributions include J. Leclercq, *Monks and Love in Twelfth-Century France: Psycho-Historical Essays,* Oxford, 1979, esp. 27–61; and G. Bataille, *Death and Sensuality: A Study of Eroticism and the Taboo,* Salem, Mass., 1984, although, as noted by B. McGinn, "The Language of Love in Christian and Jewish Mysticism," in *Mysticism and Language,* esp. 223, "Bataille distanced himself from those psychologists who tried to give a purely sexual reading of mystical experience."

26. See J. Coakley, "Gender and the Authority of the Friars: The Significance of Holy Women for Thirteenth-Century Franciscans and Dominicans," *Church History* 60 (1991): 445–60; S. B. Spitzlei, *Liebesbriefe hinter Klostermauern: Zeugnisse geistlicher Freundschaft,* Freiburg, 1990; and Peters.

27. McGinn, 1992, esp. 210, who also cites a telling passage from the *Notebooks* of Simone Weil: "To reproach mystics with loving God by means of the faculty of sexual love is as though one were to reproach a painter with making pictures by means of colors composed of material substances. We haven't anything else with which to love" (225).

28. For the history of commentary on the Song of Songs, see Astell; Matter; Ohly, 1958; and H. Riedlinger, *Die Makellosigkeit der Kirche in den lateinischen Hoheliedkommentaren des Mittelalters,* Beiträge zur Geschichte der Philosophie und Theologie des Mittelalters, 38/3, Münster, 1958. On erotic imagery in mystical discourse, see McGinn, 1992; Bynum, 1987, 246–50; J. Blanpain, "Langage mystique: Expression du désir dans les Sermons sur le Cantique des cantiques de Bernard de Clairvaux," *Collectanea Cisterciensia* 36 (1974): 45–68 and 226–47; R. Grégoire, "Il matrimonio mistico," in *Il matrimonio nella società altomedievale,* 2 vols., Settimane di Studio del Centro Italiano di Studi sull'Alto Medioevo 1976, 2 vols., Spoleto, 1977, vol. 2, 701–94; and P. Dinzelbacher, "Die Entdeckung der Liebe," *Saeculum* 32 (1981): 185–208.

29. In contrast to medieval exegetes, Reformation interpreters sought to extinguish the literal sense; see G. L. Scheper, "Reformation Attitudes toward Allegory and the Song of Songs in the Middle Ages," *PMLA* 89 (1974): esp. 557; and M. Engammare, "Der *sensus litteralis* des

Hohen Liedes im Reformationszeitalter: Interessante Indizien am Rande der Exegese," *Archiv für Reformationsgeschichte* 83 (1992): 5–30.

30. For the availability of translations and paraphrases of the Song of Songs in medieval German, see, in addition to Küsters, H. U. Schmid, "Eine spätmittelalterliche Übersetzung des Hohen Liedes," in *Latein und Volkssprache,* 199–207, both with additional bibliography.

31. A pun noted by W. Riehle, *The Middle English Mystics,* London, 1981, 44–46. As Robertson acknowledges, however, "whether or not the medieval reader identified the vagina as a wound is difficult to say" (65–66).

32. For one such reductive reading, see M. Camille, "The Image and the Self: Unwriting Late Medieval Bodies," in *Framing Medieval Bodies,* esp. 76–77, who suggests that Christ's wound "becomes a vast vagina-like object of desire, a transference of the dangerously open body of woman in all her horrifying 'difference.'" If anything, the process of transference works in the opposite and—to our way of seeing things—much more alien direction, from the Passion, understood as the pain inflicted on Christ's body, to the modern meaning of the term, understood simply as ardent desire. Auerbach remains the critical study of this process.

33. Stanbury and Spearing apply the terminology of the "gaze" to medieval literature. As observed by Spearing, however, the terms "cannot be transferred without modification from modern semiotics, psychoanalysis and film-theory to [medieval] texts" (25). As for feminist theory, numerous alternative constructions have been proposed since L. Mulvey's landmark article, "Visual Pleasure and Narrative Cinema," *Screen* 16 (1975): 6–18, including her own "Afterthoughts on 'Visual Pleasure and Narrative Cinema' Inspired by *Duel in the Sun,*" *Framework* 6 (1981): 12–21 (both reprinted in *Feminism and Film Theory,* ed. C. Penley, New York, 1988, 57–59). Some of the more important are listed by Jay, 1994, 490.

34. See Bynum, 1987, who explores the association of Christ's wound with the lactating breast of the Virgin. To the extent nuns identified the perforation in Christ's side with a woman's sexual organs, their culture would have conditioned them to associate it less with pleasure than with the pain and bleeding of menstruation and childbirth. Elaborating a proposal made by Trexler, Schmitt, 268–69, suggests a possible identification of the blood issuing from the side wound with the bleeding of menstruation, a line of thought, however, not easily reconciled with the connotations of impurity associated with that bodily function in the Middle Ages. Instead, prayers associate the wound's bleeding with the cleansing and purifying power of the sacraments. See, e.g., the prayer in the *Waldburg-Gebetbuch,* dated 1476, Stuttgart, Württembergische Landesbibliothek, Ms. brev. 12, f. 15r (opposite an image of the Christ Child standing inside the side wound surrounded by the *arma Christi*), which begins: "Die sele gottes heilige mich, Der lichnam gottes behalt mich, Das blůt gottes trenk mich, Das wasser der syten gottes wasch mich"; reproduced in *Das Gebetbuch Georg II. von Waldburg, Cod. brev. 12 der Württembergischen Landesbibliothek,* 2 vols., Süssen, 1986–87.

35. For the body as enclosure in writings addressed to religious women, see J. Wogan-Browne, "Chaste Bodies: Frames and Experiences," in *Framing Medieval Bodies,* 24–42. The same images persist in Pietist tracts well into the modern period; see Schrader, 65–66, who quotes a poem by J. M. de Geusay, baroness of Gersdorf, published in 1745: "So ruh ich denn getrost, mein Heil! in deinen Wunden, / die du mir heute hast von neuem aufgethan; / dein armes Täublein hat die Ritzen wiederfunden, / da es für Sturm und Bliz so sicher sitzen kan. / Ach lass es nimmer nicht aus diser Höle treiben, / und gib mir Kraft und Lust beständig drinn zu bleiben."

36. M. Miles, *Carnal Knowing: Female Nakedness and Religious Meaning in the Christian West,* Boston, 1989, 184.

37. As in J. G. Milhaven, "A Medieval Lesson on Bodily Knowing: Women's Experience and Men's Thought," *Journal of the American Academy of Religion* 57 (1989): 341–72.

38. Miles, 1989, 185. L. Lomperis and S. Stanbury in the introduction to *Feminist Approaches to the Body in Medieval Literature,* ed. Lomperis and Stanbury, Philadelphia, 1993, take a contrary view.

39. See R. H. Bloch, *Medieval Misogyny and the Invention of Western Romantic Love,* Chicago, 1991; J. Dalarun, "The Clerical Gaze," in *A History of Women in the West,* vol. II, *The Silences of the Middle Ages,* ed. C. Klapisch-Zuber, Cambridge, Mass., 1992, 15–42; and C. W. Bynum, *The Resurrection of the Body in Western Christianity, 200–1336,* New York, 1995, esp. 90–91, 216, and 219.

40. Bynum, 1987.

41. See, e.g., J. Kristeva, "*Stabat mater,*" in *The Kristeva Reader,* ed. T. Moi, New York, 1986, 160–86; and, for further discussion, O. Langer, "Vision und Traumvision in der spätmittelalterlichen dominikanischen Frauenmystik," in *Traum und Träumen: Inhalt, Darstellung, Funktion einer Lebenserfahrung im Mittelalter und Renaissance,* Studia humaniora, 24, Düsseldorf, 1994, esp. 67–70.

42. A. Borst, "Frauen und Kunst im Mittelalter," in *Barbaren, Ketzer und Artisten: Welten des Mittelalters,* Munich, 1990, esp. 407, notes that the enforced self-reliance of nuns often led to a remarkable originality.

43. As noted by J. Bossy, "Prayers," *Transactions of the Royal Historical Society* 1, 6th ser. (1990): 137–50, who nonetheless characterizes late medieval prayer practice in terms as highly prejudicial as those of the historians he takes to task. Katz pointedly critiques the "commonplace of the study of mysticism" that "see[s] it as the paradigm of religious individualism and radicalism" (3).

44. Thc phrase is C. W. Bynum's: "The Mysticism and Asceticism of Medieval Women: Some Comments on the Typologies of Max Weber and Ernst Troeltsch," in idem, 1991, 63. For recent representatives of this line of thought, see D. Müller, "Beginenmystik als ketzerische Frauentheologie?" in *Auf der Suche nach der Frau im Mittelalter: Fragen, Quellen, Antworten,* ed. B. Lundt, Munich, 1991, 213–32; U. Weinmann, *Mittelalterliche Frauenbewegungen: Ihre Beziehungen zur Orthodoxie und Häresie,* Frauen in Geschichte und Gesellschaft, 9, Pfaffenweiler, 1990; and K. Elm, "Frömmigkeit und Ordensleben in deutschen Frauenklöstern des 13. und 14. Jahrhunderts," in *Vrouwen en mystiek in de Nederlanden (12de–16de eeuw): Lezingen van het congres "Van Hadewijch tot Maria Petyt," Antwerpen, 5–7 september 1989* [= *Ons Geestelijk Erf,* 66], ed. T. Mertens, Antwerp, 1992, esp. 44–45.

45. B. Acklin-Zimmermann, "Mittelalterliche Frauenmystik: 'Feministische Theologie des Mittelalters' als Korrektiv an der *herrschenden* Theologie?" in *Frauen zwischen Anpassung und Widerstand: Beiträge der 5. Schweizerische Historikerinnentagung,* 13–23, provides a recent expression of this point of view, a way of construing the history of mysticism that, as noted by Bynum, 1982, 171, has been especially prevalent among Protestant historians. For mysticism as resistance to cultural norms, see also Dinzelbacher, 1993, 27–78 and 251–84.

46. Although as noted by K. Elm, "Verfall und Erneuerung des Ordenswesens im Spätmittelalter: Forschungen und Forschungsaufgaben," *Untersuchungen zu Kloster und Stift,* Veröffentlichungen des Max-Planck-Instituts für Geschichte, 68, Göttingen, 1980, esp. 233 n. 108: "Eine spezielle Untersuchung des Wandels der Frömmigkeit in den Orden liegt abgesehen von den Gesamtdarstellungen . . . noch nicht vor." For the state of research, see U. Köpf, "Monastische Theologie im 15. Jahrhundert," *Rottenburger Jahrbuch für Kirchengeschichte* 11 (1992): 117–35. Important groundwork has been laid by G. Constable, "Twelfth-Century Spirituality and the Late Middle Ages," *Medieval and Renaissance Studies* 5 (1971): 27–60, and "The Popularity of Twelfth-Century Spiritual Writers in the Later Middle Ages," in *Renaissance Studies in Honor of Hans Baron,* ed. A. Molho and J. Tedeschi, De Kalb, Ill., 1971, 5–28.

47. See Williams-Krapp, 1993, 301–13. For the broader context, see *Reformbemühungen und*

Observanzbestrebungen im spätmittelalterlichen Ordenswesen, ed. K. Elm, Berliner historische Studien, 14 (Ordensstudien, 6), Berlin, 1989.

48. One of the important implications of P. D. Johnson, *Equal in Monastic Profession: Religious Women in Medieval France,* Chicago, 1991; and idem, "*Mulier et monialis:* The Medieval Nun's Self-Image," *Thought* 64 (1989): 242–53. See also S. Heimann, " 'Gode to synem denste': Urkundliche Nachrichten über Beginenkonvente im spätmittelalterlichen Wismar," in *Der frauwen buoch: Versuche zu einer feministischen Mediävistik,* Göppinger Arbeiten zur Germanistik, 517, ed. I. Bennewitz, Göppingen, 1989, esp. 289: "Auch hier ist der Freiheitsbegriff nicht von der Idee individueller Freiräume im Sinne der modernen Emanzipation geprägt, sondern 'er ist korporativ gefaßt.' "

49. Quoted in B. Stock, "*Antiqui* or *Moderni?*" *New Literary History* 10 (1978–79): esp. 392; emphasis mine.

50. J. Huizinga, *The Waning of the Middle Ages: A Study of the Forms of Life, Thought and Art in France and the Netherlands in the Fourteenth and Fifteenth Centuries,* New York, 1954, 151.

BIBLIOGRAPHY

The bibliography lists only works with multiple citations. Short titles are used in the notes for printed primary sources and anthologies.

Die Abtei St. Walburg 1035–1935, Eichstätt, 1935.

Achten, G., *Das christliche Gebetbuch im Mittelalter: Andachts und Stundenbücher in Handschrift und Frühdruck,* 2d ed., Berlin, 1987a.

———, "De gebedenboeken van de Cisterciënserinnenklosters Medingen en Wienhausen," in *Miscellanea Neerlandica: Opstellen voor Dr. Jan Deschamps ter gelegenheid van zijn 70ste verjaardag,* ed. E. Cockx-Indestege and F. Hendrickx, Louvain, vol. 3, 1987b, 173–88.

Analecta sacri ordinis Fratrum Praedicatorum seu vetera ordinis monumenta, vol. 3, Rome, 1897.

Altdeutsche Predigten, 3 vols., ed. A. E. Schönbach, Graz 1886–91.

Altdeutsche und altniederländische Mystik, Wege der Forschung, 23, ed. K. Ruh, Darmstadt, 1964, 386–436.

Appuhn, H., *Einführung in die Ikonographie der mittelalterlichen Kunst in Deutschland,* Darmstadt, 1985.

———, "Das private Andachtsbild: Ein Vorschlag zur kunstgeschichtlichen und volkskundlichen Terminologie," in *Museum und Kulturgeschichte: Festschrift für Wilhelm Hansen,* Münster, 1978, 289–92.

Appuhn, H., and C. von Heusinger, "Der Fund kleiner Andachstbsilder des 13. bis 17. Jahrhunderts im Kloster Wienhausen," *Niederdeutsche Beiträge zur Kunstgeschichte* 4 (1965): 157–238.

Astell, A. W., *The Song of Songs in the Middle Ages,* Ithaca, N.Y., 1990.

Auerbach, E., "Gloria passionis," in *Literary Language and Its Public in Late Latin Antiquity and in the Middle Ages,* trans. R. Manheim, intro. J. M. Ziolkowski, Princeton, N.J., 1993, 67–81.

"Aufzeichnungen über das mystische Leben der Nonnen von Kirchberg bei Sulz, Predigerordens, während des XIV. und XV. Jahrhunderts," ed. F. W. E. Roth, *Alemannia* 21 (1893): 103–48.

Barth, M., "Die Haltung beim Gebet in elsässischen Dominikanerinnenklöstern des 15. und 16. Jahrhunderts," *Archiv für elsässische Kirchengeschichte* 13 (1938): 141–48.

———, "Zur Herz-Mariä-Verehrung des deutschen Mittelalters," *Zeitschrift für Aszese und Mystik* 4 (1929): 193–219.

Bauer, G., *Claustrum animae: Untersuchungen zur Geschichte der Metapher vom Herzen als Kloster,* Munich, 1973.

———, "Herzklosterallegorien," [2]VL, 2d ed., vol. III, 1153–69.

Beissel, S., "Religiöse Bilder für das katholische Volk," *Stimmen aus Maria Laach* 33 (1887): 456–72.

Belting, H., *Bild und Kult: Eine Geschichte des Bildes vor dem Zeitalter der Kunst,* Munich, 1990.

———, *Das Bild und sein Publikum im Mittelalter: Form und Funktion früher Bildtafeln der Passion,* Berlin, 1981.

Beriger, A., *Johannes Butzbach Odeporicon (eine Autobiographie aus dem Jahre 1506): Zweisprachige Ausgabe,* Weinheim, 1991.

Bériou, N., "De la lecture aux épousailles: Les Images dans la communication de la Parle de Dieu au XIIIe siècle," *Christianesimo nella storia* 14 (1993): 535–68.

Bertaud, E., and A. Rayez, "Échelle spirituelle," DS, vol. 14, 62–86.

Bilder und Bildersturm im Spätmittelalter und in der frühen Neuzeit, Wolfenbüttler Forschungen, 46, ed. R. Scribner, Wiesbaden, 1990.

Blumenberg, H., "Light as a Metaphor for Truth at the Preliminary Stage of Philosophical Concept Formation," in *Modernity and the Hegemony of Vision,* ed. D. M. Levin, Berkeley and Los Angeles, 1993, 30–62.

Bonaventuras Legenda Sancti Francisci in der Übersetzung der Sibilla von Bondorf, ed. D. Brett-Evans, Texte des späten Mittelalters, 12, Munich, 1960.

Bonaventure, *Opera theologica selecta,* vol. 5, Florence, 1964.

———, *Works of Saint Bonaventure,* 2 vols., trans. P. Boehner and M. F. Laughlin, St. Bonaventure, N.Y., 1955–56.

"Briefe der Aebtissin Sabina im Kloster zum heiligen Kreuz in Bergen an ihren Bruder Willibald Pirckheimer," ed. [no initial] Lochner, *Zeitschrift für die historische Theologie* 36 (1866): 518–66.

Bryson, N., *Word and Image: French Painting of the Ancien Régime,* 2d ed., New York, 1983.

Bühlmann, J., *Christuslehre und Christusmystik des Heinrich Seuse,* Lucerne, 1942.

Bühring, J., and K. Maier, *Die Kunstdenkmale des Landkreises Celle im Regierungsbezirk Lüneburg,* Die Kunstdenkmale des Landes Niedersachsen 34, 2 vols., Hannover, 1970.

Büttner, F. O., "Das Christusbild auf niedrigster Stilhöhe: Ansichtigkeit und Körpersichtigkeit in narrativen Passionsdarstellungen der Jahrzehnte um 1500," *Wiener Jarhbuch für Kunstgeschichte* 46–47 (1993–94): 99–130 and 397–400.

———, "Die Illumination mittelalterlicher Andachtsbücher," in *Mittelalterliche Andachtsbücher: Psalterien-Stundenbücher-Gebetbücher, Zeugnisse europäischer Frömmigkeit,* ed. H.-P. Geh and G. Römer, Karlsruhe, 1992, 11–54.

———, *Imitatio pietatis: Motive der christlichen Ikonographie als Modele der Verähnlichung,* Berlin, 1983.

Butzbach, J., *Libellus de praeclaris picturae professoribus (mit der Urschrift in Nachbildung),* ed. O. Pelka, Heidelberg, 1952.

Bynum, C. W., *Fragmentation and Redemption: Essays on Gender and the Human Body in Medieval Religion,* New York, 1991.

———, *Holy Feast and Holy Fast: The Religious Significance of Food to Medieval Women,* Berkeley and Los Angeles, 1987.

———, *Jesus as Mother: Studies in the Spirituality of the High Middle Ages,* Berkeley and Los Angeles, 1982.

Caritas Pirckheimer 1467–1532: Kloster und Klosterleben in der Herausforderung der Zeit, ed. L. Kurras and F. Machilek, Munich, 1982.

Carruthers, M. J., *The Book of Memory: A Study of Memory in Medieval Culture,* Cambridge, England, 1990.

Christus und die minnende Seele: Zwei mittelalterliche mystische Gedichte. Im Anhang ein Prosadisput verwandten Inhaltes. Untersuchungen und Texte, Germanistische Abhandlungen, 29, ed. R. Banz, Breslau, 1908.

Chronik und Totenbuch des Klosters Wienhausen, 3d rev. ed., ed. H. Appuhn, Wienhausen, 1986.

"Die Chronik von Anna von Munzingen," ed. J. König, *Freiburger Diözesan-Archiv* 13 (1880): 129–236.

Die Chroniken des Klosters Ribnitz, ed. F. Techen, Mecklenburgsche Geschichtsquellen, 1, Schwerin, 1909.

Cline, R. H., "Heart and Eyes," *Romance Philology* 25 (1971–72): 263–97.

Corbin, S., "Les Offices de la Sainte Face," *Bulletin des Études Portugaises* NS 11 (1947): 1–65.

Cornelius, R. D., *The Figurative Castle: A Study in the Medieval Allegory of the Edifice with especial Reference to Religious Writings,* Bryn Mawr, Pa., 1930.

Dinzelbacher, P., *Mittelalterliche Frauenmystik,* Paderborn, 1993.

———, "Zur Interpretation erlebnismystischer Texte des Mittelalters," *Zeitschrift für deutsches Altertum und deutsche Literatur* 117 (1988): 1–23.

Dray, M. E., "Alte und neue Buchmalerei in St. Walburg, Eichstätt," *Sankt Wiborada: Ein Jahrbuch für Bücherfreunde* 3 (1936): 61–68.

Durian-Ress, S., *Meisterwerke mittelalterliche Textilkunst aus dem Bayerischen Nationalmuseum: Auswahlkatalog,* Munich, 1986.

Die Eichstätter Bischöfschronik des Grafen Wilhelm Werner von Zimmern, Veröffentlichungen der Gesellschaft für Fränkische Geschichte, I. Reihe: Fränkische Chroniken, 3, ed. W. Kraft, Würzburg, 1956.

Falkenburg, R. L., *The Fruit of Devotion: Mysticism and the Imagery of Love in Flemish Paintings of the Virgin and Child, 1450–1550,* Oculi, 5, trans. S. Herman, Amsterdam and Philadelphia, 1994.

Faszination eines Klosters: 750 Jahre Zisterzienerinnen-Abtai Lichtenthal, ed. H. Siebenmorgen, Sigmaringen, 1995.

Feld, H., *Der Ikonoklasmus des Westens,* Studies in the History of Christian Thought, 41, Leiden, 1990.

Field, R. S., ed., *German Single-Leaf Woodcuts before 1500: Anonymous Artists,* 4 vols., *The Illustrated Bartsch:* Supplement 161–64, New York, 1987–92.

Floss, N. N., "Die Kloster Rolandswerth," *Annalen des historischen Vereins für den Niederrhein insbesondere die alte Erzdiöceze Köln* 19 (1868): 76–219.

Framing Medieval Bodies, ed. S. Kay and M. Rubin, Manchester, England, 1994.

Frauen-Bilder-Männer-Mythen: Kunsthistorische Beiträge, ed. I. Barta, Berlin, 1987.

Frauenfelder, R., "Spätmittelalterliche Ordungen für das Benediktinerinnenkloster St. Agnes in Schaffhausen," *Zeitschrift für Schweizerische Kirchengeschichte* 58 (1964): 107–18.

Frauenmystik im Mittelalter, ed. P. Dinzelbacher and D. R. Bauer, Ostfildern bei Stuttgart, 1985.

Freedberg, D., *The Power of Images: Studies in the History and Theory of Response,* Chicago, 1989.

Fries, W., "Kirche und Kloster zu St. Katharina in Nürnberg," *Mitteilungen des Vereins für Geschichte der Stadt Nürnberg* 25 (1924): 1–134.

Frugoni, C., *Francesco e l'invenzione delle stimmate: Una storia per parole e immagini fino a Bonaventura e Giotto,* Turin, 1993.

Füglister, R. L., *Das lebende Kreuz: Ikonographische-ikonologische Untersuchung der Herkunft und Entwicklung einer spätmittelalterlichen Bildidee und ihrer Verwurzelung im Wort,* Einsiedeln, 1964.

Gepeinigt, begehrt, vergessen: Symbolik und Sozialbezug des Körpers im späten Mittelalter und in der frühen Neuzeit, ed. K. Schreiner and N. Schnitzler, Paderborn, 1992.

Gerhardt, C., "Meditationsbilder aus dem ehemaligen Klarissenkloster Ribnitz (Bez. Rostock, DDR)," *Trierer theologische Zeitschrift* 98 (1989): 95–112.

Gertrude of Helfta, *Les Exercices,* Sources chrétiennes, 127, ed. J. Hourlier and A. Schmitt, Paris, 1967.

———, *Œuvres spirituelles,* Sources chrétiennes, vol. 255, ed. J.-M. Clément, B. de Vregille, and the nuns of Wisques, Paris, 1978.

———, *Spiritual Exercises,* ed. G. J. Lewis and J. Lewis, Kalamazoo, Mich., 1989.

The Golden Age of Dutch Manuscript Painting, intro. J. H. Marrow, ed. H. L. M. Defoer, A. S. Korteweg, and W. W. C. Wüstefeld, Stuttgart, 1989.

Greenspan, K., "A Medieval Iconographic Vernacular," in *So Rich a Tapestry: The Sister Arts and Cultural Studies,* ed. A. Hurley and K. Greenspan, Lewisburg, Pa., 1995, 200–215.

Grundmann, H., *Religiöse Bewegungen im Mittelalter: Untersuchungen über die geschichtlichen Zusammenhänge zwischen Ketzerei, den Bettelorden und der religiösen Frauenbewegungen im 12. und 13. Jahrhundert und über die geschichtlichen Grundlagen der deutschen Mystik,* 1935, reprinted Darmstadt, 1977.

Haas, A. M., *Geistliches Mittelalter,* Fribourg, 1984.

———, *Gottleiden-Gottlieben: Zur volkssprachlichen Mystik im Mittelalter,* Frankfurt, 1989, 127–52.

———, "Mechthild von Hackeborn: Eine Form zisterziensischer Frauenfrömmigkeit," in *Die Zisterzienser: Ordensleben zwischen Ideal und Wirklichkeit. Ergänzungsband,* Cologne, 1982, 221–39.

———, " 'Trage leiden geduldiglich': Die Einstellung der deutschen Mystik zum Leiden," in *Lerne leiden: Leidensbewältigung in der Mystik,* ed. W. Böhme, Karlsruhe, 1985, 35–55.

Hale, R., "*Imitatio Mariae:* Motherhood Motifs in Devotional Memoirs," *Mystics Quarterly* 16 (1990): 193–203.

Hamel, C. de, *Catalogue of Western Manuscripts and Miniatures,* Sotheby's, London, June 23, 1992.

Hamburger, J. F., "Art, Enclosure, and the *Cura monialium:* Prolegomena in the Guise of a Postscript," *Gesta* 31 (1992): 108–34.

———, "The *Liber miraculorum* of Unterlinden: An Icon in Its Convent Setting," in *The Sacred Image East and West,* ed. R. Ousterhout and L. Brubaker, Champaign-Urbana, Ill., 1995, 147–90.

———, "A *Liber precum* in Sélestat and the Development of the Illustrated Prayer Book in Germany," *Art Bulletin* 73 (1991): 209–36.

———, *The Rothschild Canticles: Art and Mysticism in Flanders and the Rhineland ca. 1300,* New Haven, Conn., 1990.

———, "Texts vs. Images, or the Reformation of History: The Literature of Female Spirituality from an Art Historian's Perspective," forthcoming.

———, "The Use of Images in the Pastoral Care of Nuns: The Case of Heinrich Suso and the Dominicans," *Art Bulletin* 71 (1989a): 20–46.

———, "The Visual and the Visionary: The Changing Role of the Image in Late Medieval Monastic Devotions," *Viator* 20 (1989b): 161–82.

Hartig, M., "Das deutsche Herz-Jesu Bild," *Das Münster* 2 (1948): 76–99.

Haussherr, R., "Über die Christus-Johannes-Gruppen: Zum Problem 'Andachtsbilder' und deutsche Mystik," in *Beiträge zur Kunst des Mittelalters: Festschrift für Hans Wentzel zum 60. Geburtstag,* Berlin, 1974, 79–103.

Heider, J., "Das Benediktinerinnenkloster Bergen und sein Archiv," *Neuburger Kollektaneen-*

blatt: Jahresschrift des Heimatvereins Neuburg/Donau 117 (1964) [= *Das Benediktinerinnenkloster Bergen und seine Urkunden*]: 7–17.

Heilige Walburga: Leben und Wirken, Eichstätt, 1979.

Heitz, P., *Neujahrswünsche des XV. Jahrhunderts,* Strasbourg, 1909.

Hendrix, G., "Drukgeschiedenis van het Traktaat *De doctrina cordis,*" *Archives et bibliothèques de Belgique* 49 (1978): 224–39.

Hengevoss-Dürkop, K., *Skulptur und Frauenkloster: Studien zu Bildwerken der Zeit um 1300 aus Frauenklöstern des ehemaligen Fürstentums Lüneburg,* Artefact, 7, Berlin, 1994.

Henry, A., *Biblia Pauperum: A Facsimile and Edition,* Ithaca, N.Y., 1987.

Hernad, B., *Die Graphik Sammlung der Humanisten Hartmann Schedel,* Munich, 1990.

Das Herz, 3 vols., Biberach an der Riss, 1965, 1966, 1969.

Hilpisch, S., *Aus deutschen Frauenklöstern,* Vienna, 1931.

Hl. Willibald, 787–1987: Künder des Glaubens, Pilger, Mönch, Bischof, ed. B. Appel, E. Braun, and S. Hofmann, Eichstätt, 1987.

Hogg, J., *An Illustrated Yorkshire Carthusian Religious Miscellany, British Library London Additional MS. 37049,* vol. III, *The Illustrations,* Analecta Cartusiana, 95, Salzburg, 1981.

Holter, K., "Die spätmittelalterliche Buchmalerei in Stift St. Florian," *Oberösterreichische Heimatblätter* 40 (1986): 301–24.

Höltgen, K. J., "*Arbor, Scala,* und *Fons Vita:* Vorformen devotionaler Embleme in einer mittelenglischen Handschrift (B.M. Add. 37049)," in *Chaucer und seine Zeit: Symposium für Walter F. Schirmer,* Tübingen, 1968, 355–91.

Holzbauer, H., *Mittelalterliche Heiligenverehrung: Heilige Walpurgis,* Eichstätter Studien, NF 5, Kevelaer, 1972.

Hoppeler, G., "Ein Erbauungs- und Andachtsbuch aus dem Dominikanerinnenkloster Ötenbach in Zürich vom Jahre 1436," *Zeitschrift für schweizerische Kirchengeschichte* 18 (1924): 210–16.

Hunkeler, L., "Ein Chorwochenbüchlein aus dem Engelberger Frauenkloster," in *Angelomontana: Blätter aus der Geschichte von Engelberg: Jubiläumsgabe für Abt Leodegar II.,* Gossau and St. Gall, 1914.

L'Image et la production du sacré: Actes du colloque de Strasbourg (20–21 janvier 1988) organisé par le Centre d'Histoire des Religions de l'Université de Strasbourg II, groupe "Théorie et pratique de l'image culturelle," ed. F. Dunand, J.-M. Spieser, and J. Wirth, Paris, 1991.

Jay, M., *Downcast Eyes: The Denigration of Vision in Twentieth-Century French Thought,* Berkeley and Los Angeles, 1994.

Katz, S. T., "The 'Conservative' Character of Mystical Experience," in *Mysticism and Religious Traditions,* ed. S. T. Katz, New York, 1983, 3–60.

Kern, P., *Trinität, Maria, Inkarnation: Studien zur Thematik der deutschen Dichtung des späteren Mittelalters,* Philologische Studien und Quellen, 55, Berlin, 1971.

Kessler, H. L., "'Facies bibliothecae revelata': Carolingian Art as Spiritual Seeing," in *Testo e immagine nell'alto medioevo (15–21 aprile 1993),* Settimane di Studio del Centro Italiano di Studi sull'alto medioevo, 41, 2 vols., Spoleto, 1994, vol. II, 534–94.

Kieckhefer, R., *Unquiet Souls: Fourteenth-Century Saints and Their Religious Milieu,* Chicago, 1984.

Klapisch-Zuber, C., "Holy Dolls: Play and Piety in Quattrocento Florence," in *Women, Family, and Ritual in Renaissance Italy,* ed. L. Cochrane, Chicago, 1985, 310–29.

Klosterfrauenarbeiten: Kunsthandwerk aus bayerischen Frauenklöstern, Munich, 1987.

Kloster Bergen bei Neuberg an der Donau und seine Fresken von Johann Wolfgang Baumgartner, Kunst in Bayern und Schwaben, 3, Weißenhorn, 1981.

Koepplin, D., "'Kommet her zu mir alle': Das tröstliche Bild des Gekreuzigten nach dem Verständnis Luthers," in *Martin Luther und die Reformation in Deutschland: Vorträge zur Ausstellung im Germanischen Nationalmuseum, Nürnberg, 1983,* ed. K. Löcher, Schriften des Vereins für Reformationsgeschichte, 1984, 153–99.

Körner, H., *Der früheste deutsche Einblattholzschnitt,* Mittenwald, 1979.

Kraft, H., *Die Bildallegorie der Kreuzigung Christi durch die Tugenden,* Frankfurt, 1976.

Krämer, S., *Handschriftenerbe des deutschen Mittelalters,* Mittelalterliche Bibliothekskataloge Deutschland und der Schweiz: Ergänzungsband 1, 3 vols., Munich, 1989.

Kroos, R., *Niedersächsische Bildstickereien des Mittelalters,* Berlin, 1970.

Künstlerischer Austausch: Akten des XXVIII. Internationalen Kongresses für Kunstgeschichte, Berlin, 15.–20. Juli 1992, 3 vols., ed. T. W. Gaehtgens, Berlin, 1993.

Küsters, U., *Der verschlossene Garten: Volkssprachliche Hohelied-Auslegung und monastische Lebensform im 12. Jahrhundert,* Studia Humaniora, 2, Düsseldorf, 1985.

LaCapra, D., "Rethinking Intellectual History and Reading Texts," in *Rethinking Intellectual History: Texts, Contexts, Language,* Ithaca, N.Y., 1983, 23–71.

Latein und Volkssprache im deutschen Mittelalter 1100–1500: Regensburger Colloquium 1988, ed. N. Henkel and N. F. Palmer, Tübingen, 1992.

Das Leben der Schwestern zu Töß beschrieben von Elsbet Stagel samt der Vorrede von Johannes Meier und dem Leben der Prinzessin Elisabet von Ungarn, ed. F. Vetter, Deutsche Texte des Mittelalters, 6, Berlin, 1906.

"Lebensbeschreibung der sel. Christina von Retters," ed. P. Mittermaier, *Archiv für mittelrheinische Kirchengeschichte* 17–18 (1965–66): 209–51 and 203–38.

Lechner, G. M., *Maria gravida: Zum Schwangerschaftsmotiv in der bildenden Kunst,* Münchener Kunsthistorische Abhandlungen, 9, Munich, 1991.

Lechner, J., *Die spätmittelalterliche Handschriftengeschichte der Benediktinerinnenabtei St. Walburg / Eichstätt (By.),* Münster, 1937.

Lee, A., *Materialien zum geisten Leben des späten fünfzehten Jahrhunderts im Sankt Katharinenkloster zu Nürnberg, mit besonderer Berücksichtigung der Predigten Johannes Diemars,* Heidelberg, 1969.

Lehrs, M., *Geschichte und kritischer Katalog des deutschen, niederländischen und französischen Kupferstichs im XV. Jahrhundert,* 9 vols., Vienna, 1908–34.

Lentes, T., "Die Gewände der Heiligen: Ein Diskussionsbeitrag zum Verhältnis von Gebet, Bild und Imagination," in *Hagiographie und Kunst: Der Heiligenkult in Schrift, Bild und Architektur,* ed. G. Kerscher, Berlin, 1993, 120–51.

Lewinsohn, R., *Histoire entière du cœur: Érotisme, symbolisme, chirurgie, physiologie, psychologie,* Hamburg, 1959.

Lewis, G. J., F. Willaert, and M.-J. Govers, *Bibliographie zur deutschen Frauenmystik des Mittelalters mit einem Anhang zu Beatrijs van Nazareth und Hadewijch,* Bibliographien zur deutschen Literatur des Mittelalters, 10, Berlin, 1989.

Il libro della Beata Angela da Foligno, ed. L. Thier and A. Calufetti, Spicilegium Bonaventurianum, 25, 2d ed., Rome, 1985.

Luitpold Herzog in Bayern, *Die Fränkische Bildwirkerei,* 2 vols., Munich, 1926.

Ludolf of Saxony, *Vita Jesu Christi,* 4 vols., Paris, 1870.

Mader, F., *Die Kunstdenkmäler von Mittelfranken I: Stadt Eichstätt,* Munich, 1924.

Margareta Ebner und Heinrich von Nördlingen: Ein Beitrag zur Geschichte der deutschen Mystik, ed. P. Strauch, Freiburg, 1882, reprinted Amsterdam, 1966.

Maria-Hilf: Ein Cranach-Bild und seine Wirkung, Katalogreihe Marmelsteiner Kabinett, 13, Würzburg, 1994.

Marrow, J. H., "Symbol and Meaning in Northern European Art of the Late Middle Ages and Early Renaissance," *Simiolus* 15 (1986): 150–72.

———, "Two Newly Identified Leaves from the Missal of Johannes von Giltlingen: Notes on

Late Fifteenth-Century Manuscript Illumination in Ausburg," *Anzeiger des Germanischen Nationalmuseums* (1984): 27–31.
Martin Luther und die Reformation in Deutschland, Ausstellung zum 500. Geburtstag Martin Luthers, Nuremberg, 1983.
Matter, E. A., *The Voice of My Beloved: The Song of Songs in Western Medieval Christianity,* Philadelphia, 1990.
Mauquoy-Hendrickx, M., *Les Estampes des Wierix conservées au Cabinet des Estampes de la Bibliothèque Royale Albert Ier: Catalogue raisonné,* 3 vols., Brussels, 1978.
Mayer, A. L., "Die heilbringende Schau in Sitte und Kult," in *Heilige Überlieferung,* Beiträge zur Geschichte des alten Mönchtums und des Benediktinerordens, ed. I. Herwegen, Münster, 1938, 235–62.
Mayer, J. G., "Tauler in der Bibliothek der Laienbrüder von Rebdorf," in *Überlieferungsgeschichtliche Editionen und Studien zur deutschen Literatur des Mittelalters,* ed. K. Kunze, J. G. Mayer, and B. Schnell, Tübingen, 1989, 365–90.
McGinn, B., *The Growth of Mysticism: Gregory the Great through the Twelfth Century,* New York, 1994.
———, "Resurrection and Ascension in the Christology of the Early Cistercians," *Cîteaux: Commentarii Cistercienses* 330 (1979): 5–22.
Mechthild of Hackeborn, *Revelationis Gertrudianae ac Mechthildianae,* ed. L. Paquelin, 2 vols., Poitiers and Paris, 1875–77.
Meister Eckhart: Sermons and Treatises, trans. M. O'C. Walshe, Longmead, Dorset, 1987.
Meisterwerke massenhaft: Die Bildhauerwerkstatt des Niklaus Weckmann und die Malerei in Ulm um 1500, Stuttgart, 1993.
Mengs, M., ed., *Schrifttum zum Leben und zur Verehrung der Heiligen Walburga († 779),* Eichstätt, 1979.
Menhardt, H., "Nikolaus von Dinkelsbühls deutsche Predigt vom Eigentum in Kloster," *Zeitschrift für deutsche Philologie des Mittelalters* 73 (1954): 1–39 and 268–91, and 74 (1955): 36–41.
Metz, R., *La Consécration des vierges dans l'église romaine: Étude d'histoire de la liturgie,* Paris, 1954.
Meyer, J., *Buch der Reformacio Predigerordens,* Quellen und Forschungen zur Geschichte des Dominikanerordens in Deutschland, 2–3, ed. B. M. Reichert, Leipzig, 1908–9.
Michalski, S., *The Reformation and the Visual Arts: The Protestant Image Question in Western and Eastern Europe,* London, 1993.
Michel, P., *Formosa deformitas: Bewältigungsformen des Häßlichen in mittelalterlichen Literatur,* Studien zur Germanistik, Anglistik und Komparatistik, 57, Bonn, 1976.
Michler, J., review of A. Knoepfli, *Die Kunstdenkmäler des Kantons Thurgau IV: Das Kloster St. Katharinenthal,* Basel, 1989, *Zeitschrift für Kunstgeschichte* 4 (1990): 587–94.
Miles, M. R., *Carnal Knowing: Female Nakedness and Religious Meaning in the Christian West,* Boston, 1989.
———, *Image as Insight: Visual Understanding in Western Christianity and Secular Culture,* Boston, 1985.
Miscellanea Neerlandica: Opstellen voor Dr. Jan Deschamps ter gelegenheid van zijn Zeventigste Verjaardag, ed. E. Cockx-Indestege and F. Hendrickx, 3 vols., Louvain, 1987.
Modernes Mittelalter: Neue Bilder einer populären Epoche, ed. J. Heinzle, Frankfurt, 1994.
Modernity and the Hegemony of Vision, ed. D. M. Levin, Berkeley and Los Angeles, 1993.
Morgan, N., "Longinus and the Sacred Heart," *Wiener Jahrbuch für Kunstgeschichte* (Beiträge zur mittelalterliche Kunst: Festschrift Gerhard Schmidt) 46–47 (1993–94): 507–18 and 817–20.
"Mystisches Leben in dem Dominikanerinnenkloster Weiler bei Eßlingen im 13. und 14.

Jahrhundert," ed. K. Bihlmeyer, *Württembergische Vierteljahrshefte für Landesgeschichte* NF 25 (1916): 61–93.

Mysticism and Language, ed. S. T. Katz, Oxford, 1992.

Die nicht mehr schönen Künste: Grenzphänomene des Ästhetischen, ed. H. R. Jauß, Poetik und Hermeneutik: Arbeitsergebnisse einer Forschungsgruppe, 3, Munich, 1968.

Ochsenbein, P., *Das Grosse Gebet der Eidgenossen: Überlieferung, Text, Form und Gehalt,* Bibliotheca Germanica, 29, Bern, 1989.

Ohly, F., "Cor amantis non angustum: Vom wohnen im Herzen," in *Gedenkschrift für William Foerste,* ed. D. Hofmann, Niederdeutsche Studien, 18, Cologne, 1970, 454–76.

———, *Gesetz und Evangelium: Zur Typologie bei Luther und Lucas Cranach. Zum Blutstrahl der Gnade in der Kunst,* Schriftenreihe der Westfälischen Wilhelms-Universität Münster, NF 1, Münster, 1985.

———, "Haus als Metapher," *Reallexikon für Antike und Christentum* 13 (1986): 905–1063.

———, *Hohelied-Studien: Grundzüge einer Geschichte der Hoheliedauslegung des Abendlandes bis um 1200,* Wiesbaden, 1958.

———, *Süsse Nagel der Passion: Ein Beitrag zur theologischen Semantik,* Saecvla spiritalia, 21, Baden-Baden, 1989.

O'Reilly, J., "Early Medieval Text and Image: The Wounded and Exalted Christ," *Peritia* 6–7 (1987–88): 72–118.

———, *Studies in the Iconography of the Virtues and Vices in the Middle Ages,* New York, 1988.

Ott, N. H., *Rechtspraxis und Heilsgeschichte: Zu Überlieferung, Ikonographie und Gebrauchssituation des deutschen "Belial,"* Münchener Texte und Untersuchungen zur deutschen Literatur des Mittelalters, 80, Munich, 1983.

Die Passion Christi in Literatur und Kunst des Spätmittelalters, ed. W. Haug and B. Wachinger, Fortuna Vitrea, 12, Tübingen, 1993.

Peters, U., *Religiöse Erfahrung als literarisches Faktum: Zur Vorgeschichte und Genese frauenmystischer Texte des 13. und 14. Jahrhunderts,* Hermea: Germanistische Forschungen, NF 56, Tübingen, 1988.

Pez, B., *Bibliotheca Ascetica Antiquo-Nova,* 8 vols., Regensburg, 1725.

Das "Pontifikale Gundekarianum": Faksimile-Ausgabe des Codex B4 im Diözesan-Archiv Eichstätt, ed. A. Bauch and E. Reiter, 2 vols., Wiesbaden, 1987.

Rahner, H. "De Dominici pectoris fonte potavit," *Zeitschrift für katholische Theologie* 55 (1931): 103–8.

———, "'Flumina de ventre Christi': Die patristische Auslegung von Joh. 7:37–38," *Biblia* 22 (1941): 269–302 and 367–401.

Rapp Buri, A., and M. Stucky-Schnürer, "Klosterfleiß im Dienste der Gegenreformation: Die Bildteppiche von St. Johann bei Zabern im Elsaß," *Zeitschrift für die Geschichte des Oberrheins* 137, NF 98 (1989): 290–326.

———, *"Zahm und wild": Basler und Straßburger Bildteppiche des 15. Jahrhunderts,* Mainz, 1990.

R.D., "Religiös-Volkskundliches aus St. Walburg: Das volkstümliche Andachtsbild des 15. Jahrhunderts," *Walburgis-Blätter* 24 (1936): 54–57.

Reformbemühungen und Observanzbestrebungen im spätmittelalterlichen Ordenswesen, ed. K. Elm, Berliner Historischer Studien, 14 (Ordenstudien, 6), Berlin, 1989.

"Die Regensburger Klarissenregel: Mitteilungen aus altdeutschen Handschriften, 10," ed. A. E. Schönbach, *Sitzungsberichte der philosophisch-historischen Klasse der Kaiserlichen Akademie der Wissenschaften* 160/6, Vienna, 1909, reprinted Hildesheim, 1976.

Religiöse Frauenbewegung und mystische Frömmigkeit im Mittelalter, ed. P. Dinzelbacher and D. R. Bauer, Cologne and Vienna, 1988.

Resmini, B., *Die Benediktinerabtei Maria Laach,* Germania Sacra, NF 31, Erzbistum Trier, 7, Berlin, 1993.

Richstätter, K., *Die Herz-Jesu-Verehrung des deutschen Mittelalters,* Regensburg, 1924.

Ringler, S., *Viten- und Offenbarungsliteratur in Frauenklöstern des Mittelalters: Quellen und Studien,* Münchener Texte und Untersuchungen zur deutschen Literatur des Mittelalters, 72, Zurich and Munich, 1980.

Ritzinger, E., and H. C. Scheeben, "Beiträge zur Geschichte der Teutonia in der zweiten Hälfte des 13. Jahrhunderts," *Archiv der Deutschen Dominikaner* 3 (1941): 11–95.

Robertson, E., *Early English Devotional Prose and the Female Audience,* Knoxville, Tenn., 1990.

Rubin, M., *Corpus Christi: The Eucharist in Late Medieval Culture,* Cambridge, England, 1990.

Ruh, K., *Frauenmystik und Franziskanische Mystik der Frühzeit,* Geschichte der abendländischen Mystik, 2, Munich, 1993.

———, *Meister Eckhart: Theologe, Prediger, Mystiker,* 2d ed., Munich, 1989.

Rüthing, H., "Die mittelalterliche Bibliothek des Zisterzienserinnenklosters Wöltingerode," in *Zisterzienische Spiritualität: Theologische Grundlagen, funktionale Vorraussetzungen und bildhafte Ausprägungen im Mittelalter,* 1. Himmelroder Kolloquium, Studien und Mitteilungen zur Geschichte des Benediktiner-Ordens und seiner Zweige: Ergänzungsband, 34, ed. C. Kasper and K. Schreiner, Ottobeuron, 1990, 189–216.

The Sacred Image East and West, ed. R. Ousterhout and L. Brubaker, Champaign-Urbana, Ill., 1995.

Sauvy, A., *Le Miroir du coeur: Quatre siècles d'images savantes et populaires,* Paris, 1989.

Sax, J., *Die Bischöfe und Reichsfürsten von Eichstätt, 754–1806: Versuch einer Deutung ihres Waltens und Wirkens nach den neuesten Quellen zusammengestellt,* 2 vols., Landshut, 1884–85.

———, *Geschichte des Hochstiftes und der Stadt Eichstätt,* Nuremberg, 1857.

Scharfe, M., *Evangelische Andachtsbilder: Studien zur Intention und Funktion des Bildes in der Frömmigkeitsgeschichte vornehmlich des schwäbischen Raumes,* Stuttgart, 1968.

Schawe, M., "*Fasciculus myrrhae:* Pietà und Hoheslied," *Jahrbuch des Zentralinstituts für Kunstgeschichte* 5–6 (1989): 161–212.

Schiewer, H.-J., "Die beiden Sankt Johannsen, ein dominikanischer Johannes-Libellus und das literarische Leben im Bodenseeraum um 1300," *Oxford German Studies* 22 (1993): 21–54.

Schiller, G., *The Iconography of Christian Art,* vol. II, *The Passion of Jesus Christ,* trans. J. Seligman, Greenwich, Conn., 1972.

Schlecht, J., "Beiträge zur Kunstgeschichte der Stadt Eichstätt," *Sammelblatt des historischen Vereins Eichstätt* 14 (1899): 32–69.

———, "Zur Kunstgeschichte von Eichstätt," *Sammelblatt des historischen Vereins Eichstätt* 14 (1899): 77–114.

Schleusener-Eicholtz, G., *Das Auge im Mittelalter,* Münstersche Mittelalter-Schriften, 35, 2 vols., Munich, 1985.

Schmidt, M., "Mechthild von Hackeborn," ²VL, vol. VI, 251–60.

Schmidtke, D., *Studien zur dingallegorischen Erbauungsliteratur am Beispiel der Gartenallegorie,* Hermea NF 43, Tübingen, 1982.

Schmitt, J.-C., "Cendrillon crucifiée: À propos du *Volto Santo* de Lucques," in *Miracles, prodiges et merveilles au Moyen Âge,* Paris, 1995, 241–69.

Schneider, K., *Die deutschen Handschriften der Bayerischen Staatsbibliothek München, Cgm. 351–500,* Catalogus codicum manu scriptorum Bibliothecae Monacensis, vol. V, pt. 3, Wiesbaden, 1973.

Schnürer, G., and J. M. Ritz, *Sankt Kümmernis und Volto Santo: Studien und Bilder,* Forschungen zur Volkskunde, 13–15, Düsseldorf, 1934.

Schrader, H.-J., "Le Christ dans le cœur de ses fidèles: Quelques aspects 'poétiques' de la christologie du piétisme," in *Le Christ entre orthodoxie et Lumières: Actes du colloque tenu à Genève en août 1993,* ed. M.-C. Pitassi, Histoire des idées et critique littéraire, 332, Geneva, 1994, 49–76.

Schraut, E., *Stifterinnen und Künstlerinnen im mittelalterlichen Nürnberg,* Nuremberg, 1987.

Schreiber, W. L., *Handbuch der Holz- und Metallschnitte des XV. Jahrhunderts,* 8 vols., Leipzig, 1926–30.

Schreyl, K. H., *Der graphische Neujahrsgruße aus Nürnberg,* Nuremberg, 1979.

Schuppisser, F. O., "Schauen mit den Augen des Herzens: Zur Methodik der spätmittelalterlichen Passionsmeditation, besonders in der *Devotio moderna* und bei den Augustinern," in *Die Passion Christi in Literatur und Kunst des Spätmittelalters,* ed. W. Haug and B. Wachinger, Fortuna Vitrea, 12, Tübingen, 1993, 169–210.

Scott, J. W., "The Evidence of Experience," *Critical Inquiry* 17 (1991): 773–97.

Schultz, A., "Joahnnes Butzbach's 'Libellus de preclaris picture professoribus' aus der Bonnenser Handschrift veröffentlicht," *Jahrbücher für Kunstwissenschaft,* ed. A. von Zahn, 2 (1869): 60–72.

Seebass, G., *Die Himmelsleiter des hl. Bonaventura von Lukas Cranach d.Ä.: Zur Reformation eines Holzschnitts,* Sitzungsberichte der Heidelberger Akademie der Wissenschaften, Phil.-Hist. Kl. 1985/4, Heidelberg, 1985.

Seuse, Heinrich [Henry Suso], *Heinrich Seuse: Deutsche Schriften,* ed. K. Bihlmeyer, Stuttgart, 1907, reprinted Frankfurt, 1961.

———, *Heinrich Seuses Horologium Sapientiae,* Spicilegium Friburgense: Texte zur Geschichte des kirchlichen Lebens, 23, ed. P. Künzle, Fribourg, 1977.

Spamer, A., *Das Kleine Andachtsbild vom XIV. bis zum XX. Jahrhundert,* Munich, 1930.

Spätgotik in Salzburg: Die Malerei, Salzburger Museum Carolino Augusteum: Jahresschrift, 17, Salzburg, 1972.

Spearing, A. C., *The Medieval Poet as Voyeur: Looking and Listening in Medieval Love Narratives,* Cambridge, England, 1993.

Stammler, W., *Prosa der deutschen Gotik: Eine Stilgeschichte in Texten,* Berlin, 1933.

———, "Studien zur Geschichte der Mystik in Norddeutschland," in *Altdeutsche und altniederländische Mystik,* Wege der Forschung, 23, ed. K. Ruh, Darmstadt, 1964, 386–436.

Stanbury, S., "The Virgin's Gaze: Spectacle and Transgression in Middle English Lyrics of the Passion," *PMLA* 106 (1991): 1083–93.

St. Benedict's Rule for Monasteries, trans. L. J. Doyle, Collegeville, Minn., 1948.

Das "St. Katharinentaler Schwesternbuch": Untersuchung, Edition, Kommentar, ed. R. Meyer, Münchener Texte und Untersuchungen zur deutschen Literatur des Mittelalters, 104, Tübingen, 1995.

Stock, B., "The Self and Literary Experience in Late Antiquity and the Middle Ages," *New Literary History* 25 (1994): 839–52.

Straganz, M. "Die ältesten Statuten des Klarissenklosters zu Brixen (Tirol)," *Franziskanische Studien* 6 (1919): 143–70.

Suckale, R., "*Arma Christi:* Überlegungen zur Zeichenhaftigkeit mittelalterlicher Andachtsbilder," *Städel-Jahrbuch* 6 (1977): 177–208.

Suso, Henry, *Henry Suso: The Exemplar, with Two German Sermons,* trans. and ed. F. Tobin, intro. B. McGinn, New York, 1989.

Testo e immagine nell'alto medioevo (15–21 aprile 1993), Settimane di Studio del Centro Italiano di Studi sull'alto medioevo, 41, 2 vols., Spoleto, 1994.

Trexler, R. C., "Habiller et déshabiller les images: Esquisse d'une analyse," in *L'Image et la production du sacré: Actes du colloque de Strasbourg (20–21 janvier 1988) organisé par le Centre*

d'Histoire des Religions de l'Université de Strasbourg II, group "Théorie et pratique de l'image culturelle," ed. F. Dunand, J.-M. Spieser, and J. Wirth, Paris, 1991, 195–231.
Vandenbroeck, P., *Le Jardin clos de l'âme: L'Imaginaire des religieuses dans les Pays-Bas du Sud, depuis le 13e siècle,* Brussels, 1994.
van Engen, J., "Theophilus Presbyter and Rupert of Deutz: The Manual Arts and Benedictine Theology in the Early Twelfth Century," *Viator* 11 (1980): 147–63.
Vauchez, A., "Les Stigmates de saint François et leurs détracteurs dans les derniers siècles du Moyen Âge," *Mélanges d'archéologie et d'histoire* 80 (1968): 595–625.
Verfasserlexikon: Die deutsche Literatur des Mittelalters: Verfasser Lexikon, ed. K. Ruh et al., 2d rev. ed., Berlin, 1978–.
Das Vermächtnis der Abtei: 900 Jahre St. Peter auf dem Schwarzwald, ed. H.-O. Mühleisen, Karlsruhe, 1993.
Vetter, E. M., *Die Kupferstiche zur Psalmodia Eucaristica des Melchor Prieto von 1622,* Spanische Forschungen der Görresgesellschaft, 2d ser., 15, Münster, 1972.
———, *Speculum salutis,* Abtei Münsterschwarzach, 1995.
Vision and Visuality, Dia Art Foundation Discussion in Contemporary Culture, 2, ed. H. Foster, Seattle, 1988.
Visual Culture: Images and Interpretations, ed. N. Bryson, M. A. Holly, and K. Moxey, Hanover, N.H., 1994.
"Vita venerabilis Lukardis monialis ordinis Cisterciensis in superiore Wimaria," ed. J. de Backer, *Analecta Bollandiana* 18 (1899): 305–67.
Volksreligion im hohen und späten Mittelalter, Quellen und Forschungen aus dem Gebiet der Geschichte, NF 13, ed. P. Dinzelbacher and D. R. Bauer, Paderborn, 1990.
von Heusinger, C., "Spätmittelalterliche Buchmalerei in oberrheinischen Frauenklöstern," *Zeitschrift für die Geschichte des Oberrheins* 107 (1959): 136–60.
———, "Studien zur oberrheinischen Buchmalerei und Graphik im Spätmittelalter," Ph.D. diss., Albert-Ludwigs-Universität, Freiburg, 1953.
Webber, P. E., *A Late Medieval Devotional Anthology from Salzburg ("Nonnberg Passion": Huntington Library HM 195): Commentary and Edition,* Göppingen Arbeiten zur Germanistik, 531, Göppingen, 1990.
Wegener, H., *Beschreibendes Verzeichnis der deutschen Bilderhandschriften des späten Mittelalters in der Heidelberger Universitäts-Bibliothek,* Leipzig, 1927.
———, *Beschreibendes Verzeichnis der Miniaturen-Handschriften der preußischen Staatsbibliothek zu Berlin, V: Die deutschen Handschriften,* Leipzig, 1928.
Weinberger, M., *Die Formschnitte der Katharinenklosters zu Nürnberg: Ein Versuch über die Geschichte der frühesten Nürnberger Holzschnitten,* Munich, 1925.
"Das Wienhausen Liederbuch," ed. P. Alpers, *Jahrbuch des Vereins für Niederdeutsche Sprachforschung* 60–70 (1943–47): 1–40.
Wilckens, L. von, "Die Teppiche mit der Heiligen Walburga," *Studien und Mitteilungen zur Geschichte des Benediktiner-Ordens und seiner Zweige* 90 (1979): 81–96.
———, *Die textilen Künste von der Spätantike bis um 1500,* Munich, 1991.
Wilkens, E., *The Rose-Garden Game: The Symbolic Background to the European Prayer-Beads,* London, 1969.
Williams-Krapp, W., "Bilderbogen-Mystik: Zu 'Christus und die minnende Seele' mit Editionen der Mainzer Überlieferung," in *Überlieferungsgeschichtliche Editionen und Studien zur deutschen Literatur des Mittelalters: Kurt Ruh zum 75. Geburtstag,* Texte und Textegeschichte, 31, ed. K. Künze, Tübingen, 1989, 350–64.
———, "Frauenmystik und Ordensreform im 15. Jahrhundert," *Literarische Interessenbildung im Mittelalter,* DFG-Symposion 1991, ed. J. Heinzle, Stuttgart, 1993, 301–13.

———, "Ordensreform und Literatur im 15. Jahrhundert," *Jahrbuch der Oswald von Wolkenstein-Gesellschaft* 4 (1986): 41–51.

Wirth, K.-A., "Religiöse Herzenemblematik," in *Das Herz,* vol. II, *Im Umkreis der Kunst,* Biberach an der Riss, 1966, 65–105.

Wormald, F., "Some Popular Miniatures and Their Rich Relations," in *Miscellanea pro arte: Hermann Schnitzler zur Vollendung der 60. Lebensjahres,* Düsseldorf, 1965, 279–85.

Wyss, R. L., "Die Handarbeiten der Maria: Eine ikonographische Studie unter Berücksichtigung der Techniken," in *Artes minores: Dank an Werner Abegg,* ed. M. Stettler and M. Lemberg, Bern, 1973, 113–88.

Ziegler, J. E., *Sculpture of Compassion: The Pietà and the Beguines in the Southern Low Countries c. 1300–c. 1600,* Institute Historique Belge de Rome: Études d'Histoire de l'Art, 6, Brussels, 1992.

Zimmer, P., *Die Funktion und Ausstattung des Altares auf der Nonnenempore: Beispiele zum Bildgebrauch in Frauenklöstern aus dem 13. bis 16. Jahrhundert,* Cologne, 1991.

Zum 900jährigen Jubiläum der Abtei St. Walburg in Eichstätt: Historische Beiträge, ed. K. Ried, Paderborn, 1935.

INDEX OF BIBLICAL CITATIONS

INDEX OF MANUSCRIPTS CITED

GENERAL INDEX

Designer: Barbara Jellow
Compositor: G&S Typesetters, Inc.
Text and Display: Bembo
Printer and Binder: Data Reproductions Corp.